Allegories of Reading

Allegories of Reading

Figural Language
in Rousseau, Nietzsche, Rilke, and Proust

Paul de Man

New Haven and London
Yale University Press
1979

Published with assistance from the Kingsley Trust Association Publication Fund established by the Scroll and
Key Society of Yale College.

Designed by Thos. Whitridge and set in Zapf International type. Printed in the United States of America by
The Murray Printing Company, Westford, Massachusetts.

Published in Great Britain, Europe, Africa, and Asia (except Japan) by Yale University Press, Ltd., London. Distributed in Australia and New Zealand by Book & Film
Services, Artarmon, N.S.W., Australia; and in Japan by
Harper & Row, Publishers, Tokyo Office.

Library of Congress Cataloging in Publication Data

De Man, Paul.
  Allegories of reading.

  Includes index.
   1. French literature—History and criticism.
  2. Rousseau, Jean Jacques, 1712-1778—Style.
  3. German literature—History and criticism.
  4. Figures of speech.   5. Allegory.   I. Title.
PQ145.D45   809   79-64075
ISBN 0-300-02322-7

Quand on lit trop vite ou trop doucement on n'entend rien.

Pascal

Contents

Preface

ALLEGORIES OF READING STARTED OUT AS A HISTORICAL study and ended up as a theory of reading. I began to read Rousseau seriously in preparation for a historical reflection on Romanticism and found myself unable to progress beyond local difficulties of interpretation. In trying to cope with this, I had to shift from historical definition to the problematics of reading. This shift, which is typical of my generation, is of more interest in its results than in its causes. It could, in principle, lead to a rhetoric of reading reaching beyond the canonical principles of literary history which still serve, in this book, as the starting point of their own displacement. The principles underlying the thematic diversity of Rousseau, the chronology of Rilke and Nietzsche, the rhetoric of Proust, are not left intact by the reading, but this critical result remains dependent on the initial position of these very principles. Whether a further step, which would leave this hermeneutic model behind, can be taken should not *a priori* or naïvely be taken for granted.

In Part II, on Rousseau, I have attempted the elaboration and the undoing of a system of tropological transformations in the form of a sustained argument. Part I establishes a similar pattern in a more fragmented way by moving between several authors rather than staying within a single corpus. The choice of Proust and of Rilke as examples is partly due to chance, but since the ostensible pathos of their tone and depth of their statement make them particularly resistant to a reading that is no longer entirely thematic, one could argue that if *their* work yields to such a rhetorical scheme, the same would necessarily be true for writers whose rhetorical strategies are less hidden behind the seductive powers of identification.

What emerges is a process of reading in which rhetoric is a disruptive intertwining of trope and persuasion or—which is not quite the same thing—of cognitive and performative language. The implications of this conclusion are not easy to unfold, nor can they be stated in summary fashion, separated from the intricacies of specific readings. Nevertheless, opponents of such an approach have been more eager to attack what they assume to be its ideological motives rather than the technicalities of its procedure. This is particularly true with regard to the term "deconstruction," which has rapidly become a label as well as a target. Most of this book was written before "deconstruction" became a bone of contention, and the term is used here in a technical rather than a polemical sense—which does not imply that it therefore becomes neutral or ideologically innocent. But I saw no reason to delete it. No other word states so economically the impossibility to evaluate positively or negatively the inescapable evaluation it implies. Something is lost when the same process is described by a purely negative term, as when Nietzsche speaks of the destruction (*Zertrümmerung*) of conceptual constructs or Pascal of the demolition (*démolition*) of a conviction that is itself already a destruction. I consciously came across "deconstruction" for the first time in the writings of Jacques Derrida, which means that it is associated with a power of inventive rigor to which I lay no claim but which I certainly do not wish to erase. Deconstruction, as was easily predictable, has been much misrepresented, dismissed as a harmless academic game or denounced as a terrorist weapon, and I have all the fewer illusions about the possibility of countering these aberrations since such an expectation would go against the drift of my own readings.

Allegories of Reading was a long time in the writing, and the list of institutions to which I am indebted is even longer. I began to write on Rousseau and Nietzsche with the assistance of a Guggenheim Fellowship in 1969 and wrote the main part of the book during a year's leave from Yale University in 1972–73, with the assistance of a Yale Senior Faculty Fellowship supplemented by a grant from the Merrit Foundation and a grant-in-aid from the American Council for Learned Societies. Final verifications were completed in 1978 with the help of a travel grant from the Griswold Fund at Yale. I wish to thank the numerous colleagues whose support helped me in securing this aid. As for my intellectual indebtedness, I feel indeed unable to enumerate what is beyond number and to disentangle, in so many cases, the part of influence from the part of friendship.

Parts of this book have appeared in print before. The section on Proust was originally a contribution to a *Festschrift* for Georges Poulet entitled *Mouvements premiers* (Paris: José Corti, 1972) and the Rilke chapter was written as an introduction to the French edition of Rilke's poems (Paris: Editions du Seuil, 1972). Other chapters appeared entirely or in part in *Critical Inquiry*, *Diacritics*, *The Georgia*

Review, Glyph, Studies in Romanticism, and *Yale French Studies.* Permission to reprint is gratefully acknowledged. I have myself translated the two sections originally written in French.

I wish to thank Ellen Graham and Sheila Huddleston of the Yale University Press for particularly efficient and speedy copyediting, certain to cleanse the final text of all mistakes but my own.

All translations of French and German quotations are my own unless otherwise indicated.

P. d. M.

New Haven, April 1979

Part I

Rhetoric

1 Semiology and Rhetoric

TO JUDGE FROM VARIOUS RECENT PUBLICATIONS, THE spirit of the times is not blowing in the direction of formalist and intrinsic criticism. We may no longer be hearing too much about relevance but we keep hearing a great deal about reference, about the nonverbal "outside" to which language refers, by which it is conditioned and upon which it acts. The stress falls not so much on the fictional status of literature—a property now perhaps somewhat too easily taken for granted—but on the interplay between these fictions and categories that are said to partake of reality, such as the self, man, society, "the artist, his culture and the human community," as one critic puts it. Hence the emphasis on hybrid texts considered to be partly literary and partly referential, on popular fictions deliberately aimed towards social and psychological gratification, on literary autobiography as a key to the understanding of the self, and so on. We speak as if, with the problems of literary form resolved once and forever, and with the techniques of structural analysis refined to near-perfection, we could now move "beyond formalism" towards the questions that really interest us and reap, at last, the fruits of the ascetic concentration on techniques that prepared us for this decisive step. With the internal law and order of literature well policed, we can now confidently devote ourselves to the foreign affairs, the external politics of literature. Not only do we feel able to do so, but we owe it to ourselves to take this step: our moral conscience would not allow us to do otherwise. Behind the assurance that valid interpretation is possible, behind the recent interest in writing and reading as potentially effective public speech acts, stands a highly respectable moral imperative that strives to reconcile the internal, formal, private structures of literary language with their external, referential, and public effects.

I want, for the moment, to consider briefly this tendency in itself, as an undeniable and recurrent historical fact, without regard for its truth or falseness or for its value as desirable or pernicious. It is a fact that this sort of thing happens, again and again, in literary studies. On the one hand, literature cannot merely be received as a definite unit of referential meaning that can be decoded without leaving a residue. The code is unusually conspicuous, complex, and enigmatic; it attracts an inordinate amount of attention to itself, and this attention has to acquire the rigor of a method. The structural moment of concentration on the code for its own sake cannot be avoided, and literature necessarily breeds its own formalism. Technical innovations in the methodical study of literature only occur when this kind of attention predominates. It can legitimately be said, for example, that, from a technical point of view, very little has happened in American criticism since the innovative works of New Criticism. There certainly have been numerous excellent books of criticism since, but in none of them have the techniques of description and interpretation evolved beyond the techniques of close reading established in the thirties and the forties. Formalism, it seems, is an all-absorbing and tyrannical muse; the hope that one can be at the same time technically original and discursively eloquent is not borne out by the history of literary criticism.

On the other hand—and this is the real mystery—no literary formalism, no matter how accurate and enriching in its analytic powers, is ever allowed to come into being without seeming reductive. When form is considered to be the external trappings of literary meaning or content, it seems superficial and expendable. The development of intrinsic, formalist criticism in the twentieth century has changed this model: form is now a solipsistic category of self-reflection, and the referential meaning is said to be extrinsic. The polarities of inside and outside have been reversed, but they are still the same polarities that are at play: internal meaning has become outside reference, and the outer form has become the intrinsic structure. A new version of reductiveness at once follows this reversal: formalism nowadays is mostly described in an imagery of imprisonment and claustrophobia: the "prison house of language," "the impasse of formalist criticism," etc. Like the grandmother in Proust's novel ceaselessly driving the young Marcel out into the garden, away from the unhealthy inwardness of his closeted reading, critics cry out for the fresh air of referential meaning. Thus, with the structure of the code so opaque, but the meaning so anxious to blot out the obstacle of form, no wonder that the reconciliation of form and meaning would be so attractive. The attraction of reconciliation is the elective breeding-ground of false models and metaphors; it accounts for the metaphorical model of literature as a kind of box that separates an inside from an outside, and the reader or critic as the person who opens the lid in order to release in the open what was secreted but inaccessible inside. It matters little whether we call the inside of the box the content or the form, the outside the meaning or the appearance. The recurrent debate opposing intrinsic to extrinsic criticism stands under the aegis of an inside/outside metaphor that is never being seriously questioned.

Metaphors are much more tenacious than facts, and I certainly don't expect to dislodge this age-old model in one short try. I merely wish to speculate on a different set of terms, perhaps less simple in their differential relationships than the strictly polar, binary opposition between inside and outside and therefore less likely to enter into the easy play of chiasmic reversals. I derive these terms (which are as old as the hills) pragmatically from the observation of developments and debates in recent critical methodology.

One of the most controversial among these developments coincides with a new approach to poetics or, as it is called in Germany, poetology, as a branch of general semiotics. In France, a semiology of literature comes about as the outcome of the long-deferred but all the more explosive encounter of the nimble French literary mind with the category of form. Semiology, as opposed to semantics, is the science or study of signs as signifiers; it does not ask what words mean but how they mean. Unlike American New Criticism, which derived the internalization of form from the practice of highly self-conscious modern writers, French semiology turned to linguistics for its model and adopted Saussure and Jakobson rather than Valéry or Proust for its masters. By an awareness of the arbitrariness of the sign (Saussure) and of literature as an autotelic statement "focused on the way it is expressed" (Jakobson) the entire question of meaning can be bracketed, thus freeing the critical discourse from the debilitating burden of paraphrase. The demystifying power of semiology, within the context of French historical and thematic criticism, has been considerable. It demonstrated that the perception of the literary dimensions of language is largely obscured if one submits uncritically to the authority of reference. It also revealed how tenaciously this authority continues to assert itself in a variety of disguises, ranging from the crudest ideology to the most refined forms of aesthetic and ethical judgment. It especially explodes the myth of semantic correspondence between sign and referent, the wishful hope of having it both ways, of being, to paraphrase Marx in the German Ideology, a formalist critic in the morning and a communal moralist in the afternoon, of serving both the technique of form and the substance of meaning. The results, in the practice of French criticism, have been as fruitful as they are irreversible. Perhaps for the first time since the late eighteenth century, French critics can come at least somewhat closer to the kind of linguistic awareness that never ceased to be operative in its poets and novelists and that forced all of them, including Sainte Beuve, to write their main works "contre Sainte Beuve." The distance was never so considerable in England and the United States, which does not mean, however, that we may be able, in this country, to dispense altogether with some preventative semiological hygiene.

One of the most striking characteristics of literary semiology as it is practiced today, in France and elsewhere, is the use of grammatical (especially syntactical) structures conjointly with rhetorical structures, without apparent awareness of a possible discrepancy between them. In their literary analyses, Barthes, Genette, Todorov, Greimas, and their disciples all simplify and regress from Jakobson in letting grammar and rhetoric function in perfect continuity, and in passing from grammatical to rhetorical structures without difficulty or interruption. Indeed, as the study of grammatical structures is refined in contemporary theories of generative, transformational, and distributive grammar, the study of tropes and of figures (which is how the term *rhetoric* is used here, and not in the derived sense of comment or of eloquence or persuasion) becomes a mere extension of grammatical models, a particular subset of syntactical relations. In the recent *Dictionnaire encyclopédique des sciences du langage*, Ducrot and Todorov write that rhetoric has always been satisfied with a paradigmatic view over words (words substituting for each other), without questioning their syntagmatic relationship (the contiguity of words to each other). There ought to be another perspective, complementary to the first, in which metaphor, for example, would not be defined as a substitution but as a particular type of combination. Research inspired by linguistics or, more narrowly, by syntactical studies, has begun to reveal this possibility—but it remains to be explored. Todorov, who calls one of his books a *Grammar of the Decameron*, rightly thinks of his own work and that

of his associates as first explorations in the elaboration of a systematic grammar of literary modes, genres, and also of literary figures.
Perhaps the most perceptive work to come out of this school, Genette's studies of figural modes, can be shown to be assimilations of
rhetorical transformations or combinations to syntactical, grammatical patterns. Thus a recent study, now printed in *Figures III* and
entitled *Metaphor and Metonymy in Proust,* shows the combined
presence, in a wide and astute selection of passages, of paradigmatic,
metaphorical figures with syntagmatic, metonymic structures. The
combination of both is treated descriptively and nondialectically
without considering the possibility of logical tensions.

One can ask whether this reduction of figure to grammar is
legitimate. The existence of grammatical structures, within and beyond the unit of the sentence, in literary texts is undeniable, and their
description and classification are indispensable. The question remains if and how figures of rhetoric can be included in such a
taxonomy. This question is at the core of the debate going on, in a
wide variety of apparently unrelated forms, in contemporary poetics.
But the historical picture of contemporary criticism is too confused
to make the mapping out of such a topography a useful exercise. Not
only are these questions mixed in and mixed up within particular
groups or local trends, but they are often co-present, without apparent contradiction, within the work of a single author.

Neither is the theory of the question suitable for quick exposi-
tory treatment. To distinguish the epistemology of grammar from
the epistemology of rhetoric is a redoubtable task. On an entirely
naïve level, we tend to conceive of grammatical systems as tending
towards universality and as simply generative, i.e., as capable of
deriving an infinity of versions from a single model (that may govern
transformations as well as derivations) without the intervention of
another model that would upset the first. We therefore think of the
relationship between grammar and logic, the passage from grammar to propositions, as being relatively unproblematic: no true propositions are conceivable in the absence of grammatical consistency or
of controlled deviation from a system of consistency no matter how
complex. Grammar and logic stand to each other in a dyadic relationship of unsubverted support. In a logic of acts rather than of
statements, as in Austin's theory of speech acts, that has had such a
strong influence on recent American work in literary semiology, it is
also possible to move between speech acts and grammar without

difficulty. The performance of what is called illocutionary acts such as ordering, questioning, denying, assuming, etc., within the language is congruent with the grammatical structures of syntax in the corresponding imperative, interrogative, negative, optative sentences. "The rules for illocutionary acts," writes Richard Ohman in a recent paper, "determine whether performance of a given act is well-executed, in just the same way as *grammatical* rules determine whether the product of a locutionary act—a sentence—is well formed. . . . But whereas the rules of grammar concern the relationships among sound, syntax, and meaning, the rules of illocutionary acts concern relationships among people."[1] And since rhetoric is then conceived exclusively as persuasion, as actual action upon others (and not as an intralinguistic figure or trope), the continuity between the illocutionary realm of grammar and the perlocutionary realm of rhetoric is self-evident. It becomes the basis for a new rhetoric that, exactly as is the case for Todorov and Genette, would also be a new grammar.

Without engaging the substance of the question, it can be pointed out, without having to go beyond recent and American examples, and without calling upon the strength of an age-old tradition, that the continuity here assumed between grammar and rhetoric is not borne out by theoretical and philosophical speculation. Kenneth Burke mentions *deflection* (which he compares structurally to Freudian displacement), defined as "any slight bias or even unintended error," as the rhetorical basis of language, and deflection is then conceived as a dialectical subversion of the consistent link between sign and meaning that operates within grammatical patterns; hence Burke's well-known insistence on the distinction between grammar and rhetoric. Charles Sanders Peirce, who, with Nietzsche and Saussure, laid the philosophical foundation for modern semiology, stressed the distinction between grammar and rhetoric in his celebrated and so suggestively unfathomable definition of the sign. He insists, as is well known, on the necessary presence of a third element, called the interpretant, within any relationship that the sign entertains with its object. The sign is to be interpreted if we are to understand the idea it is to convey, and this is so because the sign is not the thing but a meaning derived from the thing by a process here

1. "Speech, Literature, and the Space in Between," *New Literary History* 4 (Autumn 1972): 50.

called representation that is not simply generative, i.e., dependent on a univocal origin. The interpretation of the sign is not, for Peirce, a meaning but another sign; it is a reading, not a decodage, and this reading has, in its turn, to be interpreted into another sign, and so on *ad infinitum*. Peirce calls this process by means of which "one sign gives birth to another" pure rhetoric, as distinguished from pure grammar, which postulates the possibility of unproblematic, dyadic meaning, and pure logic, which postulates the possibility of the universal truth of meanings. Only if the sign engendered meaning in the same way that the object engenders the sign, that is, by representation, would there be no need to distinguish between grammar and rhetoric.

These remarks should indicate at least the existence and the difficulty of the question, a difficulty which puts its concise theoretical exposition beyond my powers. I must retreat therefore into a pragmatic discourse and try to illustrate the tension between grammar and rhetoric in a few specific textual examples. Let me begin by considering what is perhaps the most commonly known instance of an apparent symbiosis between a grammatical and a rhetorical structure, the so-called rhetorical question, in which the figure is conveyed directly by means of a syntactical device. I take the first example from the sub-literature of the mass media: asked by his wife whether he wants to have his bowling shoes laced over or laced under, Archie Bunker answers with a question: "What's the difference?" Being a reader of sublime simplicity, his wife replies by patiently explaining the difference between lacing over and lacing under, whatever this may be, but provokes only ire. "What's the difference" did not ask for difference but means instead "I don't give a damn what the difference is." The same grammatical pattern engenders two meanings that are mutually exclusive: the literal meaning asks for the concept (difference) whose existence is denied by the figurative meaning. As long as we are talking about bowling shoes, the consequences are relatively trivial; Archie Bunker, who is a great believer in the authority of origins (as long, of course, as they are the right origins) muddles along in a world where literal and figurative meanings get in each other's way, though not without discomforts. But suppose that it is a *de*-bunker rather than a "Bunker," and a de-bunker of the arche (or origin), an archie Debunker such as Nietzsche or Jacques Derrida for instance, who asks the question "What is the Difference"—and we cannot even tell from his grammar whether he "really" wants to know "what" difference is or is just telling us that we shouldn't even try to find out. Confronted with the question of the difference between grammar and rhetoric, grammar allows us to ask the question, but the sentence by means of which we ask it may deny the very possibility of asking. For what is the use of asking, I ask, when we cannot even authoritatively decide whether a question asks or doesn't ask?

The point is as follows. A perfectly clear syntactical paradigm (the question) engenders a sentence that has at least two meanings, of which the one asserts and the other denies its own illocutionary mode. It is not so that there are simply two meanings, one literal and the other figural, and that we have to decide which one of these meanings is the right one in this particular situation. The confusion can only be cleared up by the intervention of an extra-textual intention, such as Archie Bunker putting his wife straight; but the very anger he displays is indicative of more than impatience; it reveals his despair when confronted with a structure of linguistic meaning that he cannot control and that holds the discouraging prospect of an infinity of similar future confusions, all of them potentially catastrophic in their consequences. Nor is this intervention really a part of the mini-text constituted by the figure which holds our attention only as long as it remains suspended and unresolved. I follow the usage of common speech in calling this semiological enigma "rhetorical." The grammatical model of the question becomes rhetorical not when we have, on the one hand, a literal meaning and on the other hand a figural meaning, but when it is impossible to decide by grammatical or other linguistic devices which of the two meanings (that can be entirely incompatible) prevails. Rhetoric radically suspends logic and opens up vertiginous possibilities of referential aberration. And although it would perhaps be somewhat more remote from common usage, I would not hesitate to equate the rhetorical, figural potentiality of language with literature itself. I could point to a great number of antecedents to this equation of literature with figure; the most recent reference would be to Monroe Beardsley's insistence in his contribution to the *Essays* to honor William Wimsatt, that literary language is characterized by being "distinctly above the norm in ratio of implicit [or, I would say rhetorical] to explicit meaning."[2]

2. "The Concept of Literature," in *Literary Theory and Structure: Essays in Honor of William K. Wimsatt*, ed. Frank Brady, John Palmer, and Martin Price (New Haven, 1973), p. 37.

Let me pursue the matter of the rhetorical question through one more example. Yeats's poem "Among School Children" ends with the famous line: "How can we know the dancer from the dance?" Although there are some revealing inconsistencies within the commentaries, the line is usually interpreted as stating, with the increased emphasis of a rhetorical device, the potential unity between form and experience, between creator and creation. It could be said that it denies the discrepancy between the sign and the referent from which we started out. Many elements in the imagery and the dramatic development of the poem strengthen this traditional reading; without having to look any further than the immediately preceding lines, one finds powerful and consecrated images of the continuity from part to whole that makes synecdoche into the most seductive of metaphors: the organic beauty of the tree, stated in the parallel syntax of a similar rhetorical question, or the convergence, in the dance, of erotic desire with musical form:

> O chestnut-tree, great-rooted blossomer,
> Are you the leaf, the blossom or the bole?
> O body swayed to music, O brightening glance,
> How can we know the dancer from the dance?

A more extended reading, always assuming that the final line is to be read as a rhetorical question, reveals that the thematic and rhetorical grammar of the poem yields a consistent reading that extends from the first line to the last and that can account for all the details in the text. It is equally possible, however, to read the last line literally rather than figuratively, as asking with some urgency the question we asked earlier within the context of contemporary criticism: *not* that sign and referent are so exquisitely fitted to each other that all difference between them is at times blotted out but, rather, since the two essentially different elements, sign and meaning, are so intricately intertwined in the imagined "presence" that the poem addresses, how can we possibly make the distinctions that would shelter us from the error of identifying what cannot be identified? The clumsiness of the paraphrase reveals that it is not necessarily the literal reading which is simpler than the figurative one, as was the case in our first example; here, the figural reading, which assumes the question to be rhetorical, is perhaps naïve, whereas the literal reading leads to greater complication of theme and statement. For it turns out that the entire scheme set up by the first reading can be undermined, or deconstructed, in the terms of the second, in which the final line is read literally as meaning that, since the dancer and the dance are not the same, it might be useful, perhaps even desperately necessary—for the question can be given a ring of urgency, "Please tell me, how *can* I know the dancer from the dance"—to tell them apart. But this will replace the reading of each symbolic detail by a divergent interpretation. The oneness of trunk, leaf, and blossom, for example, that would have appealed to Goethe, would find itself replaced by the much less reassuring Tree of Life from the Mabinogion that appears in the poem "Vacillation," in which the fiery blossom and the earthly leaf are held together, as well as apart, by the crucified and castrated God Attis, of whose body it can hardly be said that it is "not bruised to pleasure soul." This hint should suffice to suggest that two entirely coherent but entirely incompatible readings can be made to hinge on one line, whose grammatical structure is devoid of ambiguity, but whose rhetorical mode turns the mood as well as the mode of the entire poem upside down. Neither can we say, as was already the case in the first example, that the poem simply has two meanings that exist side by side. The two readings have to engage each other in direct confrontation, for the one reading is precisely the error denounced by the other and has to be undone by it. Nor can we in any way make a valid decision as to which of the readings can be given priority over the other; none can exist in the other's absence. There can be no dance without a dancer, no sign without a referent. On the other hand, the authority of the meaning engendered by the grammatical structure is fully obscured by the duplicity of a figure that cries out for the differentiation that it conceals.

Yeats's poem is not explicitly "about" rhetorical questions but about images or metaphors, and about the possibility of convergence between experiences of consciousness such as memory or emotions—what the poem calls passion, piety, and affection—and entities accessible to the senses such as bodies, persons, or icons. We return to the inside/outside model from which we started out and which the poem puts into question by means of a syntactical device (the question) made to operate on a grammatical as well as on a rhetorical level. The couple grammar/rhetoric, certainly not a binary opposition since they in no way exclude each other, disrupts and confuses the neat antithesis of the inside/outside pattern. We can transfer this scheme to the act of reading and interpretation. By reading we get, as we say, *inside* a text that was first something alien to us and which we now make our own by an act of understanding. But this understanding becomes at once the representation of an extra-textual meaning; in Austin's terms, the illocutionary speech act becomes a perlocutionary actual act—in Frege's terms, *Bedeutung* becomes *Sinn.* Our recurrent question is whether this transformation is semantically controlled along grammatical or along rhetorical lines. Does the metaphor of reading really unite outer meaning with inner understanding, action with reflection, into one single totality? The assertion is powerfully and suggestively made in a passage from Proust that describes the experience of reading as such a union. It describes the young Marcel, near the beginning of Combray, hiding in the closed space of his room in order to read. The example differs from the earlier ones in that we are not dealing with a grammatical structure that also functions rhetorically but have instead the representation, the dramatization, in terms of the experience of a subject, of a rhetorical structure—just as, in many other passages, Proust dramatizes tropes by means of landscapes or descriptions of objects. The figure here dramatized is that of metaphor, an inside/outside correspondence as represented by the act of reading. The reading scene is the culmination of a series of actions taking place in enclosed spaces and leading up to the "dark coolness" of Marcel's room.

> I had stretched out on my bed, with a book, in my room which sheltered, tremblingly, its transparent and fragile coolness from the afternoon sun, behind the almost closed blinds through which a glimmer of daylight had nevertheless managed to push its yellow wings, remaining motionless between the wood and the glass, in a corner, poised like a butterfly. It was hardly light enough to read, and the sensation of the light's splendor was given me only by the noise of Camus . . . hammering dusty crates; resounding in the sonorous atmosphere that is peculiar to hot weather, they seemed to spark off scarlet stars; and also by the flies executing their little concert, the chamber music of summer: evocative not in the manner of a human tune that, heard perchance during the summer, afterwards reminds you of it but connected to summer by a more necessary link: born from beautiful days, resurrecting only when they return, containing some of their essence, it does not only awaken their image in our memory; it guarantees their return, their actual, persistent, unmediated presence.
>
> The dark coolness of my room related to the full sunlight of

the street as the shadow relates to the ray of light, that is to say
it was just as luminous and it gave my imagination the total
spectacle of the summer, whereas my senses, if I had been on a
walk, could only have enjoyed it by fragments; it matched my
repose which (thanks to the adventures told by my book and
stirring my tranquility) supported, like the quiet of a motionless
hand in the middle of a running brook the shock and the motion
of a torrent of activity. [*Swann's Way*. Paris: Pléiade, 1954, p.
83.]

For our present purpose, the most striking aspect of this passage
is the juxtaposition of figural and metafigural language. It contains
seductive metaphors that bring into play a variety of irresistible
objects: chamber music, butterflies, stars, books, running brooks,
etc., and it inscribes these objects within dazzling fire- and water-
works of figuration. But the passage also comments normatively on
the best way to achieve such effects; in this sense, it is metafigural: it
writes figuratively about figures. It contrasts two ways of evoking the
natural experience of summer and unambiguously states its preference for one of these ways over the other: the "necessary link" that
unites the buzzing of the flies to the summer makes it a much more
effective symbol than the tune heard "perchance" during the summer. The preference is expressed by means of a distinction that
corresponds to the difference between metaphor and metonymy,
necessity and chance being a legitimate way to distinguish between
analogy and contiguity. The inference of identity and totality that is
constitutive of metaphor is lacking in the purely relational metonymic contact: an element of truth is involved in taking Achilles
for a lion but none in taking Mr. Ford for a motor car. The passage is
about the aesthetic superiority of metaphor over metonymy, but this
aesthetic claim is made by means of categories that are the ontological ground of the metaphysical system that allows for the aesthetic to
come into being as a category. The metaphor for summer (in this
case, the synesthesia set off by the "chamber music" of the flies)
guarantees a presence which, far from being contingent, is said to be
essential, permanently recurrent and unmediated by linguistic representations or figurations. Finally, in the second part of the passage,
the metaphor of presence not only appears as the ground of cognition but as the performance of an action, thus promising the reconciliation of the most disruptive of contradictions. By then, the in-

vestment in the power of metaphor is such that it may seem sac-
rilegious to put it in question.

Yet, it takes little perspicacity to show that the text does not
practice what it preaches. A rhetorical reading of the passage reveals
that the figural praxis and the metafigural theory do not converge
and that the assertion of the mastery of metaphor over metonymy
owes its persuasive power to the use of metonymic structures. I have
carried out such an analysis in a somewhat more extended context
(pp. 59–67, below); at this point, we are more concerned with the
results than with the procedure. For the metaphysical categories of
presence, essence, action, truth, and beauty do not remain unaffected by such a reading. This would become clear from an inclusive reading of Proust's novel or would become even more explicit
in a language-conscious philosopher such as Nietzsche who, as a
philosopher, has to be concerned with the epistemological consequences of the kind of rhetorical seductions exemplified by the Proust
passage. It can be shown that the systematic critique of the main
categories of metaphysics undertaken by Nietzsche in his late work,
the critique of the concepts of causality, of the subject, of identity, of
referential and revealed truth, etc., occurs along the same pattern of
deconstruction that was operative in Proust's text; and it can also be
shown that this pattern exactly corresponds to Nietzsche's description, in texts that precede *The Will to Power* by more than fifteen
years, of the structure of the main rhetorical tropes. The key to this
critique of metaphysics, which is itself a recurrent gesture throughout the history of thought, is the rhetorical model of the trope or, if
one prefers to call it that, literature. It turns out that in these
innocent-looking didactic exercises we are in fact playing for very
sizeable stakes.

It is therefore all the more necessary to know what is linguistically involved in a rhetorically conscious reading of the type here
undertaken on a brief fragment from a novel and extended by
Nietzsche to the entire text of post-Hellenic thought. Our first examples dealing with the rhetorical questions were rhetorizations of
grammar, figures generated by syntactical paradigms, whereas the
Proust example could be better described as a grammatization of
rhetoric. By passing from a paradigmatic structure based on substitution, such as metaphor, to a syntagmatic structure based on
contingent association such as metonymy, the mechanical, repetitive
aspect of grammatical forms is shown to be operative in a passage

that seemed at first sight to celebrate the self-willed and autonomous inventiveness of a subject. Figures are assumed to be inventions, the products of a highly particularized individual talent, whereas no one can claim credit for the programmed pattern of grammar. Yet, our reading of the Proust passage shows that precisely when the highest claims are being made for the unifying power of metaphor, these very images rely in fact on the deceptive use of semi-automatic grammatical patterns. The deconstruction of metaphor and of all rhetorical patterns such as mimesis, paranomasis, or personification that use resemblance as a way to disguise differences, takes us back to the impersonal precision of grammar and of a semiology derived from grammatical patterns. Such a reading puts into question a whole series of concepts that underlie the value judgments of our critical discourse: the metaphors of primacy, of genetic history, and, most notably, of the autonomous power to will of the self.

There seems to be a difference, then, between what I called the rhetorization of grammar (as in the rhetorical question) and the grammatization of rhetoric, as in the readings of the type sketched out in the passage from Proust. The former end up in indetermination, in a suspended uncertainty that was unable to choose between two modes of reading, whereas the latter seems to reach a truth, albeit by the negative road of exposing an error, a false pretense. After the rhetorical reading of the Proust passage, we can no longer believe the assertion made in this passage about the intrinsic, metaphysical superiority of metaphor over metonymy. We seem to end up in a mood of negative assurance that is highly productive of critical discourse. The further text of Proust's novel, for example, responds perfectly to an extended application of this pattern: not only can similar gestures be repeated throughout the novel, at all the crucial articulations or all passages where large aesthetic and metaphysical claims are being made—the scenes of involuntary memory, the workshop of Elstir, the septette of Vinteuil, the convergence of author and narrator at the end of the novel—but a vast thematic and semiotic network is revealed that structures the entire narrative and that remained invisible to a reader caught in naïve metaphorical mystification. The whole of literature would respond in similar fashion, although the techniques and the patterns would have to vary considerably, of course, from author to author. But there is absolutely no reason why analyses of the kind here suggested for Proust would not be applicable, with proper modifications of tech-

nique, to Milton or to Dante or to Hölderlin. This will in fact be the
task of literary criticism in the coming years.

It would seem that we are saying that criticism is the deconstruction of literature, the reduction to the rigors of grammar of
rhetorical mystifications. And if we hold up Nietzsche as the
philosopher of such a critical deconstruction, then the literary critic
would become the philosopher's ally in his struggle with the poets.
Criticism and literature would separate around the epistemological
axis that distinguishes grammar from rhetoric. It is easy enough to
see that this apparent glorification of the critic-philosopher in the
name of truth is in fact a glorification of the poet as the primary
source of this truth; if truth is the recognition of the systematic
character of a certain kind of error, then it would be fully dependent
on the prior existence of this error. Philosophers of science like
Bachelard or Wittgenstein are notoriously dependent on the aberrations of the poets. We are back at our unanswered question: does the
grammatization of rhetoric end up in negative certainty or does it,
like the rhetorization of grammar, remain suspended in the ignorance of its own truth or falsehood?

Two concluding remarks should suffice to answer the question.
First of all, it is not true that Proust's text can simply be reduced to
the mystified assertion (the superiority of metaphor over metonymy)
that our reading deconstructs. The reading is not "our" reading,
since it uses only the linguistic elements provided by the text itself;
the distinction between author and reader is one of the false distinctions that the reading makes evident. The deconstruction is not
something we have added to the text but it constituted the text in the
first place. A literary text simultaneously asserts and denies the authority of its own rhetorical mode, and by reading the text as we did
we were only trying to come closer to being as rigorous a reader as
the author had to be in order to write the sentence in the first place.
Poetic writing is the most advanced and refined mode of deconstruction; it may differ from critical or discursive writing in the economy
of its articulation, but not in kind.

But if we recognize the existence of such a moment as constitutive of all literary language, we have surreptitiously reintroduced the
categories that this deconstruction was supposed to eliminate and
that have merely been displaced. We have, for example, displaced
the question of the self from the referent into the figure of the
narrator, who then becomes the *signifié* of the passage. It becomes

again possible to ask such naïve questions as what Proust's, or Marcel's, motives may have been in thus manipulating language: was he fooling himself, or was he represented as fooling himself and fooling us into believing that fiction and action are as easy to unite, by reading, as the passage asserts? The pathos of the entire section, which would have been more noticeable if the quotation had been a little more extended, the constant vacillation of the narrator between guilt and well-being, invites such questions. They are absurd questions, of course, since the reconciliation of fact and fiction occurs itself as a mere assertion made in a text, and is thus productive of more text at the moment when it asserts its decision to escape from textual confinement. But even if we free ourselves of all false questions of intent and rightfully reduce the narrator to the status of a mere grammatical pronoun, without which the narrative could not come into being, this subject remains endowed with a function that is not grammatical but rhetorical, in that it gives voice, so to speak, to a grammatical syntagm. The term *voice*, even when used in a grammatical terminology as when we speak of the passive or interrogative voice, is, of course, a metaphor inferring by analogy the intent of the subject from the structure of the predicate. In the case of the deconstructive discourse that we call literary, or rhetorical, or poetic, this creates a distinctive complication illustrated by the Proust passage. The reading revealed a first paradox: the passage valorizes metaphor as being the "right" literary figure, but then proceeds to constitute itself by means of the epistemologically incompatible figure of metonymy. The critical discourse reveals the presence of this delusion and affirms it as the irreversible mode of its truth. It cannot pause there however. For if we then ask the obvious and simple next question, whether the rhetorical mode of the text in question is that of metaphor or metonymy, it is impossible to give an answer. Individual metaphors, such as the chiaroscuro effect or the butterfly, are shown to be subordinate figures in a general clause whose syntax is metonymic; from this point of view, it seems that the rhetoric is superseded by a grammar that deconstructs it. But this metonymic clause has as its subject a voice whose relationship to this clause is again metaphorical. The narrator who tells us about the impossibility of metaphor is himself, or itself, a metaphor, the metaphor of a grammatical syntagm whose meaning is the denial of metaphor stated, by antiphrasis, as its priority. And this subject-metaphor is, in its turn, open to the kind of deconstruction to the second degree, the rhetorical deconstruction of psycholinguistics, in which the more advanced investigations of literature are presently engaged, against considerable resistance.

We end up therefore, in the case of the rhetorical grammatization of semiology, just as in the grammatical rhetorization of illocutionary phrases, in the same state of suspended ignorance. Any question about the rhetorical mode of a literary text is always a rhetorical question which does not even know whether it is really questioning. The resulting pathos is an anxiety (or bliss, depending on one's momentary mood or individual temperament) of ignorance, not an anxiety of reference—as becomes thematically clear in Proust's novel when reading is dramatized, in the relationship between Marcel and Albertine, not as an emotive reaction to what language does, but as an emotive reaction to the impossibility of knowing what it might be up to. Literature as well as criticism—the difference between them being delusive—is condemned (or privileged) to be forever the most rigorous and, consequently, the most unreliable language in terms of which man names and transforms himself.

2　Tropes

(Rilke)

RILKE IS ONE OF THE FEW POETS OF THE TWENTIETH century to have reached a large and worldwide audience. Even in France, where Yeats, Eliot, Wallace Stevens, Montale, Trakl, or Hofmannsthal are not widely known, Rilke is more read than most of the French poets of this century. More than fifty years after his death, a Rilke myth still lives well beyond the borders of the German-speaking world.

The reasons for this degree of public prominence are not obvious, for Rilke is not an easy or a popular poet. His work resists translation, his themes are intimate, and his discourse often oblique. Yet he has been received with a great deal of fervor, as if what he had to say was of direct concern even to readers remote from him in their language and in their destinies. Many have read him as if he addressed the most secluded parts of their selves, revealing depths they hardly suspected or allowing them to share in ordeals he helped them to understand and to overcome. Numerous biographies, reminiscences, and letters bear witness to this highly personal mode of reception. Rilke seems to be endowed with the healing power of those who open up access to the hidden layers of our consciousness or to a delicacy of emotion that reflects, to those capable of perceiving its shades, the reassuring image of their own solicitude. Rilke has himself often played on the ambiguity of a double-faced relationship toward others, leaving in abeyance which of the two, the poet or his reader, depended on the other to nourish his strength. "I wish to help and expect to be helped. Everyone's eternal mistake is to take me for a healer when, in fact, I am only attracting others, for my own profit, in the trap of a simulated assistance."[1] Rilke confides this self-insight in connection with a love affair, but it summarizes a mood encouraged by some aspects of the work. The initial seduction, the first intimacy

1. Letter from Rilke to the Princess of Thurn and Taxis, February 24, 1915, in *Briefwechsel Rilke / Maria von Thurn und Taxis* (Zürich, 1951), 1:399.

between Rilke and his readers almost inevitably occurs as an ambiguous complicity in shared confrontation with "the near-impossibility of living."[2] Some passages of *Malte*, large fragments of the correspondence, the general tonality of *The Book of Hours*, or a somewhat hasty reading of the *Duino Elegies*—all orient the reading in that direction. This tendency, which Rilke did nothing to discourage, contributed much to the formation and the success of the personal myth. It also left extensive traces in Rilke studies: it is sometimes difficult to discover the memory of the original texts under the abundant confessional discourse that it generates in the commentators. Rilke's considerable audience is in part based on a relationship of complicity, on shared weaknesses.

It is not difficult, for a reader alerted to the ambivalences of the relationship between the self and its language, to demystify this seduction. The intersubjective reading grounded in a common sentiment, in the "transparency of the heart," does not allow one to reach the area of Rilke's poetry that is not affected by this demystification. In the case of this poet, readings that start out from the most self-directed passages in the letters, the novels, or the confessional texts fail to uncover the poetic dimension of the work. The reason for this is not the bad faith which Rilke confesses in the letter from which I have just quoted; his poetry does not escape from sympathetic understanding because, under the guise of being solicitous and disinterested, he does not hesitate, at times, to use others rather coldly. The mechanics of this bad faith would be easy to describe and, if they were indeed at the center of his consciousness, they would be an effective way of access to his inner being. But they are in fact peripheral and secondary. It has not been difficult to call into question the image of Rilke as a healer of soul and to prove that he was both less generous in practical and less stable in psychological matters than one might have suspected.[3] Rilke's intimate self remains in fact quite invisible and, far from being its driving force, it tends to vanish from the poetry altogether—which does not mean that this poetry is deprived of a certain mode of inwardness that remains to be defined. But the poet Rilke is less interested in his own person than one might gather from his tone and from his pathos.

2. ". . . des Lebens Fast-Unmöglichkeit," same letter, p. 399.
3. See, for example, Peter Demetz, *René Rilkes Prager Jahre* (Düsseldorf, 1953), and Erich Simenauer, *R. M. Rilke, Legende und Mythos* (Bern, 1953).

The narcissism that is often ascribed to him no doubt exists, but on a very different level from that of a reader using him as a reflector for his own inner image. The personal seduction is certainly an important component of the work, but it functions, so to speak, as its zone of maximal opacity. One could approach and interpret a sizeable part of his poetry by way of the negative road that would analyze this seduction. It may be preferable however to try to understand the work in a less antithetical way and to read the poetic texts themselves, rather than letters and confessional prose that may well turn out to be of contingent importance.

On a somewhat more advanced level of understanding, the attractiveness of Rilke stems from his themes. This is obvious, first of all, in the most superficial of ways: the poetry puts on display a brilliant variety of places, objects, and characters. As in Baudelaire, the categories of the beautiful and the ugly are subsumed, in Rilke, under the common rubric of the interesting. His poetic universe has something dazzling, as if it consisted of rare items in a collection or a museum, well set off against the background of a world that emphasizes their singularity. Repugnant and terrifying themes have the same seductive power as the numberless objects of beauty and of light—fountains, toys, cathedrals, cities of Spain and Italy, roses, windows, orchards—that appear throughout the work. A form of poetic decorum, itself a mixture of caution and of genuine reserve, holds the violent images at a distance and prevents them from acquiring a presence strong enough to undo the fiction or to dislocate the language. No matter which of the uncanny figures one singles out, be it the epileptic in *Malte*, the stylite of the *New Poems*, or the sinister acrobats of the Fifth Elegy, one will always encounter this picturesque and surprising element mixed with the horror and interposing, between the reader and the theme, the screen of a language that controls its own representational mastery. Even in what appears to be Rilke's most personal poem, the poem written a few days before his death and dealing with his physical pain, the pain remains "embellished" by the virtuosity of a perfectly prepared and executed conceit.

It would be a mistake to dismiss this concern for attractive surfaces all too hastily as a form of aestheticism. The reference to Baudelaire should suffice to stress that more is involved. Aesthetic refinement is for Rilke, as for the author of the *Fleurs du mal*, an Apollonian strategy which allows him to state what would otherwise by unsayable. On this level of experience, the aesthetics of beauty and of ugliness can no longer be distinguished from each other. Nor is it possible to think of these seductive surfaces as merely superficial.

For the thematic attraction also functions on a more generally inclusive level of understanding. Beyond the brightness of the settings, Rilke's work dares to affirm and to promise, as few others do, a form of existential salvation that would take place in and by means of poetry. Few poets and thinkers of our century have dared to go so far in their affirmations, especially in affirmations that refuse to be anchored in established philosophical or theological certainties, or to have recourse to ethical imperatives that might directly lead to modes of action. It may seem surprising to characterize Rilke's work as positive and affirmative when it puts such stress on the main negative themes of modern consciousness. Rilke has an acute awareness of the alienated and factitious character of human reality, and he goes far in his refusal to grant any experience the power to suspend this alienation. Neither love nor the imagining power of the deepest nostalgias can overcome the essential barrenness of the self and of the world. Severed forever from the plenitudes of self-presence, Rilke's figure of humanity is the frailest and most exposed creature imaginable. He calls man "the most ephemeral" (Ninth Elegy), "the most fleeting" (Fifth Elegy), the creature "that is incessantly departing" (Eighth Elegy), and that can never establish itself in an appeased presence to itself or to the world. The promise that the work contains is therefore anything but facile. But this makes it all the more convincing.

On the thematic level, the existence of this promise is undeniable. The large affirmations of the *Elegies*, gnomic as they are, bear witness to this assertion, all the more so since they promise a salvation that could take place here and now: "Hiersein ist herrlich" ("To be here is glorious" [Seventh Elegy]); "*Hier* ist des *Säglichen* Zeit, *hier* seine Heimat" ("*Here* is the time for the *Tellable, here* is its home" [Ninth Elegy]); "Supernumerous existence / wells up in my heart" (idem). This emphatic *here* designates the poetic text itself and thus affirms that it escapes the fragmentation of number and of time. In the audacity of his assertion, Rilke assumes for poetry the furthest-reaching promise conceivable. The evolution of his own poetry seems to fulfil this promise. After being announced in the *Elegies*, it comes about in the appeased tonality of the later work, the *Sonnets to Orpheus*, and many of the poems written after 1912 and published posthumously. It can be said of these poems that they perform the transition from elegy to hymn, from complaint [*Klage*] to praise [*Rühmen*].

One can understand therefore that Rilke not only claims the right to state his own salvation but to impose it, as it were, on others. The imperative mode that often appears in his poetry ("You must change your life"; "Demand change"; "Sing the world to the Angel" . . .) is not only addressed to himself but asks for the acquiescence of his reader. The exhortation is rooted in an authority confirmed by the possibility of its poetic existence. Far from putting this assurance in jeopardy, the insistence of the negative themes certifies its veracity. A too easily granted promise would be suspect and would not convince, but a promise of salvation that could only be deserved by endless labor and sacrifice, in suffering, renunciation, and death, is a different matter. One can begin to understand Rilke's poetry only if one is willing to entertain this conviction. As for deciding whether it is a legitimate promise, whether it is a truth or a seduction, the question must remain open, not only as a matter of caution but because a rigorous reading must determine whether or not the work itself asks this question.

The interpreters who read Rilke's work as a radical summons to transform our way of being in the world are therefore not misrepresenting him; such a summons is indeed a central theme of the poetry. Some respond to it without reservations. Others have suggested that Rilke is still in the grip of ontological presuppositions which even the most extreme of his experiences cannot reach and that the reversal he demands, difficult as it may be, is still premature and illusory. Rilke's good faith is not being questioned, but his blindness could be demonstrated by the critical analysis of his thought. Heidegger had oriented the reading of Rilke in this direction, in an essay published in 1949 which Rilkean studies have not yet entirely assimilated.[4] But it may be that the positivity of the thematic assertion is not entirely unambiguous and that Rilke's language, almost in spite of its own assertions, puts it in question.

This does not, at first sight, seem to be the case. The advanced level of reflexive self-knowledge that informs Rilke's poetry nowhere conflicts with the mastery of his poetic invention. The meaning of the statement dovetails perfectly with the mode of expression, and since

4. "Wozu Dichter . . ." in *Holzwege* (Frankfurt am Main, 1950).

this meaning possesses considerable philosophical depth, poetry and thought here seem to be united in a perfect synthesis.

For that reason, even the best interpretations of Rilke seem to have remained, by and large, on the level of paraphrase, a paraphrase that is often subtle and careful but that does not question the convergence of the meaning with the linguistic devices used to convey it.[5] The statements are rich enough in their content to saturate the full range of meaning. The fact that these highly reflected statements directly implicate language as a constitutive category of meaning and thematize some of the lexicological and rhetorical aspects of poetical diction by no means troubles the assumed convergence between statement and *lexis*, between what is being said and the mode of its saying. Rilke's propositions about language are in fact carried out in his poetry, thus allowing one to move freely between poetry and poetics. The possibility of a conflict between both never seems to arise. Thus one of Rilke's commentators can write: "The poetic 'content' and the poetic 'form' are so perfectly united in Rilke's work that it becomes impossible to object against the value of this poetry in the name of a possible divergence between 'thought' and 'poetry'."[6] Such a divergence is inconceivable because Rilke is claimed to state, in and through his poetry, the very essence of poetry as the truth of this essence. "The true essence of poetry . . . is identical with the structures of its poetic 'content'." In the author from whom we borrow these formulations, this truth is equated with an existential decision that does not necessarily involve language. But the existential stance must eventually lead to decisions that function on the level of the language, even if these decisions appear to be of secondary importance. The same commentator is naturally led to consider formal aspects of the poetry, such as rhyme or metaphor, but he at once curbs their potential autonomy by fully identifying them with the theme they convey: "The fundamental poetic practice, namely the elaboration of a metaphorical language, also derives from the experience of suffering. The metaphor is an act of identification: the actual suffering of the poet is made 'equal' with that of his symbolic

5. The studies of Rilke that come closest to raising this question, without however considering it directly, are the work of Beda Alleman, *Zeit und Figur beim späten Rilke* (Pfüllingen, 1961), and Maurice Blanchot's considerations on Rilke in *L'espace littéraire* (Paris, 1955).

6. Hermann Mörchen, *Rilkes Sonette an Orpheus* (Stuttgart, 1958), p. 20.

figures. . . ."[7] The ontological alienation that Rilke so eloquently evokes would then not implicate language in any way. Language is the unmediated expression of an unhappy consciousness that it does not cause. This implies that language is entirely ancillary in its relation to a fundamental experience (the pain and the pathos of being) which it merely reflects, but that it is also entirely truthful, since it faithfully reproduces the truth of this pathos. The poet can thus abandon himself without fear to his language, even to its most formal and outward features:

> The logic of sounds [*Lautlogik*] to which the poet yields when he allows himself to be governed by the power of his language can be meaningful only when it stands in the service of the truth which this language uses in order to conserve it. Poetry can be truth only when its trust in language—a trust that is not confined to acoustic affinities but that includes linguistic structures in general, including etymological relationships—is indeed attuned to this justification of existence which language, in the region of its authentic origin, is always in the process of formulating.[8]

With very few exceptions, similar presuppositions underlie the best available critical readings of Rilke.[9] One may well ask whether the poetry indeed shares in the conception of language that is attributed to it. Such a question differs entirely from a concentration on the "form" of Rilke's poetry, in the narrowly aesthetic sense of the term; several careful studies have taken this approach but failed to reach major exegetic results.[10] By suggesting that the properly poetic dimension of Rilke's work has been neglected in favor of his themes, we do not wish to return to the seduction of the forms. The question is rather whether Rilke's text turns back upon itself in a manner that

---

7. Mörchen, p. 21; see also p. 15.

8. Mörchen, p. 21.

9. The remark applies, with qualifications too complex to enumerate here, to the writings on Rilke of Heidegger, Guardini, Bollnow, Mason, and Jacob Steiner.

10. Such as, for instance, H. W. Belmore, *Rilke's Craftmanship: An Analysis of His Poetic Style* (Oxford, 1954); Ulrich Fülleborn, *Das Strukturproblem der späten Lyrik Rilkes* (Heidelberg, 1960); Frank H. Wood, *Rainer Maria Rilke: The Ring of Forms* (Minneapolis, 1958); Brigitte L. Bradley, *Rainer Maria Rilkes neue Gedichte: Ihr zyklisches Gefüge* (Bern, 1968).

puts the authority of its own affirmations in doubt, especially when these affirmations refer to the modes of writing that it advocates. At a time when the philosophical interest of Rilke's thought has perhaps somewhat declined, the present and future signification of his poetry depends upon the answer to this question.

Rilke's work is often said to be divided by a clear break that corresponds approximately to the passage from *The Book of Hours* to *The Book of Images*; it is also from this moment on that a degree of mastery is achieved and that his manner reaches a certain stability.[11] The break marks an important modification in the metaphorical and dramatic texture of the poetry. The more properly phonic elements are less affected by it. Before and after this date, Rilke persists in giving considerable importance to rhyme, assonance, and alliteration; in this respect, one can hardly speak of a major change, except for a greater degree of refinement and control in the expressive use of acoustic effects of language.

It is not easy to interpret this change. Commentators agree neither on the meaning nor on the evaluation of *The Book of Hours*, and they have difficulty locating it within the corpus of the complete work. Certain characteristics of the situation and of the tone (a prayer addressed to a transcendental entity) seem to prefigure the *Duino Elegies*; the volume also contains the first mention of symbolic objects and privileged words which will later acquire a central importance, whereas many of the other themes of *The Book of Hours*

11. This bipartite division of the work does not correspond to a strict chronology in the composition of the poems. The texts that make up Parts I and II of *The Book of Hours (The Book of Pilgrimage* and *The Book of Poverty and Death)* date from September 1901 and from April 1903 respectively, whereas some of the texts included in *The Book of Images* go back as far as July 1899 and thus at times antedate even *The Book of Monastic Life* which was written in September 1899. Yet taking the manner and the style of the subsequent work as a norm, *The Book of Images* certainly appears more "advanced" than *The Book of Hours*. Rather than a genetic development, we are dealing with two distinct poetic manners that can exist side by side. According to the same stylistic criteria, *The Life of Mary*, which dates from 1912, would belong to Rilke's youthful work. This proves that the distinction between what is called "early" and "late" work is often not as simple as a genetic terminology would lead one to believe. Still, the break to which we are here alluding offers a convenient point of reference for the organization of the work. As long as one does not confer upon it the power that belongs to origins, the division has a certain validity.

disappear from the later work.[12] The fervor with which the poems address a power that is given the name of "God" raises the question of their theocentric structure, a question that never stops haunting the exegesis of Rilke without, however, receiving a satisfactory answer.[13] Like iron filings under the power of a magnet, the verbal mass turns towards a single object that causes the eclosion of an abundant poetic discourse. The following poem, a typical instance of Rilke's poetry at this time, can both give us some notion of this discourse and serve as an introduction to the general problematics of the work. Since we have to allude to sound elements that cannot be translated, I quote in German:

> Ich liebe dich, du sanftestes Gesetz,
> an dem wir reiften, da wir mit ihm rangen
> du grosses Heimweh, das wir nicht bezwangen,
> du Wald, aus dem wir nie hinausgegangen,
> du Lied, das wir mit jedem Schweigen sangen,
> du dunkles Netz,
> darin sich flüchtend die Gefühle fangen.

> Du hast dich so unendlich gross begonnen
> an jenem Tage, da du uns begannst,—
> und wir sind so gereift in deinen Sonnen,
> so breit geworden and so tief gepflanzt,
> dass du in Menschen, Engeln und Madonnen
> dich ruhend jetzt vollenden kannst.

> Lass deine Hand am Hang der Himmel ruhn
> und dulde stumm, was wir dir dunkel tun.

> > > > > > > [1:24]

---

12. As in the figure of the ball, metaphor for God and addressed as "Ding der Dinge" in a poem from *The Book of Monastic Life* (*Rainer Maria Rilke, Werke in drei Bänden* [Frankfurt am Main: Insel Verlag, 1966], 1:21. All quotations from Rilke's poems refer to this edition). The passage can be read as an early version of some of the *New Poems*.

13. Else Buddeberg, *Rainer Maria Rilke, eine innere Biographie* (Stuttgart, 1954), observes, with reference to *The Book of Hours*, "that the evaluation of [its] merit is still being much discussed today" and quotes two critics to illustrate the wide divergences of opinion. One of them speaks of a "relinquishing of the self to God . . . as the German language had not known since Hölderlin," whereas the other asserts that it would be a "sentimental confusion . . . to find the slightest trace of serious religious feeling in this book" (Buddeberg, p. 531).

By its setting, which follows the convention of the ode as a series of reiterated apostrophes that are as many metaphors, the poem indeed seems to be fully centered on the entity it attempts to name. But the periphrastic designation is so diverse that it becomes vague: the entity is addressed as "law," "homesickness," "forest," "song," and "net," a sequence that cannot easily be reduced to a common denominator. Moreover, the entity is never itself designated by one of the attributes that properly belong to it. The play of personal pronouns is balanced between "I" (or "we") and "you," thus establishing a nearly perfect symmetry from which the third person is practically excluded; after the "ihm" in the second line, the "ich/du" or "du/wir" pattern is close to perfect.[14] The object of the apostrophe is only addressed in terms of an activity that it provokes in the addressing subject: if it is said to be a forest, it is only with reference to our behavior towards this forest; the net exists only as an obstacle to *our* flight; law is, per definition, that which governs our behavior and the song is at once identified as *our* song (or silence). The metaphors therefore do not connote objects, sensations, or qualities of objects (there is practically no third person in the grammar of the poem[15]), but refer to an activity of the speaking subject. The dominating

14. The difficulty of translation, especially in the earlier Rilke poems, remains visible in the version produced by J. B. Leishman (Rainer Maria Rilke, *Selected Works* [London, 1960], p. 38):

> I love you, gentlest law, through which we yet
> were ripening while with it we contended,
> you great homesickness we have not transcended,
> you forest out of which we never wended,
> you song that from our silence has ascended,
> you somber net
> where feelings taking flight are apprehended.
>
> You made yourself a so immense beginning
> the day when you began us too,—and we
> beneath your suns such ripeness have been winning
> have grown so broadly and deep-rootedly,
> that you, in angels, men, madonnas inning,
> can now complete yourself quite tranquilly.
>
> Let your right hand on heaven's slope repose
> and mutely bear what darkly we impose.

15. An exception occurs in line 7, where the third person [*die Gefühle*] precisely refers to the feelings, to the interiority of the subject.

center, the "du" of the poem, is present in the poem only to delegate, so to speak, its potential activity to the speaking voice; this becomes the explicit theme of the poem in the two concluding lines. The purpose of the text is not to reunite the two separate entities but to evoke a specific activity that circulates between them.

The poem does not mention this activity by name. It states instead, in its final sentence, that it must remain obscure and invisible: "dunkel tun." That it is called a fulfillment [*Vollendung*] and that the will of the "du" is said to be accomplished by this act does not allow for its definition but repeats in fact the relationship of immanence between the two "persons" that is being staged in the text. A more implicit reading permits however some further specification. The beginning of the poem indicates that the activity in question is first perceived as a constraint and provokes the vain attempts to escape from its power. This is being openly stated in the first two lines and more suggestively evoked in the two following ones: the homesickness is oppressive, but we cannot evade it; there can be no escape from the forest that surrounds us; silence itself cannot prevent us from singing. The sequence culminates in the figure of the net: feelings that try to escape into forgetting or into indetermination are imprisoned and coerced, by this activity, to remain present to us.

But the constraint changes to acquiescence. In the second stanza, the relationship between the "I" and the "you," instead of being paradoxical and dialectical as in the first section, blossoms out in the luminous image of the tree. The promise of the beginning fulfills itself as naturally and harmoniously as the ripening of fruit in the sunshine. The transformation designates the acquisition of a greater mastery in the activity that the poem symbolizes. This mastery is thematically asserted in the reversal that has taken place between the beginning and the end of the poem: the subject that was at first compelled to obey can now act in full freedom and can conform its will to that of the "law." The central will of the poem has been transformed from constraint into a benevolent sun, with only the repetition of the word "dark" (dunkles Netz, dunkel tun) as a reminder of the original violence. Besides, the mention of "hand" in the next-to-last line strengthens the impression that we are dealing with an action involving skills that the initially reluctant student now fully masters.

The proof of this mastery can only be hidden in the text. The relationship between the two subjects or grammatical "persons" is so tight that it leaves no room for any other system of relationships. It is their interlacing that constitutes the text. There is therefore nothing in the poem that would entitle us to escape beyond its boundaries in search of evidence that would not be part of it: the freedom that is affirmed at the end is precisely a freedom within bondage that can prevail only because it is tolerated by the authority of the power which allows it to exist. It remains subjected to the single authority, to the single achievement, of the text.

This achievement, however, is primarily phonic in kind. The last stanza, in which the mastery is asserted, is also the one in which effects of euphony reach their highest point of elaboration. The poem comes to rest in the lines

> Lass deine Hand am Hang der Himmel ruhn
> und dulde stumm, was wir dir dunkel tun.

It can easily be verified that, in this last line of verse, there appears rigorously no syllable that does not fulfill an effect of euphony. The main rhymes and assonances (dulde stumm, wir dir, dunkel tun) are interconnected by syllables that are themselves assonant (und dulde) or alliterated (was wir) and thus enclose each sound-effect into another, as a larger box can enclose in its turn a smaller one. The mastery of the poem consists in its control over the phonic dimensions of language. A reading of the other poems in *The Book of Monastic Life* confirms this conclusion. The "God" that the poems circumscribe by a multitude of metaphors and changing stances corresponds to the ease that the poet has achieved in his techniques of rhyme and of assonance. It is well known that these poems were written very quickly in a kind of euphoria which Rilke will remember when, more than twenty years later, he will write the *Sonnets to Orpheus*; what the poems celebrate is primarily this euphoria. The metaphors connote in fact a formal potential of the signifier. The referent of the poem is an attribute of their language, in itself devoid of semantic depth; the meaning of the poems is the conquest of the technical skills which they illustrate by their acoustic success.

It may seem preposterous to associate such a near-mechanical procedure with the name of God. Yet, the apparent blasphemy can just as well be considered as the hyperbole of an absolute phonocentrism. A poem of *The Book of Monastic Life* (1:20) asserts the possibility of overcoming death itself by means of euphony, and it fulfills this prophecy in its own texture, in the "dark interval" [*im dunklen Intervall*] that in its assonance both separates and unites the two words "Tod" (death) and "Ton" (sound). Once we succeed in hearing the song hidden in language, it will conduct us by itself to the reconciliation of time and existence. This is indeed the extravagant claim made by these poems when they pretend to designate God by means of a medium which deprives itself of all resources except those of sound. Possibilities of representation and of expression are eliminated in an askesis which tolerates no other referent than the formal attributes of the vehicle. Since sound is the only property of language that is truly immanent to it and that bears no relation to anything that would be situated outside language itself, it will remain as the only available resource. The Cratylic illusion, which is held by some to constitute the essence of poetry and which subordinates the semantic function of language to the phonic one, is doubtlessly at work in *The Book of Monastic Life*. In a manner that is not yet entirely convincing, this early volume already partakes of the Orphic myth.

In these texts, in which a measure of technical mastery alternates with moments of clumsiness, the failure of the claim is as evident as is its presence. In order to give a coherent framework to the sequence of poems, Rilke is forced to substitute a subject that tells the story of its experience for the unmediated beauty of the poetic sound. The poems thus acquire a meaning that does not entirely coincide with their actual intent. They introduce an autonomous subject that moves in the forefront and reduces the euphony to the function of ornament. In the first version of *The Book of Monastic Life*, this impression was still heightened by the brief narrative sections inserted between the poems, like a journal commenting upon the daily progress of the poet's work.[16] The fact that Rilke was obliged to invent a fictional character, a monk surrounded by his ritualistic paraphernalia, well illustrates his inability, at that time, to dispense with the conventional props of poetic narration. And since the subject is confined to being an artisan of euphony, it has only a

16. This first version of *The Book of Monastic Life* appears under the title *Die Gebete* in the third volume of the *Complete Works* published in six volumes by Ernst Zinn (*Sämtliche Werke* [Frankfurt am Main: Insel Verlag, 1955–66], 3:305–73).

rather thin story to tell. In the two subsequent volumes of *The Book of Hours*, especially in *The Book of Poverty and of Death*, Rilke abandons the claim to a self-referential diction and returns to the direct expression of his own subjectivity. The texts lose most of their formal rigor and acquire the obvious interest of a self-narrating sensibility. These poems are easy of access and often moving, but measured by Rilke's final and initial ambition they represent the least exalted moment of his poetic production. It will take the long labors of *Malte* and of *The New Poems* to reconquer the impersonality that was proclaimed and lost in *The Book of the Monastic Life*.

While he was writing *The Book of Hours*, Rilke was also working at a very different kind of poem that would find a place in *The Book of Images*, itself a work of transition leading up to the masterful *New Poems*. The development that takes place in these texts is decisive for the entire mature work. It can be described by the reading of one of the poems characteristic of this period. The poem entitled "Am Rande der Nacht" ("At the borderline of the night") is a somewhat arbitrarily chosen but typical instance:

Am Rande der Nacht

> Meine Stube und diese Weite,
> wach über nachtendem Land,—
> ist Eines. Ich bin eine Saite,
> über rauschende breite
> Resonanzen gespannt.
>
> Die Dinge sind Geigenleiber,
> von murrendem Dunkel voll;
> drin träumt das Weinen der Weiber,
> drin rührt sich im Schlafe der Groll
> ganzer Geschlechter . . .
> Ich soll
> silbern erzittern: dann wird
> Alles unter mir leben,
> und was in den Dingen irrt,
> wird nach dem Lichte streben,
> das von meinem tanzenden Tone,
> um welchen der Himmel wellt,

durch schmale, schmachtende Spalten
in die alten
Abgründe ohne
Ende fällt . . .

[1:156][17]

Instead of being caught in the "somber net" of a pseudo-dialectic between pseudo-subjects, we are at once within a much more familiar poetic landscape. From the beginning, the poem announces itself as naming the unity, the complementarity of an inside/outside polarity: the inner seclusion of the "room" (which introduces a subject by the possessive of "my" room) and the infinitely wide expanse of the night outside. They are decreed to be *one* by categorical assertion, as if this unity were the sudden revelation of a single moment, a specific accord between the self of the poet and the world that surrounds him. But the poem does not remain within the instantaneous stasis of this accord. The initial oneness undergoes a transformation announced in lines 11 and 12: "Ich soll / silbern erzittern." This event triggers a transformation which is experienced as a movement of expansion. It is no longer the static unity of inside and outside that is being asserted, but the metamorphosis of an oppressive and constraining inwardness into a liberating outside world. The positive valorization of the movement is marked by the ascending motion of darkness towards light: ". . . was in den Dingen irrt, / wird nach dem Lichte streben." Upon the synchronic axis of an inside/outside polarity is juxtaposed a dynamic axis which transforms the inside/outside opposition into a successive polarity of the type night/day.

For a reader accustomed to Romantic and post-Romantic poetry, this type of poem is most familiar, both by what it asserts and by the antithetical couples that it sets into play. It tries to evoke and accomplish the synthesis, the unity of a consciousness and of its objects, by means of an expressive act, directed from inside to out-

17. Translated as literally as the text allows: "My room and this wide space / watching over the night of the land—/ are one. I am a string / strung over wide, roaring resonances. // Things are hollow violins / full of a groaning dark; / the laments of women / the ire of generations / dream and toss within . . . / I must tremble / and sing like silver: then / All will live under me, / and what errs in things / will strive for the light / that, from my dancing song, / under the curve of the sky / through languishing narrow clefts / falls / in the ancient depths / without end . . ."

side, which fulfills and seals this unity. The subject/object polarity, which remained vague and ambivalent at the beginning, is clearly designated when the poem explicitly confronts the subject, no longer with the indefinite immensity of the first line, but with the objects, the particular things that are contained in this wide space. The unity, which was only asserted as *a priori* at the start, actually occurs before our eyes when the subject, claiming to be the string of a violin, meets and adapts itself perfectly to objects which, in a metaphor that is truly Rilkean in its seductive audacity, are said to be the "body" of this same violin, "Geigenleiber." The totality of the One thus consists of a perfect complementarity: without the sounding board of the violin, the string is devoid of value, but it suffices to bring them together to make the "somber and deep unity" of the world vibrate and shine. Everything seems to confirm that this poem can be considered a later version of the "correspondence" between the inwardness of the subject and the outside world. The exteriority is further confirmed by the assimilation of the sky's immensity, in the first line, to a thing; it is indeed the resonance of its space ("Ich bin eine Saite, / über rauschende breite Resonanzen gespannt") which is transformed in the musical *body* of things ("Die Dinge sind Geigenleiber"). The poem is an example of the most classical of metaphors, conceived as a transfer from an inside to an outside space (or vice versa) by means of an analogical representation. This transfer then reveals a totalizing oneness that was originally hidden but which is fully revealed as soon as it is named and maintained in the figural language. One could stop here, and confine oneself to the discovery of further analogical parallels (such as the convergence of the spatial with the musical theme by way of an erotic connotation—since the body of the violin is that of a woman as well) and especially by stressing the perfect coalescence of the metaphorical narration with the sound-pattern of the poem. The moment of synthesis corresponds exactly to the modulation of the assonances from the ī sound (ten times repeated in the first eight lines) to the ĕ sound (ten times repeated in the four last ones). One should also draw attention to the detailed precision in Rilke's selection of metaphorical analogons.

But if one allows oneself to be guided by the rigorous representational logic of the metaphors, whose clarity of outline indeed distinguishes a poem like this one from those of *The Book of Hours*, then one should follow their guidance to the end. For Rilke's singularity becomes manifest in a displacement that distorts the habitual relationship between theme and figure. The pattern we have just schematized does not appear quite in this shape in the text. The inwardness that should belong, per definition, to the subject is located instead within things. Instead of being opaque and full, things are hollow and contain, as in a box, the dark mass of sentiments and of history. The interiority of the speaking subject is not actively engaged; whatever pathos is mentioned refers to the suffering of others: the woes of women, the ire of historical generations. By a curious reversal, this subjectivity is invested from the start, before the figural transfer has taken place, in objects and in things. This subjective experience is said to be dark to the extent that it is unable, by itself, to find expression; it exists in a condition of error and of blindness ("was in den Dingen irrt . . .") until the subject, the "I" of the poem, confers upon it the clarity of entities that are available to the senses by giving it the attribute of voice. The usual structure has been reversed: the outside of things has become internalized and it is the subject that enables them access to a certain form of exteriority. The "I" of the poem contributes nothing of its own experience, sensations, sufferings, or consciousness. The initial model of the scene is not, as one might think at first, that of an autonomous subject confronting nature or objects, as is the case, for example, in Baudelaire's poem "l'Homme et la mer." The assimilation of the subject to space (as the string of a violin) does not really occur as the result of an analogical exchange, but by a radical appropriation which in fact implies the loss, the disappearance of the subject as subject. It loses the individuality of a particular voice by becoming neither more nor less than the voice of things, as if the central point of view had been displaced into outer things from the self. By the same token, these outer things lose their solidity and become as empty and as vulnerable as we are ourselves. Yet, this loss of the subject's autonomy and of the resilience of the natural world is treated as if it were a positive event, as a passage from darkness to light. It would be mistaken to interpret this light as the clarity of a self-knowledge. In the logic of the figure, it is nothing of the sort: the light is the transformation of a condition of confusion and of non-awareness (dream, sleep, erring) in the sound-version of this same, unchanged condition. The figure is a metaphor of a becoming-sound, not of a becoming-conscious. The title, "At the borderline of the night," should not be read as the dawn of a new lucidity but rather as a persistent condition of confusion and dispersion from which there is no escape. The end of the poem confirms this reading: the rising light turns out to be a fall in "the ancient / depth without / end . . ." of the night. The totalization takes place by a return to the emptiness and the lack of identity that resides in the heart of things. The unity affirmed at the beginning of "Am Rande der Nacht" is a negative unity which deprives the self of any illusion of self-insight. By becoming a musical string, the self partakes forever in the erring of things. Yet, it gives voice to this errancy.

This reversal of the figural order, itself the figure of chiasmus that crosses the attributes of inside and outside and leads to the annihilation of the conscious subject, bends the themes and the rhetoric from their apparently traditional mode towards a specifically Rilkean one. It is difficult to comprehend this reversal on the level of the themes. The notion of objects as containers of a subjectivity which is not that of the self that considers them is incomprehensible as long as one tries to understand it from the perspective of the subject. Instead of conceiving of the poem's rhetoric as the instrument of the subject, of the object, or of the relationship between them, it is preferable to reverse the perspective and to conceive of these categories as standing in the service of the language that has produced them. The metaphor of the violin fits the dramatic action of the text so perfectly and the image seems so flawlessly right because its external structure (box, string, cleft that produces and liberates the sound) triggers and orders the entire figural play that articulates the poem. The metaphorical entity is not selected because it corresponds analogically to the inner experience of a subject but because its structure corresponds to that of a linguistic figure: the violin is *like* a metaphor because it transforms an interior content into an outward, sonorous "thing." The openings in the box (so fittingly shaped like the algorithm of the integral calculus of totalization) correspond precisely to the outside-directed turn that occurs in all metaphorical representations. The musical instrument does not represent the subjectivity of a consciousness but a potential inherent in language; it is the metaphor of a metaphor. What appears to be the inwardness of things, the hollow inside of the box, is not a substantial analogy between the self and world of things but a formal and structural analogy between these things and the figural resources of words. The coming into being of metaphor corresponds point by point to the apparent description of the object. But it is not surprising that, in evoking the details of the metaphorical instrument or vehicle (the perfect fit of the string to the box, the openings in the sounding-board, etc.), the metaphor comes into being before our eyes, since the object has been chosen exactly for this purpose. The correspondence does not confirm a hidden unity that exists in the nature of things and of entities; it is rather like the seamless encasement of the pieces in a puzzle. Perfect adjustment can take place only because the totality was established beforehand and in an entirely formal manner.

The poem "Am Rande der Nacht" still disguises this strategy by simulating the birth of metaphor as the confirmation and the proof of the unity apodictically announced at the beginning of the text. But a careful reading can reveal the stratagem without having recourse to outside information. The poem, which first appeared to be a confrontation between man and nature, is in fact the simulacrum of a description in which the structure of the described object is that of a figural potential of language. Moreover, one should not forget that the metaphor of the metaphor is represented as an acoustical process: the metaphorical object is, literally, a musical instrument. The perfect encasing of the figures makes language sing like a violin. The priority of the phonic element that was stressed with regard to *The Book of Monastic Life* has not been abandoned. Not only is it audible in the parallel between the symbolic action and the euphony of the assonances, but it extends to the play of figuration. *The Book of Images* is not less "phonocentric" than *The Book of Hours*—far from it, since now the imperatives of euphony govern not only the choice of words but the choice of figures as well.

The linguistic strategy of this still relatively early poem (which has several equivalences among the other texts that make up *The Book of Images*) will dominate the work until the end. The determining figure of Rilke's poetry is that of chiasmus, the crossing that reverses the attributes of words and of things. The poems are composed of entities, objects and subjects, who themselves behave like words, which "play" at language according to the rules of rhetoric as one plays ball according to the rules of the game. "Am Rande der Nacht" is particularly revealing because it still makes use of the classical schema of a subject/object dialectic. The linguistic character of one of the poles involved in the inversion is therefore relatively easy to perceive, whereas it will often be hidden in the later work. At the same time, the almost programmatic tonality of the poem, the unity first asserted and then "demonstrated" by the transformations of the figures, will also disappear. In the *New Poems (Neue Gedichte)* the same poem would have been constructed differently. It might have been called "The Violin"; the two first lines would in all probability have been replaced by a description that reverses the "real" schema of events: instead of being the result of their union, it might have been music itself that brought the string and the violin in contact with each other. A poem like the following, the entrance text to *The Book of Images* ("Eingang," 1:127), clearly indicates the structure of the reversal. In the evocation of what could be called an abridged landscape, the reversal appears in the fact that the eyes of the person who is being addressed constitute a world of objects, instead of the objects directing their glance:

> Mit deinen Augen . . .
> hebst du ganz langsam einen schwarzen Baum
> und stellst ihn vor den Himmel: schlank, allein.
> Und hast die Welt gemacht.[18]

The world which is thus created is then explicitly designated as a verbal world. Contact with this world is comparable to the discovery of meaning in an interpretation, and the interpretation engenders the text by appearing to describe the object:

> Und hast die Welt gemacht. Und sie ist gross
> und wie ein Wort, das noch im Schweigen reift.
> Und wie dein Wille ihren Sinn begreift,
> lassen sie deine Augen zärtlich los . . .[19]

But this poem is something of an exception. In the vast majority of the *New Poems*, only the structure of reversal is maintained, and its orientation towards the pole of language remains implicit. This remark gives access to the dominant pattern of the mature work, but it also implies the possibility of a misreading which will become an integral part of the poetry till well into its latest developments.

18. "With your eyes . . . / You slowly lift up a black tree / and stand it, thin, alone, before the sky. / You made the world."

19. "You made the world. And it is wide / and like a word that ripens still in quiet / And once you vouch to understand their sense / They'll gently let your eyes go free . . ."

By showing the prevalence, in the *New Poems*, of this reversal, one can also isolate the poles around which the rotation of the chiasma takes place. As is clear from the titles of the individual poems that make up the *New Poems*, they are often centered on natural or man-made objects. When they describe personages or settings, they have often been so caught in a stylized perception that they have become like icons, emblems of a feeling or of a destiny as sharply circumscribed as are the properties of things. It soon appears that all these objects share a similar fundamental structure: they are conceived in such a way as to allow a reversal of their categorical properties, and this reversal enables the reader to conceive of properties that would normally be incompatible (such as inside/outside, before/after, death/life, fiction/reality, silence/sound) as complementary. They engender an entity, like the violin and the string of "Am Rande der Nacht," which is also a closed totality. If we question why such or such an object inscribed in the *New Poems* has compellingly attracted Rilke's attention (or why he deliberately selected it), the answer will always be that it forced itself upon him because its attributes allow for such a reversal and for such an (apparent) totalization.

A particularly clear and concrete instance of such a structural reversal would be, for example, the specular reflection. The poem "Quai du Rosaire" (1:290) is a fine case in point. Taking advantage of a light effect at dusk, Rilke can, without seeming to be fantastic, decree that the upside-down world that is reflected in the still water of the canals is more substantial and more real than the ordinary world of the day:

> das abendklare Wasser . . .
>
> darin . . .
> die eingehängte Welt von Spiegelbildern
> so wirklich wird wie diese Dinge nie.[20]

The description of the details of this upside-down city, although it maintains the realism of the local color (Estaminets, l. 16) one expects in a poem that is also like a postcard, thus acquires a somewhat uncanny and as it were surreal character. The reversal of the

---

20. "the clear evening water . . . / in which . . . / the suspended world of mirrored images / becomes more real than things ever were."

attribute of reality (the text stresses indeed reality, "Wirklich[keit]") was prepared from the first part on. In an apparent personification, which is in fact a prosopopoeia based on the language-embedded idiom according to which, in German as in English, streets are said to "go" from here to there, the auxiliary condition for an action (the streets, auxiliary device for the action of going) becomes the agent of this same action. The slight note of absurdity sounded in the first evocation of the walking streets ("Die Gassen haben einen sachten Gang / . . . und die an Plätze kommen, warten lang / auf eine andre, die mit einem Schritt / über das abendklare Wasser tritt . . .")[21] prefigures the reversal of the reflection which might otherwise seem too brusque or artificial.

The surreality is not limited to the reflected world. We saw that the reversal acquires poetic value only when it leads to a new totalization; this is why, after having traversed the surface of the looking glass and entered the reflected world, the poem has to return, in the last stanza, to the real world "above." By the same token, the temporal nature of an event that, up till then, was described in spatial and ocular terms, becomes manifest. The blurring of the outlines, which at first seems to be due entirely to the play of light and shadow, takes on a temporal dimension when one remembers that the poem is about "Brugge," "Bruges la morte" as it is called by the poet Georges Rodenbach, a city that used to be prestigious but has become, by the loss of its natural harbor and medieval glory, an emblem for the transience of human achievement, a figure of mutability. The question that introduced the temporal dimension, "Verging nicht diese Stadt?" ("Did not this city perish?"), a question reiterated in line 17: "Und oben blieb?" ("And what remained above?"), is answered at the end: the real world "above" has not been entirely dissolved in the reflection of things past, since the final perception (the bells of the carillon) reach us from above. But this reality is then no longer solidly anchored on the ground. The reflection has emptied it out; its illusory stability has been replaced by the surreal irreality of the mirror image. The descent in the underworld of the mirror uplifts the real and suspends it in the sky, like a constellation. The final totalization takes place within this constellation, which could

21. "The streets go with a gentle walk / . . . and when they reach the squares they wait / forever for another which, in one sole step / crosses the clear evening water . . ."

not have come about without the passage through the fiction of the specular world.

This new totality is itself temporal in kind: the sound of the carillon, the real totality *that remains*, also has for its function to measure the passage of time. By thinking of Brugge no longer as a stable reality but as the figure of temporal loss and erosion, the reality lost in the everyday world of unreflected surfaces is recovered: the live Brugge is much less "real" than "Bruges la morte."[22] Finally, the temporal constellation that functions as a resolution manifests itself, in the last analysis, as *sound*. Perceived in the truth of its mutability, time becomes an audible reality.

This experience of time is highly paradoxical. It acquiesces to all that ordinarily appears as the opposite of permanence and of duration. The affirmation is retained in the seductive but funereal image of a temporal annihilation which is enjoyed as if it were a sensuous pleasure, "der Süssen Traube / des Glockenspiels" ("The sweetened cluster of grapes / of the carillon"), which actually is the death knell that reduced the city to a ghostly memory. Similarly, the sound of this new temporality will have all the attributes of its opposite: at the end of the poem, a new chiasmus crosses the attributes of silence and of sound and·designates the sound of the carillon by the properties of silence:

> Und oben blieb? —Die Stille nur, ich glaube,
> und kostet langsam und von nichts gedrängt
> Beere um Beere aus der süssen Traube
> des Glockenspiels, das in den Himmeln hängt.[23]

22. Rilke himself says just about exactly the opposite in a prose text entitled *Furnes* (*Werke in drei Bänden*, 3:498), which begins with considerations on the city of Brugge. The prose text hardly invalidates our reading. All it proves is that this text, which is a kind of travel journal, does not say the same thing on a given entity (the city of Brugge, in this case) as the poetry. The passage is a good example of the danger inherent in a too literal use made of the "sources" derived from the prose works or from the letters. The specific moment that Rilke wished to retain for the poem also appears in the prose passage: "It is constantly vanishing, like a fresco eaten by the lacework of dampness . . ." (3:498). *Furnes* also contains the explicit reference to *Bruges la Morte* by the Flemish symbolist poet (who wrote in French) Georges Rodenbach.

23. "And what remained above?—Only silence, I believe, / which tastes slowly and unhurriedly / grape by grape the sweetened cluster / of the carillon, suspended in the skies."

The evocation of Brugge as the image of mutability is in itself banal; if it were to be reduced to this theme alone, the poem would be of minor interest. The recovery of duration by means of the subject's acquiescence to the temporal erosion that threatens it is more challenging: it combines the audacity of a paradox with a promise of beauty or even, in the image of the grapes, of sensuous gratification on the far side of the grave. Yet the true interest of the poem does not stem from these thematic statements, but rather from the intricacy and the wealth of movements triggered by the original chiasmus. The crossing of the categories of reality and of specular reflection articulates a sequence of similarly structured reversals: reversal of agent and instrument, of ascent and descent, of inside and outside, of loss and recuperation, death and life, time and sound, sound and silence. A great deal of rhetorical agitation is contained in a brief poetic text which also has the innocent appearance of a picturesque description, of a picture postcard.

Versions of this same pattern reappear in each of the *New Poems*. Each of these poems is closed off in its own self-sufficiency as the description of a particular object or scene, and each poem states in its own terms the enigma of the chiasmus that constitutes it. "L'ange du méridien," for example (to refer only to the best known of the *New Poems*, 1:253), culminates in the totalization of a temporality which can, in opposition to the lacunary time of everyday experience, be said to be full; this total time is evoked by means of the figure of a sundial which, during the night, registers time that would be as entirely imaginary as might be invisible light. The temporal totalization is brought about by the chiasmic reversal of the categories night/day and light/dark. "Der Ball" (1:395) is a strictly descriptive version of a totalization that includes the contradictory motions of rising and falling [*Flug und Fall*].[24] It is brought about by means of an object which, like the violin in "Am Rande der Nacht," has become the depository of an inwardness which is not simply that of the subject.[25] The moment of reversal is graphically represented

24. The totalization of rise and fall is one of the fundamental tropes of Rilke's poetry. It is thematically asserted at the end of the Tenth Elegy but recurs persistently throughout the work. "Das Kapitäl" (1:257) would be a characteristic instance among others. The theme is present in *The Book of Monastic Life*, although it would be premature to speak of totalization in this case.

25. It goes without saying that this movement, which occurs in the lines ". . . was in den Gegenständen / nicht bleiben kann . . . / das glitt in dich . . ." ("what

when the subject becomes, in its turn, a thing whose motion is determined by another thing at the precise instant when the ball reaches the apogee of its own trajectory:

> [der Ball] . . . und sich neigt
> und einhält und den Spielenden von oben
> auf einmal eine neue Stelle zeigt,
> sie ordnend wie zu einer Tanzfigur, . . .[26]

The reversal makes it possible to consider the falling motion as if it were an event that partakes, to some degree, in the joyful upsurge of the ball's first trajectory. And this rising motion, by prospective anticipation, already contains within itself the future decline to which the subject can acquiesce. A kinetic totality is evoked by a reversal of the subject/object, free/determined polarities within a purely spatial and representational schema.

In "Archaischer Torso Apollos" (1:313) the reversal is ocular. The observer is, in its turn, being observed by the fragmentary statue which has been transformed into a single, large eye: "denn da ist keine Stelle, / die dich nicht sieht." The reversal is possible only because the sculpture is broken and fragmentary; if the statue had actually represented the eye of Apollo, the chiasmus could not have come about. The absent eye allows for an imaginary vision to come into being, and it makes the eyeless sculpture into an Argus eye capable of engendering, by itself, all the dimensions of space. We always re-encounter versions of the same negative moment: the hollow of the violin, the irreality of the mirrored image, the darkness of a sundial at night, the falling ball, the missing eye. The absences create the space and the play needed for the reversals and finally lead to a totalization which they seemed, at first, to make impossible. The broken statue becomes more complete than the intact one, decadent

---

could not remain in objects / . . . that glided into you") (that is to say, in the ball, object of the apostrophe), is a great deal more complex in the poem than in the schematic summary we give here for reasons of economy. A detailed reading of "Der Ball" would show that we are indeed dealing with such a reversal of the subjective "content."

26. "[the ball] . . . bows down / lingers and suddenly, from above, / points the player to a new place / ordering place and player as in a figured dance . . ."

Brugge richer than the prosperous reality of the past, the falling ball "happier" than the rising one, the nocturnal dial a more complete timepiece than the sundial at midday, etc.

The unifying principle of the *New Poems* resides in the homology of their rhetorical structure. Even when they evoke entities which, unlike a ball, a fountain, a cat, or a gazelle, are no longer relatively ordinary but transcendental or even divine, the structure remains the same. As a matter of fact the predicates of ordinariness and transcendence are themselves one of the most striking reversals. Rilke describes the rose window of the Chartres cathedral both as the reabsorption of all existence into the oneness of God and as the eye of a cat ("Die Fensterrose," 1:257). The shock of this juxtaposition does not actually deepen our knowledge and understanding of reality and of God, but it seduces the mind by the surprise of its precision. It captures and fascinates attention by the same skill that allows for the virtuosity of its play. It would therefore be a mistake to follow till the end those commentators who read the *New Poems* as a messianic text,[27] seeing them as a hierarchized network of symbolic relationships that ascend towards the parousia of an omnipresent being. The numerous successful poems that appear in the volume are primarily successes of language and of rhetoric. This is hardly surprising, since it has been clear from the start that the Rilkean totalizations are the outcome of poetic skills directed towards the rhetorical potentialities of the signifier.

This reversal of the traditional priority, which located the depth of meaning in a referent conceived as an object or a consciousness of which the language is a more or less faithful reflection, asserts itself in Rilke's poetry by disguising itself at once into its opposite. Very few of the *New Poems* openly refer to language (as was the case with the "Eingang" poem of *The Book of Images*), but the priority of *lexis* over *logos* is always apparent in their structure. Rilke's vocabulary retains this shift in the emphasis and in the authority of the figural struc-

27. Such as, for example, the most attentive interpreter of *New Poems*, Hans Berendt, in *Rainer Maria Rilkes Neue Gedichte: Versuch einer Deutung* (Bonn, 1957). The recent study by Brigitte Bradley, *Rainer Maria Rilkes Neue Gedichte: Ihr zyklisches Gefüge* (Bern, 1968), is not messianic but does not attempt an interpretation of the book as a whole.

tures when he uses, with considerable precision, the term "figure" (Figur) to distinguish his rhetorical strategy from that of classical metaphors.[28] By suggesting the potential identification of tenor and vehicle, the traditional metaphor stresses the possible recuperation of a stable meaning or set of meanings. It allows one to see language as a means towards a recovered presence that transcends language itself. But what Rilke calls figure is, on the thematic level, anything but a recuperation. The allegory of figuration in a text such as "Orpheus. Eurydice. Hermes" (1:298) contributes to the understanding of this distinction.

The poem explicitly describes the poetic vocation by means of a thematized version of chiasmic reversal, source of Rilke's affinity with the myth of Orpheus. The theme appears twice in the text and allows one to distinguish the "right" reversal at the end from the "wrong" reversal described in section III:

> Und seine Sinne waren wie entzweit:
> indes der Blick ihm wie ein Hund vorauslief,
> umkehrte, kam und immer wieder weit
> und wartend an der nächsten Wendung stand,—
> blieb sein Gehör wie ein Geruch zurück.[29]

This mode of reversal, to which Orpheus will finally succumb, indicates the impatience and the desire for a possession within presence. The absence of being—the death of Eurydice—is the origin of a desire which expresses itself in the elegiac tonality of the complaint. In a passage that prefigures the central theme of the Tenth Duino Elegy, the complaint is defined as a language capable of creating and filling an entire poetic universe:

> Die So-Geliebte, dass aus einer Leier
> mehr Klage kam als je aus Klagefrauen;

28. On the concept of figure in Rilke, the study by Beda Alleman, *Zeit und Figur beim späten Rilke*, remains indispensable. (See note 5 above.)

29. "And his senses were as doubled: / because his sight, like a dog, ran ahead of him, / turned around, came back to him and stood / waiting for him at the next roadbend,— / his hearing tarried as if it were an odor."

dass eine Welt aus Klage ward, in der
alles noch einmal da war: . . .[30]

[1:300]

However, since it stems from a desire for presence, the complaint is almost inevitably transformed into the impatience of a desire. It tends to consider the fictional world it engenders as an absent reality, and it tries to repossess what it lacks as if it were an exterior entity. The confusion can only lead to the loss of language which, in the symbolism of the poem, corresponds to Orpheus's increased inability to perceive sounds to the point of forgetting the existence of his lyre. To the extent that metaphor can be thought of as a language of desire and as a means to recover what is absent, it is essentially anti-poetic. The genuine reversal takes place at the end of the poem, when Hermes turns away from the ascending movement that leads Orpheus back to the world of the living and instead follows Eurydice into a world of privation and nonbeing. On the level of poetic language, this renunciation corresponds to the loss of a primacy of meaning located within the referent and it allows for the new rhetoric of Rilke's "figure." Rilke also calls this loss of referentiality by the ambivalent term of "inwardness" (*innen* entstehen, Welt*innen*raum, etc.), which then does not designate the self-presence of a consciousness but the inevitable absence of a reliable referent. It designates the impossibility for the language of poetry to appropriate anything, be it as consciousness, as object, or as a synthesis of both.

From the perspective of the language of figuration, this loss of substance appears as a liberation. It triggers the play of rhetorical reversals and allows them the freedom of their play without being hampered by the referential constraints of meaning: Rilke can assert, for instance, that the reflection is more real than reality, or that the sundial records the hours of the night, because his statement now exists only in and by itself. The same freedom also allows him to prefigure a new totality in which the figures will perfectly complement each other, since the totality does not have to take into account

30. "Beloved, so-beloved, that from one lyre / Came more woe than ever came from wailing women / and thus arose a world of woe in which / all things once more were present . . ."

any empirical or transcendental veracity that might conflict with its principle of constitution. And it also allows for a perfect articulation of the semantic with the rhetorical and phonic function of language, thus preserving the initial sound-centered manner as a principle of poetic composition. From *New Poems* on, Rilke's poetry will live off the euphoria of this recovered freedom. A constant refinement, which goes far enough to recover a semblance of simplicity, will reduce the diversity of figuration that appears in *New Poems* to a small number of elective figures that are particularly productive in their internal reversals as well as capable of combining with each other in at times dazzling constellations. But the poetry will be able to achieve this mastery only at the cost of a subterfuge to which it finds itself necessarily condemned.

For this "liberating theory of the Signifier"[31] also implies a complete drying up of thematic possibilities. In order to be a pure poetry of what Rilke calls "figures," it should start on the far side of the renunciation which opens up its access to this new freedom. But could any poetry, including Rilke's, lay claim to the purity of such a semantic askesis? Some of Rilke's allegorizing poems, such as "Orpheus. Eurydice. Hermes" or the Tenth Duino Elegy, programmatically thematize the renunciation in a narrative mode, by telling the story of this renunciation. In a more lyrical vein, Rilke attempted poems that tend towards the impersonality and the detachment that should characterize a poetics of pure "figure." In those poems, an emblematic object is revealed to be a figure without the need of any discourse, by the very structure of its constitution. Such poems appear in his work from *New Poems* on and will recur till the end, including some of the poems written in the French language. These poems are by necessity brief and enigmatic, often consisting of one single sentence. One might well consider them to be Rilke's most advanced poetic achievement. It is through them that he is related to poets such as Trakl or Celan. The figure stripped of any seduction besides that of its rhetorical elasticity can form, together with other figures, constellations of figures that are inaccessible to meaning and to the senses, located far beyond any concern for life or for death in the hollow space of an unreal sky.

But next to these short and necessarily enigmatic tests, Rilke has

---

31. The expression comes from Roland Barthes and appears on the cover of *S/Z* (Paris, 1970).

also produced works of a wider, at times monumental, scope that are more accessible to understanding. The example of predecessors such as Hölderlin or Baudelaire may well have guided him in this direction. The trend is apparent in some of the longer *New Poems* and it culminates in the *Duino Elegies*, the work that, more than any other, has determined the reading of Rilke as a messianic poet. For rather than being themselves poetic figures, the *Elegies* state a genuine existential philosophy of figuration, presented as if it were a coherent principle of inner behavior, with rules and precepts that could be set up as exemplary. In principle, the imperative tone of the *Elegies* is totally incompatible with the very notion of pure figure, which implies the complete renunciation of any normative pathos or ethical coercion. But there representational and subjective elements openly play a determining part. Although they advocate a conception of language that excludes all subjective or intersubjective dimensions, the *Duino Elegies* constantly appeal to the reader's emotion and participation.

This paradox is not due to bad faith or to deliberate deception on the part of Rilke; it is inherent in the ambivalence of poetic language. The primacy of the signifier, on which Rilke's phonocentric poetics of chiasmus is predicated, is not just one property of language among others that would have remained unnoticed during several centuries until particularly perceptive poets such as Mallarmé or Rilke would have rediscovered it. The notion of a language entirely freed of referential constraints is properly inconceivable. Any utterance can always be read as semantically motivated, and from the moment understanding is involved the positing of a subject or an object is unavoidable. In Rilke's major works, the *Duino Elegies* and, to a lesser extent, the *Sonnets to Orpheus*, the relapse from a rhetoric of figuration into a rhetoric of signification occurs in a way that the structural description of the *New Poems* made predictable.

Chiasmus, the ground-figure of the *New Poems*, can only come into being as the result of a void, of a lack that allows for the rotating motion of the polarities. As long as it is confined to objects, this structural necessity may seem harmless enough: the declining motion of a fountain or of a ball, the reflection of a mirror or the opening of a window casement have, in themselves, nothing of pathos about them. But Rilke's figuration must also involve subject/object polarities, precisely because it has to put in question the irrevocability of this particularly compelling polarity. This implies

the necessity of choosing as figures not only things but personal
destinies or subjective experiences as well, with the avowed purpose
of converting them into impersonal over-things, but without being
able (or wanting) to prevent that the subjective moment first function on the level of meaning. However, these experiences, like the
figural objects, must contain a void or a lack if they are to be con-
verted into figures. It follows that only negative experiences can be
poetically useful. Hence the prevalence of a thematics of negative
experiences that will proliferate in Rilke's poetry: the insatiability of
desire, the powerlessness of love, death of the unfulfilled or the
innocent, the fragility of the earth, the alienation of consciousness—
all these themes fit Rilke's rhetoric so well, not because they are the
expression of his own lived experience (whether they are or not is
irrelevant) but because their structure allows for the unfolding of his
patterns of figuration. And just as the kinetic totalization had to
encompass rising and falling motions into one single trope, or just as
the reflective totalization must include both sides of the mirror, so
the totalization of subjective experience must lead to a positive assertion that only chiasmus can reveal. The reversal of a negativity into a
promise, the ambivalent thematic strategy of the *Duino Elegies*, allows for a linguistic play that is analogous to that in the most discreet
of the *New Poems*. They call, however, for a very different tone,
whose pathos, fervor, and exaltation make one forget the formal and
fictional nature of the unity they celebrate. It is inevitable that the
Elegies are being read as messianic poems: all their thematic assertions confirm this claim, and it is borne out by the virtuosity of the
figuration.[32] Yet the promise asserted by these texts is grounded in a
play of language that can only come about because the poet has
renounced any claim to extra-textual authority. In conformity with
a paradox that is inherent in all literature, the poetry gains a
maximum of convincing power at the very moment that it abdicates
any claim to truth. The *Elegies* and the *Sonnets* have been the main

32. Jacob Steiner, the most exhaustive interpreter of the *Elegies* (*Rilkes
Duineser Elegien* [Bern, 1962]), constantly warns against the tendency to read too
literally many of the passages which allow for an interpretation of the *Elegies* as a
type of secular salvation (see Steiner, pp. 160, 210, among others). The fact remains,
for Steiner, that the convergence between the poetic achievement and the existential
depth is never in question. The final affirmation is seen in all its difficulty, to the
point of making its formulation impossible, but this only strengthens its affirmative
power.

source of evidence in trying to prove the adequation of Rilke's rhetoric to the truth of his affirmations, yet his notion of figural language eliminates all truth-claims from his discourse.

It would be a mistake to believe that a demystifying reading of Rilke could reduce this contradiction to a passing aberration. The messianic reading of Rilke is an integral part of a work that could not exist without it. The full complexity of this poetry can only appear in the juxtaposition of two readings in which the first forgets and the second acknowledges the linguistic structure that makes it come into being. The question remains whether Rilke himself considered his work under this double perspective or whether he followed the example of his commentators in systematically stressing the former at the expense of the latter.

Some of the particularly enigmatic poems from Rilke's last period cannot easily be reconciled with the positive tonality that is generally associated, even at this same late date, with the theme of the figure. This is the case of the following poem from the *Sonnets to Orpheus*, a text that has proven to be very resistant to interpretation:

> Sieh den Himmel. Heisst kein Sternbild "Reiter"?
> Denn dies ist uns seltsam eingeprägt:
> dieser Stolz aus Erde. Und ein Zweiter,
> der ihn treibt und hält und den er trägt.
>
> Ist nicht so, gejagt und dann gebändigt,
> diese sehnige Natur des Seins?
> Weg und Wendung. Doch ein Druck verständigt.
> Neue Weite. Und die zwei sind eins.
>
> Aber *sind* sie's? Oder meinen beide
> nicht den Weg, den sie zusammen tun?
> Namenlos schon trennt sie Tisch und Weide.
>
> Auch die sternische Verbindung trügt.
> Doch uns freue eine Weile nun
> der Figur zu glauben. Das genügt.
>
> [*Sonnets*, 1:493][33]

33. "Behold the sky. Is there no constellation called 'Horseman'? / For we have been taught, singularly, to expect this: / this pride of earth, and his companion / who drives and holds him, and whom he carries. // Is he not, thus spurred and then

Although it does not have the somewhat doctrinal tone of some texts with a similar theme, the poem is important for an understanding of Rilke's poetics, since it deals with the recurrent and central figure of the constellation. The constellation signifies the most inclusive form of totalization, the recuperation of a language that would be capable of naming the remaining presence of being beyond death and beyond time.

The recovered unity comes into being in the play of polarities in the two quatrains, in which we pass from a movement of constraint and opposition to the condition of acquiescence which we have frequently encountered in our readings. The horseman and his steed are first shown in a relationship of duality in which their wills combat each other. The horse's pride rebels against the will of the rider, despite the fact that he is entirely at the mercy of the natural and earthlike power that carries him.[34] The track [*Weg*], the path freely chosen by the animal, and the turn [*Wende*], which designates the will to direct it in a direction of the rider's choice, are at first in conflict with each other. This way of being in the world is characteristic of man, a creature that exists in constant opposition to the spirit of the earth that inhabits plants, animals, and innocent beings. The theme of this alienation, of a human destiny constantly opposed to the natural motion of things, runs through the entire work:

> Dieses heisst Schicksal: gegenüber sein
> und nicht als das und immer gegenüber.
> [Eighth Elegy, 1:471][35]

---

reined in, / like the nervelike nature of Being? / Track and turn. But a pressure brings them together. / New expanse—and the two are one. // But *are* they truly? Or is the track they / travel together *not* the meaning of their way? / Table and pasture part them more than names. // Star-patterns may deceive / but it pleases us, for a while, / to believe in the figure. That is enough."

34. The syntax of the passage is difficult and has made the task of the commentators and of the translators an uncertain one. In agreement with Jacob Steiner, we read "Dieser Stolz aus Erde" as meaning "this pride made of earth," and as designating the horse. "Ein Zweiter" then refers to the rider. The literal meaning is "and a second one (the rider) who spurs and reins in (the horse) that carries him." The rest of the interpretation differs from that of Steiner and of Mörchen on several points.

35. "This is called destiny: to be opposite things / and nothing else and always opposite."

Such a mode of existing is said to conform to the "nervelike" (sehnig), tough, and resistant nature of being, which lines 5 and 6 put into question:

> Ist nicht so, gejagt und dann gebändigt,
> diese sehnige Natur des Seins?

The answer to this question has to be negative, for Rilke never conceives of his relationship to the world, nor especially of his relationship, as poet, to words, as a dialectical one. His entire strategy is instead to let the poetic meaning be carried by the rhetorical and the phonic dimensions of language: the seductions of the syntax and of the figuration have to make even the most extreme paradoxes appear natural. The "track" of the meaning and the "turn" of the tropes have to be reconciled by and within the figure. The poem isolates and retains this moment in the paradox of a beneficent constraint: "doch ein Druck verständigt." The phrase seizes the instant where the contrary wills are reconciled by a virtuosity that acquires the graceful ease of an apparent freedom. The contrary wills cross over and change place, following the same shift in point of view that made the player acquiesce to the descending motion of the ball. The freedom at once opens up a new free space and reveals a new totality: "Neue Weite. Und die zwei sind eins." This new totality prefigures the passage from the earthlike couple to the figural constellation of "The Horseman."

Once this point has been reached, most of Rilke's poems would stop and celebrate the new relationship to the world which the figuration has revealed. This is what happens, for instance, in the poem from the *Sonnets to Orpheus* that immediately follows upon this one:

> Heil dem Geist, der uns verbinden mag;
> denn wir leben wahrhaft in Figuren.
> [1:494][36]

The second part of the Horseman sonnet, however, puts in question all that has been achieved and reduces the unified totality to a

---

36. "Hail to the spirit that may bring us together / for we live truly among figures."

mere illusion of the senses, as trivial and deceiving as the optical illusion which makes us perceive the chaotic dissemination of the stars in space as if they were genuine figures, genuine designs traced upon the background of the skies. "Auch die sternische Verbindung trügt": the imaginary lines that make up actual as well as fictional constellations (the figural constellations of Rilke's poems) are mere deceit, false surfaces. The final affirmation, "Das genügt," especially when compared to the fervent promises that appear in other poems, seems almost derisive. Far from being, as is the case in the opening lines of the Ninth Elegy, a celebration of the moment, it sounds like a disenchanted concession. One can understand the disappointment of one of Rilke's fervent commentators, a true believer in his poetic annunciation: "What are we to think of this odd complacency, which suddenly seems to satisfy itself, and 'for a moment,' with provisional and deceptive hopes?"[37]

What is most important in this unexpected thematic turn is that it comes about at the precise instant when the text states its awareness of its linguistic structure and designates the event it describes as an event of language. Not only is the horseman referred to by the metalinguistic term "figure," but the unity is stated in terms that are borrowed from the semantic function of language: "Oder *meinen* beide / nicht den Weg, den sie zusammen tun?" The lines are difficult to interpret, but the emphasis on signification and on meaning is undeniable.

The failure of figuration thus appears as the undoing of the unity it claimed to establish between the semantic function and the formal structure of language. Again, one of the *New Poems* may be the most economical way to make the figure of the "road," which horseman and steed are said to travel together, more comprehensible. The poem entitled "Der Ball" describes the road, the trajectory of the ball; one could say that it *signifies* this trajectory, that the trajectory is the meaning of the poem as its referent. Moreover, the formal, syntactical structure of the single sentence that makes up the text exactly mimics the meaning: the sentence climbs and falls, slows down, hesitates, and speeds up again in a manner that parallels at all points the signified motion. The manner of enunciation corresponds exactly with what is being said. In other poems, the same convergence will be achieved by way of phonic rather than syntacti-

37. Mörchen, p. 122.

cal elements. The logical meaning and the *lexis* indeed travel along the same road.

But can it be asserted that this parallelism signifies, in the full meaning of the term, the unity that it constitutes? Is it not rather a play of language, an illusion as arbitrary as the shape of the constellations which share a common plane only as the result of an optical appearance? The Horseman sonnet confirms that Rilke knew this to be the case: the figure's truth turns out to be a lie at the very moment when it asserts itself in the plenitude of its promise. The sonnet is not the only instance of such a retreat. In a late text entitled "Gong" (2:186) Rilke attempts the ultimate reversal, not just the visual reversal that takes place in "Archaischer Torso Apollos," but the reversal within the phonic dimension, within the ear, itself: "Klang, / der, wie ein tieferes Ohr, / uns, scheinbar Hörende, hört. . . ."[38] Yet, in this poem, the accumulation of the most extreme paradoxes and of ultimate reversals does not lead to the expected totality, but ends instead in the ignominy of a fall which has nothing in common with the happy descent of the ball. It suggests instead the denunciation of the ultimate figure, the phonocentric Ear-god on which Rilke, from the start, has wagered the outcome of his entire poetic success, as error and betrayal:

> Wanderers Sturz, in den Weg,
> unser, an Alles, Verrat . . . : Gong![39]

Among Rilke's French poems which, by their use of a foreign language, correspond to the renunciation of the euphonic seductions of language, one finds the same definition of the figure as the conversion of representational and visual into purely auditive rhetoric:

> Il faut fermer les yeux et renoncer à la bouche,
> rester muet, aveugle, ébloui:
> L'espace tout ébranlé, qui nous touche
> ne veut de notre être que l'ouie.[40]

38. "Sound, / which, as a deeper ear, / hears us, who appear to be hearing. . . ."

39. "Fall of the wanderer, on the roadside / Our, of everything, betrayal . . . : Gong!"

40. "We must close our eyes and renounce our mouths, / remain mute, blind, dazzled: / Vibrating space, as it reaches us / demands from our being only the ear."

At the moment of its fulfillment, this figure announces itself by its real name:

> Masque? Non. Tu es plus plein,
> mensonge, tu as des yeux sonores.[41]

More still than the thematic statement, which can always be interpreted as a recuperation of the posited theme beyond its most absolute negation, the shift to French indicates not only the knowledge but the advent of the disruption. The promise contained in Rilke's poetry, which the commentators, in the eagerness of their belief, have described in all its severe complexity, is thus placed, by Rilke himself, within the dissolving perspective of the lie. Rilke can only be understood if one realizes the urgency of this promise together with the equally urgent, and equally poetic, need of retracting it at the very instant he seems to be on the point of offering it to us.

41. "Mask? No. You are fuller / you lie, you have sonorous eyes."

3   **Reading**

(Proust)

GEORGES POULET HAS TAUGHT US TO CONSIDER, IN
A la recherche du temps perdu, the juxtaposition of different temporal
layers rather than the unmediated experience of an identity, given or
recovered by an act of consciousness (involuntary memory, proleptic
projection, etc.).[1] The specificity of Proust's novel would instead be
grounded in the play between a prospective and a retrospective
movement. This alternating motion resembles that of reading, or
rather that of the re-reading which the intricacy of every sentence as
well as of the narrative network as a whole constantly forces upon
us. Moreover, as Poulet describes it, the moment that marks the
passage from "life" to writing corresponds to an act of reading that
separates from the undifferentiated mass of facts and events, the
distinctive elements susceptible of entering into the composition of a
text. This occurs by means of a process of elision, transformation, and
accentuation that bears a close resemblance to the practice of critical
understanding. The intimate relationship between reading and criticism has become a commonplace of contemporary literary study.

What does *A la recherche du temps perdu* tell us about reading? I
approach the question in the most literal and, in fact, naïve way
possible by reading a passage that shows us Marcel engaged in the
act of reading a novel. This procedure in fact begs the question, for
we cannot *a priori* be certain to gain access to whatever Proust may
have to say about reading by way of such a reading of a scene of
reading. The question is precisely whether a literary text is *about* that
which it describes, represents, or states. If, even at the infinite distance of an ideal reading, the meaning *read* is destined to coincide
with the meaning *stated,* then there would in fact be no real problem. All that would be left to do would be to allow oneself to be
brought nearer to this ideal perfection by taking Marcel for our

---

1. See Poulet's essay "Proust prospectif" in *Mesure de l'instant* (Paris, 1968)
and also his *L'espace Proustien* (Paris, 1963).

model. But if reading is truly problematic, if a nonconvergence between the stated meaning and its understanding may be suspected,
then the sections in the novel that literally represent reading are not
to be privileged. We may well have to look elsewhere, in Marcel's
erotic, political, medical, or worldly experiences, to discover the distinctive structures of reading, or we may have to go further afield still
and use a principle of selection that is no longer thematic. This
circular difficulty should not, however, prevent us from questioning
the passage on actual reading, if only to find out whether or not it
does make paradigmatic claims for itself. The uncertainty as to
whether this is indeed the case creates a mood of distrust which, as
the later story of Marcel's relationship with Albertine makes clear,
produces rather than paralyzes interpretative discourse. Reading has
to begin in this unstable commixture of literalism and suspicion.

The main text on reading occurs early in the novel, in the first
volume of *Du Côté de chez Swann* (1:82–88).[2] It stands out as distinctly
marked in the narrative of "Combray" where it follows immediately
upon the young Marcel's visit to his uncle, the first explicit example of
his ritualistic initiation to the ambivalences of good and evil. The
scene is set within a thematic of closeted and hidden spaces, the
"temple of Venus" of Françoise's bower (p. 72), the "dark and fresh"
smelling closet in which Uncle Adolphe retires (p. 72) which will
engender a chain of associations that will articulate the entire middle
part of the book,[3] the "dark freshness" of the room in which Marcel
will hide in order to read (p. 83, l. 28), the "little sentry-box" where
he finds refuge when his grandmother orders him to go outside
(p. 83, l. 42). The symbolic significance of this setting is summarized
in the interiorized image of the mind as a "cradle at the bottom of
which I remained sheltered, even in order to observe what was
happening outside" (p. 84, ll. 4–5). The first section of the passage
(p. 80, l. 18 to p. 82, l. 41) does not deal with reading; it is three
pages later when Marcel will climb to his room with a book (p. 83,
l. 5), and only when he has been sent into the garden (p. 83, l. 41) will
the principal and very systematically structured discourse on reading

2. Quotations are from Marcel Proust, *A la recherche du temps perdu* (Paris:
Bibliothèque de la Pléiade, 1954), edited by Pierre Clarac and André Ferré, in 3
volumes. Pages 82–88 of Volume 1 have been numbered line by line.

3. By way of the "fresh and closeted smell" of the public lavatory (1:492),
which is also the place where the extended narrative of the grandmother's death will
begin.

be allowed to develop (p. 84, l. 3 to p. 88, l. 16). But this preliminary section is solidly linked to the main body of the passage by a transitional scene centered on the characters of Françoise and the kitchen maid (p. 82, l. 18) who was the main figure in the first section: "While the kitchen maid—unwittingly making Françoise's superiority shine at its brightest, just as Error, by contrast, makes the triumph of Truth more dazzling—served coffee which, in my mother's judgment, was mere hot water and then carried to our rooms hot water that was barely tepid, I had stretched out on my bed, with a book . . ."[4] The allegorical pair of Truth and Error crowns a passage that will be particularly rich in rotating polarities. But here, in this context of comedy, the chain of substitutions in no way preserves the integrity of the point of origin: the tepid liquid is a lowly version of genuine hot water, itself a degraded substitute for coffee. The kitchen maid is only a pale reflection of Françoise; in substituting for truth, error degrades and outwears it, causing a sequence of lapses that threatens to contaminate the entire section. All the later polarities will have to be on the defensive when placed under the aegis of the initial antithesis between truth and error.

Thus reading is staged, from the beginning of the text, as a defensive motion in a dramatic contest of threats and defenses: it is an inner, sheltered place (bower, closet, room, cradle) that has to protect itself against the invasion of an outside world, but that nevertheless has to borrow from this world some of its properties. The inside room "tremblingly shelters . . . its transparent and fragile coolness from the afternoon sun" (p. 83, l. 6). The inner world is unambiguously valorized as preferable to the outside, and a consistent series of attractive attributes are associated with the well-being of the enclosed space: *coolness,* the most desirable of qualities in this novel of the "solar myth" in which the barometer so often indicates fine weather, itself linked to the restorative *darkness* of shaded light (Marcel being never so happy as when he dwells in the shade of the vegetal world), and finally *tranquility,* without which no time would be available for contemplation. But Marcel cannot rest satisfied with these positive aspects of a sedentary solitude. The truly seductive force of the passage is revealed only when the confinement to the obscure, private existence of inward retreat turns out to be a highly

4. A good two pages earlier (1:80, l. 21) Françoise has said: "I'll let my kitchen maid serve coffee and bring up hot water . . ."

effective strategy for the retrieval of all that seemed to have been sacrificed. The text asserts the possibility of recuperating, by an act of reading, all that the inner contemplation had discarded, the opposites of all the virtues necessary to its well-being: the *warmth* of the sun, its *light*, and even the *activity* that the restful immobility seemed to have definitively eliminated. Miraculously enriched by its antithetical properties, the "dark coolness" of the room thus acquires the light without which no reading would be possible, "the unmediated, actual, and persistent presence" of the summer warmth and finally even ". . . the shock and the animation of a flood of activity [*un torrent d'activité*]." The narrator is able to assert, without seeming to be preposterous, that by staying and reading in his room, Marcel's imagination finds access to "the total spectacle of Summer," including the attractions of direct physical action, and that he possesses it much more effectively than if he had been actually present in an outside world that he then could only have known by bits and pieces.

Two apparently incompatible chains of connotations have thus been set up: one, engendered by the idea of "inside" space and governed by "imagination," possesses the qualities of coolness, tranquility, darkness as well as totality, whereas the other, linked to the "outside" and dependent on the "senses," is marked by the opposite qualities of warmth, activity, light, and fragmentation. These initially static polarities are put in circulation by means of a more or less hidden system of relays which allows the properties to enter into substitutions, exchanges, and crossings that appear to reconcile the incompatibilities of the inner with the outer would.[5] Proust can

5. Similar figures, often polarized around systems of light/dark and inside/outside, are so frequent that they could be said to make up the entire novel. They occur from the first sentence, which has to do with light and dark, truth and error, wake and sleep, perception and dream, and which turns on a literalization of the fundamental epistemological metaphor of understanding as seeing. One of the most interesting examples, also involving Giotto, occurs in the later part of the novel, in a passage from *La fugitive*, during Marcel's visit to Venice, in the company of his mother, after Albertine's death (3:648). Gérard Genette ("Métonymie chez Proust," now in *Figures III* [Paris, 1972], p. 48) quotes the passage as an example of diegetic metaphor, metaphors in which the selection of the vehicle is dictated by the proximity of a detail that happens to be present in the narrative context. The blue color of the backgrounds in the Giotto frescoes at the Arena of Padua are said to be "so blue that it looks as if the radiant daylight had crossed the threshold in the company of the visitor, and would have housed for a moment its pure sky in the coolness of the shade, a pure sky hardly darkened by being rid of [débarassé] the golden sunlight, as

affect such confidence in the persuasive power of his metaphors that he pushes stylistic defiance to the point of stating the assumed synthesis of light and dark in the incontrovertible language of numerical ratio: "The dark cool of my warm room was to the full sunlight of the street what the shadow is to the sunray, that is to say equally luminous . . ." (p. 83, l. 28). In a logic dominated by truth and error the equation is absurd, since it is the difference of luminosity that distinguishes between shadow and light: "that is to say" ("c'est à

---

in these brief moments of respite that interrupt the most beautiful days when, without having seen a single cloud, the sun having turned its eye elsewhere [le soleil ayant tourné ailleurs son regard] for a moment, the blue of the sky softens and turns darker." The comparison of the two blues (Giotto's background and the sky) stems indeed from the proximity of the previous narrative setting in the phrase "after having traversed the garden of the Arena under the full sunlight" (3:648) and can thus legitimately be called a diegetic metaphor. But it is clear that more is at stake in the passage. The initial situation is very similar to that of the section we are dealing with, since the positive valorization of coolness and shelter (as marked, for instance, by the negative connotations of the word "débarassé" which characterizes the full light as undesirable) indicates that the metaphor attempts a reconciliation of such incompatible polarities as hot/cold, inside/outside, light/dark, as well as nature/art. For the light of art, which is devoid of natural warmth and therefore potentially devoid of life, to be like nature, it must be able to borrow, by analogy, the attribute of warmth from the sun without losing its desirable coolness. Natural light has to cross the threshold of its specular representation; this illusion is convincing enough since at least some natural light, however shaded, has to penetrate into the building for the frescoes to be visible. The burden of the passage is therefore not so much to inject warmth into art as to inject coolness into nature; otherwise the symmetry of the totalizing chiasmus could not come about. Hence the necessity for an analogical description in which the heat of the sunlight would not be incompatible with a degree of coolness. What makes the passage remarkable and takes it well beyond Genette's model of a reconciled system of metaphor and metonymy (of "liaison" and "marriage"), is that Proust refuses to avail himself of the simple natural analogy that immediately comes to mind and goes out of his way to insist that the cool darkening of the sun is *not* caused by a cloud. The sentence "le soleil ayant tourné ailleurs son regard" thus becomes pure nonsense from the naturalistic point of view that the logic of the passage, structured as a nature/art dialectic, demands. The implications are far-reaching, not only for Genette's model of happy totalization, but for the entire notion of tropology as a closed system. Such systems depend on the necessary link between the existence and the knowledge of entities, on the unbreakable strength of the tie that unites the sun (as entity) with the eye (as the knowledge of the entity). The sentence "the sun having turned its eye elsewhere" is therefore, from a tropological point of view, the most impossible sentence conceivable. Its absurdity not only denies the intelligibility of natural metaphors but of all tropes; it is the figure of the unreadability of figures and therefore no longer, strictly speaking, a figure.

dire") in the quotation is precisely what cannot be said. Yet the logic of sensation and of the imagination easily remains convinced of the accuracy of the passage and has not the least difficulty in accepting it as legitimate. One should ask how a blindness comes into being that allows for a statement in which truth and falsehood are completely subverted to be accepted as true without resistance. There seems to be no limit to what tropes can get away with.

Structures and relays of this kind, in which properties are substituted and exchanged, characterize tropological systems as being, at least in part, paradigmatic or metaphorical systems. Not surprisingly, therefore, this introductory passage on reading that was placed, from the beginning, under the auspices of the epistemological couple of truth and error, also contains statements claiming the priority of metaphor in a binary system that opposes metaphor to metonymy.[6] The passage reflects on the modality of the sun's presence in the room: it is first represented in visual terms by means of the metaphor of a "reflection of light which . . . succeeded in making its yellow wings appear [behind the blinds], and remained motionless . . . poised like a butterfly"; then in aural terms by the resonance of "blows struck . . . against the dusty crates" in the street, and finally, still in aural terms, by the buzzing of the flies, generalized into "the chamber music of summer" (p. 83, l. 20).[7] The crossing of sensory attributes in synaesthesia is only a special case of a more general pattern of substitution that all tropes have in common. It is the result of an exchange of properties made possible by a proximity or an analogy so close and intimate that it allows the one to substitute for the other without revealing the difference necessarily introduced by the substitution. The relational link between the two entities involved in the exchange then becomes so strong that it can be called necessary: there could be no summer without flies, no flies without summer. The "necessary link" that unites flies and

6. The study of this polarity has been masterfully begun by Gérard Genette (see note 5 above). Proust himself at times makes use of rhetorical terms such as metaphor, alliteration, and anacoluthon, but never uses, to my knowledge, the word metonymy.

7. For the purpose of this reading "chamber music" is taken at face value. It is of course, in this novel, a highly marked term singled out from the first page ("un quatuor" [1:3]) to the various key episodes involving the Vinteuil sonata, the septuor, Morel, etc. In this passage, and for our specific purposes, it suffices to stress the soothing connotations of music that obliterates whatever unpleasant association may be evoked by swarms of buzzing flies; the image functions as a reconciliation of the classical antinomy of art and nature.

summer is natural, genetic, unbreakable; although the flies are only one minute part of the total event designated by "summer," they nevertheless partake of its most specific and total essence. The synecdoche that substitutes part for whole and whole for part is in fact a metaphor,[8] powerful enough to transform a temporal contiguity into an infinite duration: "Born of the sunny days, resurrected only upon their return, containing some of their essence, [the buzzing of the flies] not only reawakens their image in our memory but certifies their return, their actual, persistent, unmediated presence." Compared to this compelling coherence, the contingency of a metonymy based only on the casual encounter of two entities that could very well exist in each other's absence would be entirely devoid of poetic power. "The tune of human music [as opposed to the "natural" flies] heard perchance during summertime . . . ." may be able to stimulate memory in a mechanical way, but fails to lead to the totalizing stability of metaphorical processes. If metonymy is distinguished from metaphor in terms of necessity and contingency (an interpretation of the term that is not illegitimate), then metonymy is per definition unable to create genuine links, whereas no one can doubt, thanks to the butterflies, the resonance of the crates, and especially the "chamber music" of the flies, of the presence of light and of warmth in the room. On the level of sensation, metaphor can reconcile night and day in a *chiaroscuro* that is entirely convincing. But the passage plays for higher stakes.

For it does not suffice for the sound of the flies to bring the outside light into the dark room; if it is to achieve totalization, the inwardness of the sheltered reader must also acquire the power of a concrete action. The mental process of reading extends the function of consciousness beyond that of mere passive perception; it must acquire a wider dimension and become an action.[9] The light

8. Classical rhetoric generally classifies synecdoche as metonymy, which leads to difficulties characteristic of all attempts at establishing a taxonomy of tropes; tropes are transformational systems rather than grids. The relationship between part and whole can be understood metaphorically, as is the case, for example, in the organic metaphors dear to Goethe. Synecdoche is one of the borderline figures that create an ambivalent zone between metaphor and metonymy and that, by its spatial nature, creates the illusion of a synthesis by totalization.

9. The use of the term "action" (which stems from Proust's text) does not mean that metaphor is here conceived as a speech act. "Activité" has the meaning of *actus exercitus* in a classical polarity of mental contemplation versus physical action. A reading of Proust in terms of speech-act theory would have to proceed along different lines.

metaphors are powerless to achieve this: it will take the intervention of an analogical motion stemming from a different property, this time borrowed not from the warmth of the light but from the coolness of the water: "The dark coolness of my room . . . matched my repose which (thanks to the adventures narrated in my book, which stirred my tranquility) supported, like the quiet of a hand held motionless in the middle of a running brook, the shock and the animation of a flood of activity" ("mon repos . . . supportait, pareil au repos d'une main immobile au milieu d'une eau courante, le choc et l'animation d'un torrent d'activité"). The persuasive power of the passage depends on the play on the verb "supporter" which must be strong enough to be read not just as "tolerate" but as "support," suggesting that the repose is indeed the foundation, the ground that makes activity possible. Repose and action are to merge as intimately as the "necessary link" that ties the column to its pedestal.

The ethical investment in this seemingly innocent narrative description is in fact considerable enough to match the intricacy of the rhetorical strategy. For the burden of the text, among other things, is to reassure Marcel about his flight away from the "real" activity of the outer world. The guilty pleasures of solitude are made legitimate because they allow for a possession of the world at least as virile and complete as that of the hero whose adventures he is reading. Against the moral imperative speaking through the grandmother who "begs Marcel to go outside," Marcel must justify his refusal to give up his reading, together with all the more or less shameful pleasures that go with it. The passage on reading has to attempt the reconciliation between imagination and action and to resolve the ethical conflict that exists between them. If it were possible to transform the imaginary content of the fiction into actions performed by the reader, then the desire would be satisfied without leaving a residue of bad conscience. An ethical issue that is obviously involved in the success of the metaphor is connected to the central Proustian motive of guilt and betrayal that governs the narrator's relationship to himself and to those united to him by ties of love or affection. Guilt is always centered on reading and on writing, which the novel so often evokes in somber tones. This connection between metaphor and guilt is one of the recurrent themes of autobiographical fiction.

One should not conclude that the subjective feelings of guilt motivate the rhetorical strategies as causes determine effects. It is not more legitimate to say that the ethical interests of the subject determine the invention of figures than to say that the rhetorical potential of language engenders the choice of guilt as theme; no one can decide whether Proust invented metaphors because he felt guilty or whether he had to declare himself guilty in order to find a use for his metaphors. Since the only irreducible "intention" of a text is that of its constitution, the second hypothesis is in fact less unlikely than the first. The problem has to be left suspended in its own indecision. But by suggesting that the narrator, for whatever reason, may have a vested interest in the success of his metaphors, one stresses their operational effectiveness and maintains a certain critical vigilance with regard to the promises that are being made as one passes from reading to action by means of a mediating set of metaphors.

In this passage, the metaphorical relay occurs by way of the flowing water: repose supports action "like the quiet of a hand, held motionless in the middle of a running brook." In the sunny mood of the text, the image is convincing enough: nothing could be more attractive than this feeling of freshness rising from the clear water. But coolness, it will be remembered, is one of the attributes of the "inner" world, associated with shelter, bowers, and closed rooms. The analogical image of the hand is therefore not able to cross over, by its own power, towards a life of action. The water carries with it the property of coolness, but this quality, in the binary logic of the passage, belongs to the imaginary world of reading. To gain access to action, the trope should capture one of the properties that belongs to the antithetical chain such as, for example, warmth. The cool repose of the hand should be made compatible with the heat of action. This transfer occurs, still within the space of a single sentence, when it is said that repose supports "un torrent d'activité." In French, this expression is not—or is no longer—a metaphor but a cliché, a dead or sleeping metaphor which has lost its literal connotations (in this case, the connotations associated with the word "torrent") and has only kept a proper meaning.[10] "Torrent d'activité" properly signifies a

---

10. Thus illustrating the tripartite structure of all metaphors, often stressed by theoreticians of rhetoric, but not clearly embodied in ordinary English language, which distinguishes only vaguely between literal and "proper" meaning. When Homer calls Achilles a lion, the literal meaning of the figure signifies an animal of a yellowish brown color, living in Africa, having a mane, etc. The figural meaning signifies Achilles and the proper meaning the attribute of courage or strength that Achilles and the lion have in common and can therefore exchange. In the cliché "torrent d'activité" (as when I say of a hyperactive Mr. X that he is "un torrent

lot of activity, the quantity of activity likely to agitate someone to the point of making him feel hot. The proper meaning converges with the connotation supplied, on the level of the signifier, by the "torride" ("hot") that one can choose to hear in "torrent." Heat is therefore inscribed in the text in an underhand, secretive manner, thus linking the two antithetical series in one single chain that permits the exchange of incompatible qualities: if repose can be hot and active without however losing its distinctive virtue of tranquility, then the "real" activity can lose its fragmentary and dispersed quality, and become whole without having to be any less real.

The transfer is made seductive and convincing by a double-faced play on the cliché "torrent d'activité." The neighboring image of flowing water (the hand suspended "in a running brook") re-awakens, so to speak, the dozing metaphor which, in the cliché, had become the mere contiguity of two words ("torrent" and "activité") syntagmatically joined by repeated usage and no longer by the constraints of meaning. "Torrent" functions in at least a double semantic register: in its reawakened literal sense, it relays and "translates" the property of coolness actually present in the water that covers the hand, whereas in its figural meaning it designates an amplitude of action suggestive of the contrary quality of heat.

The rhetorical structure of this part of the sentence ("repose . . . supported . . . the shock and the animation of a flood of activity") is therefore not simply metaphorical. It is at least doubly metonymic: first because the coupling of two terms, in a cliché, is not governed by the "necessary link" of a resemblance (and potential identity) rooted in a shared property, but dictated by the mere habit of proximity (of which Proust, elsewhere, has much to say[11]), but also because the reanimation of the numbed figure takes place by means of a statement ("running brook") which happens to be close to it, without however this proximity being determined by a necessity that would exist on the level of transcendental meaning. To the contrary, the property stressed by the neighboring passage is precisely not the

---

d'activité") the literal meaning of torrent has been lost and only the shared attribute of "muchness" remains. I. A. Richards's distinction between ground, tenor, and vehicle designates this same structure. It is part of our argument that such numerical and geometrical models, assuming the specificity of each particular trope, though unavoidable, are in the long run intenable.

11. See, for instance, the lengthy development on "habitude" at the beginning of the second part of A l'ombre des jeunes filles en fleurs (1:643 ff.).

property that served in the coinage of the original metaphor, now degraded and become a cliché: the figure "torrent d'activité" is based on amplitude and not on coolness. This property functions in fact against the quality that the text desires.

The structure is typical of Proust's language throughout the novel. In a passage that abounds in successful and seductive metaphors and which, moreover, explicitly asserts the superior efficacy of metaphor over that of metonymy, persuasion is achieved by a figural play in which contingent figures of chance masquerade deceptively as figures of necessity. A literal and thematic reading that takes the value assertions of the text at their word would have to favor metaphor over metonymy as a means to satisfy a desire all the more tempting since it is paradoxical: the desire for a secluded reading that satisfies the ethical demands of action more effectively than actual deeds. Such a reading is put in question if one takes the rhetorical structure of the text into account.

The central text on reading (p. 83, l. 38 to p. 88, l. 16) develops in the wake of this initial complication. It has all the appearances of a set piece, so firmly constructed that it constantly attracts attention to its own system and invites representation by means of synoptic diagrams. The text follows "from inside to outside the layers simultaneously juxtaposed in [the] consciousness . . ." of the reader (p. 87, l. 22). It extends the complexity of a single moment in time upon an axis oriented from maximum intimacy to the external world. This construct is not temporal, for it involves no duration. The diachrony of the passage, as the narrative moves from a center towards a periphery, is the spatial representation of a differential but complementary articulation within one single moment. For a novel that claims to be the narrative extension of one single moment of recollection, the passage undoubtedly has paradigmatic significance. The transposition of the present moment into a consecutive sequence would correspond to the act of fiction-writing as the narration of the moment. This act would then be coextensive with the act of self-reading by means of which the narrator and the writer, now united in one, fully understand their present situation (including all its negative aspects) by means of the retrospective recapitulation of its genesis. Nor would it differ from the response available to the reader of *A la recherche du temps perdu* who, mediated by Proust's novel, understands the narrative voice as the dispenser of a true knowledge that also includes him.[12] The "moment" and the "narration" would be complementary and symmetrical, specular reflections of each other that could be substituted without distortion. By an act of memory or of anticipation, the narrative can retrieve the full experience of the moment. We are back in the totalizing world of the metaphor. Narrative is the metaphor of the moment, as reading is the metaphor of writing.

The passage is indeed ordered around a central, unifying metaphor, the "single and unbending projection of all the forces of my life" ("même et infléchissable jaillissement de toutes les forces de ma vie") within which the various levels of reading are said to constitute "sections at the different levels of an iridescent fountain that appeared to be motionless"[13] (p. 87, ll. 18–19). The figure aims at the most demanding of reconciliations, that of motion and stasis, a synthesis that is also at stake in the model of narrative as the diachronic version of a single moment. The continuous flow ("jaillissement") of the narrative represents an identity that is beyond the senses and beyond time as something accessible to sight and sensation and therefore comprehensible and articulated, just as the unique and timeless[14] fascination of reading can be divided into consecutive layers shaped like the concentric rings of a tree trunk. Within a closed system of part and whole, the complementarity of the vertical juxtaposition and the horizontal succession is firmly established. With regard to the narrative, the proof of this complementarity will be the absence of interruptions, the lack of jagged edges which allows for the characterization of the novel's narrative texture as a play of fragmentation and reunification that can be called "fondu," (i.e., smooth [Gérard Genette]) or "soudé," (i.e., welded [Proust]).[15] The

12. "In truth, each reader is, when he reads, the actual [*propre*] reader of himself" (3:911).

13. In a famous passage of *The Prelude*, Wordsworth speaks of "The stationary blast of waterfalls" (VI, l. 626). A more literal and less benevolent version of this same waterspout appears in *Sodome et Gomorrhe*: the fountain designed by Hubert Robert that splashes Mme. d'Arpajon to the great merriment of the grand duke Wladimir (2:657).

14. ". . . the concentration of my reading, like the magic of a deep sleep . . . had erased the ringing of the golden church bells on the sky-blue surface of silence" (1:88, ll. 2–5).

15. For example, in a passage referring to Vinteuil's septuor: ". . . two entirely different modes of questioning, the one breaking up a pure and continuous line into brief requests, the other welding [*soudant*] stray fragments into one single, sturdy

continuity is not only apparent in the fluency of the transitions or in the numberless symmetries of the composition, but also in the strict coherence between meaning and structure. The passage is a persuasive case in point: to the stated assertion that reading is grounded in a firm relationship between inside and outside corresponds a text that is structured in a particularly rigorous and systematic way. But if the complementarity were to be an illusion, a very different story would ensue, more like the loss of entropy that occurs as one moves from Françoise's hot coffee to the kitchen maid's tepid shaving water.

The persuasive value of the passage depends on one's reading of the fountain as an entity which is both immobile and iridescent. The iridescence is prefigured a few pages earlier in the description of consciousness as a "shimmering screen" ("un écran diapré") (p. 84, l. 13). The miraculous interference of water and light in the refracted rainbow of the color spectrum makes its appearance throughout the novel, infallibly associated with the thematics of metaphor as totalization.[16] It is the perfect analogon for the figure of complementarity, the differences that make up the parts absorbed in the unity of the whole as the colors of the spectrum are absorbed in the original white light. The solar myth of *A la recherche du temps perdu* would then be condensed in the scarf of Iris, as when the flower metaphors associated with girls and women are said to "appear at once on their two sides, like complementary colors" (p. 86, l. 20). The "necessary link" between the imagined figure and its sensory qualities make it more seductive than the empirical, "real" landscape of Combray.

---

frame" (3:255). Gérard Genette ("Métonymie chez Proust," p. 60) mentions a passage from Proust's correspondence (*Correspondence* [Paris, 1970], 2:86) which uses the expression "espèce de fondu."

16. Some examples among many others: Elstir's workshop is compared to a "block of rock-crystal, of which one of the facets, already cut and polished, shines like an iridescent mirror" (1:835); Françoise's famous asparagus "reveal in their nascent colors of early dawn, in their suggestions of rainbows . . . [their] costly essence" (1:121); "if I could have analyzed the prism [of the duchess de Guermante's eyes] . . . the essence of the unknown life that appeared in them might have been revealed to me" (2:53); "the art of Vinteuil, like that of Elstir, reveals [the ineffable character of individuality] by expressing into the colors of the spectrum the intimate being of the worlds we call individuals . . ." (3:258); "just as the spectrum represents for us the composition of light, the harmony of a Wagner or the color of an Elstir allows us to know the qualitative essence of another individual's sensations . . ." (3:159).

Unlike this real landscape, the symbolic one is "a true part of Nature itself, worthy of study and meditation" (p. 86, l. 34).

The superiority of the "symbolic" metaphor over the "literal," prosaic, metonymy is reasserted in terms of chance and necessity. Within the confines of the fiction, the relationship between the figures is indeed governed by the complementarity of the literal and the figural meaning of the metaphor. Yet the passage seems oddly unable to remain sheltered within this intra-textual closure. The complementarity is first asserted with reference to the narrator's relationship to the landscape he inhabits, but it soon extends towards another binary set of themes, those of "love" and "voyage": "Therefore, if I always imagined, surrounding the woman I loved, the landscape I most keenly wished to see at that moment . . . it was not because a mere association of ideas existed between them. No, it is because my dreams of love and of travel were only moments— which I now artificially disentangle . . .—in the single and unbending projection of all the forces of my life" (p. 87, ll. 11–21). But what is here called "love" and "travel" are not, like the narrator and his natural setting, two intra-textual moments in a fiction, but rather the irresistible motion that forces any text beyond its limits and projects it towards an exterior referent. The movement coincides with the need for a meaning. Yet at the beginning of the passage Marcel has stated the impossibility for any consciousness to get outside itself, suggesting this very ideality, paradoxically enough, by means of an analogy derived from a physical phenomenon: "When I saw something external, my awareness of the fact that I was seeing it remained between the object and myself, bordering it as with a thin spiritual layer that prevented me from touching it directly; the object would evaporate, so to speak, before I could come into contact with it, just as a red-hot body that approaches a wet object is unable to touch its humidity, since it is always preceded by a zone of vapor" (p. 84, ll. 5–13). Three pages further on, it seems that the language of consciousness is unable to remain thus ensconced and that, like so many objects and so many moments in Proust's novel, it has to turn itself out and become the outer enveloping surface:[17] "For if we have

17. The metonymy by which the covered-up entity becomes its own cover [enveloppé becoming enveloppant] is much in evidence in the concluding section of this passage, where "the afternoons have gradually surrounded and enclosed" the hours: the spatial container becomes the temporally contained, and vice versa. The famous passage on the "carafes de la Vivonne" (1:168) is the locus classicus of this

the impression of being constantly surrounded by our consciousness [*âme*], it is not as by an unmovable prison; much rather, we feel carried by it in a perpetual impulse to move beyond itself and to reach outside . . ." (p. 86, ll. 39–42). The epistemological significance of this impulse is clearly stated when, a few paragraphs earlier, we heard of a "central belief . . . that made ceaseless motions from inside outward, toward the discovery of truth" (p. 84, ll. 36–37). Like Albertine, consciousness refuses to be captive and has to take flight and move abroad. This reversal by which the intra-textual complementarity chooses to submit itself to the test of truth is caused by "the projection of all the forces of life."

Proust's novel leaves no doubt that this test must fail; numberless versions of this failure appear throughout the pages of the *Recherche*. In this section, it is stated without ambiguity: "We try to find again, in things that have thus become dear to us, the reflection that our consciousness [*âme*] has projected upon them; we are disappointed in discovering that, in their natural state, they lack the seduction that, in our imagination, they owed to the proximity of certain ideas . . ." (p. 87, ll. 2–7). Banal when taken by itself, the observation acquires considerable negative power in context, when one notices that it occurs at the center of a passage whose thematic and rhetorical strategy it reduces to naught. For if the "proximity" between the thing and the idea of the thing fails to pass the test of truth, then it fails to acquire the complementary and totalizing power of metaphor and remains reduced to "the chance of a mere association of ideas." The co-presence of intra- and extra-textual movements never reaches a synthesis. The relationship between the literal and the figural senses of a metaphor is always, in this sense, metonymic, though motivated by a constitutive tendency to pretend the opposite.

The image of the iridescent fountain is a clear case in point. Everything orients the trope towards the seduction of metaphor: the sensory attractiveness, the context, the affective connotations, all cooperate to this aim. As soon however as one follows Proust's own

---

figure. Gérard Genette quotes it, and it has since been much commented upon, without however exhausting the connotations of its context and of its tropological significance. Walter Benjamin well perceived the importance of this metonymy when he compared Proust's figures to a rolled-up sock which is its own outside and which, when unrolled, like the Möbius strip, is also its own inside ("Zum Bilde Proust," *Illuminationen* [Frankfurt am Main, 1955], p. 308).

injunction to submit the reading to the polarity of truth and error (a gesture that can be repressed but never prevented), statements or strategies that tended to remain unnoticed become apparent and undo what the figure seemed to have accomplished. The shimmering of the fountain then becomes a much more disturbing movement, a vibration between truth and error that keeps the two readings from converging. The disjunction between the aesthetically responsive and the rhetorically aware reading, both equally compelling, undoes the pseudo-synthesis of inside and outside, time and space, container and content, part and whole, motion and stasis, self and understanding, writer and reader, metaphor and metonymy, that the text has constructed. It functions like an oxymoron, but since it signals a logical rather than a representational incompatibility, it is in fact an aporia. It designates the irrevocable occurrence of at least two mutually exclusive readings and asserts the impossibility of a true understanding, on the level of the figuration as well as of the themes.

The question remains whether by thus allowing the text to deconstruct its own metaphors one recaptures the actual movement of the novel and comes closer to the negative epistemology that would reveal its hidden meaning. Is this novel the allegorical narrative of its own deconstruction? Some of its most perceptive recent interpreters seem to think so when they assert, like Gilles Deleuze, the "powerful unity" of the *Recherche* despite its inherent fragmentation or, like Genette, stress the "solidity of the text" despite the perilous shuttle between metaphor and metonymy.[18]

What is at stake is the possibility of including the contradictions of reading in a narrative that would be able to contain them. Such a narrative would have the universal significance of an allegory of reading. As the report of the contradictory interference of truth and error in the process of understanding, the allegory would no longer be subject to the destructive power of this complication. To the extent that it is not itself demonstrably false, the allegory of the play of truth and falsehood would ground the stability of the text.

One would have to untie the complex interlacing of truth and lie in *A la recherche du temps perdu* to decide whether or not the work corresponds to this model. But the passage on reading gives a first

18. Gilles Deleuze, "Antilogos," in *Proust et les signes*, 2d ed. (Paris, 1970), and Genette, "Métonymie chez Proust," p. 60.

indication how such an analysis would have to proceed. It is preceded by an episode (p. 80, l. 18 to p. 82, l. 24) which deals, as by coincidence, with the question of allegory and which can serve as a warning for the difficulties that any attempt to reach an inclusive allegorical reading of the novel are bound to encounter. The passage consists of Marcel's meditation on the nickname "Giotto's Charity" by which Swann is accustomed to refer to the kitchen maid persecuted with such cruelty by Françoise, the cook.

Slave of a slave, pathetic emblem of servitude, the kitchen maid is first described as what one could call, with Goethe, *Dauer im Wechsel*, the element that remains permanent in the midst of change. She is characterized as "a permanent institution, whose unchanging attributes guaranteed an appearance of continuity and identity, beyond the succession of transitory forms in which she was incarnated . . ." (p. 80, ll. 25–28). Swann, the personification of metaphor, is endowed with a particular knack for the discovery of resemblances, and he has observed the near-emblematic quality of this particular kitchen maid. She carries the "humble basket" of her pregnancy in a manner that, by its resemblance to the surcoat of the allegorical frescoes painted by Giotto in the Arena of Padua, reveals her universal essence. All the agonies and all the humiliations of the successive kitchen maids are concentrated in this particular trait of her physiognomy, thus raised to the level of an emblem. An allegory thus conceived is in no way distinguished from the structure of metaphor, of which it is in fact the most general version. In the same manner, metaphor warrants the identity of art as a "permanent institution" that transcends the singularity of its particular incarnations. What may appear surprising is that Proust selected servitude as the essence intended and reached by the figure. More surprising still, the allegorical figure that Swann's sagacity has singled out is Charity, a virtue whose relationship with servitude is not one of mere resemblance. By generalizing itself in its own allegory, the metaphor seems to have displaced its proper meaning.

Marcel, who has a more literary (that is to say, rhetorically less naïve) mind than Swann, has observed that the kitchen maid and Giotto's Charity resemble each other in still another way than physical shape. Their resemblance also has a dimension linked to reading and understanding, and in this capacity it is a curiously negative one. The property shared by the maid and by Charity is that of a nonunderstanding: both distinguish themselves by features they display "without seeming to understand their meaning." Both seem to be condemned to the same dyslexia.

The passage describes with great precision this shared inability to read. The allegorical image or icon has, on the one hand, a representational value and power: Charity represents a shape whose physical attributes connote a certain meaning. Moreover, it makes gestures or (in the case of a verbal icon that would no longer be pictorial) it tells tales that are particularly conspicuous in their intent to convey meaning. The figures have to be endowed with a semantic intensity that confers upon them a particularly effective representational function. The allegorical icon must attract attention; its semantic importance must be dramatized. Marcel insists that the kitchen maid and the Giotto frescoes resemble each other by their common claim to focus our attention on an allegorical detail: "Envy's attention—and, by the same token, our own—[is] entirely concentrated on the action of her lips . . ." just as "with the poor kitchen maid, [one's] attention is ceaselessly brought back to her belly by the load that weighs it down. . . ." In a metaphor, the substitution of a figural for a literal designation engenders, by synthesis, a proper meaning that can remain implicit since it is constituted by the figure itself. But in allegory, as here described, it seems that the author has lost confidence in the effectiveness of the substitutive power generated by the resemblances: he states a proper meaning, directly or by way of an intra-textual code or tradition, by using a literal sign which bears no resemblance to that meaning and which conveys, in its turn, a meaning that is proper to it but does not coincide with the proper meaning of the allegory. The facial expression of the "heavy and mannish" matron painted by Giotto connotes nothing charitable and even when, as in the case of Envy, one could perhaps detect a resemblance between the idea and the face of Envy, the stress falls on an iconic detail that sidetracks our attention and hides the potential resemblance from our eyes.

The relationship between the proper and the literal meaning of the allegory, which can be called "allegoreme" and "allegoresis" respectively (as one distinguishes between "noeme" and "noesis"), is not merely a relationship of non-coincidence. The semantic dissonance goes further. By concentrating the attention of Envy's beholder on the picturesque details of the image, he has, says Marcel, "no time for envious thoughts." Hence the didactic effectiveness of allegory since it makes one forget the vices it sets out to represent—a little as when Rousseau pretends to justify the theater because it distracts, for a while, vile seducers from their evil pursuits.[19] It actually turns out that, in the case of Envy, the mind is distracted towards something even more threatening than vice, namely death. From the structural and rhetorical point of view, however, all that matters is that the allegorical representation leads towards a meaning that diverges from the initial meaning to the point of foreclosing its manifestation.

In the case of the allegorical figuration of Charity, things are even more specific, especially if one takes the origins of the passage into account. Proust does not start out from a direct encounter with Giotto's frescoes, but from Ruskin's commentary on Giotto's Vices and Virtues of Padua.[20] The commentary is of considerable interest in many respects but it is especially striking in this context because it deals with an error of reading and interpretation. Ruskin describes Charity brandishing, in her left hand, an object that looks like a heart; he first assumes that the scene represents God giving his own charitable heart to her, but he corrects himself in a later note: "There is no doubt that I misread this action: she *gives* her heart to God, while she makes offerings to mankind."[21] Ruskin also discusses the painter's ambivalent rhetoric, which is, he says, "quite literal in [its] meaning as well as figurative." Describing the same gesture, Marcel follows Ruskin's rectified reading but displaces the meaning by adding a comparison which, at first sight, appears quite incongruous: "she stretches her incandescent heart towards God or, better, she hands it over to him,[22] as a cook would hand a corkscrew through a window of her basement to someone who asks for it at street-level" (p. 81, ll. 22–25). The comparison seems to be chosen merely to

19. Préface à *Narcisse*, in J. J. Rousseau, *Oeuvres completes*, ed. Bernard Gagnebin and Marcel Raymond (Paris: Gallimard [Bibliothèque de la Pléiade], 1961), 2:973.

20. On this question, see J. Theodore Johnson, Jr., "Proust and Giotto: Foundations of an Allegorical Interpretation of *A la recherche du temps perdu*," in *Marcel Proust: A Critical Panorama* (Urbana, Ill., 1973). That Mr. Johnson's and my conceptions of allegory have little in common is clear from his insistence, against textual evidence, on "the perfect blending of reality and symbol in the cycle of the Virtues and Vices" (Johnson, p. 202).

21. John Ruskin, *Fors Clavigera* in *The Works of John Ruskin*, ed. E. T. Cook and A. Wedderburn (London, 1907), 27:130.

22. The French text says "elle le lui *passe* . . ." with "passe" italicized, which suggests various colloquial associations. For our purposes, one can confine oneself to the connotative field suggested by the "lowly" implications of the term.

stress the homely quality of the gesture, but one of its other functions is to bring about the re-entry into the text of "the cook," that is to say, Françoise. The kitchen maid resembles Giotto's Charity, but it appears that the latter's gesture also makes her resemble Françoise. The first resemblance is not entirely unlikely: the sufferings of the hapless girl are vividly enough evoked to inspire a feeling of pity that could easily be confused with charity. But the further resemblance, with Françoise, is harder to understand: if the image, as a representation, also connotes Françoise, it widely misses its mark, for nothing could be less charitable than Françoise, especially in her attitude toward the kitchen maid. The neighboring episode (pp. 120–24), which narrates in great detail the refinements of Françoise's methods of torture, makes very clear that the literal sense of this allegory treats its proper sense in a most uncharitable manner. The rhetorical interest of the section, which culminates in the tragicomic scene where Françoise is seen weeping hot tears upon reading, in a book, a description of the very symptoms that prompt her most savage violence when she literally encounters them in her slave, is that a single icon engenders two meanings, the one representational and literal, the other allegorical and "proper," and that the two meanings fight each other with the blind power of stupidity. With the complicity of the writer, the literal meaning obliterates the allegorical meaning; just as Marcel is by no means inclined to deprive himself of Françoise's services, so the writer has no intention of doing without the thematic powers of literal representation and, moreover, would not be able to do so if he tried.

In the ethical realm of Virtue and Vice, the ambivalences of the allegorical figure thus lead to strange confusions of value. And if one bears in mind that, in Proust's allegory of reading, the couple Françoise/kitchen maid also enacts the polarity of truth and falsehood, then the epistemological consequences of the passage are equally troubling. Since any narrative is primarily the allegory of its own reading, it is caught in a difficult double bind. As long as it treats a theme (the discourse of a subject, the vocation of a writer, the constitution of a consciousness), it will always lead to the confrontation of incompatible meanings between which it is necessary but impossible to decide in terms of truth and error. If one of the readings is declared true, it will always be possible to undo it by means of the other; if it is decreed false, it will always be possible to demonstrate that it states the truth of its aberration. An interpretation of *A la recherche du temps perdu* which would understand the book as being the narrative of its own deconstruction would still operate on this level. Such an interpretation (which is indispensable) accounts for the textual coherence postulated by Genette, Deleuze, and by Marcel's own critical theories and, at the far end of its successive negations, it will recover the adequation between structure and statement on which any thematic reading depends. But when it is no longer a matter of allegorizing the crossing, or chiasmus, of two modes of reading but Reading itself, the difficulty brought to light by the passage on Giotto's Charity is much greater. A literal reading of Giotto's fresco would never have discovered what it meant, since all the represented properties point in a different direction. We know the meaning of the allegory only because Giotto, substituting writing for representation, spelled it out on the upper frame of his painting: *KARITAS*. We accede to the proper meaning by a direct act of reading, not by the oblique reading of the allegory. This literal reading is possible because the notion of charity, on this level of illusion, is considered to be a referential and empirical experience that is not confined to an intra-textual system of relationships. The same does not apply to the allegorical representation of Reading which we now understand to be the irreducible component of any text. All that will be represented in such an allegory will deflect from the act of reading and block access to its understanding. The allegory of reading narrates the impossibility of reading. But this impossibility necessarily extends to the word "reading" which is thus deprived of any referential meaning whatsoever. Proust may well spell out all the letters of *LECTIO* on the frames of his stories (and the novel abounds in gestures aimed in that direction), but the word itself will never become clear, for according to the laws of Proust's own statement it is forever impossible to read Reading. Everything in this novel signifies something other than what it represents, be it love, consciousness, politics, art, sodomy, or gastronomy: it is always something else that is intended. It can be shown that the most adequate term to designate this "something else" is Reading. But one must at the same time "understand" that this word bars access, once and forever, to a meaning that yet can never cease to call out for its understanding.

The young Marcel is at first displeased by the discordance between the literal and the proper meaning of the allegory, but the maturity of his literary vocation is dated by his ability to come to admire it: "Later on, I understood that the uncanny attraction, the specific beauty of these frescoes was due to the prominent place taken up by the symbol, and that the fact that it was not represented symbolically (since the symbolized idea was not expressed) but as something real, actually experienced or materially handled, gave to the meaning of the work something more literal and more precise . . ." (p. 82, ll. 7–14). This formulation, "plus tard, j'ai compris," is very familiar to readers of the *Recherche*, for it punctuates the entire novel like an incantation. Literary criticism has traditionally interpreted this "later on" as the moment of fulfillment of the literary and aesthetic vocation, the passage from experience to writing in the convergence of the narrator Marcel with the author Proust. In fact, the unbridgeable distance between the narrator, allegorical and therefore obliterating figure for the author, and Proust, is that the former can believe that this "later on" could ever be located in his own past. Marcel is never as far away from Proust as when the latter has him say: "Happy are those who have encountered truth before death and for whom, however close it may be, the hour of truth has rung before the hour of death."[23] As a writer, Proust is the one who knows that the hour of truth, like the hour of death, never arrives on time, since what we call time is precisely truth's inability to coincide with itself. *A la recherche du temps perdu* narrates the flight of meaning, but this does not prevent its own meaning from being, incessantly, in flight.

23. 3:910.

4 Genesis and Genealogy
(Nietzsche)

IN LITERARY STUDIES, STRUCTURES OF MEANING ARE FRE-
quently described in historical rather than in semiological or rhetorical terms. This is, in itself, a somewhat surprising occurrence, since
the historical nature of literary discourse is by no means an *a priori*
established fact, whereas all literature necessarily consists of linguistic and semantic elements. Yet students of literature seem to shy
away from the analysis of semantic structures and feel more at home
with problems of psychology or of historiography. The reasons for
this detour or flight from language are complex and go far in revealing the very semiological properties that are being circumvented.
They explain the methodological necessity of approaching questions
of literary meaning by ways of the nonlinguistic referential models
used in literary history. This is one of the means, among others, to
gain access to the enigmas that lie hidden behind the more traditional problems of literary classification and periodization.

One recurring such problem is that of the genetic pattern of
literary history and of literary texts that are assumed to reflect, by
analogy or by imitation, this pattern—as in the narrative shape of
stories that also purport to be histories (*The* History *of Tom Jones, La
Vie de Marianne*), or of histories so neatly framed that they seem to
consist of a single narrative unit (From *Baudelaire* to *Surrealism*,
From *Classic* to *Romantic*). The question is prevalent in attempts at
self-definition with relation to the past, as when the contemporary
mind is said to be, for instance, "post-Romantic" or "anti-idealist."
Romanticism itself is generally understood as the passage from a
mimetic to a genetic concept of art and literature, from a Platonic to
a Hegelian model of the universe. Instead of being mere copies of a
transcendental order, Nature or God, "all things below" are said to
be part of a chain of being underway to its teleological end. The
hierarchical world of Ideas and Images of Ideas becomes a world of
means moving towards an end and ordered in the prospective tem-

porality of a genetic movement. The existence of this *end* justifies the claim of the Romantics not to be a mere repetition of former perfection but a true birth, a beginning. "Das Resultat," says Hegel, "ist nur darum dasselbe, was der Anfang, weil der *Anfang Zweck* ist" (*Phenomenology of the Mind*, Introduction). The English translation of the words italicized by Hegel illustrates the interdependence and potential identity of end and beginning that characterizes a genetic concept of time: "The outcome is the same as the beginning only because the beginning is an *end*."

It would be tempting to document the emergence of the genetic pattern within the Romantic imagination and Romantic rhetoric. The prevalence of this pattern is not yet understood in all its implications and many studies of Romanticism are still in a pre-Hegelian stage. The tradition is caught in a non-dialectical notion of a subject-object dichotomy, revealing a more or less deliberate avoidance of the moment of negation that coincides, for Hegel, with the emergence of a true Subject. Such a study could lead us far in undoing a system that puts a natural, organic principle at the center of things and constructs a series of analogical emanations around this center, ending up with an altogether un-Hegelian concept of the subject as an irrational, unmediated experience of particular selfhood (or loss of selfhood). It would show that a dialectical conception of time and history can very well be genetic and that the abandonment of an organic analogism by no means implies the abandonment of a genetic pattern. When a contemporary philosopher like Michel Foucault characterizes nineteenth-century late-Romantic historicism as "lodged within the distance between particular histories and universal History, between singular events and the Origin of all things, between evolution and the first division within the source, between forgetting and return,"[1] then the vocabulary of source, origin, distance, memory, indicates that we are more than ever dealing with a genetic model defined in terms of an intent oriented towards an "end." The allegorization and ironization of the organic model leaves the genetic pattern unaffected.

It also leaves unaffected the genetic structure of the historiography that deals with Romanticism itself, as it developed during the nineteenth and the twentieth century. Within an organically determined view of literary history, Romanticism can appear as a high

---

1. *Les Mots et les choses* (Paris, 1966), p. 231.

point, a period of splendor, and the subsequent century as a slow receding of the tide, a decay that can take on apocalyptic proportions. A reversed image of the same model sees Romanticism as a moment of extreme delusion from which the nineteenth century slowly recovers until it can free itself in the assertion of a new modernity; Nietzsche himself, violently anti-Romantic in his cultural ideology, invariably adopts that perspective when he writes organic or, in his terminology, *monumental* history. The critical "deconstruction" of the organic model changes this image: it creates radical discontinuities and disrupts the linearity of the temporal process to such extent that no sequence of actual events or no particular subject could ever acquire, by itself, full historical meaning. They all become part of a process that they neither contain nor reflect, but of which they are a moment. They can never be the source or the end of the movement, but since the movement consists of their totalization, they can still be said to share in the experience of this movement. No father, no son can be God, but the history of the struggle between fathers and sons remains in essence divine. As a diachrony animated by a teleological intent, such a movement remains genetic. The intentional principle is no longer some ideal model or hypostasis but the law of the ultimate conformity of the end to the origin. Any particular subject or event, including texts, can be ordered as a moment within this conformity; this interpretative act of ordering and of classification both understands the event and locates it within the diachrony of the movement. In such a system, history and interpretation coincide, the common principle that mediates between them being the genetic concept of totalization.

To write a history of Romanticism that would no longer be organic but still genetic would be very useful, all the more since no truly dialectical history of Romanticism has as yet been written. Hegel's outlines of literary or art history bypass, as is well known, the contemporary moment entirely and this predictable blindness is repeated in later works that are the products of genuinely dialectical minds, such as Auerbach's *Mimesis* or Walter Benjamin's *Ursprung des deutschen Trauerspiels*. But the question remains whether such a dialectical history of Romanticism could do justice to its object. Can the genetic pattern be said to be "truly" characteristic of Romanticism? Does this system, with all the conceptual categories that it implies (subject, intent, negation, totalization, supported by the underlying metaphysical categories of identity and presence) remain as unchallenged in writers of the late eighteenth century as it remains unchallenged in most of their later interpreters? It could be that the so-called Romantics came closer than we do to undermining the absolute authority of this system. If this were the case, one may well wonder what kind of historiography could do justice to the phenomenon of Romanticism, since Romanticism (itself a period concept) would then be the movement that challenges the genetic principle which necessarily underlies all historical narrative. The ultimate test or "proof" of the fact that Romanticism puts the genetic pattern of history in question would then be the impossibility of writing a history of Romanticism. The abundant bibliography that exists on the subject tends to confirm this, for a curious blindness seems to compel historians and interpreters of Romanticism to circumvent the central insights that put their own practice, as historians, into question.

One way of progressing in this difficult question involves the examination of texts which, by their own structure and their own statement, lay the foundation for the genetic conception of history. From the eighteenth to the very recent twentieth century, one could select from a wide variety of such texts, from Montesquieu's *Esprit des lois* to Rousseau's *Discours sur l'origine de l'inégalité*, from Hegel's *Phenomenology of the Mind* to Heidegger's "The Origin of the Work of Art" ("Der Ursprung des Kunstwerkes," in *Holzwege*). Even such recent examples as Michel Foucault's or Jacques Derrida's attempts to see the conceptual crisis of language that figures so prominently in contemporary philosophy, as closing off a historical period, sometimes specifically designated as the "époque de Rousseau," fall within this pattern.

The choice of Nietzsche's *The Birth of Tragedy* as a text particularly well suited for this purpose needs little justification. Within the system of historical periodization implied by an "époque de Rousseau," Nietzsche represents an important articulation. Together with Marx and Freud, in a triumvirate that has become a cliché of intellectual history, his work participates in the radical rejection of the genetic teleology associated with Romantic idealism. Within the corpus of his own work, the pattern is repeated in the development that is said to lead from the early *Birth of Tragedy* (1871) to the entirely different tone and manner that prevails, in the published work, from *Human all too Human* (1876–78), on. In its own structure as well as in its historical function, his work would be a critique of the Romantic ideology, concluding the period that can be said to start with Rousseau. And it would indeed be difficult to find a text in which the genetic pattern is more clearly in evidence than in *The Birth of Tragedy*: it operates on various levels that all spring from a common source and converge toward a common end. We can take time to examine only some of these levels, but this should suffice to give this exercise in genetic "deconstruction" a more than heuristic significance.

The Birth of Tragedy is rightly considered to be one of Nietzsche's most unified texts. "It would be, in the final analysis, Nietzsche's only genuine 'Book,' " says Philippe Lacoue-Labarthe,[2] in a comment that fails perhaps to do justice to the coherence of *A Genealogy of Morals*, but that still faithfully reflects the first impression of any Nietzsche reader. Compared to the near-contemporary *Philosophenbuch*[3] or to the subsequent *Human all too Human*, *The Birth of Tragedy* seems to defend a well-rounded thesis, supported by relevant argument and illustration. As the title suggests, the principle of this coherence is unquestionably genetic, a classical example of the mode: the history of a birth and a rebirth, like Dante's *Vita nuova* but also like Nietzsche's favorite novel, *Tristram Shandy*. The text is held together by the psuedo-polarity of the Apollo/Dionysos dialectic that allows for a well-ordered teleology, because the ontological cards have been stacked from the beginning. With unquestionable fidelity to the dynamics of the text, Gilles Deleuze can say: "In a tragedy, Dionysos is the tragic essence [*le fond du tragique*]. He is the only tragic character, the 'suffering and glorified deity'; his sufferings are the only tragic subject, the sufferings of individuation reabsorbed in the joy of original oneness."[4] What is being said here about tragedy in general would seem to apply to Nietzsche's text as well. Truth, Presence, Being are all on Dionysos's side, and history can only occur as

2. "Le Détour," *Poétique* 5 (1971): 52.

3. A series of fragments and aphorisms that failed to coalesce into a completed book and now appear in Volume 6 of the so-called Musarion edition of Nietzsche's complete works (Friedrich Nietzsche, *Gesammelte Werke* [Munich: Musarion Verlag, 1920]). Page numbers of quotations from *The Birth of Tragedy* are from the Musarion edition, *Gesammelte Werke*, Volume 3. The numbers that follow the volume and page numbers refer to the numbered sections in which the text is divided.

4. *Nietzsche et la philosphie* (Paris, 1962), p. 13.

the birth and rebirth of a father in whose absence no son could ever exist. The starting point, Dionysos, contains within itself the endpoint, the Apollonian work of art, and governs the dialectical pathway that leads from the one to the other. Any cross-section made in the diachrony of the history can be valorized in terms of the greater or lesser manifestation or presence of Dionysos, the original "ground" by means of which distance and proximity can be measured: Sophocles is glorified, Plato and Euripedes cast as near-villains because of their greater or lesser proximity to Dionysos. The same criteria apply in the modern period, in the criticism of Florentine opera, of imitative music, and of the modern drama, or reversely, in the extravagant claims made for Wagnerian opera.

The imagery of depth and foundation used by Deleuze to convey the priority of Dionysos receives support from many statements throughout the text. It is less dependent, however, on the diachronic narrative than is the case in other genetic works such as Rousseau's *Discourse on Inequality* or his *Essay of the Origin of Language*. In these texts, the narrative articulations become themselves important thematic categories and the genetic moments are presented as cosmic catastrophes or divine interventions. By contrast, the outward narrative transitions in *The Birth of Tragedy* often consist of mere formal symmetries devoid of thematic weight. Thus the rebirth of Dionysos in the person of Wagner, crucial as the event may be, is described as a mere reversal of the regressive movement that destroyed the Hellenic world into a symmetrical movement of regeneration by which the modern, Germanic world is to be reborn.[5] Passages of this kind are valueless as arguments, since they assume that the actual events of history are founded in formal symmetries easy enough to achieve in pictorial, musical, or poetic fictions, but that can never predict the occurrence of a historical event. The narrative links are so weak that one may feel tempted to put the unity of the text in question for purely philological reasons, on the grounds that

5. "If we have rightly . . . linked the disappearance of the Dionysian spirit to an obvious but still unexplained transformation and degeneration of the Greeks, what hopes should not be kindled in us when we observe unmistakable auspices that *the reversed process, the gradual reawakening of the Dionysian spirit*, is taking place in our contemporary world!" (*Birth of Tragedy*, 3:133; 19) "we are reexperiencing analogically the great Hellenic periods *in reversed order* . . . and for example now seem to be moving backwards from the Alexandrian age into the period of tragedy" (ibid, 3:135; 19).

the complex inception of *The Birth of Tragedy* makes the final product into a patchwork of disconnected fragments or, as Nietzsche
himself put it, into a "centaur."[6]

The relative weakness of the narrative coherence becomes much
less important when one realizes that the diachronic, successive
structure of *The Birth of Tragedy* is in fact an illusion. We normally
think of genetic patterns as successive in time, and *The Birth of
Tragedy* indeed often describes the Apollonian and Dionysian phases
as "always new successive births" (3:39; 4). It can be shown, however, that whenever an art form is being discussed, the three modes
represented by Dionysos, Apollo, and Socrates are always simultaneously present and that it is impossible to mention one of them
without at least implying the others. The Dionysian moments always
occur in revolt against the tyranny or as a result of the failure of the
Socratic claim to knowledge; the Dionysian insight must always be
doubled at once by the Apollonian shelter of appearances; and the
Apollonian vision is always the vision of "the eternal contradiction, of
the father of all things" (3:37; 4). Yet this simultaneity does not
disprove the persistence of a genetic model, since parental relationship can be described as synchronic structures without in the least
denying their genetic nature. As long as the Dionysos/Apollo relationship is referred to, as in the previous quotation, in an imagery of
parenthood, successiveness and simultaneity are in fact mirror-like
versions of the same ontological hierarchy. And although the structure of parental imagery in *The Birth of Tragedy* is inconsistent, the
metaphors nevertheless remain familial throughout.

The genetic structure of the text is confirmed by layers of meaning that are sturdier than the formal symmetries of the narrative
plot. Other genetic linkages are at play, often based on genuine
philosophical insight rather than on the manipulation of geometrical
metaphors. Thus the transition to Wagnerian modernity finds its
thematic equivalence in the movement from science to art, from the
most extreme forms of epistemological constraint to the liberating
influence of German music. The myth of Socrates makes this movement into a historical development since Socrates, undoer of Greek
tragedy and founder of modern epistemology, represents the decadence that a new modernity has to overcome. The transformation of

6. Letter to Rohde, February 1870, *Briefe* 2; 3:183, also quoted in the editor's
postface [Nachbericht] to *The Birth of Tragedy*, Musarion, 3:401.

the epistemological into an aesthetic model is not to be thought of as a mere value assertion, an uncritical preference for the irrational rather than the rational faculties of man. The relationship between science and art is a great deal more complex from the start and, already in *The Birth of Tragedy*, Nietzsche advocates the use of epistemologically rigorous methods as the only possible means to reflect on the limitations of these methods. One cannot hold against him the apparent contradiction of using a rational mode of discourse—which he, in fact, never abandoned—in order to prove the inadequacy of this discourse. At the time of *The Birth of Tragedy*, Nietzsche is entirely in control of this problem and can state it with full thematic clarity, precisely in describing the transformation of the Socratic into the Wagnerian man. He uses and remains faithful to the Kantian element in Schopenhauer's terminology and this allegiance is itself epistemologically founded: "great men, capable of truly general insight, were able to use the devices of science itself in order to reveal the limits and relativity of all knowledge, thus decisively putting into question the scientific claim to universal validity and purpose. Their demonstration undid for the first time the illusion that the essence of things can be reached by means of causality" (3:123; 18). These "great men" are identified as Kant and Schopenhauer, and the reference to the laws of causality orients the remark towards the most rigorous epistemological sections of the *Critique of Pure Reason*. The same strategy and programmatic outline for the later work, in which the word "science" will reappear with a positive valorization (as in the title *The Gay Science*), is contained in a fragment that dates from the same period as *The Birth of Tragedy*: "Control over the world by means of positive action: first through science, as the destroyer of the illusion, then through art, as the only remaining mode of existence, because it cannot be dissolved by logic" (Musarion, 3:212, Fragment 44).

In *The Birth of Tragedy*, the problem of the relationship between art and epistemology functions within a genetic as well as a philosophical perspective: the ambivalence of the epistemological moment, as the critical undoer of its own claim at universal veracity, is represented as a genetic development from the Alexandrian to the truly modern man, and undoubtedly owes some of its persuasiveness to the narrative, sequential mode of presentation. It does not however, in this text, put this mode explicitly or implicitly into question. The genetic structure of *The Birth of Tragedy* is not affected, literally or rhetorically, by the epistemological paradox that it contains. Instead, the logical complication can rightly be said to be one of the principal articulations of the narrative. We must look further in order to discover whether the genetic pattern of *The Birth of Tragedy* is substantial (i.e., motivated by thematic statement considered as *meaning*) or rhetorical (i.e., motivated by thematic statement considered as *structure*).

There may well be an underlying, deeper pattern of valorization that confers genetic coherence and continuity upon the text and that transcends the thematics of the Apollo/Dionysos or the Socrates/Dionysos dialectic. A great deal of evidence points to the likelihood that Nietzsche might be in the grip of a powerful assumption about the nature of language, bound to control his conceptual and rhetorical discourse regardless of whether the author is aware of it or not. By the very choice of its literary theme, *The Birth of Tragedy* seems concerned, of its own volition, with what a text is or ought to be. Yet, in the final version, little is explicitly being said about the nature of literary language. We hear a lot about various subjects, mostly historical and cultural: a not entirely original or respectable theory about the importance of the chorus in Greek tragedy; considerations on the parallel rise and fall of the Greek theater and the Greek state and on the use and abuse of the sciences and of philology in contemporary education; aggresively polemical attacks on certain art forms written with a curious rancor; a highly personal and exalted plea for Wagner with strongly nationalistic overtones—all enclosed within the general framework of a mythological narrative involving two entities, Dionysos and Apollo, that are explicitly said to exist on a purely physiological as well as on a linguistic level. Throughout the main text and the preparatory fragments, the importance of language is consistently undercut: we are told that we can have no idea what Greek tragedy was like in the absence of the nonverbal components of the performance; in listening to vocal music, the text is an obstacle to the pure sound of the voice and it should never be understood in the first place; the outline for an elaborate theory of the work of art, reminiscent of the speculations of another post-Wagnerian, Mallarmé, is entirely directed towards the suppression of text in favor of mime and symphonic music. When the topic itself requires that literary language be considered, the chosen art form, Greek tragedy, carries with it such a weight of ideological, cultural, and theological experience, that it is nearly impossible to work one's way back to linguistic elements. The main theoretical speculations on language and art that originated at the time of *The Birth of Tragedy* have not been included in the final version. Nietzsche alludes to this in a letter to Rohde that accompanies the manuscript of the lecture "Socrates and Tragedy": "a curious metaphysics of art, which serves as background [to the main text of *The Birth of Tragedy*], is more or less my property, that is to say *real* estate [*Grundbesitz*], though not yet circulating, monetary, and consumed property. Hence the 'purple darkness,' an expression that pleased me more than I can say" (postface, 3:401).

What is this "real estate" that supports the phantasm, the rhetorical currency that the final version of *The Birth of Tragedy* puts in circulation? It must be something more fundamental than the dialectical interplay of Dionysos and Apollo, since the polarities would themselves be rooted in it. Everything seems to suggest that this "property" stems indeed from the dispossesion of the word in favor of music. The property rights over truth that belong, by philosophical authority, to the power of language as statement, are transferred to the power of language as voice and melody. Jacques Derrida has identified this gesture, which he calls "logocentric," as the perennial movement of all metaphysical speculation and has traced some of its versions in Plato, Hegel, Rousseau, Heidegger, Saussure, and others. Far from weakening the grounding of philosophy in ontology and in a metaphysics of presence, the transfer that favors voice over writing, art over science, poetry over prose, music over literature, nature over culture, symbolical over conceptual language (the chain of polarities could be extended at length and could also be put in a less naïve terminology), serves in fact to strengthen the ontological center (theocentric, melocentric, logocentric) and to refine the claim that truth can be made present to man. It also recovers the possibility of language to reach full and substantial meaning. A great number of passages from *The Birth of Tragedy* seem to place the text forcefully within the logocentric tradition. The later evolution of Nietzsche's work could then be understood as the gradual "deconstruction" of a logocentrism that receives its fullest expression in *The Birth of Tragedy*.

The logocentric valorization necessarily implies the persistence of the genetic model as its only possible representation in temporal or hierarchical terms. The propositions by means of which Nietzsche seems to identify himself most forcefully with music are always stated in terms of genetic filiation, as when he compares the absurdity of having music originate out of poetry to the absurdity of having the father originate out of the son ("Trying to illustrate a poem by means of music . . . what an upside-down world! A procedure that strikes me as if a son wanted to sire his father!" [3:343]). Within the reading of *The Birth of Tragedy* as a logocentric (or melocentric) text, the relative weakness of the main thematic articulations is of little importance, since the pattern is rooted in a deep-seated generative conception of language that is bound to control all the movements of the work, regardless of whether they belong to the highly self-reflective or to the loosely rhetorical levels of the discourse.

The most recent readings of *The Birth of Tragedy* are still oriented in this direction and do not question its logocentric ontology. Thus for Philippe Lacoue-Labarthe, who has admirably documented the importance of rhetoric for Nietzsche: "one would finally have to admit that, at the point which Nietzsche's 'deconstruction' [i.e., of the logocentric discourse] is able to reach, we are still standing under the aegis of truth; the labor of truth goes on, since we are trying to recall something that has been forgotten, to reveal something unconscious, to find the path of a 'reminiscence.'"[7] And Sarah Kofman states the same position in a more apodictic tone in her discussion of Nietzsche's concept of metaphor at the time of *The Birth of Tragedy*, as compared to his later concept of 'interpretation." In the early text, the stress on the symbolical nature of the language is still part of a binary system that opposes metaphorical to literal meaning and that reasserts, willy nilly, the authority of meaning. "To conceive of the essence of language as rhetorical implies the reference to a 'truthful' form of language, and a devalorization of the rhetorical in favor of literal language."[8] Later on, well after *The Birth of Tragedy*, this assumption presumably disappears: "the concept of metaphor becomes entirely un-proper [*impropre*], for it no longer refers to an absolute proper meaning but always already to an interpretation." It would seem that, in *The Birth of Tragedy*, this "absolute" or "truthful" meaning is the melocentric God Dionysos. The relationship between Dionysos and Apollo is again stated, by Sarah Kofman, in the genetic language of a father/son relationship and the

7. Lacoue-Labarthe, "Le Détour," p. 73.

8. "Nietzsche et la métaphore," *Poétique* 5 (1971): 78.

historical version of this relationship reappears in the development of
Nietzsche's later works. The same pattern is always repeated: within
Nietzsche's complete works, in the history of Romanticism, in the
relationship between Rousseau and Nietzsche, in the relationship
between Romanticism and modernity, etc. We now begin to see what
is at stake in the reading of *The Birth of Tragedy*, what problem
stands behind the *a priori* assertion of the genetic structure: the
relationship between language and music, between literal and
metaphorical diction, between narrative (diegesis) as representation
and narrative as temporality. Nietzsche was certainly right when he
referred to the nature of the Dionysos/Apollo relationship as "*the*
capital question [*die Hauptfrage*]" (Musarion, 3:357).

In moving from a thematic to a more rhetorical reading of *The Birth
of Tragedy*, we can take our clue from an explicit statement in which
Nietzsche asserts that the relationship between music and images
(Dionysos and Apollo) is not comparable to the relationship between
body and soul, but that it must be understood as "the opposition between appearance and the thing itself" ("Gegensatz der
Erscheinung und des Dinges" [3:146; 21]). "Thing" is not just what
we usually call reality but *Ding an sich*, the entity as substance in its
identity with itself. This terminology faithfully reproduces the principle of articulation that functions throughout the text. The successive incarnations of the Apollonian and the Dionysian spirit, from the
physiological description of the Apollonian as dream to the highly
evolved form of the Wagnerian drama, are always structured in
terms of these categories.

   The genetic version of the polarity Appearance/Thing is that of
an entity that can be said to be identical with itself and that would
engender, through a process of mediation, an appearance of which it
is the origin and the foundation. Such a model can be understood in
linguistic terms as the relationship between figural and proper
meaning in a metaphor. The metaphor *is* not "really" the entity it
literally means, but it can be understood to refer to something in
which meaning and being coincide. The meaning engenders and
determines the metaphor as the appearance or sign of this meaning.
This also seems to be how Nietzsche conceives of metaphor when he
writes: "The metaphor, for the true poet, is not a rhetorical figure,
but a substitute image that actually exists for him [*das ihm wirklich
vorschwebt*], instead of a concept" (3:60; 8). The metaphor does not

mean what it says but, in the last analysis, it says what it means to
say, since it remains controlled by and oriented towards a specific
meaning or set of meanings. Such a concept of metaphor coincides
with the very notion of language conceived as a system of symbolic
meaning, and *The Birth of Tragedy* offers many convincing reasons
why the detour through the metaphorical realm of appearances is
necessary.

There is little difficulty in matching the two mythological poles,
Dionysos and Apollo, with the categories of appearance and its antithesis, or with the relationship between metaphorical and proper
language. From its first characterization as dream, Apollo exists
entirely within the world of appearances. The dream is not, in *The
Birth of Tragedy*, the emergence of a "deeper" truth hidden by the
distraction of the wakeful mind; it is a mere surface, a mere play of
forms and associations, an imagery of light and color rather than the
darkness of the "nether Sphere." Far from being a loss of consciousness, it remains persistently aware, even in its "sleep," of its illusory,
fictional character, and it delights in this illusion. It is not a revealed
consciousness, since what it shows was never hidden. And it is not a
false consciousness, since it does not for a moment have the illusion
that its illusions are reality.

It complicates but does not, at least from our point of view, alter
the situation that this state of illusion happens to coincide with what
is usually called "reality" in everyday speech, the empirical reality in
which we live. In this reality, we must view ourselves "as the truly
nonexistent, i.e., as a constant becoming in time, space, and causality, or, in other words, as empirical reality" (3:36; 4). The quotation
comes from the section on the epic and serves to stress the doubly
fantastic quality of all narrative realism: not only is it the representation of an event and not the event itself, but the event itself is already
a representation, because all empirical experience is in essence fantastic. As mere appearance of appearance [*Schein des Scheins*],
Apollo dwells unquestionably in the realm of appearance.

All appearance, as the concept implies, is appearance of something that, in the last analysis, no longer seems to be but actually is.
This "something" can only be Dionysos. Contrary to the dream, devoid of actuality, the intoxication which is said to be the physiological
equivalence of Dionysos takes us back to the origin of things, precisely to the extent that it awakens us from the sleep of empirical
reality. As such, the Dionysian condition is an insight into things as

they are and it reaches truth by a negative road, by revealing the illusory nature of all "reality." The Apollonian appearance is the metaphorical statement of this truth; the actual meaning of the Apollonian appearance is not the empirical reality it represents but the Dionysian insight into the illusory quality of this reality.

If this is the case, then the priority of the musical, nonrepresentational language of Dionysos over the representational, graphic language of Apollo is beyond dispute. Dionysos becomes indeed the father of all art, including the plastic arts. Painting becomes a preliminary art form that prefigures truth and only waits for Dionysos to give it voice. A fragmentary passage not included in the final version states the inevitable triumph of music over painting:

> Let us people the air with the fantasies of a Raphael and watch, as he did, Saint Cecilia listening ecstatically to the choirs of angels. Not a sound emanates from this world apparently lost in music. Indeed, if we imagine that, by some miracle, these harmonies suddenly became audible, Cecilia, Paulus, and Magdelena, even the Heavenly choir, would suddenly disappear into nothing. We would at once stop being Raphael and, as on this painting the worldly instruments lie shattered on the floor, our painter's vision, defeated by a higher power, would pale away and vanish like a shadow. [Musarion, 3:343]

A different version of the same statement occurs in the description of Wagnerian opera: although the relationship between Dionysos and Apollo is then said to be a fraternal equality. Nietzsche insists, on the other hand, that Dionysos "is powerful enough ultimately to push the Apollonian drama into a sphere where it begins to speak with Dionysian insight, denying itself and its Apollonian phenomenality" (3:147; 21). The *telos* of this ultimate denial is what matters: seen from that perspective, all previous alliances between Dionysos and Apollo, marital, fraternal, paternal, or merely structural, are superseded by the genetic power vested in Dionysos as the father of all art, of all appearances.

Why then, if all truth is on Dionysos's side, is Apollonian art not only possible but even necessary? Why the need for metaphorical appearance since the proper meaning is all that counts? The question can still be answered from within the genetic logic of *The Birth of Tragedy* and without having to undo the pattern of this logic. It follows directly from the characterization of Dionysian insight as *tragic* insight. The discovery that all empirical reality is illusory is called a tragic discovery; no man, it seems, would be able to withstand its destructive power. Nietzsche can only bring us closer to it by a series of mythological approximations. The one who has reached it is, like Hamlet, frozen forever in the madness of inaction. Like Silenus, the best companion of Dionysos, he knows that "what is best of all lies forever beyond your reach: not to have been born, not to *be*, to be *nothing*. The second best however is for you—to die soon" (3:32; 3). He realizes, like Oedipus, that truth can only be reached at the cost of ultimate moral transgression and, like Prometheus, he experiences the essentially contradictory nature of the world in a state of endless rebellion devoid of hope. The entire semi-popular "existential" reading of Nietzsche takes off from this particular tonality. All readers of *The Birth of Tragedy* know by means of what ruse the destructiveness of unmediated truth is avoided: instead of being directly experienced it is represented. We are rescued by the essential theatricality of art. "Only as an *aesthetic phenomenon* is existence and the world forever *justified*" (3:46; 5, and 3:261; 24): the famous quotation, twice repeated in *The Birth of Tragedy*, should not be taken too serenely, for it is an indictment of existence rather than a panegyric of art. It accounts however for the protective nature of the Apollonian moment. The Apollonian light, says Nietzsche in one of his most striking metaphors, is the mirror image of a well-known optical phenomenon: "When, in a determined attempt to look directly at the sun, we have to turn away blinded, we'll have dark spots before our eyes to shelter them from the sunrays. Conversely, the brightly projected images of the Sophoclean hero, the Apollonian mask, are the necessary consequences of a glance into the inside and terrors of nature, bright spots to heal eyes wounded by the fearful night" (3:65; 9).

It is time to start questioning the explicit, declarative statement of the text in terms of its own theatricality. The system of valorization that privileges Dionysos as the truth of the Apollonian appearance, music as the truth of painting, as the actual meaning of the metaphorical appearance, reaches us through the medium of a strongly dramatized and individualized voice. Still more than Rousseau's *Discourse on the Origin of Inequality*, *The Birth of Tragedy* is indeed a discourse, a harangue that combines the seductive power of a genetic narrative with the rhetorical complicity of a sermon. A revealing self-critical statement about his own literary manner, in the *Philosophenbuch*, speaks of Nietzsche's resolution "to write, in general, in an impersonal and cold manner. Avoid all mention of 'us' and 'we' and 'I.' Also limit the number of sentences with relative clauses" (Musarion, 6:62). The opposite happens, of course, in *The Birth of Tragedy*. The complicity between the "I" of the narrator and the collective "we" of his acquiescing audience functions relentlessly, underscored by the repeated address of the audience as "my friends." The orator has our best interests at heart and we are guaranteed intellectual safety as long as we remain within the sheltering reach of his voice. The same seductive tone safeguards the genetic continuity throughout the text, easing the listener over difficult transitions by means of helpful summaries, marking out the truly important points by attention-catching signals. The more delirious passages are clearly marked off as digressions, after which "we glide back into the mood befitting contemplation" (3:139; 21), thus gaining at once our confidence with the reassuring thought that someone who allowed himself such verbal excesses in his digressions must be very cool and contemplative indeed in his argumentations. The voice is not beyond crediting us, the readers, with praise that it lavishes upon itself, as when we are endowed with Dionysian insight in being told that "we penetrate, with piercing clarity, into an inner world of motives" (3:159; 24). A longer enumeration of examples is superfluous, since they are as numerous as they are obvious in their strategy: this orator is in need of a very benevolent audience if it is to accept a shaky system of valorization.

The need to dramatize emphatically the stance of the convinced man is indeed imperative, for the genetic valorization of Dionysos reintroduces within the text all the categories that had originally been put into question, including the notion of an ontologically-rooted system of values. For all its genetic continuity, the movement of *The Birth of Tragedy*, as a whole as well as in its component parts, is curiously ambivalent with regard to the main figures of its own discourse: the category of representation that underlies the narrative mode and the category of the subject that supports the all-pervading hortatory voice.

Representation (mostly referred to, in this text, as *Vorstellung* or *Abbild*) functions throughout with a negative value-emphasis. From a purely historical point of view, *The Birth of Tragedy* could be ordered among the pre-expressionist critical documents in which a nonrepresentational art is being prepared; this may well be the text's main function in the history of criticism. The principal targets of this critique are the modern drama of the type associated with Lessing (*bürgerliches Trauerspiel*), with its Hellenic counterpart in Euripides, representational music and the Florentine opera with its Hellenic counterpart in the Attic dithyramb. All are dismissed as betrayals of the tragic origin of music. The difficult distinction between the "bad" imitation of realistic art and the "good" imitation of Wagner's music amounts, in fact, to the putting-into-question of the identity between origin and end that shapes the genetic pattern of the text itself. The condemnation of realism is first carried out by denouncing the overparticularization that reduces the godlike generality of tragedy to the trivia of imitative music, character drama, or personal lyricism. But Nietzsche reaches beyond the obvious shortcomings of this conventional view, and moves instead, with sure hermeneutic instinct, to the sensitive points of the imitation, the *beginning* and the *end* of the works, the points where the validity of the genetic pattern is at stake. In Euripides, or in his modern equivalent, we are told that the authority, the reliability of the action in terms of truth and falsehood that was implicitly given in the Sophoclean and Aeschylean tragedy now has to be made explicit: "the pathos of the exposition was lost [for Euripides]. Therefore, he put the prologue even before the exposition and had it spoken by a person one could trust. Often, some deity had to guarantee the credibility of the story and to remove all doubt about the reality of the mythological plot, just as Descartes could only demonstrate the reality of the empirical world by appealing to the truthfulness of a God incapable of telling a lie" (3:88–89; 12). The origin and beginning of the narrative is a literal, factual act of divine revelation and authority. The same is true of the end: the same god must literally reappear on the stage in order to resolve the apparently hopeless complications and confer dignity upon the confusion of human enterprise. The same "humanistic" pattern clearly applies to *The Birth of Tragedy*, a text based on the authority of a human voice that receives this authority from its allegiance to a quasi-divine figure. The prologue, an invocation to Richard Wagner, names the epiphany and vouchsafes for the truth of the narrative, because Nietzsche "communicated [with Wagner] as if he were present and could therefore write down only things worthy of this presence" (preface, 3:19). The resolution of the narrative hinges on the rebirth of this same Spirit as the *deus ex machina*, Wagner, reappearing on the scene to reverse the decadence of art and lead the essay to its triumphant conclusion. To the extent that it represents the history of tragedy as the narrative of a sequential event framed by the appearance and reappearance of the same incarnate spirit, *The Birth of Tragedy*, as text, resembles a Florentine opera or a *bürgerliches Trauerspiel* and not a Sophoclean tragedy or a Wagnerian opera. It is therefore open to criticism directed against these art forms. An intra-textual structure within the larger structure of the complete text undermines the authority of the voice that asserts the reliability of the representational pattern on which the text is based. And it weakens the figure precisely at the points that establish its genetic consistency: by weakening the authority of the power that sustains, by its presence, the unity between the beginning and the end.

No wonder therefore that we must react with suspicion when the discredited concept of representation is reintroduced in order to distinguish music from a purely imitative realism. Nietzsche cannot give up the necessity for a representational moment as a constitutive element of music. The tragic Dionysian insight is not, as for Rousseau, an absence of all meaning, but a meaning that we are unable to face for psychological or moral reasons. What Nietzsche calls, following Schopenhauer, the "Will" is still a subject, a consciousness capable of knowing what it can and what it can not tolerate, capable of knowing its own volition. The self-representing faculty of the will is a self-willed act; in music, the will wills itself as representation. Schopenhauer's definition of music as being the "unmediated image of the will [*unmittelbares Abbild des Willens*]" rests in the power and the authority of the will as subject. Nietzsche can therefore only write from the point of view, as it were, of the will. The authority of his voice has to legitimize an act by means of which the aporia of an unmediated representation, by itself a logical absurdity, would be suspended [*aufgehoben*].

"One might say," writes Lacoue-Labarthe, "that *The Birth of Tragedy* is ultimately nothing but the ambiguous commentary of this single statement by Schopenhauer [that music is the unmediated image of the Will], never accepted without reservations, but also never truly contested."[9] Given the way in which *The Birth of Tragedy* is rhetorically organized, Schopenhauer's dictum could only be "truly contested" by undermining the authority of the narrator from within

9. Lacoue-Labarthe, "Le Détour," p. 70.

the dynamics of the text. The negative valorization of representational realism and of the private lyrical voice (in Section 5) has precisely this effect on the narrator-orator of *The Birth of Tragedy*.

Nowhere is this more apparent than when the exemplary value of Wagnerian opera has to be demonstrated. A narrative mythological superstructure that awakens a feeling of pity and sympathy has to create the proper balance of distance and identification to "rescue" the audience from "the unmediated contemplation of the highest world-idea," "the unchecked effusion of the unconscious will"(3:144; 21). "The myth shelters us from the music" (3:141; 21), if the Dionysian truth of music as "Ding an sich" is to be maintained and if music is the origin and the end of all art, then "pure," nonrepresentational music has to be literally intolerable.

> I must address myself only to those who have a direct filiation with music, for whom music is like a maternal womb, and whose relationship with things is determined almost exclusively by unconscious musical ties. To these authentic musicians, I put the question if they could imagine a human being able to hear the third act of *Tristan and Isolde* without the assistance of word and image, as if it were a single, overwhelming symphonic movement? Such a listener would expire, carried away on the overexpanded wings of his soul. Could a man whose ear had perceived the world's very heart chamber, who has heard the roaring desire for existence as if it were a thundering river or the gentlest of brooks pouring out into the veins of the world, fail suddenly to break down? How could he endure to hear the echo of innumerable shouts of joy and pain, coming from "the wide spaces of the world's night" and reaching him within the miserable glass vessel of the human individual? Would not this metaphysical bacchanal compel him to flee back to his primordial home? [3:143; 21]

Who would dare admit, after such a passage, to not being one of the happy few among the "authentic musicians"? The page could only have been written with conviction if Nietzsche's personal identification would make him into the King Mark of a triangular relationship. It has all the trappings of the statement made in bad faith: parallel rhetorical questions, an abundance of clichés, obvious catering to its audience. The "deadly" power of music is a myth that can not withstand the ridicule of literal description, yet Nietzsche is compelled, by the rhetorical mode of his text, to present it in the absurdity of its facticity. The narrative falls into two parts or, what amounts to the same thing, it acquires two incompatible narrators. The narrator who argues against the subjectivity of the lyric and against representational realism destroys the credibility of the other narrator, for whom Dionysian insight is the tragic perception of original truth.

It cannot be claimed that one of the narrators is merely the Apollonian mask of the other. If this were the case, he could not be making the claims for truth that are constantly being made in the name of Dionysian wisdom. The myth, in Wagnerian opera, is not just the dreamlike illusion that makes no claim beyond that of its own beauty. It demands to be taken seriously as the only way of access to a substantial truth. It offers a necessary shelter to a full consciousness and is not, like the Apollonian dream, the consciousness of a nonconsciousness. The Dionysian myth can no longer be described and valorized in terms of appearance and illusion, as when the "will to delude" is presented as residing in a transcendental force that accomplishes its own designs without concern for the subject's own intentions. The Apollonian is by itself neither true nor false, since its horizon coincides with the awareness of its own illusory nature. It is illusion and not simulacrum, for it does not pretend to be what it is not. The categories of truth and falsehood can only be introduced by the Dionysian subject which, from that moment on, stands itself under the aegis of this polarity. Empowered, but also compelled, to decide on matters of truth and falsehood—as when it allows itself to refer to the Apollonian as a lie ("suffering is somehow being lied away out of the traits of nature"[3:113; 16])—it has to run the risk of having to decree the loss of its own claim to truth.

Have we merely been saying that *The Birth of Tragedy* is self-contradictory and that it hides its contradictions by means of "bad" rhetoric? By no means; first of all, the "deconstruction" of the Dionysian authority finds its arguments within the text itself, which can then no longer be called simply blind or mystified. Moreover, the deconstruction does not occur between statements, as in a logical refutation or in a dialectic, but happens instead between, on the one hand, metalinguistic statements about the rhetorical nature of language and, on the other hand, a rhetorical praxis that puts these statements into a question. The outcome of this interplay is not mere negation. *The Birth of Tragedy* does more than just retract its own assertions about the genetic structure of literary history. It leaves a residue of meaning that can, in its turn, be translated into statement, although the authority of this second statement can no longer be like that of the voice in the text when it is read naïvely. The nonauthoritative secondary statement that results from the reading will have to be a statement about the limitations of textual authority.

This statement cannot be read as such out of the original text, although it is sufficiently prepared there to come to the surface in the form of residual areas of meaning that cannot be fitted within the genetic totality. Certain formulations in *The Birth of Tragedy* remain enigmatic and cannot be integrated within the value-pattern of the main argument. For instance: after having been consistently distinguished from each other by a qualitative differential system founded on the polarity between illusion and nonillusion, the Dionysian, Apollonian, and Socratic modes are at least once, in what seems like a casual aside, differentiated in a purely quantitative system, in terms of their distance, as illusion, from a literal meaning. This literal meaning then has the purely structural function of a degree of zero figurality and does not, as such, coincide with tragic Dionysian insight. Contrary to all earlier claims, the Dionysian is then called one stage of delusion [*Illusionsstufe*] among others, "the metaphysical consolation that the eternal life flows unimpaired beneath the turmoil of appearances" (3:121; 18). Or what are we to make of the theory of dissonance that comes to the fore near the end of the text and functions there as a dynamic and temporal principle that can no longer be called genetic? The semantic dissonance of *The Birth of Tragedy* is precisely this residue of meaning that remains beyond the reach of the text's own logic and compels the reader to enter into an apparently endless process of deconstruction. This process is itself called "an artistic game that the will, in the eternal plenitude of its pleasure, plays with itself" (3:161; 24), a formulation in which every word is ambivalent and enigmatic, since the will has been discredited as a self, the pleasure shown to be lie, the fullness to be absence of meaning, and the play the endless tension of a nonidentity, a pattern of dissonance that contaminates the very source of the will, the will as source.

A detour outside the main text is needed, not in order to resolve the enigma, but to locate it, in its turn, within the context of its rhetoricity. The lateral material for *The Birth of Tragedy* that Nietzsche left out of the main essay contains formulations that retranslate into some kind of statement the disjunction between the semantic assertion and the rhetorical mode that occurs in the main text. We can confine ourselves, in conclusion, to two such statements. The "true rebuttal" of Schopenhauer, that Lacoue-Labarthe fails to find in *The Birth of Tragedy*, i.e., the contestation of the will as the ontological category by means of which beginning and end, origin and purpose are united in one genetic pattern, is brought to its explicit conclusion in the discarded fragments, whereas it was merely acted out theatrically in the main text. The following statement occurs in preparatory outlines for *The Birth of Tragedy*:

> Intelligence is justified in a world of aims. But if it is true that our aims are only a sort of rumination of experiences in which the actual agent remains hidden, then we are not entitled to transfer purposeful systems of action [*Handeln nach Zweckvorstellungen*] into the nature of things. This means that there is no need to imagine intelligence as capable of representation. Intelligence can only exist in a world in which mistakes occur, in which *error reigns*—a world of consciousness. In the realm of nature and of necessity, all teleological hypotheses are absurd. Necessity means that there can only be one possibility. Why then do we have to assume the presence of an intellect in the realm of things?—And if the will cannot be conceived without implying its representation, the "will" is not an adequate expression for the core of nature either. [Musarion, 3:239]

The radical separation of origin from purpose (*Ursprung* from *Zweck*) that is established here eliminates all possible claim at genetic totalization. Dionysos, as music or as language, must now belong either to the teleological domain of the text and then he is mere error and mystification, or he belongs to "nature" and then he is forever and radically separated from any form of art, since no bridge, as metaphor or as representation, can ever connect the natural realm of essences with the textual realm of forms and values. It had always been stated, also in the published text of *The Birth of Tragedy*, that Dionysos was not identical with the Will; he never *is*, in the full sense, an essence, but the possibility of an essence to exist in the guise of its represented appearance. "One should here distinguish as sharply as possible the notion of essence from that of appearance, for the very nature of music excludes that it be the will. This would eliminate it from the realm of art altogether, for the will is in essence the nonaesthetic. But music appears as will" (3:49; 6). *The Birth of Tragedy* dramatizes a variety of manners by means of which the distinction between essence and appearance can be bridged; what we have called the genetic pattern is precisely the possibility of this bridge, of this translation (Nietzsche speaks of "übersetzen" and "überbrücken"[10]) performed in the metaphorical narrative by means of which Dionysos can enter into a world of appearances and still somehow remain Dionysos. The imagery of filiation indicates that this essence is able to function as origin, and thus allows the text to unfold its symbolic story. The unpublished fragments, contemporaneous with the main text, deny this very possibility and thus reduce the entire *Birth of Tragedy* to being an extended rhetorical fiction devoid of authority. "One could object that I myself have declared that the 'Will' receives an increasingly adequate symbolic expression in music. To this I reply, in a sentence that summarizes a basic principle of aesthetics: *the Will is the object of music, but not its origin*" (Musarion, 3:344). This sentence could never have stood in the final version if *The Birth of Tragedy* had to survive as a text. It is hermeneutically satisfying however that the statement forced upon us by the deconstruction of the main text would reach us, formulated by the same author who also produced this text.

The deconstruction of the genetic pattern in *The Birth of Tragedy* is not without consequences, not only within the special field of Nietzsche interpretation, but in that of historiography and semiology as well. The dependence of narrative, continuous texts, such as *The Birth of Tragedy*, on discontinuous, aphoristic formulations, as in the fragments from which the last quotations were taken, turns out to be a recurrent structural principle of Nietzsche's work from the start. From a historiographical point of view, it is instructive to see a genetic narrative function as a step leading to insights that destroy the claims on which the genetic continuity was founded, but that

---

10. The image of the bridge appears in the main text within the same context of unresolvable paradox: "We may make the form [of the operatic representation] as visible and animate as possible, and have it glow with inner light, it still remains a mere appearance from which no bridge leads us back into true reality, into the heart of the world" (3:146; 21).

could not have been formulated if the fallacy had not been allowed to unfold. This may well turn out to be an exemplary model in trying to understand the aberrant interpretation of Romanticism that shapes the genealogy of our present-day historical consciousness. Moreover, bearing in mind the analogy that operates, in *The Birth of Tragedy*, between genetic movements in history and semiological relationships in language, the rhetorically self-conscious reading puts into question the authority of metaphor as a paradigm of poetic language. For if genetic models are only one instance of rhetorical mystification among others, and if the relationship between the figural and the proper meaning of a metaphor is conceived, as in this text, in genetic terms, then metaphor becomes a blind metonymy and the entire set of values that figures so prominently in *The Birth of Tragedy*—a melocentric theory of language, the pan-tragic consciousness of the self, and the genetic vision of history—are made to appear hollow when they are exposed to the clarity of a new ironic light.

5 Rhetoric of Tropes

(Nietzsche)

IT MAY SEEM FAR-FETCHED TO CENTER A CONSIDERATION of Nietzsche's relationship to literature on his theory of rhetoric. Why should one choose to consider what, by all evidence, appears to be an eccentric and minor part of Nietzsche's enterprise as a way of access to the complex question of his reflection on literature and on the specifically literary aspects of his own philosophical discourse? An abundance of other, less oblique approaches to the question may appear preferable. The configuration of the earlier literary examples explicitly mentioned by Nietzsche, a constellation that includes a wide variety of writers ranging from Goethe, Schiller, and Hölderlin to Emerson, Montaigne, and Sterne could certainly yield interpretative insights. Or one could consider Nietzsche's literary offspring, which is certainly even more extensive and informative than one suspects. The repertory of the revealed or hidden presence of Nietzsche in the main literary works of the twentieth century still has to be completed. It would reveal many surprises of value to an understanding of our period and literature in general.[1] For Nietzsche is obviously one of those figures like Plato, Augustine, Montaigne, or Rousseau whose work straddles the two activities of the human intellect that are both the closest and the most impenetrable to each other—literature and philosophy.

Nevertheless, the apparently crooked byways of the neglected and inconspicuous corner of the Nietzsche canon dealing with rhetoric will take us quicker to our destination than the usual itinerary that starts out from studies of individual cases and progresses from there to synthetic generalizations. That this area has been ne-

---

1. As one example among many, I was struck to find many more traces of Nietzsche in Proust than assumed, often in connection with Wagner and with the theme of music in general.

glected or discarded as a possible mainroad to central problems in the interinterpretation of Nietzsche is clear from bibliographical evidence: one of the few books dealing with the subject, a recent German work by Joachim Goth entitled *Nietzsche und die Rhetorik* (Tübingen, 1970), starting out from a suggestion that goes back to Ernst Robert Curtius, remains strictly confined to stylistic description and never pretends to engage wider questions of interpretation. That, on the other hand, the consideration of Nietzsche's theory of rhetoric, however marginal it may be, offers at least some promise, is clear from the work of some recent French commentators such as Philippe Lacoue-Labarthe, Bernard Pautrat, Sarah Kofman, and others.[2] Writing under the influence of a renewed interest, in France, in the theory of language, their work is oriented towards the philosophical implications of Nietzsche's concerns with rhetoric rather than towards the techniques of oratory and persuasion that are obviously present in his style. I do not plan to deal with these particular contributions which are still preparatory and tentative at best, but will try instead to indicate, in too broad and too hasty an outline, how the question of rhetoric can be brought to bear on some of Nietzsche's texts, early as well as late.

It is well known that Nietzsche's explicit concern with rhetoric is confined to the notes for a semester course taught at the University of Basel during the winter semester of 1872–73, with no more than two students present. Parts of these notes have been published in Volume V of the Kröner-Musarion edition. Only with their complete publication, presumably in the new Colli-Montinari edition, will we be able to judge if the former editors were justified in their claim that, after the seventh paragraph, the interest of the notes no longer warranted their publication. It is also well known that Nietzsche's course on rhetoric was not original and drew abundantly on the textbooks that were current at the time in the academic study of classical rhetoric, especially Richard Volkmann, *Die Rhetorik der Griechen und Römer in systematischer Übersicht* (1872), Gustav Gerber's *Die Sprache als Kunst* (1872) and, on the question of eloquence, the works of Blass (1868).[3] There is sufficient manipulation

2. See Bernard Pautrat, *Versions du soleil; Figures et système de Nietzsche* (Paris, 1971); Sarah Kofman, "Nietzsche et la métaphore," *Poétique* 5 (1971): 77–98; Philippe Lacoue-Labarthe, "Le détour," *Poétique* 5 (1971): 53–76.

3. See Friedrich Nietzsche, "Rhétorique et langage," texts translated, presented, and annotated by Philippe Lacoue-Labarthe and Jean-Luc Nancy in *Poétique* 5 (1971): 100.

of these sources and sufficient new emphases in Nietzsche's notes to justify their consideration despite their mixed origins. To claim, however, that they are of more than local significance takes some more elaboration. At first sight there is little in these notes to single them out for special attention.

Two main points that can be deduced from the notes deserve to be stressed. Nietzsche moves the study of rhetoric away from techniques of eloquence and persuasion [*Beredsamkeit*] by making these dependent on a previous theory of figures of speech or tropes. The notes contain explicit discussion of at least three tropes: metaphor, metonymy, and synecdoche, and announce Nietzsche's intention to follow this up with a taxonomy of tropes that would include catachresis, allegory, irony, metalepsis, etc. Eloquence and style are an applied form derived from the theory of figures. Nietzsche writes: "There is no difference between the correct rules of eloquence [*Rede*] and the so-called rhetorical figures. Actually, all that is generally called eloquence is figural language."[4]

The dependence of eloquence on figure is only a further consequence of a more fundamental observation: tropes are not understood aesthetically, as ornament, nor are they understood semantically as a figurative meaning that derives from literal, proper denomination. Rather, the reverse is the case. The trope is not a derived, marginal, or aberrant form of language but the linguistic paradigm par excellence. The figurative structure is not one linguistic mode among others but it characterizes language as such. A series of successive elaborations show Nietzsche characteristically radicalizing his remarks until they reach this conclusion:

> It is not difficult to demonstrate that what is called "rhetorical," as the devices of a conscious art, is present as a device of unconscious art in language and its development. We can go so far as to say that rhetoric is an extension [*Fortbildung*] of the devices embedded in language at the clear light of reason. No such thing as an unrhetorical, "natural" language exists that could be used as a point of reference: language is itself the result of purely rhetorical tricks and devices. . . . Language is rhetoric, for it only intends to convey a *doxa* (opinion), not an *episteme* (truth) . . . . Tropes are not something that can be added or subtracted from language at will; they are its truest nature.

4. Friedrich Nietzsche, *Gesammelte Werke* (Munich: Musarion Verlag, 1922), 5:300.

There is no such thing as a proper meaning that can be communicated only in certain particular cases.[5]

Although it may seem daringly paradoxical, the statement has affinities with similarly oriented formulations in Gerber's *Die Sprache als Kunst.* This is not so surprising if one bears in mind Gerber's own antecedents in German Romanticism, especially in Friedrich Schlegel and Jean Paul Richter; the relationship of Nietzsche to his so-called Romantic predecessors is still largely obscured by our lack of understanding of Romantic linguistic theory. Yet, the straightforward affirmation that the paradigmatic structure of language is rhetorical rather than representational or expressive of a referential, proper meaning is more categorical, in this relatively early Nietzsche text, than in the predecessors from which it stems. It marks a full reversal of the established priorities which traditionally root the authority of the language in its adequation to an extralinguistic referent or meaning, rather than in the intralinguistic resources of figures.

A passage such as this one could still be understood as a belated echo of earlier speculations, long since overcome in the post-Kantian and post-Hegelian syntheses that have put rhetoric back in its proper place, or dismissed it as a form of the aesthetic decadence that Nietzsche will be one of the first to denounce in later, anti-Wagnerian and anti-Schopenhauerian writings. The question remains however whether some of the implications of the early speculations on rhetoric are carried out in later works. At first sight, this hardly seems to be the case. The rhetorical vocabulary, still much in evidence in the *Philosphenbuch* (which dates from the fall of 1872 and thus immediately precedes the course on rhetoric) disappears almost entirely from *Human all too Human* on. It seems as if Nietzsche had turned away from the problems of language to questions of the self and to the assertion of a philosophy rooted in the unmediated sense of existential pathos which has been so prevalent in the interpretation of his work.

The validity of this scheme can be put in question by examining one single but typical passage from a later text. It dates from 1888 and is part of the posthumous fragments known as *The Will to Power.* The passage is characteristic of many later Nietzsche texts

5. Ibid.

and is not to be considered as an anomaly. I am not primarily interested in its specific "thesis" but rather in the manner in which the argument is conducted.

The passage has to do with what Nietzsche calls the phenomenalism of consciousness, the tendency to describe mental events such as recollection or emotion in terms derived from the experience of the phenomenal world: sense perception, the interpretation of spatial structures, etc. Under the heading "phenomenalism of the inner world," Nietzsche writes as follows:

> The *chronological reversal* which makes the cause reach consciousness later than the effect.—We have seen how pain is projected in a part of the body without having its origin there; we have seen that the perceptions which one naïvely considers as determined by the outside world are much rather determined from the inside; that the actual impact of the outside world is never a *conscious* one . . . The fragment of outside world of which we are conscious is a correlative of the effect that has reached us from outside and that is then projected, *a posteriori*, as its "cause" . . .[6]

The argument starts out from a binary polarity of classical banality in the history of metaphysics: the opposition of subject to object based on the spatial model of an "inside" to an "outside" world. As such, there is nothing unusual about the stress on the unreliability, the subjectivity of sense impressions. But the working hypothesis of polarity becomes soon itself the target of the analysis. This occurs, first of all, by showing that the priority status of the two poles can be reversed. The outer, objective event in the world was supposed to determine the inner, conscious event as cause determines effect. It turns out however that what was assumed to be the objective, external cause is itself the result of an internal effect. What had been considered to be a cause, is, in fact, the effect of an effect, and what had been considered to be an effect can in its turn seem to function as the cause of its own cause.

The two sets of polarities, inside/outside and cause/effect, which seemed to make up a closed and coherent system (outside

6. Friedrich Nietzsche, *Werke in drei Bänden*, ed. Karl Schlechta (Munich: Hanser Verlag, 1956), 3:804–05.

causes producing inside effects) has now been scrambled into an arbitrary, open system in which the attributes of causality and of location can be deceptively exchanged, substituted for each other at will. As a consequence, our confidence in the original, binary model that was used as a starting point is bound to be shaken. The main impact of this deconstruction of the classical cause/effect, subject/object scheme becomes clear in the second part of the passage. It is based, as we saw, on an inversion or reversal of attributes which, in this particular case, is said to be temporal in nature. Logical priority is uncritically deduced from a contingent temporal priority: we pair the polarities outside/inside with cause/effect on the basis of a temporal polarity before/after (or early/late) that remains un-reflected. The result is cumulative error, "the consequence of all previous causal fictions," which as far as the "objective" world is concerned, are forever tied to "the old error of original Cause."[7] This entire process of substitution and reversal is conceived by Nietzsche—and this is the main point for us in this context—as a linguistic event. The passage concludes as follows:

> The whole notion of an "inner experience" enters our consciousness only after it has found a language that the individual *understands*—i.e., a translation of a situation into a *familiar* situation—: 'to understand,' naïvely put merely means: to be able to express something old and familiar.[8]

What is here called "language" is the medium within which the play of reversals and substitutions that the passage describes takes place. This medium, or property of language, is therefore the possibility of substituting binary polarities such as before for after, early for late, outside for inside, cause for effect, without regard for the truth-value of these structures. But this is precisely how Nietzsche also defines the rhetorical figure, the paradigm of all language. In the Course on Rhetoric, metonymy is characterized as what rhetoricians also call metalepsis, "the exchange or substitution of cause and effect" and one of the examples given is, revealingly enough, the substitution of "tongue" for language. Later in the same notes metonymy is also defined as hypallagus and characterized as follows:

7. Ibid., 3:805.
8. Ibid.

> The abstract nouns are properties within and outside ourselves
> that are being torn away from their supports and considered to
> be autonomous entities. . . . Such concepts, which owe their
> existence only to our feelings, are posited as if they were the
> inner essence of things: we attribute to events a cause which in
> truth is only an effect. The abstractions create the illusion as if
> *they* were the entity that causes the properties, whereas they
> receive their objective, iconic existence [*bildliches Dasein*] only
> from us as a consequence of these very properties.[9]

Practically the same text that, in 1872, explicitly defines metonymy as
the prototype of all figural language, describes, in 1888, a metaphysical construct (the phenomenalism of consciousness) as susceptible of
being deconstructed as soon as one is made aware of its linguistic,
rhetorical structure. We are not here concerned with the consequences of this critique of phenomenalism which is also, in many
respects, a prefigurative critique of what will later become known a
phenomenology. Readers of *The Will to Power* know that this critique
by no means pretends to discard phenomenalism, but puts us on our
guard against the tendency to hypostatize consciousness into an authoritative ontological category. And they will also recognize that the
pattern of argument here directed against the concept of consciousness is the same pattern that underlies the critique of the main
categories that make up traditional metaphysics: the concepts of
identity, of causality, of the object and the subject, of truth, etc. We
can legitimately assert therefore that the key to Nietzsche's critique
of metaphysics—which has, perhaps misleadingly, been described as
a mere *reversal* of metaphysics or of Plato—lies in the rhetorical
model of the trope or, if one prefers to call it that way, in literature as
the language most explicitly grounded in rhetoric.

The idea of a reversal or an exchange of properties (in the
previous example, it is the exchange of the attributes of place and
causality) is constitutively paired by Nietzsche to the idea of error:
the critical deconstruction shows that philosophical models such as
the phenomenalism of consciousness are indeed aberrations whose
systematic recurrence extends throughout the entirety of classical
metaphysics. Would it not follow that, since the aberration turns out
to be based on a rhetorical substitution, it would suffice to become

9. Musarion, 5:319.

aware of this in order to undo the pattern and restore the properties to their "proper" place? If attributes of time and attributes of cause have been improperly associated with each other, one might be able to uncross, so to speak, the polarities that have been exchanged in order to recover a measure of truth. In the example at hand, we could conceivably eliminate the misleading temporal scheme that led to the confusion, and substitute for the derived cause, mistakenly assumed to have an objective existence in the outside world, an authentic cause that could be inferred from the critical deconstruction of the aberrant one. Granted that the misinterpretation of reality that Nietzsche finds systematically repeated throughout the tradition is indeed rooted in the rhetorical structure of language, can we then not hope to escape from it by an equally systematic cleansing of this language from its dangerously seductive figural properties? Is it not possible to progress from the rhetorical language of literature to a language that, like the language of science or mathematics, would be epistemologically more reliable? The ambivalence of Nietzsche's attitude towards science and literature, as it appears, for example, in the use of the term science in the title of "la gaya scienza" or in the later fragments that look back upon *The Birth of Tragedy*, indicates the complexity of his position. One can read these texts as a glorification as well as a denunciation of literature. The general drift of Nietzsche's thought, on this point, can be better understood by taking into account texts that precede the 1873 Course on Rhetoric, especially the never-completed *Philosophenbuch*.

For the very question we are considering, the possibility of escaping from the pitfalls of rhetoric by becoming aware of the rhetoricity of language, is central to the entire *Philosophenbuch* and its only completed unit, the essay *On Truth and Lie in an Extra-Moral Sense* [*Über Wahrheit und Lüge im aussermoralischen Sinn*]. This essay flatly states the necessary subversion of truth by rhetoric as the distinctive feature of all language. "What is truth?" asks Nietzsche, and he answers:

A moving army of metaphors, metonymies and anthropomorphisms, in short a summa of human relationships that are being poetically and rhetorically sublimated, transposed, and beautified until, after long and repeated use, a people considers them as solid, canonical, and unavoidable. Truths are illusions whose illusionary nature has been forgotten, metaphores that have been used up and have lost their imprint and that now operate as mere metal, no longer as coins.[10]

What is being forgotten in this false literalism is precisely the rhetorical, symbolic quality of all language. The degradation of metaphor into literal meaning is not condemned because it is the forgetting of a truth but much rather because it forgets the un-truth, the lie that the metaphor was in the first place. It is a naïve belief in the proper meaning of the metaphor without awareness of the problematic nature of its factual, referential foundation.

The first step of the Nietzschean deconstruction therefore reminds us, as in the above quotation, of the figurality of all language. In this text, contrary to what happens in *The Birth of Tragedy*, this insight is openly stated as the main theme of the essay. Does it follow that the text therefore escapes from the kind of error it denounces? And since we can make the possibility of this error distinctive of literature in general, does it then follow that the essay *On Lie and Truth* is no longer literature but something closer to science—as Wittgenstein's *Tractatus* could claim to be scientific rather than literary? Or, if we call a hybrid text like this one "philosophical," can we then define philosophy as the systematic demystification of literary rhetoric?

The text proceeds in its deconstructive enterprise by putting into question some of the concepts that will also be targets of the later critique of metaphysics in *The Will to Power*. It shows, for example, that the idea of individuation, of the human subject as a privileged viewpoint, is a mere metaphor by means of which man protects himself from his insignificance by forcing his own interpretation of the world upon the entire universe, substituting a human-centered set of meanings that is reassuring to his vanity for a set of meanings that reduces him to being a mere transitory accident in the cosmic order. The metaphorical substitution is aberrant but no human self could come into being without this error. Faced with the truth of its nonexistence, the self would be consumed as an insect is consumed by the flame that attracts it. But the text that asserts this annihilation of the self is not consumed, because it still sees itself as the center that produces the affirmation. The attributes of centrality and of selfhood are being exchanged in the medium of the language. Mak-

10. Schlechta, 3:314.

ing the language that denies the self into a center rescues the self linguistically at the same time that it asserts its insignificance, its emptiness as a mere figure of speech. It can only persist as self if it is displaced into the text that denies it. The self which was at first the center of the language as its empirical referent now becomes the language of the center as fiction, as metaphor of the self. What was originally a simply referential text now becomes the text of a text, the figure of a figure. The deconstruction of the self as a metaphor does not end in the rigorous separation of the two categories (self and figure) from each other but ends instead in an exchange of properties that allows for their mutual persistance at the expense of literal truth. This process is exactly the same as what Nietzsche describes as the exemplary "lie" of language: "The liar uses the valid designations, words, to make the unreal appear real. . . . He misuses the established linguistic conventions by *arbitrary substitutions or even reversals* of the names."[11] By calling the subject a text, the text calls itself, to some extent, a subject. The lie is raised to a new figural power, but it is nonetheless a lie. By asserting in the mode of truth that the self is a lie, we have not escaped from deception. We have merely reversed the usual scheme which derives truth from the convergence of self and other by showing that the fiction of such a convergence is used to allow for the illusion of selfhood to originate.

The pattern is perhaps clearest in the reversal of the categories of good and evil as they combine with those of truth and lie. The usual scheme derives good from truth and evil from falsehood. But Nietzsche tells the tale of the reversed pattern: in order to survive in society, man began by lying.

> [Then] man forgets that this is the case: his lying then is no longer conscious and is founded on age-old habit—and it is *by this nonawareness*, by this forgetting that he develops a sense of truth. Because he feels obliged to designate a certain thing as "red," another as "cold," a third as "mute," a moral impulse oriented towards truth is awakened: in opposition to the liar, who is trusted by no one and excluded from the group, man discovers the respectability, the reliability and the use of truth.[12]

Thus moral virtue is shown to originate out of lies. But the text cannot go to rest in this deconstruction that would justify, to some

11. Ibid., 3:311 (my italics).
12. Ibid., 3:314.

extent, the morality of deceit (as we find it, for example, within a political context, in Machiavelli or in Rousseau). For if we believe in the morality of deceit, we also have to believe in the evil of truth, and to the extent that the society is held together by means of deceit, the open assertion of this fact will also destroy the moral order. It could hardly be said, without further qualification, that a text like this one is socially or morally uplifting. Once again, the reversal of polarities has not led to a restoration of literal truth—in this case, it would be the assertion that moral education should increase one's skill at lying—but has driven us further into the complications of rhetorical delusion. We may have changed the rhetorical mode but we certainly have not escaped from rhetoric. This could hardly have been expected. The original pairing of rhetoric with error, as we encounter it from the Course on Rhetoric to *The Will to Power* was based on the cross-shaped reversal of properties that rhetoricians call chiasmus. And it turns out that the very process of deconstruction, as it functions in this text, is one more such reversal that repeats the selfsame rhetorical structure. All rhetorical structures, whether we call them metaphor, metonymy, chiasmus, metalepsis, hypallagus, or whatever, are based on substitutive reversals, and it seems unlikely that one more such reversal over and above the ones that have already taken place would suffice to restore things to their proper order. One more "turn" or trope added to a series of earlier reversals will not stop the turn towards error. A text like *On Truth and Lie*, although it presents itself legitimately as a demystification of literary rhetoric remains entirely literary, rhetorical, and deceptive itself. Does this mean that it will end up in a glorification of literature over science or, as is sometimes claimed of Nietzsche, in a purely literary conception of philosophy?

Two quotations from the *Philosophenbuch*, closely contemporary to *On Truth and Lie*, fully reveal the ambiguity inherent in the question. On the one hand, the truth-value of literature, albeit a negative one, is recognized and asserted. Art is no longer associated with the Dionysian immediacy of music but is now openly Socratic in its deconstructive function. It is therefore, of all human activities, the only one that can lay claim to truth: "Art treats appearance as appearance; its aim is precisely *not* to deceive, it is therefore *true*."[13] But the truth of appearance, unlike the truth of being, is not a threat or a passion that could be described in terms similar to those used in *The*

13. Musarion, 6:98.

Birth of Tragedy to evoke the Dionysian pathos of truth. It can therefore be said that it stands above pleasure and pain, in the ordinary
sense of these terms. The artist, who is truthful in his recognition of
illusion and of lie for what they are, thus gains a special kind of
affective freedom, a euphoria which is that of a *joyful* wisdom or of
the Homeric *Heiterkeit* and that differs entirely from the pleasure
principle tied to libido and desire. "As long as man looks for truth *in
the world,* he stands under the dominance of desire [*unter der
Herrschaft des Triebes*]: he wants pleasure, not truth; he wants the
belief in truth and the pleasurable effects of this belief."[14] Only the
artist who can conceive of the entire world as appearance is able to
consider it without desire: this leads to the feeling of liberation and
weightlessness that characterizes the man freed from the constraints
of referential truth, what Barthes, in more recent times, has referred
to as "la libération du signifiant." *On Truth and Lie* describes the
euphoria of this type of "truth":

> The intellect, this master of deceit, feels itself freed from its
> habitual servitude when it is allowed to deceive without direct
> harm. Then it celebrates its own saturnalia. It is never so rich,
> so seductive, proud, clever and outrageous: with inventive satis-
> faction, it juggles metaphores and tears out [*verrückt*] the bor-
> dermarks of abstractions. For example, he considers the river as
> if it were the moving roadway that carries man to where he
> would otherwise have to walk. . . . It imitates human exis-
> tence as if it were a fine thing and declares itself entirely pleased
> with it.[15]

This attractive pairing of Heraclites with Stendhal is however not
devoid of warning signals. It has its own psuedo-teleology, the flow
of time delighting in the self-sufficient, innocent spectacle of its own
motion. But if this movement is reduced to the mere appearance that
it is, it also loses its foundation and becomes one among the various
other metaphors of self-destruction disseminated throughout this
brief text: the insect and the fluttering light, the conceptual pyramid
that turns out to be a tomb, the painter deprived of his hands, man
asleep on the back of a tiger.[16] The implicit threat in all these images

14. Ibid.
15. Schlechta, 3:320.
16. Ibid., 3:310, 315, 317, 311, respectively.

is very similar to the threat implied in mistaking a river for a road. The critical deconstruction that leads to the discovery of the literary, rhetorical nature of the philosophical claim to truth is genuine enough and cannot be refuted: literature turns out to be the main topic of philosophy and the model for the kind of truth to which it aspires. But when literature seduces us with the freedom of its figural combinations, so much airier and lighter than the labored constructs of concepts, it is not the less deceitful because it asserts its own deceitful properties. The conclusion of the essay shows the artist in a not particularly enviable situation: he is indeed freer but "he suffers more [than the conceptual philosopher] *when* he suffers; and he suffers more often, because he does not learn from experience and always again falls in the same trap in which he fell in the first place. In his suffering, he is then just as foolish [*unvernünftig*] as in his happiness: he complains loudly and can find no consolation."[17] An aphorism that dates from exactly the same period puts it more bluntly and from a less personal point of view: it may be true that art sets the right norm for truth, but "Truth kills, indeed kills itself (insofar that it realizes its own foundation in error)."[18] Philosophy turns out to be an endless reflection on its own destruction at the hands of literature.

This endless reflection is itself a rhetorical mode, since it is unable ever to escape from the rhetorical deceit it denounces. The definition of this mode lies beyond our present scope, though we get some indication from the just-quoted description of the artist's plight in *On Truth and Lie* as well as from the general tonality and structure of this text. First of all, the description is certainly not a tragic one: the suffering described in the passage, as well as the happiness that precedes it, cannot be taken seriously, since both are so clearly the result of foolishness. The same foolishness extends to the text itself, for the artist-author of the text, as artist, is just as vulnerable to it as the artist-figure described in the text. The wisdom of the text is self-destructive (art is true but truth kills itself), but this self-destruction is infinitely displaced in a series of successive rhetorical reversals which, by the endless repetition of the same figure, keep it suspended between truth and the death of this truth. A threat of immediate destruction, stating itself as a figure of speech, thus becomes the permanent repetition of this threat. Since this repetition is

17. Ibid., 3:322.
18. Musarion, 6:93.

a temporal event, it can be narrated sequentially, but what it narrates, the subject matter of the story, is itself a mere figure. A non-referential, repetitive text narrates the story of a literally destructive but nontragic linguistic event. We could call this rhetorical mode, which is that of the "conte philosophique" *On Truth and Lie* and, by extension, of all philosophical discourse, an ironic allegory—but only if we understand "irony" more in the sense of Friedrich Schlegel than of Thomas Mann. The place where we might recover some of this sense is in Nietzsche's own work, not in that of his assumed continuators.

This conclusion as to the fundamentally ironic and allegorical nature of Nietzsche's discourse projects its effect on the works that follow and on those that precede the *Philosophenbuch* as well as on the relationship between the two segments that are thus being more or less arbitrarily isolated. How an ironic reading of an allegorical text such as *Zarathustra* or *The Genealogy of Morals*, or the allegorical reading of ironic aphoristic sequences from *The Gay Science* or *The Will to Power* would have to proceed cannot be outlined here, however sketchily. It may be more productive, in conclusion, to observe how an early text such as *The Birth of Tragedy* fits into this pattern. For one of the most persistent ways in which the illusion that rhetorical blindness can be overcome manifests itself is by the transference of what Nietzsche calls "the old error of original cause" from the *statement* to the *history* of the text. While granting the ambivalence of the later Nietzsche on the subject of truth, one may contrast this wariness with the relative naïveté of the earlier works. Particular texts from, say, *On Truth and Lie* on, can be considered to be epistemologically destructive, but by presenting them as a development moving beyond the assumed mystification of the earlier writings, the "history" of Nietzsche's work as a whole remains that of a narrative moving from false to true, from blindness to insight. But the question remains whether the pattern of this narrative is "historical," i.e., revelatory of a teleological meaning, or "allegorical," i.e., repetitive of a potential confusion between figural and referential statement. Is Nietzsche's work structured as a process, a movement of "becoming"—and Nietzsche's late reference to "the innocence of becoming" is well known—or as a repetition? The importance of the question is apparent from the near-obsessive way in which Nietzsche himself, as well as his interpreters, have been returning to the enigmas of the early *Birth of Tragedy*.

The obvious pathos and exaltation of *The Birth of Tragedy* seems entirely incompatible with irony. It is difficult not to read it as a plea for the unmediated presence of the will, for a truly tragic over an ironic art. If this were indeed the case, then one would have to assume a genuine development, even a conversion within Nietzsche's thought during the years immediately following the writing of *The Birth of Tragedy*. The conversion could have been brought about by his reflections on rhetoric as they appear in the *Philosophenbuch* and in the 1873 course notes, and it would also be apparent in the reaction against Wagner and Schopenhauer in the *Unzeitgemässe Betrachtungen*. The structure of the work as a whole would then be essentially different from that described and acted out in *On Truth and Lie*.

A more rhetorically aware reading of *The Birth of Tragedy* shows that all the authoritative claims that it seems to make can be undermined by means of statements provided by the text itself. And if one also takes into account notes written for *The Birth of Tragedy* but not incorporated in the published text, the ironization implicitly present in the final version becomes quite explicit. Moreover, the forthcoming publication, in the new critical edition of Nietzsche's works, of further lateral material for *The Birth of Tragedy*, shows that the exclusion of these notes was dictated by considerations that disrupt the system of epistemological authority even more deeply. We are told, in these fragments, that the valorization of Dionysos as the primary source of truth is a tactical necessity rather than a substantial affirmation. Nietzsche's auditors have to be spoken to in Dionysian terms because, unlike the Greeks, they are unable to understand the Apollonian language of figure and appearance. In pseudohistorical arguments, reminiscent of Hölderlin's considerations on the dialectical relationship between the Hellenic and the Western world, Nietzsche writes: "The epic fable of the Ancients represented the Dionysian in images. For us, it is the Dionysian that represents (symbolizes) the image. In Antiquity, the Dionysian was explained by the image. Now it is the image that is explained by Dionysos. We have therefore an exactly reversed relationship. . . . For them, the world of representation was clear; for us, it is the Dionysian world that we understand."[19] It follows that the entire system of valoriza-

---

19. Quoted from galley proofs of the forthcoming Colli and Montinari edition of *The Birth of Tragedy*; no reference available.

tion at work in *The Birth of Tragedy* can be reversed at will. The Dionysian vocabulary is used only to make the Apollonian mode that deconstructs it more intelligible to a mystified audience. This exchange of attributes involving the categories of truth and appearance deprives the two poles of their authority. The binary polarity that structures the narrative of the text turns out to be the same figure we have encountered in all previous examples, the same "reversal of names" that was mentioned in *On Truth and Lie*. If we read Nietzsche with the rhetorical awareness provided by his own theory of rhetoric we find that the general structure of his work resembles the endlessly repeated gesture of the artist "who does not learn from experience and always again falls in the same trap." What seems to be most difficult to admit is that this allegory of errors is the very model of philosophical rigor.

6 Rhetoric of Persuasion
(Nietzsche)

THE QUESTION OF THE RELATIONSHIP BETWEEN PHIL-
osophical and literary discourse is linked, in Nietzsche, to his critique
of the main concepts underlying Western metaphysics: the concept
of the one [*hen*], the good [*agathon*] and the true [*aletheia*].[1] This
critique is not conducted in the tone and by means of the arguments
usually associated with classical critical philosophy. It is often carried out by means of such pragmatic and demagogical value-
oppositions as weakness and strength, disease and health, herd and
the "happy few," terms so arbitrarily valorized that it becomes
difficult to take them seriously. But since it is commonly admitted
that value-seductions are tolerated (and even admired) in so-called
literary texts in a manner that would not pass muster in "philosophical" writings, the value of these values is itself linked to the possibility
of distinguishing philosophical from literary texts. This is also the
crudely empirical level on which one first encounters the specific
difficulty of Nietzsche's works: the patent literariness of texts that
keep making claims usually associated with philosophy rather than
with literature. Nietzsche's work raises the perennial question of the
distinction between philosophy and literature by way of a deconstruction of the value of values.

The most fundamental "value" of all, the principle of noncontradiction, ground of the identity principle, is the target of a posthumous passage dating from the fall of 1887:

> We are unable to affirm and to deny one and the same thing:
> this is a subjective empirical law, not the expression of any
> "necessity" *but only of an inability.*

1. Eugen Fink, *Nietzsches Philosophie* (Stuttgart, 1960).

If, according to Aristotle, the *law of contradiction* is the most certain of all principles, if it is the ultimate ground upon which every demonstrative proof rests, if the principle of every axiom lies in it; then one should consider all the more rigorously what presuppositions [*Voraussetzungen*] already lie at the bottom of it. Either it asserts something about actual entities, as if one already knew this from some other source; namely that opposite attributes *can*not be ascribed to them [*können*]. Or the proposition means: opposite attributes *should* not be ascribed to it [*sollen*]. In that case, logic would be an imperative, *not* to know the true [*erkennen*] but to posit [*setzen*] and arrange a world that *should be true for us.*

In short, the question remains open: are the axioms of logic adequate to reality or are they a means and measure for us to *create* the real, the concept of "reality," for ourselves? . . . To affirm the former one would, as already stated, have to have a previous knowledge of entities; which is certainly not the case. The proposition therefore contains no *criterion of truth*, but an imperative concerning that which *should* count as true.

Supposing [*gesetzt*] there were no self-identical A, such as is presupposed [*vorausgesetzt*] by every proposition of logic (and of mathematics), and the A were already mere *appearance*, then logic would have a merely *apparent* world as its precondition [*Voraussetzung*]. In fact, we believe in this proposition under the influence of ceaseless experience which seems continuously to *confirm* it. The "thing"—that is the real substratum of *A; our belief in things* is the precondition [*Voraussetzung*] of our belief in logic. The A of logic is, like the atom, a reconstruction [*Nachkonstruktion*] of the "thing" . . . Since we do not grasp this, but make of logic a criterion of true being, we are on the way to positing [*setzen*] as realities all those hypostases: substance, attribute, object, subject, action, etc.; that is, to conceiving a metaphysical world, that is a "true world" (—*this, however, is the apparent world once more* . . .).

The very first acts of thought, affirmation and denial, holding true and not holding true, are, in as much as they presuppose [*voraussetzen*] not only the habit of holding things true and holding them not true, but the *right* to do so, already dominated by the belief that *there is such a thing as knowledge for us and that judgments really can reach the truth:*—in short, logic does not doubt its ability to assert something about the true-in-itself (namely that it *can* not have opposite attributes).

Here *reigns* the coarse sensualistic preconception that sensations teach us *truths* about things—that I cannot say at the same time of one and the same thing that it is *hard* and that it is *soft*. (The instinctive proof "I cannot have two opposite sensations at the same time"—*quite coarse* and *false*.)

The conceptual ban on contradictions proceeds from the belief that we *can* form concepts, that the concept not only designates [*bezeichnen*] the essence of a thing but *comprehends* it [*fassen*]. . . . In fact, *logic* (like geometry and arithmetic) applies only to *fictitious truths* [*fingierte Wahrheiten*] *that we have created*. Logic is the attempt to *understand the actual world by means of a scheme of being posited* [*gesetzt*] *by ourselves, more correctly: to make it easier to formalize and to compute* [*berechnen*]. . . . .[2]

In this text, the polarities are no longer such spatial properties as inside and outside, or categories such as cause and effect, or experiences such a pleasure and pain all of which figure prominently in the many sections in which consciousness or selfhood are the targets of Nietzsche's critique. We are dealing with the more elusive oppositions between possibility and necessity, "können" and "sollen," and especially between knowing and positing "erkennen" and "setzen." To know [*erkennen*] is a transitive function that assumes the prior existence of an entity to be known and that predicates the ability of knowing by ways of properties. It does not itself predicate these attributes but receives them, so to speak, from the entity itself by merely allowing it to be what it is. To the extent that it is verbal it is *properly* denominative and constative. It depends on a built-in continuity within the system that unites the entity to its attributes, the

---

2. Friedrich Nietzsche, *Werke Kritische Gesamtausgabe (KGW)*, ed. Giorgio Colli and Mazzino Montinari (Berlin: de Gruyter, 1970), 8(2):53–58. In earlier editions, the passage appears as section 516 of *Der Wille zur Macht* (for instance, Musarion edition, 19:23–29). I quote in English from Friedrich Nietzsche, *The Will to Power*, translated by Walter Kaufmann and R. J. Hollingdale (New York: Random House, 1967), pp. 279–80, with some slight modifications for the sake of terminological consistency. All italics are Nietzsche's. The syntactical form of the German terms has been altered to avoid lenghty quotation. See also note 9.

grammar that links the adjective to the noun by predication. The specifically verbal intervention stems from the predication, but since the predicate is nonpositional with regard to the properties, it cannot be called a speech *act*. We could call it a speech *fact* or a fact that *can* be spoken and, consequently, known without necessarily introducing deviations. Such a fact *can*, on the one hand, be spoken [*können*] without changing the order of things but it does not, on the other hand, *have to be* spoken [*sollen*] since the order of things does not depend on its predicative power for its existence. Knowledge [*Erkenntnis*] depends on this noncoercive possibility and in fact enunciates it by ways of the principle of the self-identity of entities, "the self-identical *A*."

On the other hand, language can also predicate entities: in this Nietzsche text, this is called "setzen" (to posit), the key verb around which the logic of the passage twists its snakelike way. It designates genuine *acts* of speech, the question being whether the identity-principle is an obligatory speech act or a fact merely susceptible of being spoken. Classical epistemology, Nietzsche asserts, has maintained the latter at least since Aristotle: ". . . according to Aristotle, the law of contradiction is the most certain of all principles . . . , the ultimate ground upon which every demonstrative proof rests"; it is the ground of all knowledge and can only be so by being *a priori* given and not "put up," "gesetzt." The deconstruction sets out to show that this is not necessarily the case. The convincing power of the identity principle is due to an analogical, metaphorical substitution of the sensation of things for the knowledge of entities. A contingent property of entities (the fact that, as a "thing," they can be accessible to the senses) is, as Nietzsche's early treatise on rhetoric puts it, "torn away from its support"[3] and falsely identified with the entity as a whole. Like Rousseau, Nietzsche assimilates the delusive "abstraction" of the "coarse sensualist preconception" with the possibility of conceptualization: the contingent, metonymic link of the sensation [*Empfindung*] becomes the necessary, metaphorical link of the concept: "The conceptual ban on contradiction proceeds from the belief . . . that the concept not only designates the essence of a thing but *comprehends* it. . . ." The semiological moment [*bezeichnen*], which can simply be described as the metonymic deconstruction from necessity into contingency, is clearly apparent in this sentence. It asserts that, for Nietzsche as for Rousseau, concep-

3. Friedrich Nietzsche, *Gesammelte Werke* (München: Musarion; 1922), 5:319.

tualization is primarily a verbal process, a trope based on the substitution of a semiotic for a substantial mode of reference, of signification [*bezeichnen*] for possession [*fassen*]. This is, however, only one among a variety of deconstructive gestures and it is chosen for strategic and historical rather than for intrinsic reasons.

For the text goes well beyond the assertion that the claim to know is just an unwarranted totalization of the claim to perceive and to feel. Elsewhere, Nietzsche will devote considerable energy to questioning the epistemological authority of perception and of eudaemonic patterns of experience. But here he has other objectives. The unwarranted substitution of knowledge for mere sensation becomes paradigmatic for a wide set of aberrations all linked to the positional power of language in general, and allowing for the radical possibility that all being, as the ground for entities, may be linguistically "gesetzt," a correlative of speech acts. The text asserts this without equivocation: "To affirm [that logical axioms are adequate to reality] one would . . . have to have a previous knowledge of entities: *which is certainly not the case* [my italics]." It has, in truth, not been shown explicitly that we have no *a priori* knowledge of the being of entities. What has and will be shown, within the confines of this particular fragment, is the possibility of unwarranted substitutions leading to ontological claims based on misinterpreted systems of relationship (such as, for example, substituting identiy for signification). The possibility of arousing such a suspicion suffices to put into question a postulate of logical adequacy which might well be based on a similar aberration. And since this aberration is not necessarily intentional but grounded in the structure of rhetorical tropes, it cannot be equated with a consciousness, nor proven to be right or wrong. It cannot be refuted, but we can be made aware of the rhetorical substratum and of a subsequent possibility of error that escapes our control. We cannot say that we know "das Seiende" nor can it be said that we do not know it. What can be said is that we do not know whether or not we know it because the knowledge we once thought we possessed has been shown to be open to suspicion; our ontological confidence has forever been shaken.

Nietzsche seems to go further than this and concludes: "[The law of contradiction] *therefore* [my italics] contains no *criterion of truth*, but an *imperative* concerning that which should count as true." The conclusion seems irrevocable. As is stated at the beginning of the passage (in the form of a thesis), the inability to contradict—to state at the same time that A is and is not A—is not a necessity but an inadequacy, "ein Nicht-vermögen." Something one has failed to do can become feasible again only in the mode of compulsion; the performative correlate of "I cannot" is "I [or you] must." The language of identity and of logic asserts itself in the imperative mode and thus recognizes its own activity as the positing of entities. Logic consists of positional speech acts. As such, it acquires a temporal dimension for it posits as future what one is unable to do in the present: all "setzen" is "voraussetzen," positional language is necessarily hypothetical.[4] But this hypothetical "voraussetzen" is in error, for it presents a pre-positional statement as if it were established, present knowledge. This belief can be deconstructed by showing that the truths of a logic based on noncontradiction are "fictitious truths." But in so doing the temporal order has also been reversed: it now turns out that the future-projected, prospective assertion was in fact determined by earlier assumptions, that the future truth was in fact past error. All "voraussetzen" is "Nachkonstruktion" (as when it is said that the A of logic is "eine Nachkonstruktion des Dinges"). The deconstruction of the metaphor of knowledge into the metonymy of sensation is a surface manifestation of a more inclusive deconstruction that reveals a metaleptic reversal of the categories of anteriority and posteriority, of "before" and "after." The "truth" of identity, which was to become established in the future that follows its formulation turns out to have always already existed as the past of its aberrant "position."

Does this mean that we can now rest secure (though hardly safe) in the knowledge that the principle of contradiction is aberrant and that, consequently, all language is a speech act that has to be performed in an imperative mode? Can we consequently free ourselves once and forever from the constraints of identity by asserting and denying the same proposition at the same time? Is language an act, a "sollen" or a "tun," and now that we know that there is no longer such an illusion as that of knowledge but only feigned truths, can we replace knowledge by performance? The text seems to assert this without question: it acts by denying the oneness and the sameness of things. But in so doing it does not do what it claims to be entitled to do. The text does not simultaneously affirm and deny identity but it denies affirmation.[5] This is not the same as to assert

4. "man sollte erwägen was (der Satz vom Widerspruch) im Grunde schon an Behauptungen *voraussetzt.*" *KGW*, 8(2):53, ll. 9–10.

5. Perhaps more clearly, in German: "Der Text bejaht und verneint nicht ein und dasselbe sondern er verneint das Bejahen."

and to deny identity at the same time. The text deconstructs the authority of the principle of contradiction by showing that this principle is an act, but when it acts out this act, it fails to perform the deed to which the text owed its status as act.

The inconsistency can be retraced by observing the play of the same verb-root "setzen" in the following sentence: "Supposing [*gesetzt*] there were no self-identical *A*, such as is presupposed [*vorausgesetzt*] by every proposition of logic (and of mathematics), and the *A* were already mere *appearance*, then logic would have a merely *apparent* world as its precondition [*Voraussetzung*]." The deconstruction of logical and mathematical truth is based on the fact that it is not rooted knowledge but that it depends on a prior act of assumption [*Voraussetzen*]. This prior act is itself the target and the outcome of the deconstruction. But the conclusion that would seem to follow from this, namely that the principle of contradiction is to be discarded, is again formulated in a positional mode: "*Gesetzt*, es gäbe ein solches Sich-selbst-identisches A gar nicht. . . ." This terminology is eminently correct, for we saw that the negative proposition (there is no such thing as an A that is equal to A) has not been established as knowledge (proven) but merely as a possibility, a suspicion—and any hypothetical knowledge is positional, Yet all "setzen" has been discredited as unable to control the epistemological rigor of its own rhetoric, and this discredit now extends to the denial of the principle of identity as well. The burden of proof shifts incessantly back and forth between incompatible propositions such as A = A, A better be equal to A or else, or A cannot be equal to A, etc. This complication is characteristic for all deconstructive discourse: the deconstruction states the fallacy of reference in a necessarily referential mode. There is no escape from this, for the text also establishes that dèconstruction is not something we can decide to do or not to do at will. It is co-extensive with any use of language, and this use is compulsive or, as Nietzsche formulates it, imperative. Moreover, the reversal from denial to assertion implicit in deconstructive discourse never reaches the symmetrical counterpart of what it denies. In the sentence under discussion, for example, the assertion that language is an act (the symmetrical counterpart of the negative assertion that it is not a knowledge based on the principle of identity) cannot be taken as final: the term "gesetzt" functions as a marker which undermines the authority of such a conclusion. But it does not follow that, if it cannot be said of language that it is an act, that it has to be a knowledge. The negative thrust of the deconstruction remains unimpaired; after Nietzsche (and, indeed, after any "text"), we can no longer hope ever "to know" in peace. Neither can we expect "to do" anything, least of all to expurge "to know" and "to do", as well as their latent opposition from our vocabulary.

Lest we be inclined to read this text as an irreversible passage from a constative conception of language to a performative one, there are several other statements from the same general period in which the possibility of "doing" is as manifestly being deconstructed as the identity principle, the ground of knowledge, is being put in question here. This is not obviously the case: in many texts that are more clearly destined for publication than the posthumous fragments, the valorization consistently seems to privilege active forms of language over passive or merely reactive ones; the *Genealogy of Morals* is, of course, a clear case in point. Active and passive (or reactive) modes are coordinated with values of high and low or, more provocatively, with those of master and slave, aristocracy and populace, distinction and vulgarity. The passages from the *Genealogy* on *ressentiment* are well known: *ressentiment* is the state of mind of "such creatures that are denied the true reaction, that of deeds . . ."; "In order to exist, slave morality always first needs a hostile external world; it needs, physiologically speaking, external stimuli in order to act at all—its action is fundamentally reaction. The reverse is the case with the noble mode of valuation."[6] And a little further in the same work, in connection with a discussion of causality that anticipates many similar arguments in the posthumous fragments, the hypostasis of action as the horizon of all being seems to be unquestionably affirmed: "there is no 'being' behind doing, effecting, becoming; the 'doer' is merely a fiction added to the deed—the deed is everything" ["es gibt kein "Sein" hinter dem Tun, Wirken, Werden; "der Täter" ist zum Tun bloss hinzugedichtet—das Tun ist alles"[7] The use of the term "hinzugedichtet" (added by poetic invention), as well as the context, indicate that action here is conceived in close connection with linguistic acts of writing, reading and interpretation, and not within a polarity that opposes language, as speech or as writing, to action.

6. Musarion, 15:295, quoted in English from Friedrich Nietzsche, *On the Genealogy of Morals*, ed. and trans. Walter Kaufmann (New York; Random House, 1967), first essay, section 10, pp. 36–37.

7. Kaufmann, trans., *On the Genealogy of Morals*, first essay, section 13, p. 45; Musarion, 15:305.

Of course, one cannot expect the same strategy with regard to valorization in a book like the *Genealogy* explicitly designated as a pamphlet and destined to condemn and to convince, as in the more speculative treatises that Nietzsche's later book (or books) were, among other things, destined to be. On a specific question (such as the ontological authority of acts) the speculative statements should be given at least equal consideration next to the emphatic, persuasive ones. One therefore has to confront a slogan such as "Tun ist alles" with a passage like the following: "The 'Spirit', *something that thinks* . . . here we *first* imagine an act that does not exist, 'thinking', and *second* we imagine as substratum of this act a subject in which every act of thought and nothing else originates: this means that *the deed as well as the doer are fictions* [*sowohl das Tun, als der Täter sind fingiert*]."[8] The parallel that concerns us is the symmetry between this fictitious doing [*fingiertes Tun*] and the fictitious truths [*fingierte Wahrheiten*] that appear in the previously discussed passage on the principle of identity: "Logic (like geometry and arithmetic) applies only to fictitious truths"[9]: here, in section 516, truth is opposed to action as fiction is opposed to reality. In the later passage (section 477), this conception of action as a "reality" opposed to the illusion of knowledge is, in its turn, undermined. Performative language is not less ambivalent in its referential function than the language of constatation.

It could be objected that, in the passage now under discussion (section 477), it is not the reality of action in general that is being put in question but specifically the act of thinking and, furthermore, that the linkage between the act and the performing subject (the principle of intentionality) is being deconstructed rather than action as such. But Nietzsche is not concerned with the distinction between speech (or thought) acts and, on the other hand, acts that would not be verbal. He is interested in the distinction between speech *acts* and other verbal functions that would not be performative (such as knowing). Non-verbal acts, if such a thing were to be conceivable, are of no concern

8. *KGW*, 8(2):296, ll. 9–17. Previously published as section 477 of *Der Wille zur Macht* (Musarion, 19:8); Kaufmann and Hollingdale, trans., *The Will to Power*, p. 263.

9. The earlier Nietzsche editions (including the Schlecta edition in 3 volumes) all print "fingierte Wesenheiten" (fictitious *entities*) but the Colli and Montinari critical edition gives "fingierte Wahrheiten" (fictitious *truths*). The authoritative version is more germane to our argument.

to him, since no act can ever be separated from the attempt at understanding, from the interpretation, that necessarily accompanies and falsifies it. The fictional truths, which are shown to be acts, are always oriented towards an attempt "to *understand* the actual world . . . to make it easier to formalize and to compute [*berechenbar machen*] . . ." and, in the later passage, thought is also described as "an artificial adjustment for the purpose of *understanding* [*eine künstliche Zurechtmachung zum Zweck der Verständlichung*]" (1296, ll. 8–9, my italics). Even in the *Genealogy* the pure act that is said to be all there is, is conceived as verbal: its paradigm is denomination and the deconstruction of its genesis is best carried out by means of etymology.

As for the intentional link between act and subject, it has been the target of a considerable number of late texts, not to mention several earlier versions that go back at least as far as the *Birth of Tragedy*. In the posthumous texts, it is often carried out as a rhetorical deconstruction of the metalepsis of cause and effect; the well-known passage on the phenomenalism of consciousness is a good case in point.[10] This moment in the deconstructive process is undoubtedly still present in the fragment with which we are concerned: it is, after all, entitled "On psychology and epistemology"[11] and in it Nietzsche denounces the acceptance of an "unmediated and causal link between ideas" as "the crudest and clumsiest observation."[12] There is nothing new about such utterances; what gives the passage a special significance is that the fiction of a "subject-substratum" for the act is explicitly called secondary as compared to the prior fiction of the act itself ("*first* we imagine an act that does not exist . . . and *second* we imagine a subject-substratum for this act . . .). The aberrant authority of the subject is taken for granted; the new attack is upon the more fundamental notion of "act." Hence also the apparent contradiction between this text and the one on the phenomenalism of consciousness alluded to earlier (Section 479). Whereas the notions of an "inner" space or time seem to be more or less definitively reduced to the status of a deception in the latter fragment, section

10. Section 479 of *Der Wille zur Macht* (Musarion, 19:10); Kaufmann and Hollingdale, trans., *The Will to Power*, 265–66.

11. The heading appears only in the new Colli and Montinari critical edition, 8(2):295.

12. *KGW*, 8(2):295, ll. 26–30; Kaufmann and Hollingdale, trans., *The Will to Power*, p. 264.

477 begins by asserting: "I maintain the phenomenalism of the *inner* world, too . . ."; but the immediate continuation of the sentence (". . . everything of which we become conscious is arranged, simplified, schematized, interpreted through and through . . . and is perhaps purely imaginary")[13] makes clear that phenomenality is now no longer used as an authoritative term that has to be deconstructed, but as the name of a metaphysical concept considered to be aberrant. Section 477 takes for granted the deconstruction of the phenomenalism of consciousness and of the subject carried out in section 479 and it moves on to the more advanced target of "denken" as act. If Nietzsche's notes were to be reordered as a logical progression (in itself a nightmarish and absurd assignment), fragment 477 in the old classification would have to come after fragment 479.

The deconstruction of thought as act also has a different rhetorical structure from that of consciousness: it is not based on metalepsis but on synecdoche: " 'Thinking,' as epistemologists conceive of it [*ansetzen*], simply does not occur: it is a quite arbitrary fiction, arrived at by singling out one element from the process and eliminating all the rest, an artificial arrangement for the purpose of intelligibility."[14] Whereas the subject results from an unwarranted reversal of cause and effect, the illusion of thought as action is the result of an equally illegitimate totalization from part to whole.

The rhetorical structure of the figures concern us less here than the outcome of their analysis: the text on the principle of identity established the universality of the linguistic model as speech act, albeit by voiding it of epistemological authority and by demonstrating its inability to perform this very act. But the later text, in its turn, voids even this dubious assurance, for it puts in question not only that language can act rightly, but that it can be said to act at all. The first passage (section 516) on identity showed that constative language is in fact performative, but the second passage (section 477) asserts that the possibility for language to perform is just as fictional as the possibility for language to assert. Since the analysis has been carried out on passages representative of Nietzsche's deconstructive procedure at its most advanced stage, it would follow that, in

13. *KGW*, 8(2):295, ll. 15–22, Kaufmann and Hollingdale, trans., *The Will to Power*, pp. 263–64.

14. *KGW*, 8(2):296, ll. 4–8; Kaufmann and Hollingdale, trans., *The Will to Power*, p. 264.

Nietzsche, the critique of metaphysics can be described as the deconstruction of the illusion that the language of truth (*episteme*) could be replaced by a language of persuasion (*doxa*). What seems to lead to an established priority of "setzen" over "erkennen," of language as action over language as truth, never quite reaches its mark. It under- or overshoots it and, in so doing, it reveals that the target which one long since assumed to have been eliminated has merely been displaced. The *episteme* has hardly been restored intact to its former glory, but it has not been definitively eliminated either. The differentiation between performative and constative language (which Nietzsche anticipates) is undecidable; the deconstruction leading from the one model to the other is irreversible but it always remains suspended, regardless of how often it is repeated.

This conclusion takes us back to the Course on Rhetoric, which precedes the posthumous fragments by fifteen years. The course starts out from a pragmatic distinction between rhetoric as a system of tropes and rhetoric as having to do with the skills of persuasion. [*Beredsamkeit*]. Nietzsche contemptuously dismisses the popular meaning of rhetoric as eloquence and concentrates instead on the complex and philosophically challenging epistemology of the tropes. The distinction is not actually accounted for but taken over empirically from the history of rhetoric. Privileging figure over persuasion is a typically post-Romantic gesture and Nietzsche's dependance on his predecessors in the German Romantic tradition, from Friedrich Schlegel on down, has been well documented.[15] The question, however, is eternally recurrent and coincides with the term "rhetoric" itself. Within the pedagogical model of the trivium, the place of rhetoric, as well as its dignity, has always been ambivalent: on the one hand, in Plato for example and again at crucial moments in the history of philosophy (Nietzsche being one of them), rhetoric becomes the ground for the furthest-reaching dialectical speculations conceivable to the mind; on the other hand, as it appears in textbooks that have undergone little change from Quintillian to the present, it is the humble and not-quite-respectable handmaiden of the fraudulent grammar used in oratory; Nietzsche himself begins his course by pointing out this discrepancy and documenting it with examples taken from Plato and elsewhere.[16] Between the two

15. See, for instance, Philippe Lacoue-Labarthe, "Le Détour," in *Poétique* 5 (1971): 53–76.

16. Musarion, 5:298.

functions, the distance is so wide as to be nearly unbridgeable. Yet the two modes manage to exist side by side where one would least expect it. Nietzsche's philosophical contempt for oratory finds impressive confirmation in the rigor of his epistemology, yet, as any reader of *The Birth of Tragedy*, *The Genealogy of Morals*, or of that irrepressible orator Zarathustra knows, there hardly is a trick of the oratorical trade which he is not willing to exploit to the full. In a sense, Nietzsche has earned a right to this inconsistency by the considerable labor of deconstruction that makes up the bulk of his more analytical writings. For this deconstruction seems to end in a reassertion of the active performative function of language and it rehabilitates persuasion as the final outcome of the deconstruction of figural speech. This would allow for the reassuring conviction that it is legitimate to do just about anything with words, as long as we know that a rigorous mind, fully aware of the misleading power of tropes, pulls the strings. But if it turns out that this same mind does not even know whether it is doing or not doing something, then there are considerable grounds for suspicion that it does not know *what* it is doing. Nietzsche's final insight may well concern rhetoric itself, the discovery that what is called "rhetoric" is precisely the gap that becomes apparent in the pedagogical and philosophical history of the term. Considered as persuasion, rhetoric is performative but when considered as a system of tropes, it deconstructs its own performance. Rhetoric is a *text* in that it allows for two incompatible, mutually self-destructive points of view, and therefore puts an insurmountable obstacle in the way of any reading or understanding. The aporia between performative and constative language is merely a version of the aporia between trope and persuasion that both generates and paralyzes rhetoric and thus gives it the appearance of a history.

If the critique of metaphysics is structured as an aporia between performative and constative language, this is the same as saying that it is structured as rhetoric. And since, if one wants to conserve the term "literature," one should not hesitate to assimilate it with rhetoric, then it would follow that the deconstruction of metaphysics, or "philosophy," is an impossibility to the precise extent that it is "literary." This by no means resolves the problem of the relationship between literature and philosophy in Nietzsche, but it at least establishes a somewhat more reliable point of "reference" from which to ask the question.

Part II

Rousseau

7 Metaphor

(Second Discourse)

THE PLACE OF THE *Discourse on the Origins and the Foundations of Inequality among Men* (1754) in the canon of Rousseau's works remains uncertain. The apparent duality of Rousseau's complete writings, a whole that consists in part of political theory, in part of literature (fiction and autobiography), has inevitably led to a division of labor among the interpreters, thus bringing to light latent incompatibilities between political scientists, cultural historians, and literary critics. This specialization has often prevented the correct understanding of the relations between the literary and the political aspects of Rousseau's thought. As the overtly political piece of writing that it undoubtedly is, the *Second Discourse* has primarily interested historians and social scientists.[1] It does not confront them with the same difficulties as *Julie,* a book in which it is not easy to overlook the literary dimensions entirely and where it takes some degree of bad faith to reduce the text to "an intellectual experiment in the techniques and consequences of human engineering."[2] Despite the presence of at least one explicit passage on language in the *Discourse* the linguistic mediations can easily be ignored. The section on the origin of language[3] is clearly a polemical digression without organic links to the main argument, and the *Discourse* can be considered as a literal model for a theory of history and of society, that is, a model that

1. The bibliography of studies wholly or in part devoted to the *Second Discourse* is immense and one would welcome an updated *état de recherches* on the text. In his notes to the edition of the *Second Discourse* in the Pléiade Edition (Paris): Gillimard, 1964) Jean Starobinski gives several useful indications (see notes, pp. 1297, 1299, 1305, 1315, 1317, 1319, 1334, 1339, 1359, 1370, 1372, 1377). Since then (1964) there have been numerous additions.

2. Lester Crocker, *J. J. Rousseau* (New York 1968), p. 20

3. *Discourse,* pp. 146–51. All page references are to the French edition of the *Discourse: Discours sur l'origine et les fondements de l'inégalité,* texte établi et annoté par Jean Starobinski, in J. J. Rousseau, *Oeuvres complètes,* ed. Bernard Gagnebin and Marcel Raymond (Paris: Gillimard [Bibliothèque de la Pléiade], 1964), vol. 3.

could be transposed *tel quel* from the text to the political or social situation that it represents or prefigures. Once this is assumed, the *Second Discourse* becomes highly vulnerable to a list of recurrent objections that reappear with remarkable persistence in all Rousseau studies and that any reader of the text will feel compelled to make himself.

It is by no means my intention to suggest that these objections are unfounded or that they are inspired by a deliberate malice that should be met with defensive counter-malice. The Rousseau interpreter should avoid the danger of repeating the paranoid gesture of his subject. The first task is to diagnose what, if anything, is being systematically overlooked by other readers, prior to asking why this particular area of Rousseau's thought possesses the curious privilege of rendering itself invisible, as if it were wearing the ring of Gyges referred to in the sixth *Promenade*. The literal reading that fails to take into account the figural dimensions of the language (despite the fact that this particular text explicitly draws attention to these dimensions) is not to be rejected as simply erroneous or malevolent, all the more since, in the *Second Discourse*, the political terminology and the political themes postulate the existence of an extra-textual referent and raise the question of the text's relationship to this referent. Nor can we assume that this relationship is one of literal correspondence.

Consider, for instance, the status of what seems to be the inescapable *a priori* of the text itself, what Rousseau calls the "state of nature." Very few informed readers today would still maintain that Rousseau's state of nature is an empirical reality, present, past, or future.[4] Most commentators would agree that, at least up to a point, the state of nature is a state "that no longer exists, that has perhaps never existed and that probably will never come into being . . ." (3:123). It is a fiction; but in stating this, the problem has merely been displaced, for what then is the significance of this fiction with regard to the empirical world? Granted that the authority of the state of nature, the hold it has over our present thought, is no longer that of something that existed elsewhere or at other times and towards

4. For a recent statement to this effect, among many others, see Henri Gouhier, *Les méditations métaphysiques de J. J. Rousseau* (Paris, 1970), p. 23. For a clear formulation of the fictional character of the state of nature, see Herbert Dieckmann's edition of Diderot, *Supplément au voyage de Bougainville* (Geneva, 1965), pp. lxxiii-xciv.

which our relation can therefore be described in terms of nostalgia and quest; granted that the mode of being of the state of nature and the mode of being of the present, alienated state of man are perhaps radically incompatible, with no road connecting the one to the other—the question remains why this radical fiction ("We must begin by discarding all facts . . ." [3:132]) continues to be indispensable for any understanding of the present, as if its shadow controlled once and forever the degree of light allotted to us. It is a state that we must "know well" and of which "it is necessary to have a correct understanding [*des notions justes*] in order to evaluate our present condition" (3:123). What kind of epistemology can hope to "know well" a radical state of fiction? The *Second Discourse* hardly seems to provide a reliable answer. As a genetic narrative in which the state of nature functions at the very least as a point of departure or as a point of reference[5] (if no longer necessarily as a point of arrival), the *Second Discourse* seems to contradict the radical rejection of reality on which it bases its claim to free itself from the constraints of facts. Rousseau seems to want to have it both ways, giving himself the freedom of the fabulator but, at the same time, the authority of the responsible historian. A degree of impatience on the part of the historians is certainly justified towards a man who, by his own admission, escapes in speculative fantasies but who, on the other hand, claims that in so doing "one sweeps away the dust and the sands that cover the edifice [of human institutions], one reveals the solid foundations on which it is built and learns to consider them with respect" (3:127). How can a pure fiction and a narrative involving such concrete political realities as property, contractual law, and modes of government coalesce into a genetic history that pretends to lay bare the foundations of human society?

It seems difficult to avoid a prognosis of inconsistency, leading to the separation between the theoretical, literary and the practical, political aspects of Rousseau's thought. The literary faculty which, in the *Second Discourse*, invents the fiction of a natural state of man becomes an ideology growing out of the repression of the political faculty. A clear and concise statement of this recurrent critical interpretation of Rousseau—which goes back at least as far as Schiller—can be found in a recent study of the *Social Contract* by the

5. On this point, see Starobinski's preface, *Discourse*, 3:lvii. He refers primarily to an article by Eric Weil, "J. J. Rousseau et sa politique," *Critique* 56 (January 1952): 3–28.

French social philosopher Louis Althusser. He analyzes recurrent shifts [*décalages*] in the key terms of Rousseau's vocabulary and concludes that these shifts, or displacements, are

> to be explicitly understood, once and forever, as the very displacement that separates the consequences of theory from reality, a displacement between two equally impossible *praxes* [*décalage entre deux pratiques également impossibles*]. Since we now have [in the text of the *Social Contract*] reached the stage of reality and since we can only keep going around in a circle (ideology—economy—ideology, etc.) no flight remains possible into the actual, real world [*dans la réalité même*]. End of the displacement.
>
> If no other displacement is available to us . . . only one single, different road remains open: a *transference* [*transfert*] of the impossible theoretical solution into the other of theory [*l'autre de la théorie*], namely literature. The fictional triumph of an admirable, unprecedented literary work.[6]

If the political side of Rousseau's work is indeed a reductive ideology that results from a repression carried out by means of literary language, then the theoretical interest of a text like the *Second Discourse* is primarily psychological. Conversely, the political writings can then themselves become a reliable way of access to the problematics of the self in Rousseau. And here the *Second Discourse* would be particularly useful, not only because, unlike the *Social Contract*, it explicitly involves the moment of transference into literary fiction, but precisely because, unlike the autobiographical writings, it hides its self-obsessions behind a language of conceptual generality. Rousseau's ambivalence with regard to such key notions as property, civil authority, and even technology[7] could then serve as

6. Louis Althusser, "Sur le Contrat Social (Les décalages)" in *Cahiers pour l'Analyse*, 8, *L'impensé de J. J. Rousseau* (Paris, 1970), pp. 5–42.

7. The ambivalence of Rousseau's attitude towards property is one example: on the one hand, he makes it sound as if property were theft; on the other hand, law is at times glorified, in almost extravagant terms, as the defense of property (see, for example, *Discours sur l'économie politique*, in *Oeuvres complètes*, 3:248–49). One is tempted to interpret the inconsistency psychologically by referring to Rousseau's lowly birth as a social misfit who both glorifies property as something he desires but cannot possess, and poverty as a self-redeeming moral virtue. On civil authority, see

a model for an understanding of his psychological self-mysti-fications. In strictly textual terms, the problem comes down to the inconsistency between the first and the second part of the text. Between the pure fiction of the first part, dealing with theoretical problems of man, nature, and methodology, and the predominantly historical and institutional language, used in the second part, there would exist a gap, an unbridgeable "*décalage*," that Rousseau, caught in a false claim of authentic self-knowledge, would be least of all able to perceive. The reading that follows puts this scheme into question.

In the *Second Discourse*, the state of nature, though fictional, is not static. Possibilities of change are built into its description as a syn-chronic *state* of being. The potentially dynamic properties of natural man are pity, "a principle anterior to reason [that] inspires a natural reluctance to see any sensitive being, and especially our fellow-man, suffer or perish" (3:126), and freedom: "Nature alone does every-thing in the actions of animals whereas man partakes in his own actions in his quality as free agent" (3:141). The concept of pity has been definitively treated by Jacques Derrida.[8] We can therefore begin with the concept of freedom.

The ambivalent nature of the concept of freedom in Rousseau has been noticed by several interpreters. To be free, for Rousseau, is by no means a tranquil and harmonious repose within the ordained boundaries of the human specificity, the reward for a Kantian, ra-tional sense of limitations. From the start, freedom appears as an act of the will ("the will still speaks when Nature is silent" [3:141]) pitted against the ever-present obstacle of a limitation which it tries to transgress.[9] It is a consequence, or another version, of the statement at the beginning of the *Second Discourse*, that the specificity of man

---

the discrepancy between, on the one hand, the glorification of the magistrates of Geneva and of his own father in the *Dédicace* of the *Second Discourse* (3:117–18), and the caricature of the harassed magistrate in the text of the *Discourse* proper (3:192-93).

8. Jacques Derrida, *De la Grammatologie* (Paris, 1967), pp. 259–72.

9. As summarized in the admirable title of Starobinski's *Jean-Jacques Rous-seau: La transparence et l'obstacle* (Paris, 1957). Rousseau's statement to the Polish nation is well known: "Le repos et la liberté sont incompatibles: il faut opter" (*Considérations sur le Gouvernement de Pologne, Oeuvres complètes*, 3:955). This aspect of Rousseau's thought is now generally recognized in contemporary studies.

forever escapes our grasp since "the more we study man . . . the less
we are in a position to know him" (3:123). Any confinement within
the boundaries of an anthropological self-definition is therefore felt
to be a restriction beyond which man, as a being devoid of natural
specificity, will have to transgress. This will to transgress, in a pre-
Nietzschean passage, is held by Rousseau to be the very definition of
the Spirit: "the power to will or, rather, the power to choose, as well
as the feeling of this power is a purely spiritual act" (3:142). Very
little distinguishes power to will, or willpower (*puissance de vouloir*)
from "will to power," since the power to choose is precisely the
power to transgress whatever in nature would entail the end of
human power.

The direct correlative of freedom thus conceived is mentioned in
the paragraph that follows immediately upon the definition, although the transitory link is not explicitly stated: freedom is man's
will to change or what Rousseau somewhat misleadingly calls "perfectibility."[10] The potential transgression that occurs whenever the
concepts of nature and of man are associated—in the *Essay on the
Origin of Language* all examples destined to illustrate the "natural"
language of man are acts of violence[11]—transforms all human attributes from definite, self-enclosed, and self-totalizing actions into
open structures: perception becomes imagination, natural needs [*besoins*] become unfulfillable passions, sensations become an endless
quest for knowledge all of which deprive man forever of a central
identity ("the more one meditates . . . the greater the distance becomes between our pure sensations and the simplest forms of
knowledge" [3:144]). In the same consistent pattern, the discovery of
temporality coincides with the acts of transgressive freedom: time
relates to space in the same way that imagination relates to perception, need to passion, etc. The very conception of a future is linked

10. Misleadingly, since "perfectibility" is just as regressive as it is progressive.
Starobinski, in a lengthy footnote (3:1317) asserts that perfectibility is a "néologisme
savant"; the concept if not the word appears in Fontenelle's *Digression sur les anciens
et les modernes* which dates from 1688. Fontenelle speaks of "le progrès des choses."

11. See *Essai sur l'origine des Langues*, texte reproduit d'après l'édition A. Belin
de 1817 (Paris, le Graphe, supplément au No. 8 des *Cahiers pour l'Analyse*), henceforth referred to as *Essay*, p. 502. Rousseau mentions the threatening gifts sent by the
king of the Scythians to King Darius and especially the Old Testament story (Judges)
of the Levite from Ephraim who sent the body of his murdered wife, cut in twelve
pieces, to the Tribes of Israel to spur them on to revenge. The same theme is taken up
in the later story *Le lévite d'Ephraim* (1762).

with the possibility of a free imagination; the soul of the still enslaved primitive man is "without any awareness of the future, however close it may be. His projects are as narrow as are his views: they hardly extend until the end of the day" (3:144). Consciousness of mortality is similarly linked to the freedom that distinguishes man from the animal: "the knowledge and the fear of death is one of the first things acquired by man as he moves away from the animal condition" (3:143).

This existential notion of freedom is impressive enough in itself. It does not suffice, however, to make the connection with the political parts of the *Second Discourse*. It accounts for the ambivalent valorization of all historical change, since any change will always have to put into question the value-system that made it possible: any positive valorization as progress always also implies a regress, and Rousseau's text scrupulously maintains this balance.[12] The impossibility of reaching a rationally enlightened anthropology also accounts for the necessary leap into fiction, since no past or present human action can coincide with or be under way towards the nature of man. The question remains why the *Second Discourse*, in its second part, somehow manages to return to the concrete realities of political life in a vocabulary that reintroduces normative evaluations—why, in other words, the methodological paradox of the beginning (that the very attempt to know man makes this knowledge impossible) does not prevent the text from finally getting started, after many hesitations: a preface preceding a first part which is itself a methodological introduction and which, in its turn, is again introduced by another preface. What characteristic structures of freedom and perfectibility, in Part I, lead us to understand the political structures of Part II? And where are we to find a structural description of perfectibility in what seems to be a self-enclosed genetic text in which perfectibility simply functions as the organizing theme?

The section on language (3:146–51) appears as a digression destined to illustrate the impossibility of passing from nature to culture by natural means. It runs parallel to a similar development that deals with the growth of technology. As such, it serves indeed a secondary function that belongs with the polemical and not with the systematic aspects of the *Second Discourse*. Starobinski rightly em-

12. See *Discourse*, pp. 142, 162, 187, 193, especially note ix, pp. 207–08, and *passim*.

phasizes that the passage is written "less in order to formulate a coherent theory on the origin of language than to demonstrate the difficulties the question raises" (3:1322, notes). In fact, the entire passage has the tone of a mock-argument directed against those who explain the origin of language by means of causal categories that are themselves dependent on the genetic power of the origin for which they are supposed to account.[13] The constant warning against the mystification of adopting a privileged viewpoint that is unable to understand its own genealogy, a methodological theme that runs throughout the *Second Discourse*, also applies to the theory of language. But not selectively so. The science of language is one of the areas in which this type of fetishism (reducing history to nature) occurs, but it is not the only one. The same error prevails with regard to ethical judgment (Hobbes) or with regard to technology. From this point of view, the section on language seems to have a primarily critical function and it could not serve to illuminate the central problem of the text—that of the epistemological authority of the normative second part.

The passage, however, contains its own theory on the structure of language, albeit in a highly fragmentary and oblique form. More important still, Rousseau explicitly links language to the notion of perfectibility, itself derived from the primal categories of freedom and will. "Moreover," he writes, "general ideas can only enter the mind by means of words and our understanding can seize upon them only by means of propositions. This is one of the reasons why animals could never acquire such ideas, nor the perfectibility that depends on it" ("C'est une des raisons pourquoi les animaux ne sauraient se former de telles idées, ni jamais acquérir la perfectibilité qui en dépend" [3:149]). Perfectibility evolves as language evolves, moving from particular denomination to general ideas: an explicit link is established between two distinct conceptual areas in the text, the first pertaining to perfectibility, freedom, and a series of general concepts that are connected narratively and thematically but never described in terms of their internal structures, the second pertaining

13. ". . . dire que la Mère dicte à l'Enfant les mots . . . cela montre bien comment on enseigne des Langues déjà formées, mais cela n'apprend point comment elles se forment" (p. 147); "si les hommes ont besoin de la parole pour apprendre à penser, ils ont eu bien plus besoin encore de savoir penser pour trouver l'art de la parole" (p. 142). The conclusions are reached by substituting effect for cause (metalepsis).

to the structural and epistemological properties of language. Besides, freedom and perfectibility are relay-stations on the itinerary by way of which the *Second Discourse* can move from the methodological language of the first to the political language of the second part. The sentence can therefore be interpreted to mean that the system of concepts at work in the political parts of the *Second Discourse* are structured like the linguistic model described in the digression on language. This makes the passage a key to an understanding of the entire text. For nowhere else do we find as detailed a structural analysis of the concepts involved in the subsequent narrative.

Yet the passage is avoided rather than stressed in most readings of the *Second Discourse*. In his notes to the Pléiade Edition, Jean Starobinski seems to be clearly aware of some of its implications, but he at once limits its impact by means of an argument that goes to the center of the problem involved in the interpretation of this text. Commenting on Rousseau's sentence—"C'est une des raisons pourquoi les animaux ne sauraient se former des idées générales, ni jamais acquérir la perfectibilité qui en dépend"—he writes: "The relative clause [*qui en dépend*] has here a determinative and not an explicative function. Rousseau refers here to one particular kind of perfectibility that depends on language. As for Perfectibility in general, which Rousseau has told us to be an essential and primitive property of man, it is not the result of language but much rather its cause" (3:1327, notes). Since the French language does not distinguish between "which" and "that," it is impossible to decide by grammatical means alone whether the sentence should read: "animals could never acquire perfectibility, since perfectibility depends on language" or, as Starobinski would have it, "animals could never acquire the kind of perfectibility that depends on language." The correct understanding of the passage depends on whether one accepts the contention that the principle of genetic causality introduced by Starobinski, in which chronological, logical, and ontological priority coincide,[14] is indeed the system at work in Rousseau's text. Can it be said of perfectibility that it is an "essential and primitive property of man," Starobinski's phrasing rather than Rousseau's, who said only that it was "une qualité très spécifique qui distingue [l'homme]"

14. See *Oeuvres complètes*, 3:1285, notes. Starobinski writes: "Rousseau has rigorously followed [Aristotle's] method, by giving to the word origin [*arche*] a meaning in which the logical antecedent necessarily entails a *historical* antecedent."

(3:142)? Each of the terms is problematic and their combination, as if they could be freely interchanged, is the most problematic of all. Starobinski's phrasing not only assumes that the (temporally) primitive must also be the (ontological) essence, but that a property of what is presumably a substance (man) can be an essence. Since moreover the substance "man" is in this text a highly volatile concept that behaves logically much more like a property than like a substance, the essence perfectibility would then be the property of a property. Rousseau's main methodological point, his constant warning against the danger of substituting cause for effect[15] reveals at least a certain distrust of genetic continuities, for the substitution becomes aberrant only if such a continuity is in doubt. This should make us wary of accepting uncritically the common sense and admirable prudence displayed in Starobinski's reading.

Even if read to mean that perfectibility, in the general sense in which it is used when we first encounter it in the *Second Discourse* (3:142), is linked to language, the statement does not at first sight seem to be so far-reaching as to justify its repression. Why then is it being overlooked or avoided? How curious that, when a text offers us an opportunity to link a nonlinguistic historical concept such as perfectibility to language, we should refuse to follow the hint. Especially curious in the case of a text whose intelligibility hinges on the existence or nonexistence of such a link between a "literary," language-oriented method of investigation and the practical results to which the method is assumed to lead. Yet a critic of Starobinski's intelligence and subtlety goes out of his way in order to avoid the signs that Rousseau has put up and prefers the bland to the suggestive reading, although it requires an interpretative effort to do so. For there is no trace to be found in Rousseau's work of a particular, linguistic perfectibility that would be distinct from historical perfectibility in general. In the *Essay on the Origin of Language*, the perfectibility of language, which is in fact a degradation, evolves exactly as the perfectibility of society evolves in the *Second Discourse*. There must be an unsuspected threat hidden in a sentence that one is so anxious to de-fuse.

Animals have no history because they are unable to perform the specifically linguistic act of conceptualization. But how does conceptualization work, according to Rousseau? The text yields information

15. See preceding notes 13 and 14.

on this point, though not in a simple and straightforward way. It describes conceptualization as substituting one verbal utterance (at the simplest level, a common noun) for another on the basis of a resemblance that hides differences which permitted the existence of entities in the first place. The natural world is a world of pure contiguity: "all individual entities appear in isolation to the mind [of primitive man],[16] as they are in the picture of nature. If one oak tree was called *A*, another was called *B* . . ." (3:149). Within this contiguity certain resemblances appear. By substituting for *A* and *B* the word "tree" on the basis of certain properties that *A* and *B* have in common, we invent an abstraction under which the irreducible differences that separate *A* from *B* are subsumed. The perception of these resemblances is not, in itself, a conceptualization: in the case of animals, it leads to acts that satisfy needs but that remain confined to the limits of the particular action. "When a monkey goes without hesitation from one nut to another, do we think that he has in mind a general idea of this type of fruit and that he compares his archetype to these two individual entities? Certainly not . . ." (3:149). Conceptualization does not proceed on the basis of mere perception: perception and imagination (in the guise of memory)[17] intervene in recognizing the existence of certain similarities—an act of which animals are said to be as capable as men—but the actual process of conceptualization is verbal: "It is necessary to state propositions and to speak in order to have general ideas; for as soon as the imagination stops, the mind can only proceed by means of discourse" (3:150).

The description seems to remain within a binary system in which animal and man, nature and culture, acts (or things) and words, particularity (or difference) and generality, concreteness and abstraction stand in polar opposition to each other. Antitheses of this kind allow for dialectical valorizations and although this passage of the *Second Discourse* (3:149–50) is relatively free of value judgments (nothing is said about an innate superiority of nature over artifice or of practical behavior over speculative abstraction), it nevertheless invites value judgments on the part of the interpreter. The most incisive evaluations of this and of similar passages are those which

16. Rousseau says "des premiers Instituteurs," which may sound cryptic in translation. The meaning refers to "primitive" men as the "first" inventors who instituted language.

17. ". . . la vue d'une de ces noix rappelle à [l] a mémoire [du singe] les sensations qu'il a reçues de l'autre . . ." (3:150).

locate the tension within language itself by stressing that the implied
polarity exists within the structure of the linguistic sign, in the distinction established by Rousseau between the denominative and the
conceptual function of language. The text indeed distinguishes the
act of naming (tree *A* and tree *B*) which leads to the literal denomination of the proper noun, from the act of conceptualization. And
conceptualization, conceived as an exchange or substitution of properties on the basis of resemblance, corresponds exactly to the classical definition of metaphor as it appears in theories of rhetoric from
Aristotle to Roman Jakobson.[18] The text would then, in a sense,
distinguish between, on the one hand, figurative, connotative, and
metaphorical language and, on the other, denominative, referential,
and literal language, and it would oppose the two modes anti-
thetically to each other. This allows for a valorization that privileges
one mode over the other. Since Rousseau asserts the temporal priority
of the proper noun over the concept ("Each object received *first* a
particular name . . ." [3:149]; "the *first* nouns could only have been
proper nouns" [3:150], it would indeed follow, within the genetic
logic of the narrative, that he separates the literal from the metaphorical forms of language and privileges the former over the
latter. This interpretation, nearly unanimously accepted in Rousseau
studies, is well summarized, with a helpful reference to Michel
Foucault, by a recent commentator:[19] "The entire history of Rousseau's work, the passage from 'theory' to 'literature,' is the transference of the need to name the world to the prior need of naming
oneself. To name the world is to make the representation of the
world coincide with the world itself; to name myself is to make the
representation that I have of the world coincide with the representation that I convey to others."[20] Rousseau's increasingly subjective and

18. The definition from the *Poetics* (1457 b) is well known: "Metaphor is the
transfer [*epiphora*] to a thing of a name that designates another thing, a transfer
from the genus to the species or from the species to the genus or according to the
principle of analogy." Jakobson defines metaphor as substitution on the basis of
resemblance.

19. Alain Grosrichard, "Gravité de Rousseau" in *Cahiers pour l'analyse*, 8.

20. Grosrichard, "Gravité de Rousseau," p. 64. I give a free translation that
attempts to explain the more elegant but more elliptical French version: "Toute
l'histoire de l'oeuvre de Rousseau, le passage de la 'théorie' à la 'littérature,' c'est le
passage d'une exigence qui est de faire se recouvrir la représentation du monde et le
monde même, bref de le *nommer*, à l'exigence préalable de faire coincider la représentation que j'en donne à la représentation que j'en ai, bref de *me nommer*."

autobiographical discourse would then merely be the extension, within the realm of the self, of the referential linguistic model that governs his thought. The failure of this attempt to "name" the subject, the discovery that, in Grosrichard's words, "le sujet est l'innomable"[21] undercuts the authority of Rousseau's own language. It also relegates him, with Condillac and, generally speaking, with all followers of Locke, to what Foucalt subversively calls "le discours classique." As far as the *Second Discourse* is concerned, such an interpretation would have to conclude that the text is truly incoherent, since it does not control the opposition between the conceptual metaphor "state of nature" and the literal reality of civil society, an opposition asserted in the *Discourse* itself. Moreover, by starting out from the metaphor, the text reverses the priority of denomination over connotation that it advocates. In texts explicitly centered on the self, such as the *Confessions* or the *Dialogues*, this incoherence would at least be brought into the open, whereas it is merely repressed in the pseudo-conceptual language of the *Second Discourse*.

Before yielding to this very persuasive scheme, we must return to the particular passage in the *Discourse* and to the corresponding section in the *Essay on the Origin of Language*.[22] Does Rousseau indeed separate figural from literal language and does he privilege one type of discourse over the other? There is no simple answer to this question, for whereas, in the *Discourse*, it is said that "the first nouns could only have been proper nouns," the *Essay* states with

21. Ibid., p. 64.
22. On the complex debate involving the chronological and thematic relationship between the *Discourse* and the *Essay*, see J. Derrida, *De la Grammatologie*, pp. 272–78. One can consider the *Essay* as an expanded footnote to the *Discourse*. As far as this particular point is concerned (animals lacking perfectibility because they lack conceptual language), the phrasing in the *Essay* runs entirely parallel to the phrasing in the *Discourse*. The parallel is close enough to allow for an extension of the *Discourse* to include the *Essay*, at least on this particular point. "Les animaux qui parlent (les langues naturelles) les ont en naissant: ils les ont tous, et partout la Même; ils n'en changent point, ils n'y font pas le moindre progrès. La langue de convention n'appartient qu'à l'homme. Voilà pourquoi l'homme fait des progrès, soit en bien soit en mal, et pourquoi les animaux n'en font pas" (*Essay*, p. 504). That "langue de convention" has the same meaning as conceptual language is part of our argument. Starobinski is certainly right to say that "there is no contradiction between [this text] and the passage from the *Essay* . . ." (3:1327). On the combined reading of the *Essay* with the *Discourse* see also, for a divergent view, Michèle Duchet and Michel Launay, "Synchronie et diachronie; *l'Essai sur l'origine des langues* et le second *Discours*" in *Revue internationale de Philosophie*, 82 (1967): 421–42.

equal assurance that "man's first language had to be figurative" and that "figural language predates literal meaning" (*Essay*, p. 506). And when we try to understand denomination in Rousseau as, in Foucault's words, "going through language until we reach the point where words and things are tied together in their common essence,"[23] then we find that, in the *Second Discourse*, denomination is associated with difference rather than with identity. A note in the 1782 edition adds to the description of denomination ("If one oak were called A, another would be called B") the following remark: "for the first idea we derive from two things is that they are not the same; it often takes a great deal of time to observe what they have in common." We would then have to assume that an observer, so keenly aware of difference that he fails to notice the resemblance between one oak tree and another would be unable to distinguish the difference between the word *a* and the tree A, to the point of considering them as united in some "common essence." Another difficulty: following the traditional reading of Rousseau as it is here represented by Alain Grosrichard, we would want to seize upon the act of denomination in all the transparency of its nonconceptual literalness. We find instead that "the first inventors [of words] were able to give names only to the ideas they already possessed . . ." (3:150), a sentence in which the word "idea," despite all pre-Kantian empiricist concreteness, denotes the presence of some degree of conceptuality (or metaphor) from the start, within the very act of naming. We know, moreover, from the previous quotation, what this "*idée première*" must be: it is the idea of difference ("the first idea we derive from two things . . ."). But if all entities are the same, namely entities, to the extent that they differ from each other, then the substitution of sameness for difference that characterizes, for Rousseau, all conceptual language is built into the very act of naming, the "invention" of the proper noun. It is impossible to say whether denomination is literal or figural: from the moment there is denomination, the conceptual metaphor of entity as difference is implied, and whenever there is metaphor, the literal denomination of a particular entity is inevitable: "try to trace for yourself the image of a tree in general, you will never succeed. In spite of yourself, you will have to see it as small or large, bare or leafy, light or dark" or "As soon as you imagine [a triangle] in your mind, it will be one specific triangle and

23. Michel Foucault, *Les Mots et les choses* (Paris, 1966). The passage is quoted in Grosrichard, "Gravité de Rousseau," p. 64.

no other, and it would be impossible not to make its contour visible and its surface colored" (3:150). Are we forced to conclude that Rousseau's paradoxes are genuine contradictions, that he did not know, in the *Discourse*, what he stated in the *Essay*, and vice versa? Perhaps we should heed his admonition: "in order not to find me in contradiction with myself, I should be allowed enough time to explain myself" (*Essay*, p. 521).

In the third section of the *Essay on the Origin of Language*, Rousseau offers us an "example" in the form of a narrative parable, a brief allegory. It tells us how the proper name *man*, which figures so prominently at the beginning of the *Second Discourse*,[24] came into being:

> A primitive man [*un homme sauvage*], on meeting other men, will first have experienced fright. His fear will make him see these men as larger and stronger than himself; he will give them the name *giants*. After many experiences, he will discover that the supposed giants are neither larger nor stronger than himself, and that their stature did not correspond to the idea he had originally linked to the word giant. He will then invent another name that he has in common with them, such as, for example, the word *man*, and will retain the word giant for the false object that impressed him while he was being deluded. [*Essay*, p. 506]

This is a general and purely linguistic version of what Grosrichard calls "*se nommer*," in which the origin of inequality, in the most literal sense of the term, is being described. The passage was possibly inspired, as has been pointed out,[25] by Condillac, except for the fact that Rousseau refers to full-grown men and not to children. The difference is important, for the entire passage plays a complex game with qualitative and quantitative notions of similarity, equality, and difference.

In this encounter with other men, the first reaction of the primitive is said to be fear. The reaction is not obvious; it is certainly not based on objective data, for Rousseau makes it clear that the men are

---

24. "La plus utile et la moins avancée de toutes les connaissances humaines me parait être celle de l'homme . . ." (3:122). On the question of "man" in Rousseau, see especially Martin Rang, *J. J. Rousseaus Lehre vom Menschen* (Göttingen, 1959).

25. Among others by Starobinski, *Oeuvres complètes*, 3:1323, n. 3

supposed to be of equal size and strength. Neither is it the fear of a single individual confronted with a multitude, since primitive men are entirely devoid of the sense of numbers or of groups. The similarity in size and in the observable attributes of strength should, at first sight, act reassuringly and make the reaction less anxious than if the man had encountered a bear or a lion. Yet Rousseau stresses fright, and Derrida is certainly right in stating that the act of denomination that follows—calling the other man a giant, a process that Rousseau describes as a figural use of language—displaces the referential meaning from an outward, visible property to an "inward" feeling.[26] The coinage of the word "giant" simply means "I am afraid." But what is the reason for fear, if it is not due to observable data? It can only result from a fundamental feeling of distrust, the suspicion that, although the creature does not look like a lion or a bear, it nevertheless might act like one, outward appearances to the contrary. The reassuringly familiar and similar outside might be a trap. Fear is the result of a possible discrepancy between the outer and the inner properties of entities. It can be shown that, for Rousseau, all passions—whether they be love, pity, anger, or even a borderline case between passion and need such as fear—are characterized by such a discrepancy; they are based not on the knowledge that such a difference exists, but on the hypothesis that it might exist, a possibility that can never be proven or disproven by empirical or by analytical means.[27] A statement of distrust is neither true nor false: it is rather in the nature of a permanent hypothesis.

The fact that Rousseau chose fear as an example to demonstrate the priority of metaphor over denomination complicates and enriches the pattern to a considerable degree, for metaphor is precisely the figure that depends on a certain degree of correspondence between "inside" and "outside" properties. The word "giant," invented by the frightened primitive to designate his fellow-man, is indeed a metaphor in that it is based on a correspondence between inner

---

26. Jacques Derrida, *De la Grammatologie*, p. 393.

27. The assertion has to be proven by a general interpretation of "passions" in the work of Rousseau. To indicate the direction of the argument, the following quotation from *Julie* is characteristic; recapitulating the history of her passion for Saint-Preux, Julie is said to write: "Je crus voir sur votre visage les traits de l'âme qu'il fallait à la mienne. Il me sembla que mes sens ne servaient que d'organe à des sentiments plus nobles; et j'aimai dans vous, moins ce que j'y voyais que ce que je croyais sentir en moi-même . . ." (*Oeuvres complètes*, 2:340).

feelings of fear and outward properties of size. It may be objectively false (the other man is not in fact any taller) but it is subjectively candid (he seems taller to the frightened subject). The statement may be in error, but it is not a lie. It "expresses" the inner experience correctly. The metaphor is blind, not because it distorts objective data, but because it presents as certain what is, in fact, a mere possibility. The fear of falling is "true," for the potentially destructive power of gravity is a verifiable fact, but the fear of another man is hypothetical; no one can trust a precipice, but it remains an open question, for whoever is neither a paranoiac nor a fool, whether one can trust one's fellow man. By calling him a "giant," one freezes hypothesis, or fiction, into fact and makes fear, itself a figural state of suspended meaning, into a definite, proper meaning devoid of alternatives. The metaphor "giant," used to connote man, has indeed a proper meaning (fear), but this meaning is not really proper: it refers to a condition of permanent suspense between a literal world in which appearance and nature coincide and a figural world in which this correspondence is no longer *a priori* posited. Metaphor is error because it believes or feigns to believe in its own referential meaning. This belief is legitimate only within the limits of a given text: the metaphor that connotes Achilles' courage by calling him a lion is correct within the textual tradition of the *Iliad* because it refers to a character in a fiction whose function it is to live up to the referential implication of the metaphor. As soon as one leaves the text it becomes aberrant—if, for example, one calls one's son Achilles in the hope that this will make him into a hero. Rousseau's example of a man encountering another man is textually ambiguous, as all situations involving categorical relationships between man and language have to be. What happens in such an encounter is complex: the empirical situation, which is open and hypothetical, is given a consistency that can only exist in a text. This is done by means of a metaphor (calling the other man a giant), a substitutive figure of speech ("*he* is a giant" substituting for "*I* am afraid") that changes a referential situation suspended between fiction and fact (the hypothesis of fear) into a literal fact. Paradoxically, the figure literalizes its referent and deprives it of its para-figural status. The figure dis-figures, that is, it makes fear, itself a para-figural fiction, into a reality that is as inescapable as the reality of the original encounter between the two men. Metaphor overlooks the fictional, textual element in the nature of the entity it connotes. It assumes a

world in which intra- and extra-textual events, literal and figural
forms of language, can be distinguished, a world in which the literal
and the figural are properties that can be isolated and, consequently,
exchanged and substituted for each other. This is an error, although
it can be said that no language would be possible without this error.

The intricacy of the situation is obviously tied to the choice of
the example. The interplay of difference and similarity implied in the
encounter between two men is more complex than if the encounter
had been between two potentially antithetical entities such as man
and woman, as is the case in *Julie* or parts of *Émile*, or man and
things, as is the case in the example of the *Second Discourse* in which
a man is naming a tree instead of naming another man. It seems
perverse on Rousseau's part to choose an example based on a more
complex situation than that of the paradigm with which he is dealing. Should we infer, with the traditional interpreters of Rousseau,
that the intersubjective, reflective situation of self-encounter, as in
the specular self-fascination of Narcissus, is indeed for Rousseau the
paradigmatic experience from which all other experiences are derived? We must remind ourselves that the element of reflective similarity mirrored in the example of man's encounter with man is not
the representation of a paradigmatic empirical situation (as is the
case in Descartes's *cogito* or in any phenomenological reduction) but
the metaphorical illustration of a linguistic fact. The example does
not have to do with the genetic process of the "birth" of language
(told later in the text) but with the linguistic process of conceptualization. The narrative mode of the passage is itself a metaphor that
should not mislead us into transposing a synchronic, linguistic structure into a diachronic, historical event. And conceptualization, as the
passage of the *Second Discourse* on the naming of trees makes clear,
is an intralinguistic process, the invention of a figural metalanguage
that shapes and articulates the infinitely fragmented and amorphous
language of pure denomination. To the extent that all language is
conceptual, it always already speaks about language and not about
things. The sheer metonymic enumeration of things that Rousseau
describes in the *Discourse* ("if one oak was called *A*, and another was
called *B* . . .") is an entirely negative moment that does not describe
language as it is or used to be at its inception, but that dialectically
infers literal denomination as the negation of language. Denomination could never exist by itself although it is a constitutive part of all
linguistic events. All language is language about denomination, that

is, a conceptual, figural, metaphorical metalanguage. As such, it partakes of the blindness of metaphor when metaphor literalizes its referential indetermination into a specific unit of meaning. This statement about the metalinguistic (or conceptual) nature of language is the equivalent of the earlier statement, directly derived from Rousseau, according to which denomination has to postulate the concept (or idea) of difference in order to come into being.

If all language is about language, then the paradigmatic linguistic model is that of an entity that confronts itself.[28] It follows that the exemplary situation described in the *Essay* (man confronting man) is the correct linguistic paradigm, whereas the situation of the *Second Discourse* (man confronting a tree) is a dialectical derivation from this paradigm that moves away from the linguistic model towards problems of perception, consciousness, reflection, and the like. In a text that associates the specificity of man with language and, within language, with the power of conceptualization, the priority belongs to the example from the *Essay*. The statement of the *Discourse* that "the first nouns could only have been proper nouns" is therefore a statement derived from the logically prior statement "that the first language had to be figural." There is no contradiction if one understands that Rousseau conceives of denomination as a hidden, blinded figure.

This is not yet the end of the parable. Actual language does not use the imaginary word "giant"[29] but has invented the conceptual term "man" in its stead. Conceptualization is a double process: it is this complexity that allows for the successive narrative pattern of the allegory. It consists first of all of a wild, spontaneous metaphor which is, to some degree, aberrant. This first level of aberration is

28. The implication is that the self-reflective moment of the *cogito*, the self-reflection of what Rilke calls "le Narcisse exhaucé," is not an original event but itself an allegorical (or metaphorical) version of an intralinguistic structure, with all the negative epistemological consequences this entails. Similarly, Rousseau's use of "fear" as the paradigmatic passion (or need) that leads to figural language is not to be accounted for in psychological but in linguistic terms. "Fear" is exemplary because it corresponds structurally to the rhetorical model of the metaphor.

29. The actual word "giant," as we know it from everyday usage, presupposes the word "man" and is not the metaphorical figure that Rousseau, for lack of an existing word, has to call "giant." Rousseau's "giant" would be more like some mythological monster; one could think of Goliath, or of Polyphemos (leaving aside the temptation to develop the implications of Odysseus's strategy in giving his name to Polyphemos as no-man).

however not intentional, because it does not involve the interests of the subject in any way. Rousseau's man stands to gain nothing from inventing the word "giant." The distortion introduced by the term results exclusively from a formal, rhetorical potential of the language. The same is not true at the second stage. The word "man" is created, says Rousseau, "after many experiences, [when primitive man] will have discovered that the supposed giants are neither larger nor stronger than himself . . ." (*Essay*, p. 506). The word "man" is the result of a quantitative process of comparison based on measurement, and making deliberate use of the category of number in order to reach a reassuring conclusion: if the other man's height is numerically equal to my own, then he is no longer dangerous. The conclusion is wishful and, of course, potentially in error—as Goliath and Polyphemos, among others, were soon enough to discover. The second level of aberration stems from the use of number as if it were a literal property of things that truly belongs to them, when it is, in fact, just one more conceptual metaphor devoid of objective validity and subject to the distortions that constitute all metaphors. For Rousseau, as for Nietzsche, number is par excellence the concept that hides ontic difference under an illusion of identity. The idea of number is just as derivative and suspect as the idea of man:

> A primitive could consider his right and his left leg separately, or consider them together as one indivisible pair, without ever thinking of them as *two* [legs]. For the representational idea of an object is one thing, but the numerical idea that determines it is another. Still less was he able to count up to five. Although he could have noticed, in pressing his hands together, that the fingers exactly corresponded, he did not in the least conceive of their numerical equality. . . . [3:219, note 14]

The concept of man is thus doubly metaphorical: it first consists of the blind moment of passionate error that leads to the word "giant," then of the moment of deliberate error that uses number in order to tame the original wild metaphor into harmlessness (it being well understood that this numerical terminology of "first," "doubly," "original," etc., is itself metaphorical and is used only for the clarity of exposition). Man invents the concept man by means of another concept that is itself illusionary. The "second" metaphor, which Rousseau equates with the literary, deliberate and rhetorical use of the spontaneous figure[30] is no longer innocent: the invention of the word man makes it possible for "men" to exist by establishing the equality within inequality, the sameness within difference of civil society, in which the suspended, potential truth of the original fear is domesticated by the illusion of identity. The concept interprets the metaphor of numerical sameness as if it were a statement of literal fact. Without this literalization, there could be no society. The reader of Rousseau must remember that this literalism is the deceitful misrepresentation of an original blindness. Conceptual language, the foundation of civil society, is also, it appears, a lie superimposed upon an error. We can therefore hardly expect the epistemology of the sciences of man to be straightforward.

The transition from the structure of conceptual language to society is implicit in the example from the *Essay* describing the genealogy of the word "man." It becomes explicit when, at the beginning of the second part of the *Discourse*, the origin of society is described in exactly parallel terms, this time no longer as a marginal example but as the central statement of the *Second Discourse*, forging the axis of the text in the coherent movement that extends from freedom to perfectibility, from perfectibility to language, from language to man, and from man to political society. Neither the discovery of fire and technology, nor the contiguity of man's proximity to man on earth account for the origin of society. Society originates with the quantitative comparison of conceptual relationships:

> The repeated contacts between man and various entities, and between the entities themselves, must necessarily engender in the mind of man the perception of relationships. These relationships, which we express by words such as large, small, strong, weak, fast, slow, fearful, bold, and other similar ideas, when compared to man's needs, produced, almost without his being aware of it, some kind of reflection, or rather some form of mechanical prudence that taught him to take the precautions most needed for his safety. . . . The resemblances that time allowed him to observe [between his fellow men], the human female and himself, made him infer [*juger de*] those which he

30. "L'image illusoire offerte par la passion se montrant la première, le langage qui lui répondait fut aussi le premier inventé; il devint ensuite métaphorique, quand l'esprit éclairé, reconnaissant sa première erreur, n'en employa les expressions que dans les mêmes passions qui l'avaient produite" (*Essay*, p. 506).

could not perceive. Noticing that all of them behaved in the same way that he would himself have behaved in similar circumstances, he concluded that their way of thinking and feeling was entirely in conformity with his own. [3:166][31]

The passage describes precisely the same interplay between passion (fear), measurement, and metaphor (inferring invisible properties by analogy with visible ones) as the parable from the *Essay on the Origins of Language*. In the lines that follow, the principle of conformity on which the concept of man and the possibility of government is founded is called "cette importante Vérité" (3:166). We should now realize that what Rousseau calls "truth" designates, neither the adequation of language to reality, nor the essence of things shining through the opacity of words, but rather the suspicion that human specificity may be rooted in linguistic deceit.

The consequences of this negative insight for Rousseau's political theory are far-reaching. What the *Discourse on Inequality* tells us, and what the classical interpretation of Rousseau has stubbornly refused to hear, is that the political destiny of man is structured like and derived from a linguistic model that exists independently of nature and independently of the subject: it coincides with the blind metaphorization called "passion," and this metaphorization is not an intentional act. Contrary to what one might think, this enforces the inevitably "political" nature or, more correctly, the "politicality" (since one could hardly speak of "nature" in this case) of all forms of human language, and especially of rhetorically self-conscious or literary language—though certainly not in the representational, psychological, or ethical sense in which the relationship between literature and politics is generally understood. If society and government derive from a tension between man and his language, then they are not natural (depending on a relationship between man and things), nor ethical (depending on a relationship among men), nor theological, since language is not conceived as a transcendental principal but as the possibility of contingent error. The political thus becomes a

31. The translation considerably simplifies the opening lines, quite obscure in the French text: "[L]'application réitérée des êtres divers à lui-même, et les uns aux autres, dut naturellement engendrer. . . ." The immediately preceding paragraph in the text makes clear that Rousseau refers to the interplay between several physical entities in technological inventions (such as the invention of the bow and arrow) or between man and nature, as in the discovery and conservation of fire.

burden for man rather than an opportunity, and this realization, which can be stated in an infinity of sardonic and pathetic modes, may well account for the recurrent reluctance to accept, or even to notice, the link between language and society in the works of Rousseau. Far from being a repression of the political, as Althusser would have it, literature is condemned to being the truly political mode of discourse. The relationship of this discourse to political praxis cannot be described in psychological or in psycholinguistic terms, but rather in terms of the relationship, within the rhetorical model, between the referential and the figural semantic fields.

To develop the implications of this conclusion would lead to a detailed reading of the second part of the *Discourse on Inequality* in conjunction with the *Social Contract*, *Julie*, and Rousseau's other political writings. I have tried to emphasize the importance and the complexity of the transition that leads up to such a reading. Only if we are aware of the considerable ambivalence that burdens a theoretical discourse dealing with man's relation to man—"un homme [que parle] à des hommes . . . de l'homme," as the *Second Discourse* puts it (3:131)—can we begin to see how Rousseau's theory of literature and his theory of government could get translated into practical terms. The introductory analysis allows for the schematic formulation of some directives.

First of all, the passage from a language of fiction to a language oriented towards political praxis implies a transition from qualitative concepts such as needs, passions, man, power, etc., to quantitative concepts involving numbers such as rich, poor, etc.[32] The inequality referred to in the title of the *Discourse*, and which must first be understood as difference in the most general way possible, becomes in the second part the inequality in the quantitative distribution of property. The basis of political thought, in Rousseau, is economic rather than ethical, as is clear from the lapidary statement that opens the second part of the *Discourse*: "The first man who, after having fenced in a plot of land went on to say '*this belongs to me*' and found other men naïve enough to believe him [*assez simples pour le croire*], was the true founder of civil society" (3:164). The

---

32. "Que les mots de *fort* et de *faible* sont équivoques (dans le cas où l'on explique l'origine de la société par l'union des faibles entre eux); que . . . le sens de ces termes est mieux rendu par ceux de *pauvre* et de *riche*, parce qu'en effet un homme n'avait point, avant les lois, d'autre moyen d'assujettir ses égaux qu'en attaquant leur bien, ou leur faisant quelque part du sien" (3:179).

passage from literal greed to the institutional, conceptual law pro-
tecting the right to property runs parallel to the transition from the
spontaneous to the conceptual metaphor.[33] But the economic foundation of political theory in Rousseau is not rooted in a theory of needs,
appetites, and interests that could lead to ethical principles of right
and wrong; it is the correlative of linguistic conceptualization and is
therefore neither materialistic, nor idealistic, nor merely dialectical
since language is deprived of representational as well as of transcendental authority.[34] The complex relationship between Rousseau's and
Marx's economic determinism could and should only be approached
from this point of view.[35]

Second, one sees why civil order and government are, in Rousseau, such fragile and threatened constructions, since they are built
on the very sands of error.[36] "The vices that make social institutions
necessary also make the abuse of these institutions inevitable . . ."
(3:187). This circular, self-destructive pattern of all civil institutions
mirrors the self-destructive epistemology of conceptual language
when it demonstrates its inabillity to keep literal reference and
figural connotation apart. The literalism that makes language possible also makes the abuse of language inevitable. Hence the fundamental ambivalence in the valorization of literal reference throughout the *Second Discourse*. The "pure" fiction of the state of nature
precedes, in principle, all valorization, yet nothing can be more destructive than the inevitable transposition of this fictional model to
the present, empirical world in which "the subjects have to be kept

33. Thus confirming the semantic validity of the word-play, in French, on
"sens *propre*" and "*propriété*."

34. This, of course, does not mean that questions of virtue, of self, and of God
are not being considered by Rousseau; they obviously are. What is at stake is not the
existence of an ethical, psychological, or theological discourse but their authority in
terms of truth or falsehood.

35. Hints in this direction are present in the work of Lucien Sebag, *Marxisme
et structuralisme* (Paris, 1964), whereas Althusser remains short of Engels' treatment
of Rousseau in the *Anti-Dühring* (especially Chapter 13 of Part I, "Dialectics: Negation of the negation"). I am not informed on the state of Rousseau studies outside
Western Europe and the United States.

36. ". . . rien n'est permanent que la misère qui résulte de toutes ces vicis-
situdes; quand [l]es sentiments et [l]es idées [de l'homme] pourraient s'élever jusqu'à
l'amour de l'ordre et aux notions sublimes de la vertu, il lui serait impossible de faire
jamais une application sure de ses principes dans un état de choses qui ne lui
laisserait discerner ni le bien ni le mal, ni l'honnête homme ni le méchant" (*Du
Contrat social*, Ière version, *Oeuvres complètes*, 3:282).

apart" (*Essay*, p. 542) and by which one reaches "the last stage of inequality and the extreme point that closes the circle and touches again upon our point of departure (namely the state of nature): this is where all individuals again become equal because they are nothing . . ." (3:191).

Finally, the *contractual* pattern of civil government can only be understood against the background of this permanent threat. The social contract is by no means the expression of a transcendental law: it is a complex and purely defensive verbal strategy by means of which the literal world is given some of the consistency of fiction, an intricate set of feints and ruses[37] by means of which the moment is temporarily delayed when fictional seductions will no longer be able to resist transformation into literal acts. The conceptual language of the social contract resembles the subtle interplay between figural and referential discourse in a novel. It has often been said that Rousseau's novel *Julie* is also his best treatise on political science; it should be added that *The Social Contract* is also his best novel. But both depend on their common methodological preamble in the theory of rhetoric that is the foundation of the *Discourse on the Origin and the Foundations of Inequality Among Men*.

37. The furthest-reaching of these ruses being perhaps that of the legislator having to pretend that he speaks with the voice of God in order to be heard. "Voilà ce qui força de tout temps les pères des nations de recourir à l'intervention du ciel et d'honorer les dieux de leur propre sagesse, afin que les peuples soumis aux lois de l'Etat comme à celles de la nature, et reconnaissant le même pouvoir dans la formation de l'homme et dans celle de la cité, obéissent avec liberté et portassent docilement le joug de la félicité publique." The example of the true legislator is Moses and the passage concludes with a footnote reference to Machiavelli. (J. J. Rousseau, *Oeuvres complètes*, 3:383).

8   Self

(Pygmalion)

THE *SECOND DISCOURSE* IS THE STORY OF "A MAN [SPEAK-ing] of man . . . to men" (*Oeuvres Complètes*, 3:131). The situation postulates an utterance (a man speaking . . .), a meaning (*about* man), and a reading (*to* men), a threefold articulation within the single act of denomination. This structure is paradigmatic for all cognitive discourse: it always has to be about an entity such as "man" in which the noun is a conceptual metaphor that replaces a delusive play between identity and difference. The naïvely empirical formulation of this fact (which Rousseau avoids) claims that man, as a species, is defined by the possession of language as an elective attribute that is proper to him. But we do not "possess" language in the same way that we can be said to possess natural properties. It would be just as proper or improper to say that "we" are a property of language as the reverse. The possibility of this reversal is equivalent to the statement that all discourse *has to be* referential but can never signify its actual referent. It leads to the loss of knowledge that Rousseau deplores at the beginning of the *Discourse*: ". . . the least advanced of all human knowledge would seem to be the science of man" but "what is more cruel still . . . is that, in a sense, by studying man we have made ourselves unable to know him" (3:122–23), a sentence in which "studying" must be understood as any process involving definitional language. The relationship between man and his discourse is so far from being the simple possession of a natural attribute that it has to be called "cruel" whereas, in the case of natural properties such as the senses, it is the absence of the faculty rather than its existence that would arouse pity.

The *Second Discourse* also demonstrates obliquely why all denominative discourse has to be narrative. If the word "man" is a conceptual figure grafted on a blind metaphor, then the referential status of the discourse about man is bound to be curiously ambivalent. It claims to refer to an entity (man), but this entity turns out to be the substitution of a definitional for what was only a hypothetical knowledge, an epistemological metaphor substituting certitude for ignorance on the basis of an assumed resemblance between passion and perception, fear and size, inside and outside. The resulting discourse is complex not just because it has a plurality of perhaps incompatible meanings but because the semantic status of any of these meanings can never be determined. It always points to the meaning which the figure, by its very existence, decrees: man as an entity with specific properties. But the substitutive chain that links the figure to its assumedly proper meaning can always be broken, since it is grounded in hypothetical inferences that cannot be verified. In the case of such concepts as "fear," "state of nature," "passion," "perfectibility" and ultimately "man," it is impossible to decide whether they are referential names for extralinguistic entities or mere phantoms of language. And it is equally impossible to let the question remain in abeyance, since the pressure towards meaning and the pressure towards its undoing can never cancel each other out. This assymetry is suggested, in Rousseau, by the stress on passion (in which the referential element is suspended) over need (in which the referential element is determined) as the proper affective metaphor for language[1] and, among passions, for such passions as fear that remain, per definition, in an intolerably suspended state. Language can only be about something such as man (i.e., conceptual), but in being about man, it can never know whether it is about anything at all including itself, since it is precisely the *aboutness*, the referentiality, that is in question. Rousseau's anthropological discourse, as it comes to deal with questions of selfhood, of knowledge, of ethical and practical judgment, of religion and politics, will always be the restatement of this initial complication in a variety of versions that confer upon his work an appearance of consistency.

The classical polarities that shape narrative discourse, such as the distinction between showing and telling (mimesis and diegesis), or, in a more recent terminology, between *discours* and *histoire*, are correlatives of the initial complexity of denomination. Just as it is impossible to say whether discourse about man is referential or not, it is impossible to decide whether it is mimetic or diegetic. The diegetic possibility implies the hypothetical existence of a narrator, of

1. *Essai sur l'origine des langues*, in *Cahiers pour L'Analyse* 8. Chapter 2 (p. 505) is entitled "Que la première invention de la parole ne vient pas des besoins, mais des passions."

a man talking about man. It also implies the necessity of an act by which the question of the referential verifiability is raised, and this epistemological moment, which cannot be short-circuited, is readily represented in the figure of an audience or a reader. We re-find the traditional space or stage for the scene of reading as the scene of telling, the mimesis of a diegesis. But the necessary presence of the moment of utterance and of the interpretative moment of understanding has nothing to do with the empirical situation naïvely represented in this scene: the notions of audience and of narrator that are part of any narrative are only the misleading figuration of a linguistic structure. And just as the indeterminacy of reference generates the illusion of a subject, a narrator, and a reader, it also generates the metaphor of temporality. A narrative endlessly tells the story of its own denominational aberration and it can only repeat this aberration on various levels of rhetorical complexity. Texts engender texts as a result of their necessarily aberrant semantic structure; hence the fact that they consist of a series of repetitive reversals that engenders the semblance of a temporal sequence. All the constitutive categories of narration are implied in the theory of language as figuration that appears in the *Essay on the Origin of Language* and that is enacted in the fictional history of the *Second Discourse*. One should remember that they are the unfolding and not the resolution of the chaotic uncertainty which Rousseau calls "fear."

But does all this complication and cruelty not stem from an intrinsic weakness of the *Second Discourse*? Other theoretical texts such as the *Social Contract* or the *Profession de foi* are much more impersonal in tone than the hybrid *Second Discourse*, with its mixture of polemics, pathos, argument, fiction, and, at times, personal confession. On the other hand, openly autobiographical texts, from the *Letters to Malesherbes* (1762) to the *Rêveries* (1776–77), though certainly not devoid of generalizing intentions, are explicitly rooted in a strong sense of particular selfhood (one remembers Rousseau's claim at the beginning of the *Confessions*: "Si je ne vaux pas mieux, au moins je suis autre"[2]). The complications of the *Second Discourse* are unquestionably related to the overgeneral use of the word "man" as a conceptual metaphor, detached from its empirical foundation in the reflective self-experience of a subject, in the constitutive *cogito* of a

2. J. J. Rousseau, *Oeuvres complètes*, ed. Bernard Gagnebin and Marcel Raymond (Paris: Gallimard [Bibliothèque de la Pléiade], 1959), 1:5.

consciousness. If one admits, with Alain Grosrichard and many others, that the main purpose of Rousseau's work is "to make the representation I have of the world coincide with the representation I convey to others or, in brief, to name myself [*me nommer*],"[3] then this act of self-denomination remains confused, in the *Second Discourse*, with the anthropological definition of man in general. The fact that the mediations leading from the particular to the general self remain repressed [*impensé*] would then explain the extreme ambivalence, bordering on incoherence, of the *Discourse*. The problem may never be resolved in Rousseau's further work but, in compensation, the near-obsessive concentration on a partly censored self that becomes more and more evident as one moves from the main political writings to, say, the *Dialogues* (1773) leads to a refinement of self-insight that places Rousseau in the main tradition of the post-Augustinian literature of the self. He restates the Delphic "know thyself" alluded to at the onset of the *Second Discourse* in the eighteenth-century terminology of the "morale sensitive." That such acute self-understanding is by no means incompatible with pathological misinterpretations of the self's relationship to others and to the world is by now a psychological commonplace. It is also well known that the interpretation of Rousseau as a philosopher of the self has been among the most productive ways to read him in past as well as in recent times, from Hazlitt and Germaine de Stael to Jean Starobinski.

Before turning to the further development of Rousseau's figural rhetoric, we must therefore consider his own understanding of selfhood. Do we indeed avoid some of the complications of the *Second Discourse* by starting out from the particular self instead of starting out from the idea of man in general? Is the theory of metaphor derived from the *Second Discourse* still applicable in texts centered on self-reflection rather than on historical fictions? More specifically, can the self be called a metaphor in the same way that "giant" and subsequently "man" could be shown to be the result of coercive tropological displacements?

The word "metaphor" occurs rarely in Rousseau, who speaks more generally of "langage figuré" without making distinctions between particular tropes or getting involved in the pitfalls and refinements of

3. Alain Grosrichard, "Gravité de Rousseau" in *Cahiers pour l'analyse*, 8, p. 64.

such distinctions. It does appear however in a piece of dialogue spoken by a very minor character in a very minor work, the early play *Narcisse* that Rousseau claims to have written at the age of eighteen. It tells the story of a character named Valère so inebriated by vanity that he falls in love with his own portrait, barely disguised as a woman. His valet Frontin, whose inebriation, after making the rounds of the city cabarets, is a great deal more literal, is in conversation with Lucinde, Valère's sister:

Lucinde: He is drunk, I believe. Ah, Frontin, I beg you, try to get hold of yourself and to make some sense.
Frontin: Nothing could be easier. See here. It is a portrait . . . a portrait that has been metamor . . . no metaphor . . . yes, metaphorized. It's my master, it's a girl . . . you have made a certain mixture . . . I have guessed all that, I . . .

[*Narcisse*, 2:100]

The explicit association of "portrait"[4] with metaphor (leaving aside the further complications introduced by "metamorphosis" and, for that matter, by drunkenness) allows for a parallel with the fable of the *Essay*. The passion involved in *Narcisse* is not, as in section II of the Essay, "fear" but "love" or, more precisely, the interplay between self-love (*amour de soi*), vanity (*amour propre*), and the love of others that makes up the passion. Already in this early text (revised at a later moment that is hard to determine)[5] love is constitutively associated with the notion of self. The first explicit formulation of the structure of self-love, in note 15 to the *Second Discourse*, makes clear that "love" is characterized by the differential relationship between the personal and the reflexive pronoun in the paradigmatic sentence that designates self-love: je m'aime. "In the true state of nature," says Rousseau, "vanity [*amour propre*] does not exist, for each particular

4. "Portrait" will become, of course, a particularly rich and ambiguous term throughout Rousseau's work, from the early riddle (2:1133), to the portrait in *Narcisse*, the scene of Julie's portrait in the *Nouvelle Héloïse* (2:278–80), the distinction between "portrait" and "tableau" in the Second Preface to the *Nouvelle Héloïse*, and the rantings about his own portrait in the *Dialogues* (Deuxième dialogue, 1:777 ff. and notes).

5. On the complex history of *Narcisse*, see the notes of Jacques Scherer in his edition of *Narcisse* in J. J. Rousseau, *Oeuvres complètes*, ed. Bernard Gagnebin and Marcel Raymond (Paris: Gallimard [Bibliothèque de la Pléiade], 1961), 2:1858–65. "On the possible corrections made by Marivaux," writes Scherer, "one can only make conjectures" (2:1860).

man considers himself as the only spectator that takes notice of him, as the sole being in the universe that takes an interest in his existence, as the only judge of his own merit. It is therefore not possible for a feeling to burgeon in his soul that takes its origin in comparisons which he is not able to carry out . . ." (*Second Discourse*, 3:219, note 15). The specular, reflective distance is postulated as already foremarked in the fictional state of nature where Rousseau is free to set up his scene as he pleases; as in all other instances, the differential relationships that will become the articulations and tensions of the historical world are already present "en creux" and in the guise of equalities, in the so-called state of nature. Primitive man is alone and has no conception of the other whatever, yet already in this absolute and inconceivable state of solitude, he can be the spectator, the concern and the judge of his own singular being. In the apparent identity of the nominative with the reflexive "I," the differentiation is foreshadowed and the grammatical space for the future differences staked out. The statement that corresponds to this condition would have to be "je m'aime donc je suis," in which the word "aimer" is needed to posit a reflexive structure that the verb "to be" cannot provide (it is impossible to say "je me suis") and thus to produce a genuine *cogito*, the constitution of a self defined in its own self-identity by a reflexive act. The description of *amour de soi* pointedly avoids the scene that would correspond to the nonreflexive, transitive sentence "j'aime donc je suis," which would assert the transparency of the self to its own experience of selfhood, the unmediated presence of the self to itself. If the notion of transparency is at all operative in Rousseau, it is certainly not associated with the concept of selfhood defined as "amour de soi."

Self-love does not enter the dramatic world of *Narcisse*, which owes whatever comic effects it can muster to experiences at the furthest remove from "amour de soi." To a large extent, *Narcisse* exploits the hackneyed comical resources of vanity, of the *amour propre* that Rousseau sharply distinguishes from self-love. In contrast to the solitary self-concentration of self-love, *amour propre* is entirely directed towards the approval of others. It is a false consciousness, a *mauvaise foi* based on the aberrant assumption that the self, as such, is worthy of being loved by the world at large: "on m'aime" or "je suis aimable" would be the correct paraphrase for *amour propre* as opposed to the "je m'aime" of self-love.

A false consciousness of this kind can perfectly remain within the confines of an organizing self that understands and controls its dynamics. The subject may be blinded by vanity and prone to say outrageously false things about the world, yet it remains a subject and can be known as such. "What pleasure it will give me to make Angélique happy!" exclaims Valère on the eve of his wedding day; confronted with his own portrait disguised to look like a woman, he reacts by saying "I find much in her of my own countenance . . . On my word, she is charming . . . Ah! if only there is a mind to support all this . . . But her taste bears witness to her intelligence. The girl is an expert in the merits of men!" (1:984). This is certainly a grievous misreading of the text of the portrait in which some of the structures, the concern with a correspondence between outside attributes and inner qualities (*esprit*), the resemblance acting as a support for the mystification, suggest a pattern very close to metaphorical substitution. Yet, on the level of *amour propre*, the portrait is neither a metaphor nor any other trope.

The mere existence of an aberrant substitution is not sufficient to set up the specific complexity of figuration, as long as the error can be reduced to the intelligibility of an intentional act. On the level of identifiable bad faith the fantastic image that originates in the mind of the subject and that blots out the world can simply be identified with the mode of consciousness that created it; the reductive reading of the situation is also the correct one. Once the assumption is made that the character is vain, the kind of aberrations to which it is to fall prey are entirely predictable and the author's skill will consist only in the invention of more or less surprising situations in which the predictable reaction will choose to fit. The semantic pattern is straightforward: the misreading of the portrait as being the image of a pretty girl simply means: Valère is vain. The function of the portrait is to reveal a consciousness, and since this consciousness turns out to be a false one, it also serves the corrective function of revealing this falseness to the subject in the hope that he may mend his ways. The purpose of the portrait is satirical and didactic and the comical effects are of this general type. They assume an audience in willing complicity with what is being done to someone else, for his own good. This "good" is not in question, since it is clear that vanity is a very stupid way of being—stupid enough, in fact, to degrade a man into a woman ("Yes Valère, up till now it [the portrait] was a woman; but I hope that henceforth it will be a man . . ." [1:1015]). Hence, at all times, the possibility of exploiting ridicule for low comic effect: "*Valère:* What pleasure it will give me to make Angélique happy!

Frontin (his servant): Do you intend to make her a widow?" (1:982); "*Valère:* Well now, would Mr. Frontin recognize the original of this painting? *Frontin:* Phoo! You bet I would! A couple of hundred kicks in the ass and as many blows I have had the honor of receiving from him have made it a very solid acquaintance" (1:985). In these exchanges between master and servant we are far removed from Scagnarelle, or Diderot's Jacques, or Kleist's Sosias in *Amphitryon*. The effects don't have to be that crudely obvious: within some of the finer moral distinctions made in the satirical scenes, commentators have found Rousseau's play worthy of having been edited by Marivaux. But whether crude or subtle, the referential status of all these passages is unproblematic. They are statements about a consciousness considered as a single unit of meaning and susceptible therefore of being either "true" or "false"; no epistemological tension or intra-textual play is involved. On this level, the portrait resembles the deliberate word "homme" rather than the spontaneous "giant" in the parable from the *Essay on the Origins of Language*. But whereas "homme" is the manipulation of a figure, the portrait is simply the representation of a consciousness. The representation of a misreading is not itself a misreading unless the status of the representation is being questioned as such. As long as we remain in the sphere of *amour propre* this is not the case: vices of this type can be "shown" without having to be "told." One can read Rousseau's entire *Confessions* as if it were such a mimetic history and, as Starobinski and other commentators demonstrate,[6] it is possible to be both subtle and astute in the process.

The question arises whether the theme of *amour propre* (and in this case it would be entirely legitimate to speak of a "theme") fully accounts for the dramatic and linguistic effects of the text. If it does, then there is no reason to read *Narcisse* as if it were the dramatization of a linguistic figure. It is simply the mimesis of a flawed self with the existence of the flaw allowing for whatever dramatic tension the play contains: the juxtaposition of a mystified character to the clear-sighted author and audience, the gradual or sudden discovery of the subterfuge (anagnorisis), etc. As such, the portrait is not a metaphor but one element among others in a human history of general psychological and social interest.

There remains however a residue of complication that cannot

6. See especially "Le progrès de l'interprète" in Jean Starobinski, *La relation critique* (Paris, 1970), pp. 82–173.

be accounted for in these terms. *Narcisse* contains a number of grammatical plays on the reflexive mode that point to the greater degree of generality also suggested by the Ovidian title. It contains sentences of some pronominal intricacy such as "il se cherche pour s'épouser" (1:1005), or "je ne veux plus l'aimer que parce qu'il vous adore" (1:1016), or "il vaut encore mieux n'aimer rien que d'être amoureux de soi-même" (1:1002), as well as plays on the status of identity that seem to exist for their own sake, regardless of the vanity that is supposed to inspire them. The text also suggests that the introduction within the existing situation of the ambivalent portrait—part male, part female; part image, part object—creates a disturbance that no one is entirely able to control, the slightly uncanny "vent de folie" (Baudelaire) that hangs over some of the scenes, especially those most prominent in the use of linguistic and hermeneutic terminology: considerations on "galimatias," "comprendre" and "expliquer" contrasted in an opposition that is not obvious ("*Lucinde:* Comment m'expliquer ce que je ne comprends pas" [1:1006]), and finally, of course, the "portrait métaphorisé" which is supposed to explain the incomprehensible (1:1006).

The actual narcissistic moment when Valère falls in love with his own image is not a moment of pure *amour propre*. It comes closer to the situation summarized by Frontin: "il est devenu amoureux de sa ressemblance" ("he fell in love with his resemblance" [1:1006]), a moment suspended between self-love and the transitive love of others, not quite "je m'aime" or "j'aime X" but rather "je m'aime comme si j'étais X." The self/other tension, latent when the feeling, as in the *Second Discourse*, is that of pity, has become objectified in an autonomous entity, the portrait, that is not entirely fictional but exists in the mode of a simulacrum. The portrait has been substituted for the reflexive pronoun in "je m'aime" and it can do so because it is and is not the self at the same time. It both resembles the self sufficiently to allow for the possibility of self-love, but it also differs enough from it to allow for the otherness, for the "pieuse distance" (Valéry) that is a constitutive part of all passion. Valère (not Valéry) could just as well be in love with difference as with resemblance; resemblance is "loved" because it can be interpreted as identity as well as difference and is therefore unseizable, forever in flight.

In this situation, while Valère, like the legendary Narcissus, is suspended in frozen fascination before an image, the structure is a great deal more complex than in the *amour propre* of mere vanity. The portrait is a substitution, but it is impossible to say whether it substitutes for the self or for the other; it constantly vacillates between both, exactly as in the condition of fear, one constantly vacillates between the suspicion that the reassuring outside might or might not conceal a dangerous inside or, in the opposite situation, that the frightening surface may or may not be appearance rather than evidence. Whereas, in the case of fear, the substitutive oscillation occurs within an inside/outside polarity, in the case of love the polarities involve a subjective as well as a spatial model and the fluctuation occurs between self and other, between ipseity and alterity here reduced to the empirical polarity of man and woman. When it is revealed that the image is indeed the portrait of a specific person, the ambivalence disappears and mere trickery remains. The interesting moment, however, when the play says something significant about the nature and the structure of love, is when the protagonist remains suspended between his desire for the portrayed other and his seduction by reflected likeness.

Love, like perfectibility, is structured like a figure of speech. The portrait allows for the bizarre substitution of self for other, and of other for self, called love. From the moment Valère/Narcisse gives in to this fascination, he considers the portrait "beloved" and transforms the suspended vacillation into the definite identity of an other. The pattern runs parallel to that of the fictional primitive man in the *Essay* who, upon encountering another man, ended the uncertainty of his feeling by attributing to him the size corresponding to his suspicions. To the extent that the portrait partakes of *amour de soi*, albeit in the displaced version of an imagined other, it is indeed a figure (the metaphor of a metonymy), a substitution based on a reflected (contiguous) resemblance and leading to aberrant referential conclusions. And since the very notion of selfhood is grounded in self-love, the loss of epistemological stability in the figure corresponds to a loss of authority in the self, now reduced to ontological nothingness: "Il vaut encore mieux n'aimer *rien* que d'être amoureux de soi-même" (my italics).

This sentence sums up the dénouement of the action. After Valère has had it spelled out to him that he was the victim of a mystification, we seem to end up in the transcendence of narcissistic self-fixation by a normal feeling of love for another. One can expect the reflexive to become transitive and "je m'aime" to become simply "j'aime Angélique." But Rousseau does not allow for the tranquility of a transitive world. After having been "cured" by a public humiliation that reduces him to near-oblivion, Valère reaffirms in fact his self-love, though in a somewhat changed mode: "*Angélique:* Was I wrong in telling you that I love the original model for this portrait? *Valère:* As for me, I will consent to love him only because he adores you" (1:1017). From "on m'aime" to "je m'aime comme autrui," we have come to "je m'aime aimant," apparently one step further away from *amour propre* toward *amour de soi.* The final metamorphosis of the portrait into Angélique completes the movement that began when Valère was transformed into a woman. The disruptive portrait has been domesticated into a reassuring, extra-textual presence, just as the threatening giant was tamed into "man." "Je m'aime aimant" preserves a reflexive moment and combines a referential with an intra-textual structure that cannot be called self-referential, since the "self" to which it claims to point is in fact itself an infinitely deferred condition of indeterminacy between self and other, between identity and difference. To the extent that she is inscribed within this structure, Angèlique's apparent mastery over the situation becomes illusory, as will be evident when the same situation, considerably developed and enriched, will be treated from her perspective in *Julie.* The return to order, normalcy, and proper identity at the end of *Narcisse* is therefore treated as a bouffonerie, especially with regard to the authority figure of the father, Lisimon. By getting "beyond" *amour propre*, a much more disturbing structure is revealed, since it now becomes forever uncertain whether the beloved is in fact a person or a portrait, a referential meaning or a figure. "It is better still to love nothing than to be in love with oneself" becomes a very odd maxim, since "oneself" can never know whether it is anything at all, and since being in love with this non-being is precisely the aberrant hypostasis of a "nothing" into something, delusively called a self. The transitive displacement of selfhood upon the other contaminates the other's referential identity and opens up the possibility that she (or he) too is a "nothing." Once we realize that selfhood is not a substance but a figure, the either/or choice set up in the sentence loses all meaning, since it then becomes impossible to distinguish between self-love, the love of others, or the love of nothing. The rhetoric of self, like the rhetoric of "man" shows that the politics of love, like the politics of history, are rooted in the quicksands which, as *Julie* will show (or tell), make up the ethical judgments governing the relationships between self and other.

One other element in the problematics of selfhood was omitted from the consideration of *Narcisse* and, indeed, from the play itself. The portrait did not fall from the sky, but had to be painted by someone skillful enough to hide and to reveal, at the same time, the identity of the model.[7] From the action of the play we can surmise that the portrait was commissioned, or painted, by Valère's sister, but this event does not enter the text in any way. If however we consider Rousseau as the author of a text in which an action is being "portrayed," then we can call him the "painter" of the scene in the classical sense of *ut pictora poesis*. The later Preface to *Narcisse* (1753) has much more to do with the reception of the *Discourses* than with the play, but it contains several statements on the self-conscious activity of writing and invites the transference of selfhood from the fictional character into the author who invents and represents it. By the same token, the indeterminacy of the self may well be resolved since common sense tells us that the representation of an error is a necessary step in its correction. That Rousseau is not or no longer Valère is clear from the fact that he is able to paint Valère's portrait as well as the scene of the portrait's effect upon others. Does it follow that, unlike his Narcissus figure (which may be a former incarnation of his deluded self now left behind) Rousseau, as a writer, can be called a self in a more inclusive sense than the particular and empirical self lost in the confusion of his everyday existence?

The Preface to *Narcisse* seems at least to allow for the possibility: "I confess that there exist a few sublime minds [génies sublimes] able to dispel the veils with which truth hides itself, a few privileged souls who are able to withstand the stupidity of conceit, the low jealousy and the other passions generated by literary ambitions . . . If any doubt remains as to the justification [of my literary vocation], I boldly proclaim that it is not with regard to the public or with regard to my opponents; it is only towards myself, for only by observing myself can I judge whether or not I can include myself among the small number . . . I needed a test to gain complete knowledge of myself and I have taken it without hesitation" (2:970-73). Writing seems to be held up and justified as a way to recuperate a self dispersed in the world. Such a recuperation can be conceived quite pragmatically or even therapeutically, but it can also be formulated in more inclusive terms: "What distinguishes Jean-Jacques from an

---

7. "Mais le portrait exige un artiste" (Starobinski, *Jean-Jacques Rousseau: La transparence et l'obstacle*, p. 215).

ordinary neurotic," writes Starobinski, "is that the phantasm, far from staying self-enclosed, demands its own development in *actual* labor [un travail *réel*], provokes the desire to write, wants to seduce the public, etc. The decision in favor of the experience of immediacy [le parti pris de l'immédiat] becomes a literary work and betrays itself in the process of its manifestation . . . Rousseau is projected, in spite of himself, in the practical, mediated world and one has to grant that, at least in the case of this extraordinary man, the pathological regression of instincts and desires is not incompatible with the *progression* of his thought."[8] This view is not without its problems, for it is not *a priori* clear how speculative writing can be called a "travail *réel*"; the oddness of its status as a commodity is apparent from the erratic relationship between effort and value that governs the economy of its production and consumption. More interesting still is the suggestion that the experience of immediacy can be transformed into a literary work that replaces the fulfillment of an ideal vision by its representation. For this is precisely what Rousseau constantly warns us against as the most dangerous of aberrations: the danger of a lapse into a literal version of the state of nature is the main assertion of the *Second Discourse*. Starobinski himself is anyway saying something more complex since (at least in this passage) he does not describe the unmediated vision of pure transparency as a reality, nor even as a desire, but as a *parti pris*, the willful assertion of a likely aberration as well as a resignation to the possibility of this error. The gesture introduces an important nuance in the strategies of ego recuperation. It echoes the awareness, in *Narcisse*, that the referential representation of what Rousseau calls a passion (as opposed not only to a need but also to a vice such as conceit) is in fact the representation of a rhetorical structure which, as such, escapes the control of the self. Beyond this point, which is when "writing" can be said to begin its labor, one no longer starts out from a passion but from the assertion, the *parti pris*, of its nonsubjective, linguistic structure. But is this not the best way to reintroduce the authority of a self at the far end of its most radical negation, in the highly abstracted and generalized form of a deconstructive process of self-denial? The statement of the enigma that gives language its necessarily referential complexity might itself be no longer a representation but a single voice that, by the rigor of its negativity, finally coincides with what it asserts.

8. Starobinski, *Jean-Jacques Rousseau: La transparence et l'obstacle*, p. 215.

The rhetorical resources of language, regardless of whether one considers them as mere tropes or extends them to wider patterns of persuasion, are by no means, in themselves, incompatible with self-hood. On the simplest pragmatic level, they obviously offer the self the means by which it can accomplish its own designs, either in full knowledge of its purpose or with the true intent hidden from the subject by bad faith, repression, sublimation, or whatever dynamics of consciousness one wishes to imagine. Rhetoric all too easily appears as the tool of the self, hence its pervading association, in the everyday use of the term, with persuasion, eloquence, the manipulation of the self and of others. Hence also the naïvely pejorative sense in which the term is commonly used, in opposition to a literal use of language that would not allow the subject to conceal its desires. The attitude is by no means confined to the popular use of "rhetoric" but is in fact a recurrent philosophical topos, a philosopheme that may well be constitutive of philosophical language itself.[9] In all these instances, rhetoric functions as a key to the discovery of the self, and it functions with such ease that one may well begin to wonder whether the lock indeed shapes the key or whether it is not the other way round, that a lock (and a secret room or box behind it) had to be invented in order to give a function to the key. For what could be more distressing than a bunch of highly refined keys just lying around without any corresponding locks worthy of being opened? Perhaps there are none, and perhaps the most refined key of all, the key of keys, is the one that gives access to the Pandora's box in which this darkest secret is kept hidden. This would imply the existence of at least one lock worthy of being raped, the Self as the relentless undoer of selfhood.

Within the epistemological labyrinth of figural structures, the recuperation of selfhood would be accomplished by the rigor with which the discourse deconstructs the very notion of the self. The originator of this discourse is then no longer the dupe of his own wishes; he is as far beyond pleasure and pain as he is beyond good and evil or, for that matter, beyond strength and weakness. His consciousness is neither happy nor unhappy, nor does he possess any power. He remains however a center of authority to the extent that

9. Jacques Derrida's "La mythologie blanche" (in *Marges de la philosophie* [Paris, 1972], 247–324) is the most powerful recent restatement of this assertion. Among the numerous antecedents that are both the target and the confirmation of Derrida's essay, Kant's remarks on rhetoric in a footnote to the *Third Critique* (*Kritik der Urteilskraft*, 217, note) is a typical example.

the very destructiveness of his ascetic reading testifies to the validity of his interpretation. The dialectical reversal that transfers the authority from experience into interpretation and transforms, by a hermeneutic process, the total insignificance, the nothingness of the self into a new center of meaning, is a very familiar gesture in contemporary thought, the ground of what is abusively called modernity. Thus in his book on interpretation Paul Ricoeur casts Freud into the role of the rhetorical undoer and the hermeneutic recoverer of the self. Freud has divested the self of any intuitive stability whatever: "all that Freud says [of the self] assumes the forgetting and the vacillation of the self.[10] Instead, the self is a mere factor operating among others in the system of quantitative forces and ratios that Freud's dynamic metaphors describe: ". . . never does the consciousness of the Ego appear in Freud's system in the capacity of an apodictic position, but only as an economic function."[11] However, at the moment that all seems lost, all is regained: "This realism [which replaces consciousness by an economy] is unintelligible if considered by itself; the abdication [*dessaisissement*] of consciousness would be properly speaking *senseless* [*insensé*, meaningless but also insane], if its only result were to alienate reflection into the consideration of a mere thing. This is what would happen if we omitted the complex ties that bind this topico-economic explanation to the effective labor of interpretation, which makes psychoanalysis into the decyphering [*décryptage*] of a hidden meaning into an apparent meaning."[12] The Freudian deconstruction is only a necessary prelude to a "recovery of meaning in interpretation"[13] and the subject is reborn in the guise of the interpreter: "Reality of the *it* [the nonsubjective id of the unconscious] because the *it* gives food for thought to the exegete" ("Réalité du ça en tant que le ça donne à penser à l'éxégète").[14]

The part here played by Freud (and we are not now concerned with the "validity" of this interpretation with regard to Freud) could equally be assigned to literary texts, since literature can be shown to accomplish in its terms a deconstruction that parallels the psychological deconstruction of selfhood in Freud. The intensity of the interplay between literary and psychoanalytical criticism is easy

10. Paul Ricoeur, *De l'interprétation, Essai sur Freud* (Paris, 1965), p. 416.
11. Ibid., p. 416.
12. Ibid., p. 416.
13. Ibid., p. 411.
14. Ibid., p. 425.

enough to understand in these terms. The same strategy occurs in certain philosophical texts or readings, for example in Heidegger, who also locates the deconstruction of the self as substance in a hermeneutic activity which, in its turn, becomes the ground of a recovery of selfhood as the springboard of futurity: "When fully conceived, the care-structure includes the phenomenon of Selfhood. This phenomenon is clarified by interpreting the meaning of care; and it is as care that Dasein's totality of being has been defined."[15] Our present concern is merely whether Rousseau, like Ricoeur's Freud, reclaims a measure of authority for the self, grounded in its ability to understand its own failure to make such a claim.

The consistency with which Rousseau dramatizes this very question in another Ovidian text staged, like *Narcisse*, for theatrical representation, illustrates the recurrent symbiosis of the problems of understanding with those of selfhood, a pattern that is obvious in the sparse philosophical references we have mentioned but that could be extended at almost infinite length. The "scène lyrique" *Pygmalion* (1762), in contrast to the Preface to *Narcisse* written with the anticipation of an extensive productive labor ahead, looks back upon a considerable body of literary achievement, including the invention, in the figures of Emile and Julie, of convincing fictional subjects. The situation of the scene, that of an author confronting his own finished work, corresponds to the actual predicament of Rousseau at that time, just as the position of *Pygmalion* within the Rousseau corpus marks the transition from theoretical and fictional to autobiographi-

---

15. *Sein und Zeit* (Tübingen, 1927), p. 323, quoted from *Being and Time*, translated by John Macquarrie and Edward Robinson (New York, 1962), p. 370. Heidegger is however a great deal subtler (or more devious) than Ricoeur in insisting, in reference to Kant, that "the subjectum is 'consciousness in itself,' not a representation but rather the 'form' of representation. That is to say, the 'I think' is not something represented but the formal structure of representing as such, and this formal structure alone makes it possible for anything to have been represented." (*Sein und Zeit*, 319; *Being and Time*, p. 367). The "formal structure of representation" (perhaps with the omission of "as such") is what we call rhetoric or, better, rhetoricity. Ricoeur, on the other hand, considers Freud's distinction between a drive [*Trieb*] and the representation of this drive as an unquestioned extension of a valid realism: "C'est parce que ce réalisme est un réalisme des "présentations" de pulsion, et non la pulsion elle-même, qu'il est aussi un réalisme du connaissable, et non de l'inconnaissable . . ." (Ricoeur, p. 422). The epistemological integrity of the rhetorical moment remains "inpensé" whereas, in Heidegger, far from being simply repressed, it accomplishes the much more redoubtable feat of becoming the "totality of Being."

cal works. The fact that the text, as we understand it, asserts in fact the impossibility of making these facile generic distinctions should caution one against following all too confidently the hints provided by the convenient evidence of chronology.

The lyrical scene, as Rousseau calls it, starts out as a confrontation between the artist and his creation and culminates in the highly dramatic moment when the statue of Galathea comes to life. This moment is preceded and also followed by a great deal of contradictory verbal agitation, by no means clear in its dramatic and semantic function with regard to the central event. No wonder that the brief text, despite its obvious dramatic shortcomings, has engendered a minor but distinguished tradition of misreading which includes Hamann, Schiller, and Goethe.[16]

The general movement of the text is one of constant vacillation, explicitly identified as such, since Pygmalion repeatedly rejects, in a sequence of dramatic reversals, the understanding he seems to have acquired of his situation. As was already the case in *Narcisse*, the possibility of interpretational error is thematized throughout the text. Consequently, none of the statements in Pygmalion's monologues can be taken at face value; they all function within a contextual movement that stands itself in need of interpretation but without which their validity in terms of truth and falsehood cannot even be considered. The provisional syntheses that are achieved along the way in the course of the action do not necessarily mark a progression and it is the burden of the reading to decide whether the text is the teleology of a selfhood that culminates in the climactic exclamation "Moi!" or a repetitive vacillation.

The encounter between author and work with which the play begins—as the parable of language began by the encounter between two men—occurs in a complex affective mood. In the scene from the *Essay*, the emotion was fear; in *Narcisse* it was love, complicated by its various self-reflective creases; in *Pygmalion*, it is a combination of both. The presence of love accounts for the choice of this particular myth, but the finished statue, considered in retrospect, also inspires fear: "I don't know what I feel in touching this veil; I am seized by terror [*frayeur*] . . ."[17]

16. See Hermann Schlüter, *Das Pygmalion-Symbol bei Rousseau, Hamann, Schiller* (Zürich, 1968) and his bibliography.

17. *Pygmalion*, texte établi et annoté par Jacques Scherer in J. J. Rousseau,

Fear in *Pygmalion* cannot simply be equated with the discrepancy between appearance and reality, outside and inside, that organized the scene from the *Essay*. The threat that occurs here is less obvious than that of physical assault. It is rather the paralysis that afflicts Pygmalion and that reduces him, at the onset of the action, to a state of dejection. Consequently, the metaphor that it generates will have to be further-reaching than the "giant" invented by primitive man. Pygmalion is paralyzed by the feeling of awe that is characteristic, to use Kantian terminology, of the sublime. The threatening power is not something exterior that one confronts directly in an unmediated encounter: it has instead been transferred, by an act of the mind (sometimes called imagination) into the constitution of an entity, a subject, capable of reflecting upon the threatening power because it partakes of that power without however coinciding with it.[18] Awe is not directed towards a natural object since it actively involves the self,[19] nor is it directed towards something that could conceivably coincide with the self (such as "man"), since such an equation would be merely evasive. Rousseau takes his metaphor from the myth in which the work of art is presented in the guise of a goddess: ". . . I feel as if I were touching the sanctuary of a goddess . . ." (1:1226). The awesome element in the work of art is that something so familiar and intimate could also be free to be so radically different. Unlike nature, where the difference is easily conceptualized into a dichotomy of subject and object, the work of art exists as a nondialectical configuration of sameness and otherness, sufficiently uncanny to be called godlike.

The goddess metaphor is an aptly monstrous concatenation of self and other. Galathea partakes of divinity not because of her objective beauty, the Pythagorean harmony of her proportions; the rich iconography of the topic is uniformly ludicrous or at best, as in the case of Falconnet, banal. In the Rousseau text, her beauty is noticeable only in the emotional gesticulation of her maker. Her godlike quality stems from the discrepancy between her specular nature, as an act of the self in which the self is bound to be reflected, and her

---

Oeuvres complètes, ed. Bernard Gagnebin and Marcel Raymond (Paris: Gallimard [Bibliothèque de la Pléiade], 1961), 1:1224–31.

18. Immanuel Kant, *Kritik der Urteilskraft* (Stuttgart, 1924), § 28, pp. 105 ff.

19. Kant, § 28 (105): "Thus, in our aesthetic judgment, nature is not considered to be sublime because it is awesome but because it awakens our power (which is not that of nature) in ourselves . . ."

formal nature which has to be free to differ from the self as radically as can be imagined. This discrepancy produces the system of antinomies that confront each other at the beginning of the play, evoked by such traditional polarities as hot and cold ("all my fire has been extinguished, my imagination is ice cold . . ."), art and nature (". . . masterpieces of nature that my art dared to imitate . . ."), man and god ("Pygmalion, make no more Gods: you are only a common artist . . ."). Those antinomies are not rooted in natural oppositions but are coordinated in terms of the relationship between self and other that engenders them. This is true even of the most natural and "material" polarity to appear in the text, that of hot and cold.

The statue is "cold," sheer marble not because it is made of stone, but because, from the very beginning, it reflects the figural coldness of Pygmalion's condition: "All my fire has been extinguished, my imagination is ice cold, the marble comes cold out of my hands . . ." 1:1224). The original, literal coldness of the marble had been turned into figural heat at the moment of invention, and this heat had in its turn fed the enthusiasm of Pygmalion as he engaged nature in the analogical process of imitation, in which the common properties of art and of nature, of "génie" and of "amour," are revealed and exchanged; nature can then be addressed as ". . . masterpieces that my art dared imitate, . . . beautiful models that *fired* me with the *ardor* of love and of genius . . ." (1:1225, my italics). But when the action starts, we are well beyond the illusion of this "beautiful" balance between self and other. The exchange breeds its own excess, engenders its own sublimity, as the illusory presence of the self gives the object quasi-divine powers which, in turn, reduce the subject to the awestruck bafflement of a will entirely alienated from its works. This kind of awe, frozen before its own sublimity, is again called cold (by inferential contrast to the "ardor" of the imitated models): ". . . masterpieces of nature that fired me with the ardor of love and genius, since I surpassed you, you leave me entirely indifferent." But this coldness has nothing in common with the coldness of the original stone; Bachelard's thermodynamics of the material imagination would find nothing to feed on in *Pygmalion*. "Hot" and "cold" are not, in this text, derived from material properties but from a transference from the figural to the literal that stems from the ambivalent relationship between the work as an extension of the self and as a quasi-divine otherness. This was implicity asserted as soon as Galathea is said to be godlike; from the moment the sublime is involved, nature recedes in the background and, as in Kant, a terminology of selfhood an self-consciousness takes over.[20]

The divinity also has to be a god*dess*, an object of erotic desire. Ambivalences of self and other are thematized in terms of "love" and Pygmalion's awe contains self-erotic as well as transcendental elements. Galathea turns into Venus and Pygmalion's erotic self-fascination is similar to Valère's in *Narcisse*: *je m'aime aimant* is echoed in Pygmalion's "je m'adore dans ce que j'ai fait . . ." ("I worship myself in what I have produced" [1:1226]). Except that the object of his love is not just any woman, not even an angelical one, but a goddess: the sublime dimension is the product of a self awed by the knowledge that he is the agent of his own production as radically other. If, in the passage from which this sentence is quoted, this self-idolatry ("je m'adore" instead of "je m'aime") is called *amour propre* ("je m'enivre d'amour propre" [1:1226]), it is only related by hyperbole to the mere vanity for which men of letters are so frequently being blamed in Rousseau's writings.[21] Pygmalion's fascination is of a different order and the social satisfactions of recognition no longer can touch him: ". . . praise and glory no longer elevate my soul; the appreciation of those who will be cherished by posterity no longer touches me; friendship even has lost its appeal for me" (1:1224–25). For the self-idolatry, considered from the perspective of the subject, is by no means a mere mystification: the inventive power of the self is truly uncanny in its escape from any willful control. There is no limit to the wealth of its discoveries and one must assume that, for the author of *Julie*, the surprises of self-reading are inexhaustible.

The ambivalence of this scene of reading (or writing) carries over into the structure of its representation. The scene is both static, with Pygmalion locked into the fascinated concentration on a single, perfect object at the exclusion of anything else, and animated by the restlessness of a desire that disrupts all tranquil contemplation.

20. Kant, § 28 (109): "Thus the sublime is not contrived in natural things but in our consciousness [*Gemüt*] . . ."

21. "Le goût des lettres . . . naît du désir de se distinguer . . . Tout homme qui s'occupe des talents agréables veut plaire, être admiré, et il veut être admiré plus qu'un autre. Les applaudissements publics appartiennent à lui seul: je dirais qu'il fait tout pour les obtenir, s'il ne faisait encore plus pour en priver ses concurrents . . ." (Préface de *Narcisse*, 2:965, 967–68).

Pygmalion's fetishism of selfhood, inherent in his vocation as "artist," is an unstable juxtaposition of plenitude and disruption. The predicament is represented in the absurd gesticulation of a man caught within the space that immediately surrounds the statue yet unable to remain within it: "Pygmalion . . . dreams in the attitude of a restless and sad man; then suddenly rises . . ."; "Pygmalion walks dreamily around for a while, . . . sits down and looks around him . . . then rises impetuously" (1:1224–25). The same tension is evoked less naïvely in the paradox of an excess that is also a lack, the supplementary structure that Derrida has so accurately described in Rousseau. The perfection (". . . never did anything so beautiful appear in nature; I have surpassed the handiwork of the Gods . . .") stems from an excess that sets the statue apart from the merely natural world; the excess in turn engenders a lack ("Ah! her only shortcoming is her perfection"—"c'est la perfection qui fait son défaut" [1:1227]), and there is no escape from the pressure of a differentiation that never allows for a totalizing integrity. The scene has to get in motion, and the initial polarities that had been frozen in static opposition have to enter into a play of substitutions and reversals. The lyricism of the opening monologue has to become dramatic, turn into the mixed genre of a "scène lyrique," the representation of a godlike self, Dionysus on the stage.

The text is dramatically structured as a dynamic system of excess and lack (défaut) metaphorically represented in a polarity of self and other that engenders, in its turn, a chain of (as)symetrical polarities: hot/cold, inside/outside, art/nature, life/death, male/female, heart/senses, hiding/revealing ("Et toi, sublime essence qui se cache aux sens, et se fait sentir aux coeurs . . ." [1:1228]), eye/ear (in the apparent progression of the text from *seeing* the statue to *hearing* it speak in its own voice), lyric/dramatic, etc. In a passage like the following, the antinomies achieve intense condensation: "All your fires are concentrated in my heart and the cold of death remains on the marble: I perish by the excess of life that [the statue] lacks . . . Yes, two beings are lacking from the plenitude of things . . ." (1:1228). Systems of this type would evolve harmoniously by means of exchanges of properties if they stand under the aegis of a totalizing principle (here called 'sublime essence," "soul of the universe," "principle of all existence," "sacred fire," etc.) that functions according to a balanced economy, the rich spontaneously giving to the poor because benevolent nature's law is that of a distributive justice: "the natural order has been upset, nature is out-raged; give back their strength to nature's laws, restore its benevolent flow and distribute your divine influence with equanimity . . ." (1:1228). At this point in the action, these statements are made by Pygmalion at the height of his self-mystification, in the tone of a prayer that receives a by-no-means unambiguous answer. What the passage proves is that Rousseau controls the rhetoric of totalization inherent in all supplementary systems, from its most naïve to its most devious forms. Unavoidably, these are precisely the statements that will be retained as the commonplaces that become the mainstay of traditional intellectual history: equally benevolent natural economies will soon inspire Rousseau's readers, such as Herder for example,[22] and it will be almost impossible to escape from their seduction. When this finally happens, it is equally predictable that the author blamed for the aberration which he identified only in order to denounce it, would precisely be Jean-Jacques Rousseau.

The processes of substitution at work in *Pygmalion* are not all as transparently wishful as in the passage that has just been quoted and that culminates in Pygmalion's pathos-filled apostrophe to Galathea (1:1228). The text achieves a higher degree of dialectical complexity. For example, the dialectics of desire are allowed to develop along consistent lines in the first part of the scene as they evolve from literal sexual aggression to the idea of the "beautiful soul" to the dialectics of the general and the particular and finally to the apotheosis of the self by its immolation to the work.

Goethe would have grievously misread *Pygmalion* if the com-plaint that Rousseau "wanted to destroy the highest that mind and deed can produce by the most common act of sensuous lust"[23] were to be taken seriously. Pygmalion's gesture of literal sexual aggression is comically transparent: "He takes his mallet and his chisel and hesitatingly ascends the steps leading to the statue. He seems afraid to touch it. Finally, with his tool already raised, he stops. 'Such trembling! How troubled I feel! I hold the chisel with faltering hand . . . I cannot . . . I dare not . . . I would spoil everything'"

22. In his *Abhandlung über den Ursprung der Sprache*, Herder refers to the "unifying laws of Nature's economy" [*die Verbindungsgesetze der haushaltenden Natur*]. The complications of Herder's own text remain to be analyzed, in themselves as well as in relation to Hamann's subsequent attack.

23. Goethe, *Dichtung und Wahrheit*, Part 3, Book 11, in *Goethes Werke*, Ham-burger edition, edited by Lieselotte Blumenthal (Hamburg, 1955) 9:489.

(1:1226). But sexual assault is by no means incompatible with the aesthetics of the sublime, and Goethe's polarity of high and low, of "the highest" opposed to "the most common," entirely misrepresents the significance of the scene. The aggression, reminiscent of Saint-Preux's fetishistic fantasies upon receiving Julie's portrait (*Julie*, 2:278–79), simply reaffirms the referential effectiveness of any metaphor. Love as aggression, Venus and Mars, is a necessary thematic projection of any pattern of metaphorical exchange, since the representation of copulation or of murder are the most effective emblems for the moment of literal significance that is part of any system of tropes. Desire is built into the system, the only problem being whether it can be fulfilled by an exchange that would put a stop to the endless chain of substitutions. The text of *Pygmalion* suggests a general version of such a closure and this part of the play is ordered as a dialectical progression. It starts in the inside/outside analogism of the "beautiful soul" ("How beautiful must be the soul to animate such a body!" [1:1227]) in which the intrinsic quality of the self is borrowed from the surface of its physical shape. The literal sexual aggression becomes the "symbolic" adoration of Galathea's soul, a displacement rather than an intensification of the initial error, since it was never suggested that the statue was a substitute for an actual person in the first place; Galathea's divine status is affirmed from the start and is constitutive for the text. Pygmalion's problem is not that a desire for a particular person is idealized and called divine but rather that the abstraction and the generality of a linguistic figure manifests itself necessarily in the most physical of modes. In moving from the delusion of unmediated possession to the delusion of a correspondence between body and soul, we have neither progressed nor regressed towards a further degree of truth or falsehood, but merely moved to another place within the structure.

Pygmalion discovers the metaphor of the beautiful soul to be as unsatisfactory as the referentiality of the body; rather than copulating with literal meaning, it is more akin to copulating with a stone: ". . . so it is because of this inanimate object that I am unable to leave this room! . . . a piece of marble! a stone! a shapeless and hard piece of matter, worked on with this iron tool! . . . Fool, come back to your senses, lament your fate, see your error . . . see your madness . . . But no . . ." (1:1227). By conceiving of the soul analogically, by way of its assumed resemblance to a material entity, one has in fact reduced it to being one more stone among stones. But this

moment of negative insight is at once reintegrated within the process, thus allowing for a "higher" couple of antinomies to come into
play: "No, I have not taken leave from my senses; no, I am not
delirious; no, I don't have to blame myself for anything. It is not this
death marble that I love, it is a living being that resembles it; I am
entranced by the shape [*figure*] that it presents to my eyes. In whatever place this adorable shape may be, whatever body may carry it,
whatever hand may fashion it, I have given it all my heart" (1:1227).
The synthesis now returns to the level of appearances ("la figure que
l'être vivant offre *à mes yeux*"), but it takes place between a particular being and the general principle of which this being is a representation. The inside/outside metaphor of the beautiful soul is replaced by a synthesis of the particular and the general reminiscent of
what neoclassical writers refer to as "general beauty." This aesthetic
"generality" does not correspond to what Rousseau had earlier called
the "*general* will" in his political writings and especially in the *Social
Contract*;[24] here, the term "general" (which does not appear in the
text) designates a synecdochal metaphor in which the whole has
priority over the part. The *general* model is not a combination of
miscellaneous particular traits (as if Galathea were an amalgama-
tion of the various individual women that animated Rousseau's erotic
rêveries), but the attraction of the individual stems from its resemblance to a prior general model that is, in fact, an emanation of
the self. Only individuals who partake of that general principle can
be beautiful and desirable. Aesthetic generality is the precondition
for resemblance which also means that it is constitutive of metaphor.
One is reminded of Frontin's statement in *Narcisse*: "il est devenu
amoureux de sa ressemblance" (1:1006). The "progression" from the
literal to the general remains within the tropological pattern of substitution that makes *Pygmalion* into an allegory of figuration. The
various steps in this progression do not simply cancel each other out;
they are "aufgehoben," surpassed but maintained ("No, I don't have
to blame myself for anything," says Narcisse, in a statement that
nothing in the text disproves), which does not mean that they are
allowed to reach their teleological closure.

The synthesis of the general and the particular is clear enough
as long as it involves *another* rather than the self. "Je suis épris d'un
être vivant qui lui ressemble" is entirely understandable as long as

24. On "general" in the *Social Contract*, see pp. 247–49.

the "lui" refers to another, in this case feminine, identity. But if, as in *Narcisse*, the situation is rather "Je suis épris d'un être vivant qui *me* ressemble," then the crossing of generality and particularity with the categories of self and other engenders the disorder heard in Pygmalion's "passionate," "transported" speech. The ambivalence of self and other is actively at play in the mode of the sublime and the claim to generality has to extend to the self as well. This implies that the "general" shape of Galathea's statue *is* the self in a radical sense. The work no longer originates in the particular will that shaped it, but it is the work that causes the self to exist as its own source and *telos*: "What lines of fire seem to emanate from this object in order to enflame my senses and return with my soul to their source" (1:1228). The work alone is now the source of light and life, both mirror and lamp. The work reads the man and reveals his total insignificance except in his relation to the work. This apparent immolation of the self ("Ah! let Pygmalion die in order to relive in Galathea!" [1:1228]; ". . . I have given you all my being; henceforth I shall live only through you" [1:1232]) is in fact its glorification, for at its cost and only at this cost can the work be called a source and made the center of all life, the "holy fire" in which only Sages can dance. Poetry draws its most effective seductions from this temptation, from Blake's myth of the Book of Fire "displaying the infinite which was hid . . . by printing in the infernal method, by corrosives" made of "flaming fire, raging around and melting the metals into living fluids" to be "received by Men . . . and [to take] the forms of books to be arranged in libraries."[25]

Pygmalion, as a character, swerves away from this temptation as soon as it has been explicitly stated and revealed. In the central articulation that sets the dramatic pattern for the text, when the totalizing identification is about to occur, the exchange between self and other that was to abolish all polarities does not take place or, perhaps more accurately, leaves a surplus (or a deficiency) that prevents the narration from closing: "Ah! let Pygmalion die in order to relive in Galathea! . . . Heavens! What am I saying! If I were she, I would not see her, I would not be the one who loves her. No, let my Galathea live, and let me not be she. Ah! Let me always be another so that I may always wish to be she, to see her, to love her, to be loved

25. William Blake, *The Marriage of Heaven and Hell*, in *The Poetical Works of William Blake* (London, 1913), p. 255.

by her . . ." (1:1228). As a mere reassertion of "pieuse distance" the
passage (except for the high degree of pronominal condensation)
says nothing that was not already stated in Narcisse's fascination
with the portrait. But the location of the statement within the play,
after the systematic development leading from the literal to the
analogical to the general has been allowed to unfold, gives it added
significance. The totalizing symmetry of the substitutive pattern is
thrown out of balance: instead of merging into a higher, general Self,
two selves remain confronted in a paralyzing inequality. The
categories that are thus being challenged are precisely those of self
and other, the ground of the system. If these polarities have only been
posited in order to eliminate their opposition, then the failure of the
synthesis, the persistence of their antagonism, reveals the fallacy of
their position. And there can be no doubt about their continued
confrontation, in endless repetition, in the apparent conclusion of the
text. The final exchange between Galathea and Pygmalion reiterates
the situation that existed in the central passage when Pygmalion
withdraws from ultimate identification with the most generalized
form of selfhood. If Galathea's coming alive (a moment that remains
to be accounted for) confirms this interpretation, then the play
could, in principle, have come to a stop in the identifying echo of the
two "moi's" uttered by the protagonists: "*Galathea* (touches herself
and says): Moi. *Pygmalion* (transported): Moi!" (1:1230). The
supplementary exclamation mark records the imbalance acted out
in the final exchanges. Galathea setting herself apart from the material stone ("*Galathea* takes a few steps and touches a marble stone: It
is no longer I") is clear to the point of redundancy, but her statement
after touching Pygmalion is as ambiguous as Alkmene's famous
"Ach!" at the end of Kleist's play *Amphitryon:* "Galathea goes in his
direction and looks at him. He rises precipitously, stretches out his
arms toward her and looks at her ecstatically. She touches him with
one of her hands: he trembles, takes her hand, presses it against his
heart, then covers it with kisses. *Galathea* (with a sigh): Ah! encore
moi" (1:1230–31). The tone is hardly one of ecstatic union, rather of
resigned tolerance towards an overassiduous admirer. Since
Galathea is the Self as such, she has to contain all particular selves
including Pygmalion; as a statement of identity in which "encore
moi" means "aussi moi" ("me as well"), it is a true enough affirmation. This is certainly how Pygmalion understands it; it provokes in
him the same language of self-immolation that was checked earlier:

"*Pygmalion*: . . . It is you, you alone: I have given you my entire being; henceforth I shall live only through you." But the line "Ah! encore moi" spoken with a sigh that suggests disappointment rather than satisfaction can also mean "de nouveau moi" ("me again"), a persisting, repeated distinction between the general Self and the self as other. Indeed, the separation between Galathea's coldness and Pygmalion's impetuousness could not be greater, all the more so since appearances to the contrary nothing has happened that would diminish the validity of the earlier moment of withdrawal before self-destruction and prevent its repetition. It is true that by now the statue has come alive, but the text is pointedly set up in such a way that the epiphany does *not* occur as a reward for the sacrificial self-transcendence but only after the hope for the success of such an economy of all or nothing has been abandoned: "*Pygmalion*: . . . Alas! In the condition I'm in, one invokes all and nothing hears us. The hope that misleads us is more senseless than desire" (1:1224). When Pygmalion returns to a rhetoric of self-annihilation in the final lines, one can assume from the preceding movement of the text that he has again been led astray by a hope now known to be unfounded. Rousseau and his reader, together with Galathea, can now part company from the character Pygmalion (which was not the case earlier at the moment when Pygmalion reaffirmed his distance) and notice that the concluding scene is not in fact a conclusion but one more vacillation in a sequence of reversals, none of which have the power to close off the text.

The separation of the group work-author-reader from the consciousness of the protagonist indicates that we are no longer within a thematic context dominated by selfhood but in a figural representation of a structure of tropes. The coming to life of the statue does not occur in response to the most advanced stage in the dialectic of the general and the particular, in the self-sacrificing negation of the subject. It takes place after the "cold" mood which sees through this strategy has been allowed to assert itself. That this radical negation of the self is in fact its recuperation is evident from its text-producing power: even in this brief play, it engenders most of the "heat" that keeps the language alive and allows for the coinage of the paradoxes based on binary oppositions. The language of pathos is infinitely eloquent. However, the structure of priority represented in the time-sequence of the dramatic action indicates that the moment at which Galathea finally consents to borrow from Pygmalion the excess that she lacks, she feeds upon colder fires than those burning at sacrificial altars. The energy that succeeds at last in forcing the exchange is the deconstructive discourse of truth and falsehood that undoes selfhood as tragic metaphor and replaces it by the knowledge of its figural and epistemologically unreliable structure. When Galathea comes alive, Pygmalion is no longer a tragic figure but, like Ricoeur's Freud, a deconstructive interpretative process (a reading) that can no longer tolerate the pathos of the self. Galathea's coming alive rewards the access to this advanced level of understanding. The point of the text however is that even this mode of discourse fails to achieve a concluding exchange that would resolve the tension of the original dejection. The part of the action that follows Galathea's epiphany disrupts the dialectical progression that leads up to it and merely repeats its aberrant pattern. The discourse by which the figural structure of the self is asserted fails to escape from the categories it claims to deconstruct, and this remains true, of course, of any discourse which pretends to re-inscribe in its turn the figure of this aporia. There can be no escape from the dialectical movement that produces the text.

Narcisse revealed the figural structure of selfhood as it operates in the relationship between subjects. *Pygmalion*, on the other hand, represents the more complex relationship between selfhood as metaphor and the representation of this metaphor, the "formal structure," in Heidegger's words, "of representing" which is also the main concern of Kant's critique of judgment as aesthetic judgment. On this level of rhetorical awareness, the previous metaphors such as "giant" and "portrait" have been extended to become the most general, all-inclusive concept of selfhood conceivable: what remains after any "self"-interested motions of selfhood, even at their most sublime or their most rigorous have been negated. Rousseau's refusal to grant authority to even this level of discourse, despite the fact that the dialectical development that leads up to it is controlled at all its stages, indicates the impossibility of replacing the epistemology of figural language by that of the self. From the point of view of truth and falsehood, the self is not a privileged metaphor in Rousseau. This obviously has consequences for the way in which his autobiographical texts, from the *Letters to Malesherbe* to the *Rêveries*, would have to be read.[26]

26. An attempt in this direction is made in the last chapter on "Excuses."

9   **Allegory**

(Julie)

IF THE SELF IS NOT, IN PRINCIPLE, A PRIVILEGED CATE-
gory, the sequel to any theory of metaphor will be a theory of narrative centered on the question of referential meaning and not merely
on the pronominal substitutions that organized such texts as *Narcisse* and *Pygmalion*. Texts will of course always contain substitutions
of this type but they will not necessarily determine the main narrative articulations. Rousseau's most extensive narrative fiction, the
novel *Julie ou la Nouvelle Héloïse,* contains elaborate substitutive patterns involving the polarities of self and other; if this were not the
case, "love" would not be the prominent thematic element that it
obviously still is in *Julie.* But the very clearly marked division of the
novel in two parts can no longer be interpreted in terms of this
model. What is involved in this division determines one's understanding of the text as a whole and requires a further elaboration of the
general theory of figuration established in the *Second Discourse.*

For it is clear that the problematics of figural language have not
run their full course in such texts as the *Second Discourse,* anthropological fictions that carry out the deconstruction of conceptual
language. A narrative like *Julie* cannot be reduced to parables of
denomination. If the thematic prevalences are any indication (something which can only be postulated heuristically for the sake of exposition), then the major difference between *Julie* and the *Discourse* is
the presence, in the former text, of a strongly marked ethical dimension in the foreground of the action. Just as, in the *Second Discourse,*
the burden of the interpretation consisted of finding the passage
from the linguistic structure to the political assertion, the challenge,
in the reading of *Julie*, is the articulation of the figural mode with the
ethical tonality.

Much has gone astray in the critical reading of *Julie*[1] because not

---

1. All references to *Julie ou la Nouvelle Héloïse* are to J. J. Rousseau, *Oeuvres
complètes,* edited by Bernard Gagnebin and Marcel Raymond (Paris: Gallimard [Bib-

even the generalized notion of selfhood, let alone the linguistic problem of referentiality, has been recognized. I am not only thinking of
the literalism that debates the priorities between the assumedly
"real" correspondence between Mme d'Houdetot and Rousseau and
the fictional correspondence between Julie and Saint-Preux, or that
speculates and passes judgment on the psychological verisimilitude
of the *ménage à trois* at Clarens. All this is a little like speculating
whether Fichte's absolute Self rides on horseback or stands on a
mountain top, or whether Kant's schemata have blue or brown eyes.
The more Rousseau tried to avoid particularization, for example by
reducing distinctive physical traits to the minimum need for allegorical signification[2] or by making the epistolary style almost intolerably
uniform,[3] the more readers have felt compelled to fill the space thus
allotted to their fantasy with trivia.[4] The fallacy of realistic fiction
seems to have blinded us to the figural abstraction invited by the
neo-medieval title, although it should be obvious in a work in which
"characters" have little more human individuality than the theological virtues, the five senses, or the parts of the body.

But even on a much more refined level of critical awareness,
when *Julie* is read as a novel of inward self-reflection that might
anticipate *Adolphe,* say, or *Oberman,* or even some aspects of
Baudelaire or of Proust, we are still coping with a contingent and
basically irrelevant misreading. For one thing, such a reading keeps
considering *Julie*, if it considers it at all, as if it would have preferred
it to be the *Confessions* or the *Rêveries* rather than what it is. "It is
truly regrettable," writes Bernard Guyon, the latest editor of the
Nouvelle Héloïse, "that in his dialogue-preface and even in his report

---

liothèque de la Pléiade], 1961), vol. 2, text established and annotated by Bernard
Guyon. Guyon's notes bring the earlier critical editions of the *Nouvelle Héloïse*
(including Daniel Mornet's edition of 1925) up to date.

2. See Roger Kempf, *Sur le corps romanesque* (Paris, 1968), pp. 49–65.

3. Diderot's characterization of the epistolary style of Richardson would certainly not apply to *Julie:* "Un homme qui a du goût ne prendra point les lettres de
Mme Norton pour la lettre d'une des tantes de Clarisse, la lettre d'une tante pour
celle d'une autre tante ou de Mme Howe . . . Dans ce livre immortel, comme dans la
nature au printemps, on ne trouve point deux feuilles qui soient d'un même vert.
Quelle immense variété de nuances!" (Eloge de Richardson, in Denis Diderot, *Oeuvres
complètes,* chronological edition with introduction by Roger Lewinter [Paris, 1970],
5:136).

4. Bernard Guyon thinks that the deepest source of *Julie* is the "démon du
midi" of a man who has passed the age of forty (Introduction, 2:xxvi–xxvii).

on the novel in the *Confessions* [Rousseau] has put such stress on the differences that separate the two first parts from the rest of his novel . . ." (2:xlii). Something of this "il est vraiment regrettable . . ." lingers on in much less naïvely reductive readers, who still would have wished the book to be somehow different. The critics most astutely responsive to the seduction of Rousseau's reflective inwardness, Marcel Raymond and Georges Poulet,[5] have little or nothing to say about *Julie* and have to emphasize passages from the *Rêveries* at the near total expense of the rest of the work. This could, of course, be entirely legitimate and it is in accordance, moreover, with the impact of Rousseau on a literary lineage that includes prestigious names: Marcel Raymond mentions Maine de Biran, Senancour, Chateaubriand, Nodier, Nerval, Maurice de Guérin, Amiel, Baudelaire, Rimbaud, and also Gide, Proust, and Ramuz;[6] speaking of "la conscience de soi comme hantise" he refers to a tradition beginning "more precisely with Rousseau" which includes "within Romanticism, symbolism, and existentialism, Baudelaire, Amiel, Kierkegaard, Nietzsche, Mallarmé, Valéry, Kafka."[7] The historical investment in this interpretation of Rousseau is considerable, and one of the more intriguing possibilities inherent in a rereading of *Julie* is a parallel rereading of texts assumed to belong to the genealogical line that is said to start with Rousseau. The existence of historical "lines" may well be the first casualty of such a reading, which goes a long way in explaining why it is being resisted.

Serious attempts to come to terms with the structure and diction of *Julie* have always tended towards a bi-polar, pseudo-dialectical reading, the main issue being the definition of the poles that set up the tension of the textual field. Schiller referred to them as sensitivity [*Empfindung*] and intellect [*Denkkraft*] or, in terms of genre (implicitly) as idyll and elegy,[8] a more productive opposition since it is based, in his terminology, on the absence or the presence of

5. Marcel Raymond, *Jean-Jacques Rousseau, La quête de soi et la rêverie* (Paris, 1962). Numerous references to Rousseau are scattered throughout the writings of Georges Poulet; see more specifically the chapters on Rousseau in *Etudes sur le temps humain* (Paris, 1949) and in *Les métamorphoses du cercle* (Paris, 1961).

6. Raymond, *Jean-Jacques Rousseau, La quête de soi et la rêverie*, p. 154.

7. Ibid., p. 193.

8. Friedrich Schiller, *Über naïve und sentimentalische Dichtung*, in *Schillers Werke*, Nationalausgabe edited by Benno von Wiese and Helmut Koopman (Weimar, 1962), 20:451.

a referential moment.[9] Dialectizing Marcel Raymond, Starobinski reads the novel as a tension between immediacy (transparence) and mediation (obstacle). But whatever name is given to the polarities, it is generally admitted that the dialectical progression fails. The tension between immediacy and mediation allows the coordination of the experience of nature with that of an individual consciousness that overcomes its alienation by an act of love: "la transparence des coeurs restitue à la nature l'éclat et l'intensité qu'elle avait perdus" ("the transparency of the heart restores to nature the brightness and intensity that it had lost").[10] It also makes it possible to pass from individual passions such as love, to the collective and social dimensions of the state. Here difficulties begin to arise, for the political and economic theory of Clarens proves to be something of an embarrassment to anyone who attributes to Rousseau the belief that a political order is conceivable only if it allows for an unmediated presence of consciousness to itself. Some assimilate the political model of Clarens to a utopia[11] or denounce it as mere totalitarianism;[12] others, like Starobinski, try valiantly to rescue what can be rescued, but are forced to conclude that "Jean-Jacques appears to us as a restless soul that falls prey to the power of ambivalences, and not as a thinker who posits thesis and antithesis."[13] The ambivalence is at its most evident in the passage from political to religious language, in the final conflict between Julie's faith and Wolmar's atheism, which appears to be a gesture of evasion before the unresolved contradictions of the political world: "To the earthly well-being that could have been a 'reasonable' ending of the *Nouvelle Héloïse*, Rousseau opposes an alternate conclusion that is religious in nature."[14] Within this religious consciousness, the same incapacity to reach a genuine synthesis persists: on the one hand, like the Vicaire Savoyard (read superficially), Julie seems to advocate a theophany, a natural religion; on the other hand, an unmediated encounter with God is still being promised in a realm that lies beyond death: "following the laws of an almost Manichean dualism that radically sepa-

9. Ibid., 20:448–49 and note.

10. Starobinski, *Jean-Jacques Rousseau, La transparence et l'obstacle*, p. 105.

11. For example, Judith N. Shklar, *Men and Citizens, A Study of Rousseau's Social Theory* (London, 1969).

12. For example, Lester Crocker, *J. J. Rousseau* (New York, 1968).

13. Starobinski, *Jean-Jacques Rousseau, La transparence et l'obstacle*, p. 142.

14. Ibid., p. 140.

rates spirit from matter, death causes the abolition of all obstacles, the disappearance of all mediations."[15] The dialectics of love and of politics are finally superseded by a religious experience that is no longer dialectical in any sense and that simply obliterates the entire experience that precedes it: "Rousseau . . . ends his novel in a manner equivalent to a choice. Between the absolute imperative of the community and that of personal salvation, he has chosen the latter. Julie's death signifies this choice."[16] The literary consequence of this decision takes the form of a return to a confessional, Augustinian mode. In this reading too *Julie* ultimately appears as only a momentary aberration left far behind by a spiritual experience that transcends it. Or, if one asserts that Rousseau always remained tempted by the ethics of political reform and by the seductions of the novel, then he failed to make up his mind although he was able to articulate clearly the necessity for the choice. Perhaps the failure of the dialectic is not the failure of *Julie* but the unavoidable consequence of positing an antithetical model where none exists. Which compels us, however, to discover relationships which, in Wordsworth's terms, would have "another and a finer connection than that of contrast."[17]

In the very passage in which Julie speaks of an encounter with God, the encounter is not described as a transparency but by means of a metaphor, the curiously unreadable metaphor of reading which one never seems to want to read. The communication does not occur in the form of a perception ("The eternal Being . . . speaks neither to the eyes nor to the ears, but to the heart"), but the contact which can be called unmediated because it does not involve a sense perception occurs as a "reading": it is "an unmediated communication, similar to the one by which God *reads* our thoughts already in this life, and by which we will, in turn, *read* his thoughts in the afterlife, since we will see him face to face" (2:728 my italics). A note draws further attention to the verb "to read": "This seems to be very well put. For what does it mean to see God but to read in the supreme intellect?"[18]

15. Ibid., p. 145.
16. Ibid., p. 145.
17. William Wordsworth, "Essay upon Epitaphs," in *The Prose Works of William Wordsworth*, ed. W. J. B. Owen and Jane Worthington Smyser (Oxford, 1974), 2:53.
18. A further gloss appears a few paragraphs later in the same letter: Julie speculates as to whether or not she will "see" after death those who were dear to her on earth and Rousseau comments: "Il est aisé de comprendre que par le mot *voir* elle

The action which Starobinski rightly considers as the crux of the entire text (although Julie seems to speak of it with less solemnity than the commentator)[19] is represented by Rousseau as the act of reading. All the thematic problems of the work, the relationship between love, ethics, political society, religious experience, and their respective hierarchies, depend on the understanding of a term of which the meaning, for Rousseau, is by no means transparent. What does the *Nouvelle Héloïse* have to tell us about the problematics of reading?

People read a lot in this book, for there can be no better way to thematize the ever-present necessity of reading than the epistolary novel. Unlike Laclos's letters in the *Liaisons dangereuses*, which are as directly effective as bullets, the letters of the *Nouvelle Héloïse* rarely set out to accomplish anything specific beyond their own reading; apparent deviations from this norm would turn out, at more careful consideration, to be hardly exceptions at all.[20] Rousseau's text does

---

entend un pur acte de l'entendement, semblable à celui par lequel Dieu nous voit et par lequel nous verrons Dieu." The rational act of understanding (*entendement* or *Vernunft*) here called "voir" is conceived as "lire."

19. "Au reste, ajouta-t-elle en regardant le ministre d'un air assez gai, si je ne me trompe, un jour ou deux d'erreur seront bientôt passés. Dans peu j'en saurai là-dessus plus que vous-même." (2:729) or, with reference to the possible immortality of the soul: "C'est une folie, soit, mais elle est douce . . ." (2:695, note c).

20. It is obvious that the narrative does not exploit various possibilities that would equate the letters with acts rather than with meditations or discourses. There is, for example little fetishism in which the letters act as a mere substitute for the body of the beloved; in fetishistic scenes, the object is Julie's painted portrait or her house, not her letters. The facticity of the letters, when it is referred to, is not as a substitutive presence, but in a curiously literal way, as when a note is added about the frequency of mail deliveries (2:71). The discursive letters (from the Valais, from Paris, on music, etc.) are judged by Julie to be inopportune rather than seductive, and quite superfluous from the point of view of fostering the practical affairs of the two lovers. When a fetishistic substitution occurs ("Baise cette lettre et saute de joie pour la nouvelle que je vais t'apprendre . . ." [2:111]), it is precisely when something more tangible than a letter is being promised and very practical arrangements are being made. A highly dramatic exception seems to be letter 25, Part I, in which Saint-Preux threatens to kill himself ("La roche est escarpée, l'eau est profonde et je suis au désespoir . . ." [2:93]). This appears to lead to Julie's surrender and to make the letter into an effective act of seduction. But the immediacy of this cause and effect relationship is more illusory than actual. Other élements intervene and more time elapses. The point is that Julie gives in to pity rather than to the direct expression of desire and Letter 25 can be considered as part of a development on the theme of pity rather than as a seductive strategy. One could say, of course, that Julie's

not exploit the narrative possibilities of the letters as "actants," as direct plot-agents. They rather appear to be reflective and retrospective musings, interpretations of events rather than being themselves the events. This is, in part, why the novel has little difficulty in representing the facticity of reading but faces some awkward moments when it comes to writing.[21] Hence also the Ciceronian, declamatory style destined to be read aloud and heard rather than visualized—probably the main obstacle to the enjoyment of the novel by the contemporary reader. Not that the act of reading is innocent, far from it. It is the starting point of all evil. "The woman who, in spite of the title, will dare to read one single page, is a lost woman . . ." (2:6), is a sentiment echoed by Julie as the reader of Saint-Preux's letters: ". . . you wrote. Instead of throwing your first letter into the fire or taking it to my mother, I dared to open it. This was my crime and all the rest followed. I tried to force myself not to answer these nefarious letters which I could not prevent myself from reading" (2:342).

The evil of the letters can be too easily attributed to their literary mediation, to the desire they convey in the guise of fictions. As we know from the *Essay*, Rousseau claims that seduction could be much more effectively performed by mimicry and by gesture than by writing; part of the realistic oddity, bordering on the ludicrous, of the novel is that the letters are so didactic in tone, and the distance between Saint-Preux and Valmont so hard to bridge. The entire reception of *Julie* goes in a different direction, but Laclos's, Hazlitt's, or Stendhal's use of the novel almost parodies the obvious misreading predicted by Rousseau. The letters are no invitation to a shared erotic or passionate experience and to read *la Nouvelle Héloïse* the way Paolo and Francesca read Lancelot only results in its dismissal as a bourgeois version of the Tristan myth.[22] Despite the chivalric connotations of his name, Saint-Preux's literary archetype is closer to Abélard than to Lancelot or to Tristan. What Julie and Saint-Preux

---

invitation to Saint-Preux, in Letter 4 of Part IV, to join her and Wolmar at Clarens is a direct action, but this is certainly rather a mechanical need of the plot and the letter consists of only two and a half lines.

21. As in letter 15, Part I (2:147), when Saint-Preux is about to enter Julie's bedroom and interrupts his exalted anticipations with the remark "Quel bonheur d'avoir trouvé de l'encre et du papier!"

22. Denis de Rougemont, *L'amour et l'occident* (Paris, 1939).

will read together is austere fare, and it includes "neither poets, nor love stories, contrary to the usual readings destined to [Julie's] sex" (2:61).[23] Their relationship is not primarily characterized as a desire mediated by literary substitutes; there is little reason not to take Rousseau at his word when he has Saint-Preux say "What would we learn about love in books? Ah, Julie, our heart has more to tell us than they can, and the imitated language of books is cold for anyone who is himself passionate" (2:61). The temptations emanating from literary inscriptions, as in the lines from Petrarch and Tasso which Saint-Preux engraved on the rocks at Meillerie (2:519) are genuine dangers and the text tries, at the risk of heroic boredom, to avoid having a similar effect. The abundant presence of literary antecedents much in evidence throughout the novel, in direct quotation as well as by allusion, are never merely a quixotic mystification that would imply a simple displacement of a desire upon a text. When such patterns occur, they are only a minor version of a more inclusive structure. Intertextuality in *la Nouvelle Héloïse* is more than just "literary" in its complications. The danger of reading is a far-reaching and invidious threat that no conversion, however radical, could ever hope to remove.

The best place in the text of *Julie* to enrich one's understanding of "reading" is without doubt the second Preface, sometimes referred to as "Dialogue on the novel" and staging a confrontation between author and reader in the conventional form of an apologia (2:12–30). Despite its largely traditional terminology, this brief text has little in common with the habitual eighteenth-century discussions of the relative merits of fiction as compared to history.[24] It therefore demands

23. It is true that the list contains Petrarch, Tasso, Metastasis, and the French tragedians. Rousseau considers Petrarch and the Italian poets in the wake of the Augustinian rather than the chivalric tradition. In the case of Racine, one may assume that he is thinking of Esther rather than of Phèdre. The ambivalence of the literary valorizations is part of the wider ambivalence of all systems grounded in metaphor.

24. See Werner Kraus. "Zur Französischen Romantheorie des 18. Jahrhunderts" in *Nachahmung und Illusion*, Poetik und Hermeneutik I, H. R. Jauss, ed. (Munich, 1964), for a brief bibliography of the question. Some of the quotations from lesser known authors are very close to the distinction from which Rousseau starts out. In the same volume, the discussion of Kraus's paper is informative. There would, of course, be numerous English examples, perhaps well summarized in the opening chapter of Book III of Fielding's *Joseph Andrews* ("Matter prefatory in praise of biography").

a reading in its own right, much as *Julie* itself fails to conform to the norms and conventions of eighteenth-century fiction.

The central question around which the imaginary debate of the preface circles is not that of verisimilitude (granted by both interlocutors to be nonexistent in *Julie*, in realistic detail as well as in the general conception), but that of the text's referential status. Does the model for the main characters in the narrative exist outside the language of fiction or not? "Is this correspondence real or is it a fiction?" The device (presenting a fiction as if it were a history) is common enough and coincides with the emergence of the novel as a separate genre, yet Rousseau's treatment of it goes a long way in explaining its almost obsessional recurrence in the history of the novel.[25]

The dialogue starts out from what appears to be a classical antithesis: a narrative text can be either the "portrait" of an extra-textual, particular referent, or a "tableau." The "tableau" does not have a specific referent and is therefore a fiction ("tableau d'imagination," [2:9]). Common sense tells us that *Julie* is a tableau and Rousseau states as much, in no uncertain terms, in the actual, first Preface.[26] It may, of course, be a displaced portrait transferred into a fiction, but this, for the moment, is not the issue. We were never supposed to take literally the assertion of the title page that the letters of the two lovers, "inhabitants of a little town at the foothills of the Alps," have been "collected and published" (and not written) by J. J. Rousseau. This does not mean however that the reverse of this proposition, namely that Rousseau is the *author* of these letters in the full sense of the term, is simply true without any reservations. All assertions to the contrary, a "question" seems to remain and to demand exploration, as if the either/or choice between "portrait" and "tableau" were perhaps not as mutually exclusive as might seem to be the case.

If *Julie* is not simply a "portrait," a mimesis of an action or a

25. The closest antecedent for *Julie* is, of course, Richardson's *Clarissa*, but Rousseau refers most frequently to Montesquieu's *le Temple de Gnide*, which is mentioned at least once in *La nouvelle Héloïse* (2:113) and reappears in the *Fourth Rêverie*.

26. As distinguished from the Preface dialoguée. "Quant à la vérité des faits, je déclare qu'ayant été plusieurs fois dans le pays des deux amants, je n'y ai jamais ouï parler du Baron d'Etange ni de sa fille, ni de M. d'Orbe, ni de Milord Edward Bomston, ni de M. de Wolmar" (2:5).

person, what then does it mean for a text to be a tableau, a fiction? For the enlightened reader that N. seems to be (call him Marmontel or almost any writer on fiction at the time) the way back to referentiality and to meaning or truth is easy enough: fiction and the truth are reconciled through the concept of man as universal: "every human figure must possess the common traits shared by all men, otherwise the fiction [tableau] is worthless"; ". . . in the fictions [tableaux] of humanity everyone must be able to recognize Man" (2:12). That the idea of man as a well-established, stable concept has to be rejected by Rousseau is predictable enough, since the *Second Discourse* and the *Essay* chose the very word "man" as the target of their epistemological critique of concepts in general. Behind the reassuring term lurks an unknown, unpredictable, and unreliable monster or "giant." N.'s protestations bring the inferences of Rousseau's anthropology into the open: ". . . [in the absence of the universal] unheard of monsters, giants, pygmees, chimeras of all sorts, anything could specifically be admitted within nature: everything would be disfigured, we would no longer have a common model . . ." (2:21). Without taking away the terror, the same feeling of unpredictability can just as well be phrased in positive terms, as an assertion of freedom, of infinite possibilities and renewals, as in the quotation from the *Social Contract* that Hölderlin was to single out as a motto for his early "Hymn to Humanity": "The limits of the possible in spiritual matters are less narrow than we assume. Our weaknesses, our vices, our prejudices are the cause of our confinement. Lowly souls fail to believe in great men; vile slaves smile scornfully at the mention of the word freedom." (3:425). The same positive tone can be heard in the Second Preface: "Who would dare to assign precise limits to nature and assert: This is how far man can go, and not further?" (2:20), or, in the reversed value-pattern but still within the same metaphor: "O Philosophy! How you take pains to make hearts narrow and man small!" (2:28).

The pathos of these statements, regardless of whether they are expressions of terror or assertions of prophetic exaltation, stems from the referential indeterminacy of the metaphor "man." The anthropological "tableau" is indeed a fiction, bewildered by its own suspended meaning. It depicts human passions (fear, pity, love, freedom) but these passions all have, by definition, the self-deceiving structure, familiar to us from the *Second Discourse*, that forces the narrative of their deconstruction to unfold. In the case of *Julie*, the passion happens to be love, the traditional topic of romance, but one could just as well imagine novels of pure fear or, like Proust's, of pure suspicion. On the thematic level, it is not the prevalence of love rather than fear that sets apart *Julie* from the *Discourse*, since the determining structure is that of passion which both have in common.

Like "man," "love" is a figure that disfigures, a metaphor that confers the illusion of proper meaning to a suspended, open semantic structure. In the naïvely referential language of the affections, this makes love into the forever-repeated chimera, the monster of its own aberration, always oriented toward the future of its repetition, since the undoing of the illusion only sharpens the uncertainty that created the illusion in the first place. In this same affective language, the referential error is called desire, and the voice of this desire can be heard throughout Rousseau's writings: "Such is the nothingness of my chimeras that, if all my dreams had turned into realities, I would still remain unsatisfied. I would have kept on dreaming, imagining, desiring. I found in myself an unexplainable void that nothing could have filled, a longing of the heart towards another degree of fulfillment of which I could not conceive but of which I nevertheless felt the attraction" (*Letter to Malesherbes, Oeuvres complètes*, 1:1140). The Second Preface says the same thing in slightly more technical terms by establishing the link with figural diction: "Love is a mere illusion: it fashions, so to speak, another Universe for itself; it surrounds itself with objects that do not exist or that have received their being from love alone; and since it states all its feelings by means of images, its language is always figural" (2:46).

However evanescent the referent of the passion may have become ("le néant de mes chimères," "le néant des choses humaines" *Julie*, 2:693), it is clear that once the figurality of the language of passion has been established ("son langage est *toujours* figuré") we return in fact to a referential model. The unproblematic figurality of the metaphor restores its proper meaning, albeit in the form of a negating power that prevents any specific meaning from coming into being. The very pathos of the desire (regardless of whether it is valorized positively or negatively) indicates that the presence of desire replaces the absence of identity and that, the more the text denies the actual existence of a referent, real or ideal, and the more fantastically fictional it becomes, the more it becomes the representation of its own pathos. Pathos is hypostatized as a blind power or mere "puissance de vouloir," but it stabilizes the semantics of the figure by making it "mean" the pathos of its undoing. In the text of the Second Preface, the speaker referred to as R. (standing presumably for Rousseau), by unsettling the metaphor "man," shifts from anthropological generality to pure pathos, but the figurality of the language of love implies that pathos is itself no longer a figure but a substance. In the terminology of the text, the "tableau" has become a "portrait" after all, not the portrait of universal man but of the deconstructive passion of a subject. R.'s sensible interlocutor understands this very well and knows that, as soon as the return to mimetic representation is in fact granted and claimed to be internalized, the impersonal desire is again susceptible of being represented by a subject: "*R.*: So we will find men, in books, only as they wish to reveal themselves? *N.*: The author as he wishes to reveal himself; the characters he describes such as they are . . ." (2:14). R. started out by deconstructing the referential system based on the metaphor "man" but has substituted for it a new referential system based on the pathos of a temporal predicament in which man's self-definition is forever deferred. The polarity between "portrait" and "tableau" does not engender extra-textual referents. The inside is always already an outside.

In the process of this discovery, however, the original system undergoes some transformations. At the onset of the text, "tableau" and "portrait" were associated with author and editor respectively: if the work was imaginary, then Rousseau had to be the author; if it were to be an actual collection of letters, the portrait or copy of a written text, then Rousseau was merely the editor. We then move on to a work that unsettles its own referential status but find that such a work can be read as the "portrait" of its own negative gesture. It follows that, if the work indeed represents objects "qui ne sont point," then it is the "portrait" of a subject's initiation to this knowledge. But only this subject can be the author of the text, since Julie, the emblem of love, is par excellence the object that does not exist. Rousseau is then the author of what turns out to be the portrait of an impossible "tableau." The original pairing of author with "tableau" has now been reversed, and instead of being paired with editor, "portrait" is now paired with author. As such, unlike the literal portrait of the real Julie, it becomes again comprehensible and "interesting." For the original pairing was self-defeating: "'I understand you', says R. 'If these letters are portraits, they are of no interest; if they are fictions, they imitate badly'" (2:10). This original impasse is broken in deconstructive narratives of which the *Second Discourse* and the *Essay* are examples: the imitation is now, in epistemological terms, a "good" imitation for it is free of any trace of distortion or wishful mystification; on the other hand, it is "interesting" since it portrays a pathos in which all can share. Contrary to received opinion, deconstructive discourses are suspiciously text-productive.

It is not only possible but necessary to read *Julie* in this way, as putting in question the referential possibility of "love" and as revealing its figural status. Such a reading would differ from the available interpretations of the novel but would not be essentially different from our reading of the *Second Discourse* and of the *Essay*: both are deconstructive narratives aimed at metaphorical seductions. From a rhetorical point of view, nothing would distinguish the discursive language of the earlier texts from the language of the novel. Such a reading is a necessary part of the novel's interpretation, which has to start out by undoing the simply antithetical relationship between referent and figure. This does not mean however that it can stop there.

Rousseau himself, at any rate, does not, in the Second Preface, allow the reading to come to rest. The question of authorship never receives a satisfactory answer, although it would seem to be a settled matter. N. keeps pressing R. to affirm or deny his authorship but R. keeps refusing, not for reasons of prudence, modesty or shame, but in the name of truth. "*N.*: If I keep asking you whether or not you are the author of these letters, why do you avoid my question? / *R.*: For the very reason that I do not wish to tell a lie. / *N.*: But you also refuse to tell the truth? / *R.*: Declaring one's wish to keep truth unsaid is still a way to pay tribute to it . . ." (2:28). "Taire la vérité" does not mean here to conceal something one knows, but not to proclaim known something one is unable to ascertain: "Who could decide whether or not I am caught in the same doubt in which you find yourself: Whether all this mystery and evasion is not a feint in order to hide my own ignorance of what you are trying to discover?" (2:29). What can it mean, in this context, for the author of a text to claim that he doesn't know whether or not he is its author? We speak perhaps too easily nowadays of the impersonality of writing, of writing as an intransitive verb, "disparition élocutoire qui laisse l'initiative aux mots" (Mallarmé). Are these the terms in which we are to understand Rousseau's statement?

Part of the difficulty stems from a naïve distinction between "writing" and "reading," from an exclusive concentration on authorship at the exclusion of the reader. Unlike the *Second Discourse* and the *Essay*, which deal with the origination of language and consequently with "writing" the Second Preface to *Julie* deals with reading in its relationship to writing. If to read is to understand writing—and we are deliberately leaving aside, for the moment, the performative function of language—then it presupposes a possible knowledge of the rhetorical status of what has been written. To understand primarily means to determine the referential mode of a text and we tend to take for granted that this can be done. We assume that a referential discourse can be understood by whoever is competent to handle the lexicological and grammatical code of a language. Neither are we helpless when confronted with figures of speech: as long as we can distinguish between literal and figural meaning, we can translate the figure back to its proper referent. We do not usually assume, for example, that someone suffers from hallucinations merely because he says that a table has four legs; the context of common usage separates the figural meaning of the catachresis (which, in this case, leads to the referent) from its literal denotation (which, in this case, is figural). Even if, as is often said to be the case for poetic language, the figure is polysemous and engenders several meanings, some of which may even be contradictory to each other, the large subdivision between literal and figural still prevails. Any reading always involves a choice between signification and symbolization, and this choice can be made only if one postulates the possibility of distinguishing the literal from the figural. This decision is not arbitrary, since it is based on a variety of textual and contextual factors (grammar, lexicology, tradition, usage, tone, declarative statement, diacritical marks, etc.). But the necessity of making such a decision cannot be avoided or the entire order of discourse would collapse. The situation implies that figural discourse is always understood in contradistinction to a form of discourse that would not be figural; it postulates, in other words, the possibility of referential meaning as the *telos* of all language. It would be quite foolish to assume that one can lightheartedly move away from the constraint of referential meaning.

The critical thrust of Rousseau's theory of language in the *Second Discourse* and in the *Essay* undermines this model. In these texts, the discussion of denomination as the primal linguistic function in fact puts in question the status of referential language. It becomes an aberrant trope that conceals the radical figurality of language behind the illusion that it can properly mean. As a result, the assumption of readability, which is itself constitutive of language, cannot only no longer be taken for granted but is found to be aberrant. There can be no writing without reading, but all readings are in error because they assume their own readability. Everything written has to be read and every reading is susceptible of logical verification, but the logic that establishes the need for verification is itself unverifiable and therefore unfounded in its claim to truth.

In the Second Preface to *Julie*, N., as a reader, is dependent on the possibility of reference and represents this need metaphorically by the assumption that the author holds the key to the referential status of his language. Hence his tireless questioning of R.'s authorship, in itself a correct representation of the necessarily naïve component included in any act of reading, regardless of its level of competence. This elusive author is not initially a subject but the metaphor for readability in general. Since he intervenes only to the extent that he is supposed to control the rhetorical mode of the text, he becomes the metaphor of a will or of a subject. Unlike N., Rousseau is supposed to know whether the text of his novel was merely copied (or quoted?) from a previous document or whether he invented it as his own creation. Although at this particular moment in the dialogue (2:12) N. expresses a preference for the first alternative, he could accommodate himself to both possibilities. Asked whether he can respond to the pathos of the text, he replies: "I can conceive of this effect with regard to you. If you are the author, the impact is easy to understand. If you are not, I can still conceive of it . . ." (2:18). What he could not tolerate, however, is the impossibility of distinguishing between the alternatives. This would leave him dangling in an intolerable semantic irresolution. It would be worse than madness: the mere confusion of fiction with reality, as in the case of Don Quijote, is mild and curable compared to this radical dyslexia.[27]

---

27. "Voulant être ce qu'on n'est pas, on parvient à se croire autre chose que ce qu'on est, et voilà comment on devient fou. En montrant sans cesse à ceux qui les lisent les prétendus charmes d'un état qui n'est pas le leur, [les romans] les séduisent, ils leur font prendre leur état en dédain, et en faire un échange imaginaire contre celui qu'on leur fait aimer." (2:21). This is a simple figural exchange in which the two specular poles, "leur état" and "un état qui n'est pas le leur," are clearly to be distinguished. The madness can be considered the madness of another which does not threaten the sanity of the reader.

R.'s denial of the knowledge that he is the author of his own text leaves N. in a predicament that his imagination cannot even begin to grasp. He would much rather assume that R. is mystifying him deliberately by withholding information that must be in his possession. The relationship between author and reader would then be one of simple deceit. The author is a liar, an unreliable narrator open to moral censure[28] or suspect, at best, of playing a frivolous game of hide and seek. The novel would be a riddle rather than an enigma, with a definite answer known from the beginning and artificially encrypted, like the missing body in a clumsy mystery story. The text would be generated by the mere deferment of a known secret. It is painfully clear that this is not the structure of the *Nouvelle Héloïse*, a novel not distinguished by dramatic suspense.[29] The only suspense would stem from Rousseau's capricious withholding of the key to his roman à clef.

Taken literally, Rousseau's assertion that he does not know whether he or his fictional characters wrote the letters that make up *Julie* makes little sense. The situation changes when we realize that R. is merely the metaphor for a textual property (readability). Further inferences then become apparent, for example that R. is similar to N. in his inability to read *Julie* and that it is impossible to distinguish between reader and author in terms of epistemological certainty. It follows that we can reverse the priority which makes us think of reading as the natural consequence of writing. It now appears that writing can just as well be considered the linguistic correlative of the inability to read. We write in order to forget our foreknowledge of the total opacity of words and things or, perhaps worse, because we do not know whether things have or do not have to be understood.

In the Second Preface, we come closest to being drawn into the wake of this whirlpool in passing from the terminology of reference and figure (portrait and tableau) to that of textuality. In a search parallel to his quest for authorship, N. wants to find a statement within the text that establishes the margin between text and external referent, that clearly marks off an intra-textual from an extra-textual

28. See Wayne Booth, *The Rhetoric of Fiction* (Chicago, 1961), Chapters 12 and 13.

29. "N. Quant à l'intérêt, il est pour tout le monde, il est nul. Pas une mauvaise action; pas un méchant homme qui fasse craindre pour les bons. Des évènements si naturels, si simples qu'ils le sont trop: rien d'inopiné; point de coups de Théâtre. Tout est prévu longtemps d'avance; tout arrive comme il est prévu . . ." (2:13).

field. He thinks to have found it in the epigraph on the title page, a passage from Petrarch which, in Rousseau's own translation, reads as follows: "Le monde la posséda sans la connaîtra, et moi je l'ai connue, je reste ici-bas à la pleurer" (2:1338). "Don't you see," asks N., "that your epigraph gives it all away?", assuming that the author confesses in this way the existence of the live model. The authority of the quotation is, of course, anything but decisive: it is highly ambivalent in itself; it is not Rousseau's statement but is borrowed from a complex context; it is not even Petrarch's statement, since Petrarch borrows it freely from John the Evangelist where it refers to God as Logos, etc. To all these possibilities of doubt, R. adds one less likely to come to mind: "for who can know whether I found this epigraph in the manuscript or whether it is I who put it there?" (2:29). Even if Rousseau had merely copied the letters, this would in no way establish their referentiality, since they might have been written by someone who, as the use of epigraphs shows, was just as much in need of reassurance as to the status of his text as R. and N. admit to being. The author of the letters may not have acted, copied, or portrayed but merely quoted. And it is impossible to say where quotation ends and "truth" begins, if by truth we understand the possibility of referential verification. The very statement by which we assert that the narrative is rooted in reality can be an unreliable quotation; the very document, the manuscript, produced in evidence may point back, not to an actual event, but to an endless chain of quotations reaching as far back as the ultimate transcendental signified God, none of which can lay claim to referential authority.

The Second Preface to *Julie* thus links a deconstructive theory of reading with a new sense of textuality. The innumerable writings that dominate our lives are made intelligible by a preordained agreement as to their referential authority; this agreement however is merely contractual, never constitutive. It can be broken at all times and every piece of writing can be questioned as to its rhetorical mode, just as *Julie* is being questioned in the Preface. Whenever this happens, what originally appeared to be a document or an instrument becomes a text and, as a consequence, its readability is put in question. The questioning points back to earlier texts and engenders, in its turn, other texts which claim (and fail) to close off the textual field. For each of these statements can in its turn become a text, just as the citation from Petrarch or Rousseau's assertion that the letters were "collected and published" by him can be made into texts—not by simply claiming that they are lies whose opposites could be true, but by revealing their dependence on a referential agreement that uncritically took their truth or falsehood for granted. The same applies, of course, to the text of the Preface with regard to the main text of *Julie:* rarely has a preface been less able to shed light on the meaning of the text it introduces, to the point of thematizing this impotence into the knowledge of an ignorance which the main text will, in its turn, have to challenge. We can no longer be certain, at this point, whether the preface was written for the main text or the main text for the preface.

The rhetorical mode of such structures can no longer be summarized by the single term of metaphor or of any substitutive trope or figure in general, although the deconstruction of metaphorical figures remains a necessary moment in their production. They take into account the fact that the resulting narratives can be folded back upon themselves and become self-referential. By *refusing,* for reasons of epistemological rigor, to confirm the authority, though not the necessity, of this juxtaposition, Rousseau unsettles the metaphor of reading as deconstructive narrative and replaces it by a more complex structure. The paradigm for all texts consists of a figure (or a system of figures) and its deconstruction. But since this model cannot be closed off by a final reading, it engenders, in its turn, a supplementary figural superposition which narrates the unreadability of the prior narration. As distinguished from primary deconstructive narratives centered on figures and ultimately always on metaphor, we can call such narratives to the second (or the third) degree *allegories.* Allegorical narratives tell the story of the failure to read whereas tropological narratives, such as the *Second Discourse,* tell the story of the failure to denominate. The difference is only a difference of degree and the allegory does not erase the figure. Allegories are always allegories of metaphor and, as such, they are always allegories of the impossibility of reading—a sentence in which the genitive "of" has itself to be "read" as a metaphor.

In the text of the Second Preface, the point at which the allegorical mode asserts itself is precisely when R. admits the impossibility of reading his own text and thus relinquishes his power over it. The statement undoes both the intelligibility and the seductiveness that the fiction owed to its negative rigor. The admission therefore occurs *against* the inherent logic which animated the development of the narrative, and disarticulates it in a way that seems perverse, just as

Rousseau's discursiveness, or Julie's preaching, has seemed to all critics the perverse spoiling of a fine subject. The reversal seems opposed to the best interests of the narrator. It has to be thematized as a sacrifice, a renunciation that implies a shift in valorization. Before the reversal, the narrative occurs within a system governed by polarities of truth and falsehood that move parallel with the text they generate. Far from interfering with each other, the value system and the narrative promote each other's elaboration; hence the relative ease of the narrative pattern in the *Second Discourse* despite (indeed because of) its figural complications, or of the story of passion in the first part of *Julie* which is said to be "like a live source that flows forever and that never runs dry" (2:15). But in the allegory of unreadability, the imperatives of truth and falsehood oppose the narrative syntax and manifest themselves at its expense. The concatenation of the categories of truth and falsehood with the values of right and wrong is disrupted, affecting the economy of the narration in decisive ways. We can call this shift in economy *ethical*, since it indeed involves a displacement from *pathos* to *ethos*. Allegories are always ethical, the term ethical designating the structural interference of two distinct value systems. In this sense, ethics has nothing to do with the will (thwarted or free) of a subject, nor *a fortiori*, with a relationship between subjects. The ethical category is imperative (i.e., a category rather than a value) to the extent that it is linguistic and not subjective. Morality is a version of the same language aporia that gave rise to such concepts as "man" or "love" or "self," and not the cause or the consequence of such concepts. The passage to an ethical tonality does not result from a transcendental imperative but is the referential (and therefore unreliable) version of a linguistic confusion. Ethics (or, one should say, ethicity) is a discursive mode among others.

But the Preface and the main text of *Julie* are ethical not only in this wider sense. They are also moralistic in a very practical way that frequently borders on the ridiculous but that is nonetheless a necessary part of what is most consistent in Rousseau's thought. In the Preface, this tone, all too familiar to readers of *Julie* and *Emile*, is much in evidence in R.'s lengthy considerations on all the good his book will be able to do for its readers. The discrepancy between the *persona* of Rousseau as the critical moralist of rhetorical suspicion and that of the man of practical wisdom is puzzling. The relationship between the epistemologist and the voice of practical reason

(Rousseau himself speaks of "morale de pratique") is certainly, like the relationship between Rousseau and the two fictional speakers R. and N. in the Preface, a dialogical rather than a monological one. From the first, one has to expect a mental attitude that is highly self-reflective, persistently aware of the discrepancies between the formal and the semantic properties of language, fully responsive to the seductive plays of the signifier yet wary of their powers of semantic aberration. It supposes an austere analytical rigor that pursues its labors regardless of the consequences, the most rigorous gesture of all being that by which the writer severs himself from the intelligibility of his own text. Yet, while holding up this attitude as morally exemplary, Rousseau nevertheless, in the same breath, discusses its consequences in very practical utilitarian terms. The same person who is vulnerable to reproaches of sophistry and over-subtlety when he dodges simple signification with phrases such as "si elles furent, elles ne sont plus," or with hard-to-follow evasions on the status of epigraphs, also speaks naïvely about his desire to be useful: "in order to make what one wishes to say useful, one must first of all be intelligible to those who have to make use of it" (2:22); "if one wants to be useful, one should be read in the Provinces"; "perhaps husbands and wives will find in this volume views that may make their labors useful" (2:23), etc. We find back the same mixture of epistemological refinement and utilitarian naiveté that is characteristic of much of Rousseau's writing, especially when the "poetic" aspects of his discourse have to be reconciled with considerations on morality and on customs. No such problems occur with the theoretical aspects of his political thought; they arise primarily with regard to the wisdom of practical reason. The question is not the intrinsic merit or absurdity of these pieces of good advice but rather the fact that they *have to be* uttered, despite the structural discrepancy between their intellectual simplicity and the complexity of the considerations on which they are predicated.

The heterogeneous texture of Rousseau's allegorical narratives is less surprising if one keeps in mind that his radical critique of referential meaning never implied that the referential function of language could in any way be avoided, bracketed, or reduced to being just one contingent linguistic property among others, as is postulated, for example, in contemporary semiology which, like all post-Kantian formalisms, could not exist without this postulate. Rousseau never allows for a "purely" aesthetic reading in which the referential determination would remain suspended or be nonexistent. Such a reading is inconceivable on the epistemological, premoral level, where it would be the mere play of a free signifier, nor does it exist in allegory, when the undoing of signification has taken on ethical dimensions and when the object of aesthetic contemplation would be the beautiful philosophical soul. The impossibility of aesthetic judgment is built within Rousseau's linguistic model as an aberrant figure. Suspended meaning is not, for him, disinterested play, but always a threat or a challenge. The loss of faith in the reliability of referential meaning does not free the language from referential and tropological coercion, since the assertion of the loss is itself governed by considerations of truth and falsehood that, as such, are necessarily referential. Kant's concept of aesthetic freedom is, in Rousseau, a metaphor for the indeterminacy of signification and can thus never be the source of any judgment, nor a license to elaborate modes of judgment that would no longer be dependent on concepts. It is clear that Schiller's *Letters on Aesthetic Education* could never have been recommended reading for Emile. The concept, in Rousseau, always retains a referential moment, the supply of difference that the concept acknowledges by concealing it. But since the convergence of the referential and the figural signification can never be established, the reference can never be a meaning. In Rousseau's linguistics there is room only for "wild" connotation; the loss of denominational control means that every connotation has claim to referential authority but no statute in which to ground this claim. When Kant, using music and the ornamental arabesque[30] as his main example was in fact to ground aesthetic judgment in nonreferentiality, his semiological insight was gained at the cost of a repression that was to make theoretical poetics, a branch of applied linguistics, into aesthetics, a branch of applied psychology.

The persistence of the referential moment (which is to be distinguished from the noncognitive, performative function of language) prevents the confinement of allegory to an epistemological and ethical system of valorization. Since the epistemological mediation is known to be unreliable, and since the narrative of this discovery cannot be left suspended in the contemplation of its own aesthetic gratification, the allegory speaks out with the referential efficacy of

30. Kant, *Kritik der Urteilskraft*, §11 and further passages on music, §40, §42 f., etc.

a *praxis*. The ethical language of persuasion has to act upon a world that it no longer considers structured like a linguistic system but that consists of a system of *needs*. The *Nouvelle Héloïse,* for example, can be read as a thematization of the movement from symbolic, metaphorical meaning in the first part to a more contractual type of meaning in the second part, after Julie's marriage to Wolmar. At the same time however Rousseau is concerned with the practical effect of this thematization on the reader. And although what he actually says about this may be quite silly (silliness being deeply associated with reference), the co-presence of thematic, exhortative discourse with critical analytic language points to an inherent characteristic of all allegorical modes. The resulting discourse of praxis is however not only devoid of authority (since it is the consequence of an epistemological abdication), but it occurs again in the form of a text. The Second Preface, however practical it may be in its concerns, is not more of an action than the rest of the novel. Reading is a praxis that thematizes its own thesis about the impossibility of thematization and this makes it unavoidable, though hardly legitimate, for allegories to be interpreted in thematic terms.

By moving, under the guidance of the Second Preface to *Julie,* from figural deconstruction, first to the theoretical and then to the practical ethical dimension of allegory, we had to reintroduce the concept of need [besoin] which originally served Rousseau as the means to distinguish the language-structured discourse of passion from nonverbal entities. Just as it is impossible to understand the historical condition of man without positing a fictional state of nature, and just as it is impossible for a statement not to connote a referential meaning, it is impossible for a passion not to hypostatize a hypothetical need from which it would be the supplementary displacement. Passions are then conceived as pathological needs, which is also why they are affectively valorized in terms of pleasure and pain. The allegory inevitably shifts to a eudaemonic vocabulary. In its more domestic versions, this vocabulary generates the mixture of erotic sweetness and deceit, of "doux modèle" (2:13) with "âcres baisers" that hangs over much of Rousseau's fictions. He himself compared *Julie* to the "soave licor" (Tasso) that covers up the bitterness of the actual statement, and this slightly nauseating flavor catches the quintessential aroma of Rousseau's necessarily "bad" taste. One can always console oneself from this cloyness with the hygienically brisk *Social Contract.*

With the reintroduction of needs, the relapse into the seductions of metaphor is inevitable and the cycle repeats itself. Needs reenter the literary discourse as the aberrant proper meaning of metaphors *against* which the allegory constitutes itself. The reintroduction of the intentional language of needs into the allegory is not itself intentional but the result of a linguistic structure. The entire assumption of a nonverbal realm governed by needs may well be a speculative hypothesis that exists only, to put it in all too intentional terms, *for the sake of* language. But the existence of this moment of relapse in Rousseau's allegories first has to be documented and, by alluding to its existence, we have in fact moved away from the Second Preface into the main text of *Julie.*

The lengthy recapitulative letter (2:340–65) in which Julie explains to Saint-Preux the reasons for her marriage can serve as a (fallacious) synecdoche for the totality of a text which demands a much more extensive treatment. What is being "read" in this case is the structure of the passion between Julie and Saint-Preux, which has been acted out dramatically in the three books that lead up to this concluding episode.

That "passion" has to be understood as a structural system has clearly been stated in an earlier recapitulation. Passion is not something which, like the senses, belongs in proper to an entity or to a subject but, like music, it is a system of relationships that exists only in the terms of this system: "The source of happiness does not reside entirely either in the desired object or in the heart that possesses it, but in the relationship between both . . ." (2:225).[31] As we know from the reading of *Narcisse* and *Pygmalion*, texts centered on the specular structure of selfhood, this relationship can be stated in terms of a dichotomy of self and other that engenders a chain of contrasting polarities. Having moved through such a process of figural substitutions, Julie describes it as based on the presumption of an analogy between body and soul, between outside and inside. "I thought I recognized in your face the traces (traits) of a soul which

31. The statement is made within a context that brings together several of the novel's main polarities, and heavily engaged in the bad faith of what Rousseau calls "morale de pratique." It is used by Julie in an antihedonistic sermon to prove that Saint-Preux would be ill advised to substitute pleasure for love. Pleasure, as the satisfaction of needs, is indeed not founded on relationship but on possession. That her own plea is nevertheless dependent on the seductive vocabulary of pleasure is clear, but does not permit us to discard the statement.

was necessary to my own. It seemed to me my senses acted only as the organs of nobler sentiments, and I loved you, not so much for what I saw in you as for what I thought I felt in myself" (2:340). The chain of substitutions crosses from "visage" (outside) to "âme" (inside) by way of "traits" ("les traits de l'âme") which are said to be both inside and outside, an ambiguity made plausible by the fact that, despite their exteriority, the lines of a face produce a semiological as well as a physical connotation, and appear as the inscription, on the surface of the face, of the soul's meaning. Simultaneously, we pass from "sens" and "yeux" (outside) to "sentiments" by means of the synecdoche "organe" ("mes sens ne servaient que d'organe à des sentiments . . ."). "Voir" and "sentir" also accomplish the transference to the categories of self and other, since now to "see" the other is to "feel" the self ("j'aimai dans vous, moins ce que j'y voyais que ce que je croyais sentir en moi-même"). This transfer occurs because the self is said to be in need of the other, to be lacking something that only the other can provide: "les traits de l'âme qu'il *fallait* à la mienne." The void, the hole, is filled, as it were, by the soul of the other, which is of course also his body. The dynamics of the chiasmus require a valorization achieved by calling the desired feelings "noble"; the continuity from sensory to ethical hierarchies is part of the same metaphorical and analogical system. But the crossings have upset the authority of the construction and produced a constant emphasis on possible delusion: "je crus voir . . ."; "il me sembla que . . ."; "je croyais sentir . . ."; modalities that throw their shadow on the parallel verbal construction extending from "je crus voir . . ." to "il me sembla que . . ." to "je croyais sentir . . ." and finally to "j'aimai en vous. . . ." Under the impact of so many mental reservations, the verb "aimer" almost acquires an optative tone and it is indeed soon bluntly stated that all these substitutions were grounded in an aberration which now belongs to the past: "Less than two months ago, I still thought that I was not mistaken . . ." (2:340). Love must now be called blind ("l'aveugle amour") in a way that deviates considerably from the commonplace associations with the blindfolded Cupid, all the more so since blindness is stated within a (negative) context of truth and falsehood: "l'aveugle amour, me disais-je, avait raison . . ." (2:340). The self-destructive power of the passions is not due to outside causes but is grounded in unwarranted assumptions about the coherence of a world in which the resemblance of appearances would warrant the affinity of essences. The passage explicitly discards the notion that the evil consequences of passion might be the result of external obstacles, such as social prejudices or parental tyranny: "I still thought that I was not mistaken; blind love, I told myself, was right; we were made for each other; I would be his if the human order had not upset the order of nature . . ." (2:340). From a narrative point of view, the statement shifts the pattern of referential authority from a representational, mimetic mode (which has been prevalent in the unfolding of the novel up to this point) to a deconstructive diegesis. For up till this letter, the interest of the action had been primarily based on elements now found to be fallacious: Julie and Saint-Preux have been presented as stock characters in a situation of sentimental tragedy, persecuted by the social inequities of wealth and class and by the caprices of a tyrannical father. The reader's responses are solicited according to the rules of this plot, thus maintaining the homology between enunciation and understanding that characterizes monological narratives. With the discovery, in retrospect, that this symmetry is an illusion, the entire narrative has to be reconstructed along different lines. The reading has to check itself at all points, in quest of clues that puncture the surface of the discourse and reveal the holes and the traps concealed underneath. Reading now requires a vigilance that can no longer simply trust what it hears. Areas of the text obscured by the succession of predictable events and feelings become again apparent as a new network of narrative articulations replaces the first. What appeared at first as a sequence of lyrical moments, separated from each other by the well-rounded closure of each particular letter, becomes, in the recapitulation, a narrative chain of successive errors, as misleading for the reader as they were for the character—not unlike the steady degradation from invention to historical catastrophe by which, in the *Second Discourse* and in the *Essay*, mankind has been brought down to its present condition.

Like all metaphorical systems, the first part of *La nouvelle Héloïse* (Books 1 to 3) consists of a chain of substitutions and, as in all deconstructive narratives, the second reading, called forth by the recapitulation, reveals the weakness of the links by means of which the polarities were held together. The relationship between Julie and Saint-Preux is told as a substitutive movement in which self and other constantly exchange their identity, as if they were a single androgynous being whose unity could not be deranged by the internal transfers of attributes: "Come and unite with your own self" ("Viens te réunir à toi-méme" [2:146]), Julie tells Saint-Preux, and she is for him like the omnipresence, the parousia of an element finer than air: "I see you, I feel you everywhere, I breathe you in the air you have breathed; you penetrate my entire substance" (2:147) or, in another "Platonic" passage,[32] "I would imagine you to be of a higher species, if the devouring fire that penetrates my substance did not unite me with yours and made me feel that they are the same" (2:116). It is not surprising that their sexual union is linked from the start with an imagery of incest. Not very long before their first embrace, Saint-Preux will say: "I would tremble to touch your chaste body as if it were the vilest incest, and your safety is not less inviolate in my company than it would be in your father's" (2:42). "I am no longer in possession of myself," Saint-Preux had said somewhat earlier, "my estranged soul is entirely within you" (2:101), and in response Julie can see herself as totally immolated before and replaced by the other: "Be my entire being, now that I am no longer anything . . ." (2:103). These self/other substitutions are familiar from *Narcisse* and *Pygmalion* and can be transferred from the relation between the lovers to the relationship between author and work and finally between author and reader. A sentence like the following could have come directly out of *Pygmalion* or out of the tradition that stands behind it: "You have left in me something of the ineffable charm that inhabits you, and I believe that with your gentle breath you inspired a new soul within me. Hasten, I beg you, to complete your work. Take whatever remains of my soul and put yours entirely in its place" (2:150).

If the substitutions could indeed occur within the totality of a single androgynous being, they would still engender other metaphors by which this unity would be asserted, be it in the form of myths or of images. A full cosmos is an inexhaustible reservoir of complementary symbols. But the polarities that stem from an illusory plenitude will lead to ever-widening dissonances and generate a very different type of story. The first three books of *Julie* are a typical version of such a story. They include all conceivable configurations of the original oppositions, intertwined in patterns that are never allowed to stabilize, for whenever a substitution has taken place a new unbalance, by excess or by default, is revealed and requires new displacements.

It would be too lengthy a task to trace in detail the chain of transformations that make up the narrative segment ending with the last letter of the third part, but even on the simplest thematic level it

32. The reference is, of course, to *Symposium*, 189, 190.

is clearly in evidence. As a spatial, topographical structure, the first half of *La nouvelle Héloïse* is a succession of uncoordinated, erratic movements, a series of flights and returns put in motion by the very first sentence of the narrative: "il faut vous fuir, Mademoiselle, je le sens bien. . . ." Saint-Preux's incessant comings and goings, from the Valais, to la Meillerie, to Paris, finally literally to the end of the world, are reminiscent of the restless pacing up and down of Pygmalion in his atelier. They differ from *Pygmalion* however in that the motions are not comparable to the dance of a swarm of insects around a single light, which, in this case, would be Julie. This would invest all attributes of being into one of the two poles and thus create a very different, single-centered system. Even the few examples mentioned above indicate that the substitutions cannot occur in one single direction and that they have to travel from Saint-Preux to Julie as well as in the opposite direction. Saint-Preux's geographical agitation has its counterpart in the vacillations and "langueurs" of Julie's state of mind; between his "outside" and her "inside," there develops an interplay of complicated and by no means balanced exchanges.

The temporal pattern is equally unstable. Separated from Julie by the breadth of the lake, Saint-Preux writes to her the type of ode to the glories of the moment which is so familiar in the Petrarchan tradition. A recurrent theme exalting or denouncing the seductions of the moment runs through the book, reaching at times high points of lyrical intensity; speaking of his "days of pleasure and of glory" with Julie, Saint-Preux can say: "A gentle ecstasy absorbed their entire duration and condensed it into one point, like the duration of eternity. Neither past nor future existed for me and I could taste simultaneously the delights of thousand centuries" (2:317). The exaltation of the moment is counterbalanced by the contrasting appreciation of duration for its own sake: "sentiment dies away with time, but the sensitive soul remains forever" (2:16). Duration is indeed the privileged temporal mode for a system in quest of its own authority and striving for a state in which events are no longer changes but the confirmation of an identity no longer threatened by an exterior force. It is the proper temporal mode for a lengthy, monodic, and eventoned narration towards which *Julie* seems, at times, to be tending, a narrative in which the void of signification would no longer be experienced as a loss. In an allegory of this kind, duration has to be valorized as the attraction of what is known to be least attainable. The text does not however describe this dialectic of instant and duration, of sameness and of change, in which the seductions of the moment also acquire those of repose, as leading to a stable synthesis. Duration, the coincidence of an entity with its own present, requires the vocabulary of an inwardness detached from anything that is other or elsewhere, containing nothing desirable that is not already possessed. It evokes a fulfillment no longer associated with desire, since desire is organized around the moment that separates possession from its opposite. Saint-Preux describes "the time that follows the time of pleasure" (2:149), the transfer of attributes derived from desire into a new, tranquil state: ". . . I adored you and desired nothing. I could not even imagine any other bliss . . . What tranquility in all my senses! What pure, continuous, universal voluptuousness! The source of pleasure was in the soul; it never left it, it lasted forever. What a difference between this peaceful state and the agitation of love!" (2:149). Duration appears as self-enclosed and autonomous, yet it borrows "jouissance" and "volupté" from a restless outside world governed by "les fureurs de l'amour." It remains linked to this world by sensations and memories ("There is a time for experience, another for memory" [2:16]), and it is by ways of this metonymic link that the metaphorical illusion of duration is achieved. The ambiguity fully appears when consciousness, as duration, has to realize that it can come into being only at the expense of the passion that produced the experience of inwardness in the first place. At the end of the paragraph from which the previous quotation is taken, Saint-Preux has to ask the by-no-means rhetorical question: "Tell me, Julie, whether I did not love you before, or whether it is now that I no longer love you?" The exchange between properties of stability and of change engenders an unhappy consciousness: it occurs in a state of dejection, "in self-shame and self-humiliation" (2:149), and it leads to Saint-Preux's later statement that ". . . we return to life in order to return to suffering, and the consciousness of our existence is for us only a consciousness of pain" (2:326). This mood is obviously not compatible with a state of duration and repose. Neither can it compromise by substituting memories for presence, or by the aesthetic contemplation of its own soul, made "beautiful" by the sacrifice of the passion that created it. *La nouvelle Héloïse* would be a very different (and a much shorter) text, more like *Werther* or the Mignon chapter in *Wilhelm Meister* or *Sylvie*, if the narrative had been allowed to stabilize in this way.[33]

33. As suggested by Claire: "Vous vous direz (après avoir fait le sacrifice de votre amour) je sais aimer, avec un plaisir plus durable et plus délicat que vous n'en

The reversal of the allegory (peripeteia) occurs, then, as the deliberate rejection of the system of analogical exchanges that has structured the narrative of the novel's first half. The reversal is no longer, as was the case in the *Second Discourse*, left implicit in the declining movement, "la pente inévitable" (2:353), of the narrative of error. It asserts itself as an outspoken decision that sharply divides the novel in two segments, a before and an after, entirely modifies the circumstances and the setting and allows for a retrospective vision of remarkable lucidity. The allegory of unreadability begins by making its pre-text highly readable: there is not a single episode, practically not a single word, in the more than hundred letters that come before the turning point that is not clarified and accounted for by the redoubled reading that the reversal compels us to undertake. Nor does the narrative hesitate to draw conclusions from the discovery of its earlier aberrations. In the place of "love," based on the resemblances and substitutions of body and soul or self and other, appears the contractual agreement of marriage, set up as a defense against the passions and as the basis of social and political order. This decision acquires its moral dimension from the fact that it moves against the "natural" logic of the narrative and of its understanding.

This, too, is not self-evident. For it appears that the first effect of the decision is one of clarification, permitting a coherent interpretation of the first half of the novel. The complexity of the passage, which also marks the transition to the allegorical mode, stems from the fact that, at the moment when Julie acquires a maximum of insight, the control over the rhetoric of her own discourse is lost, for us as well as for her. The retrospective clarity gained at midpoint does not extend to the second part: no equivalent recapitulation is possible at the end of *Julie*, for it can be shown that the religious language of the last chapters is nowhere held up as being free of delusion, in the way the beginning of Letter 18, Part III, can be said to

---

goûteriez à dire: je possède ce que j'aime. Car celui-ci s'use à force d'en jouir; mais l'autre demeure toujours, et vous en jouirez encore, quand même vous n'aimeriez plus." The supplementary economy of an aesthetic of sacrifice (as when Claire calculates, in the same passage that "le véritable amour a cet avantage . . . qu'il *dédommage* de tout ce qu'on lui sacrifie, et qu'on jouit en quelque sorte des privations qu'on s'impose par le sentiment même de ce qu'il en *coûte* et du motif qui nous y porte" [2:320, my italics]) is exposed when, instead of to sublimation, we move on to deconstruction, as was already the case in *Pygmalion*.

be. The readability of the first part is obscured by a more radical indeterminacy that projects its shadow backwards and forwards over the entire text. Deconstructions of figural texts engender lucid narratives which produce, in their turn and as it were within their own texture, a darkness more redoubtable than the error they dispel.

In this text (Letter 18, Part III) darkness falls when it becomes evident that Julie's language at once repeats the notions she has just denounced as errors. Not only does she continue to use a metaphorical diction (which would be, by itself, of little consequence, since we are now fully aware of its dangers), but she construes the new world into which she is moving as an exact repetition of the one she claims to have left behind. If this is so, then it can be said that Julie is unable to "read" her own text, unable to recognize how its rhetorical mode relates to its meaning.[34] The repetition differs from its earlier version, not in structure, but by a thematic shift: it moves from an erotic to an ethical and religious vocabulary, to the odd stratification of pragmatic, practical reason with a language of high morality and desire that we first encountered in the Second Preface to *Julie*. Virtue is referred to in the most practical of terms,[35] yet it is also spoken of in a language of religious awe that had hardly been heard, up to this point, in the novel and that has led critics to speculate whether or not Julie is supposed to have undergone a religious conversion. Actually, there is nothing in the structure of Julie's relationship to virtue or to what she calls God that does not find its counterpart in her previous and now so rigorously demystified relationship towards Saint-Preux.

This relationship was based on the metaphor of a subject that

34. By the play of notes which allows him to acquire a distancing perspective with regard to Julie, Rousseau may seem to escape from this obfuscation at the expense of his character. But this pattern is anticipated in Julie herself, whose lucidity with regard to her past experience is never in question and who is capable of the same distance toward herself as Rousseau allows himself towards her, yet remains entirely unable to avert the repetition of her errors. R.'s statement, in the Preface, of helplessness before the opacity of his own text is similar to Julie's relapse into metaphorical models of interpretation at her moments of insight. The manipulation of point of view is a form of infinite regress inscribed within the metaphor of selfhood.

35. Adultery, for example, is denounced for the most practical of reasons: fathers should not be forced to support children they may not have sired, family life is disrupted by the constant necessity to lie and to cheat, the continuity of the succession may be upset, and one should not break the prevalent rules too lightly since it is so hard to lose the habit once one has done so.

differed from another as plenitude differs from lack, and that was able to exchange the shortcomings of the one for the excess of the other because a basic affinity compelled them to enter into a relationship of reciprocity. The text insists at length on the need for such response: "The love I have known can only be born from a reciprocal affinity and from a harmony of souls. One cannot love if one is not loved or, at least, one does not love for long" (2:341). Reciprocity or resemblance is made manifest by the analogy between inside and outside that allows Julie to recognize the affinity between herself and Saint-Preux by merely looking at his face. Having discarded this model, Julie at once has to invent an entity called God in order to repeat what she had condemned. God has to be entirely unlike herself in his self-sufficiency and omnipresence: "Nothing exists but through Him that is" (2:358) and, as such, "no model can exist among incarnate beings to which [He] could be compared" (2:358). Yet he is at once anthropomorphized by giving him the very attributes that made the substitutive exchanges with Saint-Preux possible: a language, a voice, and a face. Like Saint-Preux, he exists as a combination of traces ("traits") which make it possible to "read" his substance: " . . . all his features [traits] linked to his infinite essence are always represented to reason, and help reason to restore what error and imposture had distorted" (2:358). The configuration of these "traits" make up a face, the "inward effigy" (2:358) which is also able to speak with "the secret voice that never stopped its murmur in the depth of my heart. . . ." But this voice can have no greater authority than the voice of Saint-Preux, since its comprehension depends on the same rhetorical code that proved fallacious in the first instance. Consequently, it will be difficult to tell apart the discourses addressed to Saint-Preux from those addressed to God or to virtue. Both are based on the same "eternal simulacrum" (2:223), "divine model" (2:224, 2:358), "image that we carry within ourselves" (2:358), and that we are able to perceive and to emulate: "as soon as passion allows us to see it, we want to resemble it . . ." (2:224). Julie and God become the two-sided exchange of a dialogue in which the words carry shared substances that can be offered and received: Julie's prayer, for example, far from being a radical loss of selfhood before an unintelligible otherness, addresses a kind of overself that does not differ from her in kind. Attributes circulate freely within the transparency of a representational model of expressive voices and faces: "I see him, I feel him; his helping hand . . . restores

me to myself, in spite of myself"; "I want, I told him, the good that
you want, and of which you are the sole source"; "Render all my
actions akin to my constant will which is also your will. . . . " What
Julie wishes to receive from God are the same attributes of selfhood
and of will (the prayer repeats "je veux" six times, like an incantation) that she requested from Saint-Preux, "the soul which was
necessary to my own" in order to achieve individuation. And she can
again identify this received selfhood by recognizing the signs through
which the divinity manifests itself: a face, a voice, or most effectively
of all, certain emotions[36] that postulate a continuity between these
signs and their signification, just as her own sense of selfhood could
be read off from Saint-Preux's countenance. The concatenation between self, feeling, sign (trait), and outer appearance (visage) is a
constant network in Julie's relationship to God, as it was in her
relationship to Saint-Preux. It is therefore not surprising that, in an
apostrophe first addressed to Saint-Preux, Julie's exclamation, "Ah, I
have learned too well what it costs to lose you and will not forsake
you a second time!" (2:355), could be directed just as well to her lover
as to the actual grammatical antecedent in the sentence, divine virtue. Neither is it surprising that virtue will later be identified, by
Wolmar, as being a passion among others, with a structure similar
to that of love (2:493).

36. It will not do to interpret the love for Saint-Preux "platonically" as a
prefiguration of a transcendental love temporarily directed towards an imperfect
being: the exposure of the relationship is too radical and the difference between the
first and the second part of the novel too wide to allow for such a reading. Bernard
Guyon may be right in pointing out that a degree of similarity prevails in the
analogical structures giving rise to metaphors of inwardness, self, will, joy, etc., that
keep occuring in the second half of the novel. But this very similarity is then recognized as a pattern of error that remained hidden in the first three books; instead of
unifying the totality of the text, it undoes whatever illusion of unity the first half
tended to convey. Nor is the opposite reading more convincing: Julie's passionate
addresses to God cannot be interpreted as a simple confusion of the divine with the
erotic, a delusion akin to that of a "quixotic" character like Emma Bovary. The rigor
of Julie's insight into the aberrations of "romantic" love finds no remote equivalence
in Flaubert's heroine, neither does the ensuing control of Flaubert over his fiction find
an equivalence in Rousseau's confusion with regard to his. The problem is not that
Julie remains mystified, but that a totally enlightened language, regardless of
whether it conceives of itself as a consciousness or not, is unable to control the
recurrence, in its readers as well as in itself, of the errors it exposes. Julie, the best
conceivable critical reader, is apparently unable to read her own critical text criti-
cally.

Thus the text of the pivotal letter that concludes the first part of *Julie*, so clarifying as a recapitulation, bodes little good for the stability of what it proleptically announces. It will be followed by the lengthy description of the political order in the community of Clarens, of which it is difficult to decide whether it is an exemplary model for a state or an ambivalent family romance. When the language of selfhood returns, as in the final letters again centered on the relationship between Julie and Saint-Preux, it is in terms that are not political and not even primarily ethical, but religious. Our reading tries to account for the emergence of the ethical valorization but remains unable to answer the question raised by the interpreters of *Julie* as to the relationship between the political aspects of Clarens and the religious considerations in Julie's last letters. The question could be dealt with by an extended reading of *Julie* in its entirety, but since we dispose, in Rousseau's work, of at least two more systematic treatises involving religious and political theory (the *Profession de foi* from *Emile* and the *Social Contract*) it may be legitimate to follow his own hint and take him at his word in his assertion that the *Profession de foi* and the concluding letters of *Julie* "are in close enough accord to make it possible to explain the one by means of the other."[37]

37. *Lettres de la montagne* in *Oeuvres complètes*, 3:694.

10 Allegory of Reading

(Profession de foi)

WHEN THE SAVOYARD PRIEST HAS COMPLETED THE theoretical part of his discourse, his listener is impressed enough by the fervor of his tone to compare him to Orpheus, but less inclined to praise the originality of a doctrine conveyed with such inspired conviction: "The views you have just expressed, I said, seem more unusual to me because of what you admit you do not know than because of what you say you believe. I see in them something very close to theism or natural religion, which Christians profess to equate with atheism or irreligion, though it is actually the exact opposite" (p. 606[1]). It is indeed well known that even Voltaire, despite many reservations, expressed agreement with the doctrine of the *Profession de foi* and that William Blake could, with some justice, link Voltaire and Rousseau together as promoters of the natural religion he despised. On a first level of understanding, the *Profession de foi* is unquestionably a straightforward theistic document,[2] basing religious conviction on the manifestation of innate and natural moral

---

1. All page references are to J. J. Rousseau, *Oeuvres complètes*, ed. Bernard Gagnebin and Marcel Raymond (Paris: Gallimard [Bibliothèque de la Pléiade], 1969), vol. 4. In this edition, the text of *Emile* (of which the *Profession de foi* is a part) has been established by Charles Wirz and the commentary by Pierre Burgelin. The English translations from the *Profession de foi* are those of Lowell Bair in *The Essential Rousseau* (New York: Random House, 1974) but page references are to the French *Oeuvres complètes*.

2. For Rousseau's definition of theism, see the *Social Contract*: the religion of man, as opposed to the religion of the citizen, is ". . . without temples, altars or rites, limited to the purely inward cult of the Supreme Deity and to the eternal duties of morality. It is the pure and simple religion of the Gospel, true theism and what can be called divine natural right"—J. J. Rousseau, *Oeuvres complètes*, ed. Bernard Gagnebin and Marcel Raymond (Paris: Gallimard [Bibliothèque de la Pléiade], 1964), 3:464. The text and commentary of the *Social Contract*, in this edition, has been established by Robert Derathé.

feelings: "Let us limit ourselves to the first feelings we find within us, since inquiry always brings us back to them, when it has not led us astray. Conscience! Conscience! Divine instinct, immortal and celestial voice! You are the sure guide of a being who is ignorant and confined, but intelligent and free. You are the infallible judge of good and evil and it is through you that man resembles God . . ." (600--01). As for understanding what this voice is telling and where this guide is leading us, there seems to be no serious difficulty: "It is not enough to know that this guide exists: we must also be able to recognize and follow it. If it speaks to all hearts, why are there so few who understand it? It is because it speaks to us in the language of nature . . ." (601). This is presumably the same language in which the Book of Nature has been written: "I was never able to believe that God had ordered me, under penalty of damnation, to be so learned. I therefore closed all books. There is only one that is open to all eyes: the book of nature" (624). Hence the sublime natural setting chosen for the vicar's discourse: "Nature seemed to display all its magnificence to our eyes, as if to offer it as the text of our dialogue" (565). The *text* of nature has its equivalence in the "inner image" [*effigie intérieure*] whose voice speaks clearly enough if only we are willing to silence the distracting noises of worldliness: "Let us look into ourselves my young friend! . . . There is within our souls an innate principle of justice and virtue by which, in spite of our maxims, we judge our acts and those of others as good or bad, and it is this principle that I call conscience" (598). To the vain teaching of philosophy, the vicar opposes the innate wisdom of "inner light" (569).

The affirmation of belief in a natural religion, founded in the transcendental valorization of such concepts as inwardness, innateness [*inéité*], voice, natural language, conscience, consciousness, selfhood, etc., represents, of course, a considerable deviation from the epistemological and rhetorical critiques that are to be found elsewhere throughout the work of Rousseau. No such considerations play a part in the historical and political arguments of anthropological texts such as the *Second Discourse;* when God is mentioned in the *Discourse* it is primarily to demonstrate that there is no such thing as a natural language.[3] The conflict emerges perhaps most dramatically

3. "Whatever the origins [of language] may have been, one can see how poorly Nature has prepared men for life in society from the little care it took to bring them together by natural means or to facilitate their use of speech" (*Oeuvres complètes*, 3:151). The same is said about the development of technology: men had to learn

when one juxtaposes the vicar's natural piety with the pre-Nietzschean denunciations of Christianity, as a political force, in the chapter on civil religion (Book IV, chapter 8) of the *Social Contract:* "It was in these circumstances [paganism having become the universal religion of the Roman empire] that Jesus came to establish a spiritual kingdom on earth. By separating the theological system from the political system, this destroyed the unity of the state, and caused the internal divisions that have never ceased to agitate Christian nations. . . . What the pagans feared finally happened. Everything then became different; the humble Christians changed their tone, and the supposedly otherworldly kingdom, under a visible ruler, soon became the most violent despotism in this world."[4] "The [religion of the priests . . . which includes Roman catholicism as a major instance] is [considered politically] so obviously bad that amusing myself by demonstrating its drawbacks would be a waste of time. Anything that breaks social unity is worthless. All institutions that place man in contradiction with himself are worthless."[5] Jean-Robert Tronchin, the Procureur général of the City of Geneva, whose report led the Petit Conseil to order the burning of *Emile* and the *Social Contract* (as "tending to destroy the Christian religion and all governments") was certainly justified in referring to these texts in his cogent attack on Rousseau published under the title *Lettres de la Campagne.*

The gap between the theophany of the *Profession de foi* and the political writings, especially the *Social Contract* (*Julie* being an intermediate case, too complex for summary discussion), is too obvious to have escaped notice and remains one of the main cruxes in Rousseau interpretation. The critical rigor of the political texts contrasted with the piety of religious sentiment in the *Profession de foi* always again forces commentators, depending on their temperament and convictions, to daemonize the former or to condescend to the latter. Thus Pierre Burgelin, in his introduction to the fourth volume of the *Complete Works*, says of the discrepancies between statement and tone in the *Profession* that "these disparities stem from the distance between intellectual analysis and the impulses of the heart" (cxlii)—always and again the Schillerian dichotomy between Rousseau's *Denkkraft*

---

various techniques from the Gods "since it is impossible to conjecture how they could have taught them to themselves" (*Oeuvres complètes*, 3:145).

4. *Oeuvres complètes*, 3:462.

5. Ibid., 3:464.

and his *Empfindlichkeit*. The usual temptation arises to account for
the contradictions in various empirical and thematic ways. One can
argue that the movement of Rousseau's thought tends towards religious conversion, a hypothesis that receives some support from bio-
graphical data as well as from the fact that the *Nouvelle Héloïse* can be
read so as to make conversion the central statement of the book. Or
one can simply accuse Rousseau of inconsistency and dismiss the one
or the other half of his schizophrenic speculations. More produc-
tively, one can consider the religious aspect of his work as an ideological superstructure resulting from the repression or sublimation of
psychological or political contradictions, in a movement that runs
parallel to Althusser's diagnosis of the *literary* sublimation of Rousseau's political confusions. Before following any of these suggestions,
one should begin by establishing if, on the basis of the existing texts,
the discrepancies indeed occur in such philosophically uninteresting
ways. In the main texts, *Julie, Emile,* and the *Social Contract,* religious
and political elements are closely intertwined, but their relationship is
far from being either peaceful or simply comprehensible.

On the somewhat more specific issue of the source of legal and
moral authority, the discrepancy between the *Profession de foi* and
the *Social Contract* is not less striking. In political decisions having to
do with conflicts between the general will and individual interests,
the "inner voice" of conscience, which the Vicar held up as the source
of all truth, is of no avail: "When the general will has to be consulted
on a particular act . . . what will [common man] do to shelter
himself from error? Will he listen to the inner voice? But this voice is
said to be merely the result of judgments and feelings within the
sphere of an existing society and according to the laws of this society.
It can therefore not be used to establish these laws. Moreover, if it is
to be audible, none of the passions that speak louder than conscience, that cover up its timid voice and allow philosophers to claim
that this voice does not exist, should have arisen in the heart of
man."[6] This same "shyness" of conscience (although it is the voice of
God) is stressed in the *Profession de foi* (and in the letters to Sophie
d'Houdetot which are closely connected to the *Profession*): "Consciousness is shy, it loves retreat and peace . . ." and, in the long run,
it can even fall silent altogether: "It no longer speaks to us or answers
us, and when we have despised it so long, it becomes as difficult for

6. *Social Contract,* first version, *Oeuvres complètes,* 3:287.

us to call it back as it was to banish it" (601).[7] At other times, however, the same voice can be so loud that only the deaf fail to hear it: "[The materialists] are deaf to the inner voice that cries out to them in a tone that is difficult to ignore: A machine does not think . . ." (585). A great deal of ambivalence, historical, metaphorical, and logical, thus blurs a point that, according to all students of Rousseau, is crucially important in the interpretation of his thought.

Indeed, the entire question of the relationship between the general will and particular volition, between public and private morality Letter to Franquières), between public and private well-being (*Du bonheur public*), between the theological and the political order, hinges upon the uncanny timidity of the divine voice. Is God timid because he is so exquisitely sensitive or because he is not himself quite certain of what he has to say? There certainly is nothing timid about the laws which are supposed to be dictated by this voice and which confer, for example, the right of life and death over individuals (*Social Contract*, II, chapter 5).[8] It is difficult to see how Pierre Burgelin, as one instance among others, can slide so easily over the difficulties. Having to account for a similar discrepancy between the first and the second version of the *Social Contract* on the source of legal authority, he writes: "These two texts seem to contradict each other. But this is not the case: universal justice originates in reason enlightened by God [by conscience], and it only becomes applicable in the law. Thus the law changes from being a celestial voice to the condition of its applicability; the celestial voice is transferred to moral consciousness and finally to God" (1562). Burgelin moves from God to "voice," from divine voice to human conscience, from human conscience to practical morality, from morality to political law, in a sequence of mediations threatened at all points by numberless aberrations. For a mind as distrustful as Rousseau's, little inclined to have faith in any voice including his own, it seems unlikely that such a chain of displacements could be mastered without further complications.

The mere juxtaposition of explicit statements or the recourse to extra-textual causal explanations does nothing to resolve the difficulties. Since the question focuses precisely on the possible understanding or misunderstanding of voices that restate other voices, meanings

7. Almost the same formulation appears in Letter 6 of the *Lettres morales* (à Sophie d'Houdetot), *Oeuvres complètes*, 4:1112.

8. *Oeuvres complètes*, 3:376–77.

that reread or rewrite other meanings, the reading of the *Profession de foi* should be less monological than has been the case, with very few exceptions, in the interpretation of Rousseau's religious and political writings. It is obvious, for example, that none of the passages so frequently quoted from the *Profession* as evidence for Rousseau's theistic convictions are spoken by Rousseau himself, but by a fictional character, whose "voice" does not necessarily coincide with the author's; the same is true, of course, in Julie's letters. In the case of a so-called work of fiction, the observation is almost too self-evident to be necessary; no one will; without further question, simply equate Proust with Marcel or Flaubert with Emma Bovary. But in a discursive text like the *Profession de foi*, the use of a fictional spokesman, if it is noticed at all, is explained empirically as an alibi to shelter the writer from reprisals for his subversive opinions, a real enough problem in the case of *Emile*. Yet the presence of a fictional narrator is also a rhetorical necessity in any discourse that puts the truth or falsehood of its own statement in question. More still than epics or novels, discursive texts are necessarily dialogical—which implies, among other things, that they cannot be *quoted* without first having been *read*. The unwarranted separation between the way of reading and interpreting "literary" as opposed to "philosophical" or discursive texts—a separation due in large measure to ideologies derived from the misuse of aesthetic categories—deprives the reading of philosophical texts of elementary refinements that are taken for granted in literary interpretation. Paradoxically enough, this seems to happen even more clearly in the case of rhetorically self-conscious writers like Plato, Rousseau, or Nietzsche than in that of more formally technical philosophers.

The quotations that support the reading of the *Profession de foi* as a defense of natural religion frame an extended argument, one of the most sustained philosophical developments in the entire Rousseau corpus (567–606). The argument is in part polemical and primarily directed, as is well known, against Helvetius's *De l'esprit*, the article "Evidence" in the *Encyclopédie*, and, beyond that, the orthodoxy of a materialistic interpretation of nature associated with the works of Buffon, d'Holbach, Maupertuis, la Mettrie, and certain aspects of Diderot.[9] The place of the *Profession de foi* in the intellec-

9. The sources of the *Profession de foi* have been extensively studied, first by Pierre-Maurice Masson in *La "profession de foi du vicaire Savoyard" de Jean-Jacques*

tual history of the eighteenth century, as a belated Cartesian text[10] that resists both the Spinozistic and experiential trends of the times, has been well documented and concerns us here only on the first level of understanding. Indispensable as they are, such historical considerations have been an obstacle to the reading of the *Profession*, if only because they promote a tendency to oppose the sentimentalism of the pious passages to the rigor of enlightened rationalism and thus impose upon the text a binary system of valorization that is alien to its structure.

The argument of the *Profession de foi* begins (567) in Montaigne rather than in Descartes, in a condition of radical doubt that is more empirical than epistemological. As is consistently the case in Rousseau, the reduction to a condition of mere self-presence, be it as an individual consciousness or, as in the *Essai sur l'origine des langues*, as a political society, does not result in a constitutive *cogito*. It is a moment of genuine and intolerable confusion that allows for no statement other than its own intolerability. Consequently, it is more likely than any other moment to lead astray: tortured by doubt, "[the human mind] would rather be mistaken than believe nothing" (568). But since the original confusion is itself caused by error, by the inaccessibility of truth ("I love truth, I search for it but fail to recognize it . . ." [567]), the addition of more error to an existing state of aberration is not likely to improve things. The invocation of Descartes's name (567) has from the outset placed upon the argument an epistemological burden that makes it impossible to valorize such terms as "error" or "illusion" in a positive way. Rousseau can then reiterate the classical gesture of a *tabula rasa* and reject all existing wisdom as the product of mere conceit. But whereas this gesture should traditionally be a preliminary to the counterassertive integrity of self-reflection, it fails to lead, in this case, to any such assurance. The only claim made for the "inner light" that the mind is able to throw upon its powers is a dubious, unfounded hope for a lesser evil, entirely unable to resolve the condition of uncertainty that engen-

Rousseau, edition critique (Fribourg and Paris, 1914). Masson's findings are discussed and completed in Burgelin's introduction and notes to the *Oeuvres complètes*, with special emphasis on Helvetius and the article "Evidence" from the *Encyclopédie*, now generally believed to have been written by François Quesnay, the best known of the "physiocrats" (see 3:1129, n.1).

10. For example in Henri Gouhier, *Les méditations métaphysiques de Jean-Jacques Rousseau* (Paris, 1970), chapter 2.

dered the mental activity in the first place: ". . . I must follow the inner light, it will mislead me less than [the philosophers] do, or at least my error will be my own, and I shall be less perverted if I follow my illusions than if I believe their lies" (569). The shift to ethical valorization ("me dépraver"), suggesting that the distinction between "illusion" and "lie" is primarily a question of Rousseau's good faith as opposed to the false pride of the *philosophes*, is at the very least premature since, at this point, the question at issue is one of truth and falsehood and not of good and evil. Rousseau never claimed that good faith suffices to give authority of truth to a statement or a knowledge.

Neither does he claim it here. Still guided by the same valorization that privileges inside conviction over outside opinion, a polarity that has been introduced by the conventional rejection of all received knowledge as coming from "outside," we glide without discontinuity from sight to sound (from light to voice) and are told to follow "l'assentiment intérieur" (569) in accepting or rejecting the results of our attempts at understanding. Does this "inner assent" then acquire the paradigmatic quality of a Cartesian *cogito* as the foundation of judgment? This is hardly the case, for the description of its workings indicates that the "inner assent" operates only with regard to "ideas" that have themselves been identified (i.e., understood) by means of an act of judgment that has nothing to do with an immanent assent: "Then, turning over in my mind the various opinions that had successively swayed me since my birth, I saw that . . . my inner assent was given to them or withheld from them in varying degrees. Having made this observation, I compared all those different ideas without prejudice and found that the first and most common was also the simplest and most sensible . . ." (569). To *compare* is, for Rousseau, the distinctive quality of judgment, thus making it clear that the inner assent is itself dependent on a prior act of judgment which it does not control. The structure of the argument is in fact more deceptive, for the "first and most common idea" is identified as being precisely the theistic claim for the immanent authority of conscience, an article of faith here stated allusively by reference to the name of Samuel Clarke. The only thing to which the "inner assent" assents is itself; it sets up a tautological structure devoid of the deductive power inherent in a Cartesian *cogito*. It is true that we are being advised, in the next paragraph (570), to decide upon the truth of further units of knowledge deductively, by ascertaining their "necessary link" with the original evidence of the inner assent. But this apparent deduction is an illusion, since the necessity of the link can only be verified by means of the same rule of evidence that established the validity of the original principle and thus infinitely repeats itself without modification: assentio ergo assentio, etc.—unless one makes the principle of verification into an independent act of judgment (as was already the case in postulating the possibility of comparing ideas), but then the evidence of immanence is no longer the "first." Regardless of how one construes the passage, it indicates that the principle of immanence is in fact being superseded by an act of judgment which does not necessarily claim to possess the constitutive or generative power of a *cogito*. In this respect, the *Profession de foi* may well be a pre-Kantian rather than a neo-Cartesian text. For, despite the apparent confusion of its point of departure, it is not in fact confused by its own inconsistencies. It immediately draws the correct inferences from difficulties that could well have paralyzed the argument from the outset. The problem now becomes, not how to construe an interpretation of existence by means of a rule of inner assent, but to account, by a critical act of judgment, for the occurrence of such an assent and to establish its epistemological status. Rousseau acknowledges at once the indeterminacy of his own self-reflection by moving into a *critical* vocabulary: "But who am I? What right do I have to judge things and what determines my judgments? If they are forced upon me by the impressions I receive, it is futile for me to expend my energy in such inquiry, because they will not occur, or will occur on their own, without any effort on my part to control them. First, therefore, I must examine myself to come to know the instrument I intend to use and learn the extent to which I can rely on it" (570). The main informing concept of this text is that of *judgment*, not inner light or inner assent. The argument of the *Profession de foi* serves to reveal the structure of judgment in Rousseau and to establish its relationship to other key concepts such as will, freedom, reason, etc.

The structure of judgment, in this text, is established by opposition to that of sensation or perception. Moreover, what will be said about judgment will apply, albeit with a different and independently interesting thematic content, to three concepts shown to be correlatives of judgment: will, reason or intelligence, and freedom. No inherent priority or genetic link exists between the four terms (judgment, will, reason, and freedom) and it seems that a decision to start out the argument in terms of judgment is to a large extent arbitrary. They form a coherent conceptual chain in which each term can be derived from the other at will: "If I am asked what cause determines my *will*, I ask in turn what cause determines my *judgment*: for it is clear that those two causes are one. If we realize that man is active in his judgment and that his *intelligence* is only the power of comparing and judging, we see that his *freedom* is only a similar power, or one derived from it. He chooses good as he chooses truth; if his judgment is false, his choice is wrong. What, then, is the cause that determines his *will*? It is his *judgment*. And what is the cause that determines his judgment? It is his faculty of *intelligence*, his power to judge . . ." (586, my italics).

Rousseau's theory of judgment restates, though in a less oblique and bewildering manner, the critical theory of metaphor that underlies the argument of the *Second Discourse*. Judgment is described as the deconstruction of sensation, a model that divides the world into a binary system of oppositions organized along an inside/outside axis and then proceeds to exchange the properties on both sides of this axis on the basis of analogies and potential identities. The systems conceived by the contemporaries against whom Rousseau polemicizes are all structured according to this fundamentally metaphorical pattern: by means of empirical considerations on the nature of perception, they oppose body to soul, sensation to judgment, nature to mind (or art), *res extensa* to *res cogito*, outside to inside, death to life, and then reconcile the antinomies with varying degrees of dialectical rigor. For example, in the hylozoistic vision of a biologically alive matter, even death and life can be reconciled: to see the natural world as a live animal is to push to its limit, as Diderot will ironically suggest in *Pensées sur l'interprétation de la nature*,[11] the metaphorical model of an inside/outside correspondence. Rousseau, in the discussion of judgment, categorically rejects the unwarranted totalization of metaphorized synecdoches: "Yet this visible universe consists of matter, scattered and dead matter, which as a *whole* has none of the cohesion, organization or the common feeling of the *parts* of a living body, for it is certain that we, who are *parts*, have no feeling of ourselves in the *whole*" (575, my italics). Sensation unadulterated by judgment is in fact inconceivable, but if it is posited

---

11. Denis Diderot, *Oeuvres complètes*, chronological edition with introduction by Roger Lewinter (Paris, 1970), 2:767–71.

hypothetically (as the state of nature is posited in the *Second Discourse*), it is totally incapable of setting up any relationship between entities or of setting up entities in the first place. It would not be adequate to call the rhetorical structure of such a world of pure sensation metonymic rather than metaphorical, since such a structure could not even conceive of contiguity, let alone of resemblance. Rousseau writes as if he admitted the existence of an inside/outside polarity ("I therefore clearly understand that a sensation, which is inside me, and its cause or object, which is outside me, are not the same thing" [571]), but this "hors de moi" is then so entirely devoid of any semblance of coherence or signification as to be nothing at all, for us or in itself. To a pure sensation, it would appear entirely chaotic, contingent and unpredictable, much more so even than the picture of the organic world gone awry that Diderot conjures up in the *Lettre sur les aveugles*.[12] A universe of pure sensation would be unable to conceive of ratio or of number: "Such comparative ideas as 'larger' or 'smaller' and the numerical ideas of 'one,' 'two,' etc., are certainly not sensations, even though they are always accompanied by sensations when my mind produces them" (572). Pure "outsideness" is the only discontinuity that articulates even the smoothest appearance of identity, since it cannot be said that the sensation of a given entity in X is identical with the sensation of the same entity in Y: "When the sensations are different, the sentient being distinguishes them by their differences; when they are alike, it distinguishes them because it feels that the one is *outside* the other [*hors des autres*]" (572, my italics). Spatial models—and the same would have to apply to temporal models—are metaphorical conceptualizations of *differential* structures, which is why they engender such redoubtably effective and misleading powers of unification and categorization. Rousseau, however, introduces outsideness (with its implicit train of spatial and temporal correlatives) as a principle of differentiation that could never legitimately be made to function in the opposite direction: the "outside" in the sentence just quoted is not the outside *of* a corresponding inside. In the mode of pure sensation, everything is "outside" everything else; there is nothing but outside differences and no integration is possible.

This version of differentiation is similar to the distinction made in the *Second Discourse*, also on the basis of difference and re-

12. Ibid., 2:197–98.

semblance, between denomination and conceptualization. The act of judgment coincides with the ability to postulate relationships, the possibility of elaborating systems based on the correlation of differential with integrative moments. This activity is called "to compare" or, more explicitly, "to place one [object] over another to pronounce on their difference or on their similarity" (571). The process is a manipulation, a displacement that upsets the "truth" of things as they are, for sensation, unlike judgment, is truthful to the extent that it leaves things in their proper places and does not even conceive of making what is distinct identical: "By sensation, objects are presented to me as separate, isolated, as they are in nature . . ." (571) and therefore "I know only that truth is in things, not in the mind that judges them, and that the less of myself I put into my judgments of them, the surer I am to approach truth . . ." (573). Since judgment is also associated with what, in this same paragraph, is called "the honor of thinking," it follows that thought and truth are not necessarily coextensive notions.

Judgment, also called "attention," "meditation," "reflection," or "thought" [pensée], and always described by verbs of motion such as to move, to transport, to fold [replier], neither reveals things for what they are nor leaves them undisturbed. It moves them around, thus mimicking the etymology of the very term metaphor, of the Aristotelian epiphora: "in comparing [objects], I move and transpose them, so to speak, I place one over another . . ." (571). Judgment does this in order to create systems of relationship that are not substantial but merely structural; from a formal point of view, these systems are by no means arbitrary but since they are devoid of ontological authority, they are not controlled by considerations of truth and falsehood. Therefore, they are capable of errors which they make possible by their very existence: "Why then am I mistaken about the relation between these two sticks, especially when they are not parallel? . . . Why is the image, which is the sensation, unlike its model, which is the object? Because I am active when I judge, and the operation of comparison is faulty; in judging relations, my understanding mingles its errors with the truth of sensations, which show only objects" (572). The falsehood does not have a contingent cause that could be corrected by trial and error, by experimental or methodological refinements, since the act of thought is itself, by its very manifestation, a falsification.[13] The pattern of this falsification is the same as

13. The statement recurs frequently in Rousseau. See, for example, in *Emile:*

that of the concept in the *Second Discourse:* it uses structural resemblances in order to conceal the differences that permit the very
articulations of structure.

The consistency, or repetitiveness, of Rousseau's thought on this
point reduces the polemics of the *Profession de foi* against the
philosophes to a secondary function. The disagreement with Helvetius, la Mettrie, and to a lesser extent, Diderot, repeats the earlier
disagreement with Condillac and the tradition of Locke on the origin
of language.[14] It is a central insight of Rousseau that never varies
throughout the work and that finds its first systematic expression in
the section on language in the *Second Discourse* and in the *Essay on
the Origins of Language.* The same rhetorical vigilance determines
the disjunction between judgment and sensation in the *Profession de
foi* and that between judgment and sensation in the earlier texts. And
the equation of judgment with language is hardly less clear in the
later theological than in the earlier political text: it is asserted in a
single sentence, when it is said of judgment that "In my opinion, the
distinctive faculty of an active or intelligent being is the ability to give
meaning to the word 'to be'" (571).

The ambivalence of judgment stands fully revealed in this sentence. The stability of the natural world is by itself devoid of meaning
and cannot become a source of knowledge. Being is for us only "the
word 'to be'", and the copula has no transcendental referent by
natural or divine right. This negative insight, achieved in the differentiation between judgment and sensation, is itself an act of judgment and this act is verbal. Terms such as "to move" or "to fold" are
replaced by such verbs as "to pronounce" or "to give meaning," thus
implying that the verb "to be," as matrix of all referential language,
has no proper meaning by itself. The scene of judgment is that of a
verbal pronouncement and that of an oracular verdict. But after
having thus undone any possible association between relation and
necessity, the same judgment then proceeds to do, in its own name,
what it had undone in the name of sensation, and to set up structures, such as concepts, which lay claim to meaning in the same way
that sensation could lay claim to the existence of matter and reality:

". . . the more men know, the more they err . . .'." (3:483). In contrast to this,
Helvetius, in *De l'esprit*, will say: ". . . our false judgments are the result of accidental causes which do not imply, in the *mind*, a faculty of *judgment* that would be
distinct from a faculty of *perceiving* [faculté de *sentir*]" (quoted by Burgelin, 3:1523).

14. See Chapter 7, p. 152.

"Thus not only do I exist, but other entities exist also, namely, the objects of my sensations . . . [which] I call matter . . ." (571). Like language, judgment engenders the same possibility of reference that it also excises. Its error can therefore not be localized or identified in any way; one could not, for example, say that the error stems from language, as if language were an entity that existed independently of judgment or judgment a faculty that could exercise its activity in a nonlinguistic mode. To the extent that judgment is a structure of relationships capable of error, it is also language. As such, it is bound to consist of the very figural structures that can only be put in question by means of the language that produces them. What is then called "language" clearly has to extend well beyond what is empirically understood as articulated verbal utterance and subsumes, for instance, what is traditionally referred to as perception.

This becomes apparent in Rousseau's treatment of the Lockean problem of Molyneux and the *sensus communum*, a recurrent question in eighteenth-century philosophy of perception.[15] The *Profession de foi* distinguishes between sensation and perception as Rousseau distinguishes elsewhere between verbal and nonverbal drives ("passions" and "besoins"): "If we were purely passive in the use of our senses, there would be no communication among them; it would be impossible for us to know that the object we touch and the object we see are the same. Either we would never be aware of anything outside ourselves, or there would be for us five perceptible substances whose identity we would have no means of perceiving" (573). The unity of perception is an act of judgment which, as such, denies that the totalization of perception could be rooted in an exchange of properties held in common by mind and matter. While denying therefore that perception could ever be an access to true knowledge, the passage acknowledges that it is structured like a metaphor and thus must be considered as an act of judgment or a language. The term "language" thus includes that of perception or sensation, implying that understanding can no longer be modeled on or derived from the experience of the senses; in this respect, the *Profession de foi* occupies a pivotal position in the complex history of the relationships between empirical psychology and theories of language in the eighteenth century. We can conclude that the vicar describes judg-

15. John Locke, *An Essay Concerning Human Understanding*, ed. Alexander Campbell Fraser (New York, 1959), 1:186–87; Book 2, chapter 9, § 8.

ment as the power to set up potentially aberrant referential systems that deconstruct the referentiality of their own elaboration. This description warrants the equation of judgment with figural language, extensively conceived.

Different versions of the same aporia organize the description of the related concepts of will, mind, and freedom. In the discussion of the will (576–78), the polemical argument against Toland and la Mettrie denying the immanence of motion within matter and defining the will as the transcendental cause of all motion, reintroduces the inside/outside structure that was also adopted at the beginning of the description of judgment. Just as the vicar begins by sounding like an orthodox disciple of Locke when he asserts the truth-value of sensation, he sounds like an orthodox disciple of Fénelon in asserting the need to postulate a transcendental *primum mobile.* The transcendental outside structure becomes productive however (and potentially aberrant) only when it is conceived as a polarity rather than a mere positional relationship, that is, from the moment that a principle of articulation connects an inside with this outside in a way that allows for the exchange of properties. In the midst of so many borrowed arguments and philosophical commonplaces about the transcendental will, the specificity of Rousseau's thought manifests itself in the sudden refusal to grant intelligibility to the principle of articulation on which the possibility of understanding depends: "It is no more possible for me to conceive how my will moves my body than how my sensations affect my soul. I do not even know why one of those mysteries has seemed more explainable than the other. As for me, either when I am passive or when I am active, the means of uniting the two substances seems completely incomprehensible to me. It is strange that others take that very incomprehensibility as their point of departure for combining the two substances, as though operations so different in nature could be better explained in one subject than in two" (576). What are here called incomprehensible are precisely such notions as analogy, resemblance, sympathy, or even proximity which are the ground of understanding and which the rationalistic and theistic eighteenth century was trying to reclaim. Far from clarifying the obscure link between will and motion by means of the apparently more verifiable (because easier to observe and to quantify) link between matter and mind (or body and soul), the vicar lets the darkness of the former encroach upon the latter. We know as little about the (outside) sensation becoming (inside) affect or consciousness as about the (inside) will becoming (outside) motion. As a matter of fact, the individual will is unable ever to get outside itself and to establish a corresponding principle of exteriority: "I know the will only through the feeling of my own will, and intelligence [*entendement*] is not better known to me" (586). This does not imply that judgment is enigmatic because, like the will, it can be metaphorically represented in the guise of a self; it merely states that judgment is as enigmatic as the will, though the mode of indeterminacy or undecidability may vary depending on whether one considers the aporia from a voluntaristic or from an epistemological point of view. The patterns of error engendered by the will are not the same as those engendered by judgment, since both produce their own referential systems, and are commonly in error only to the extent that referentiality is itself their error. The referent produced specifically by the will is that of *selfhood*, which is open to the same deconstructive ambivalence as the more general *meaning* derived from judgment. The explicit linkage of judgment with error thus extends to the idea of selfhood, product of the same metaphorical illusion of proper meaning as the relational constructs of judgment.

The combination of judgment with the will engenders in turn the mental activity here called intelligence. But the more we advance in the degree of conceptualization associated with each of these terms—the text being set up in such a way that, as we move from judgment to will to intelligence and finally to freedom, we are further and further removed from the critical deconstruction that established the epistemological ambivalence of judgment at the outset—the more the aporia, still quite clearly thematized in the analysis of judgment, becomes embedded within the texture of the narrative, to the point of making the text into the dramatization of its own confusions. Examples abound, especially in the closely linked discussions of intelligence, as the systematic assertion of the power to will, and of freedom. It is in these pages (from 577 to 606) that the strongest statements in support of Rousseau's theistic orthodoxy occur: the awe expressed before the deity as a principle of natural harmony and order, pietistic statements about the innate virtue of a divine omnipresence, the definition of moral conscience as innate: "There is thus within our souls an innate principle of justice and virtue by which, in spite of our maxims, we judge our acts and those of others as good or bad, and it is this principle that I call conscience" (598). One should bear in mind that these assertions occur within a context in which the concepts that are being described are consistently equated with acts of judgment (as when it is said, in the above quotation, that "we *judge* our acts and those of others . . .") which have been shown to be constitutively associated with aberrant totalization. And one should also notice that each of these affirmations of piety and trust is always coupled, sometimes explicitly, sometimes by implication, with a statement that puts it in question. For instance, when the vicar wishes to oppose intelligence to sheer random chance, he chooses a literary text as a model for analogy. Such a text could never be the contingent result of infinitely combining the letters of the alphabet: "If I were told that printer's type had been thrown at random and the letters fallen in such a way as to spell out the entire *Aeneid*, I would not deign to take one step to investigate that falsehood" (579).[16] The statement comes in fact a lot closer to the sentence of Mallarmé which seems to be saying the reverse ("Jamais un coup de dés n'abolira le hasard"), if one takes into account that, for the "author" of the Preface to the *Nouvelle Héloïse*, the intentionality ("unité d'intention," 580) of a literary text is so undecidable that no writer can be certain of his own authorship. If God is to be present to his own creation in the same manner that a writer is present to his text, this leaves very little authority to the divine intelligence. The *Profession de foi* can therefore posit itself, so to speak, on both sides of the position taken by Diderot in the *Lettre sur les aveugles* with regard to the element of chance involved in the creation of the organic world: the natural world is here much more radically contingent, disjointed, and inarticulated than the floating organs Diderot and la Mettrie[17] are so fond of evoking, but, on the other hand, the model of a combinatory system with a very large number of elements seems equally inadequate as an analogy for the workings of the mind. The ability of the mind to set up, by means of acts of judgment, formally coherent structures is never denied, but the ontological or epistemological authority of the resulting systems, like that of texts, escapes determination.

More explicit instances of controlled contradiction also appear in this section of the *Profession de foi*. They are dramatically em-

16. Rousseau seems to have a predilection for this example which is repeated in the Letter to Franquières (3:1139), the *Letter to Voltaire* (3:1071), where he politely substitutes the *Henriade* for the *Aeneid*, and in a letter to Vernes of February 18, 1758.

17. Diderot, *Lettre sur les aveugles, Oeuvres complètes*, 2:197; la Mettrie, *Système d'Epicure, Oeuvres philosophiques de Mr. de la Mettrie* (Berlin, 1775), p. 260.

phasized in the contrast between the harmony of a universe conceived as a teleological system without known endpoint,[18] or the
glorification of man as "king of the earth" (582) and on the other
hand the utter misery of the human mind incapable of understanding the principles of its own working and torn apart by the contradictions of its condition: "Feeling myself swayed and torn by those
two conflicting tendencies, I said to myself, 'No, man is not one; I
both exert my will and fail to exert it; I feel both enslaved and free; I
see what is good, I love it, and I do evil, etc.'" (583). The contradiction comes fully into view in the way the vicar conceives of God. Since
he rejects any idea of unmediated revelation, the idea of God is
derived, by analogical extension, from the attributes of human
judgment, and not of nature (for whenever he considers the possibility of patterning the relationship between God and man on that
between man and nature, or subject and object, he rejects the possibility by means of arguments derived from the distinction between
judgment and sensation). Therefore divine activity is described by
the same terms that were used to define judgment: "Acting, comparing, and choosing are operations of an active and thinking being;
therefore that being exists . . ." (578); "The being who has both will
and power, who is active of himself, who moves the universe and
orders all things, that being, whatever he may be, I call God. I add to
that name the ideas of intelligence, power, and will . . ." (581). The
mind of God and the mind of man resemble each other; man and
God are each other's metaphor.[19] Hence the fact that they can be

18. In statements such as these: ". . . I never cease to perceive the intimate
correspondence by means of which the beings that compose the universe come to
each other's rescue" (578); ". . . I see that each part [of the machine] is made for the
others, I admire its maker in the details of his work, and I am sure that its parts all
move together for some common end . . ." (578). It is always added that this
common end is unknown, but this does not detract from the fact that the pattern
remains teleological, "the harmony and the unison of the universe [l'harmonie et
l'accord du tout]" (580).

19. The manuscript of the *Profession de foi* is more explicit on this point than
the final version: ". . . I call this being God. Does this word allow me to know the
'essence' of the being he represents. No. . . . I will never know him in his being. I
can therefore study him only in his attributes . . . I cannot even clearly conceive of
him by his attributes for how could I conceive of them if not by comparison with
human faculties" (Masson, *La "profession de foi du vicaire Savoyard" de Jean-Jacques
Rousseau*, pp. 145–46). See also the note "Dieu est intelligent; mais comment l'est-il?
L'homme" (ibid., p. 146).

substituted at will: God can be said, for example, to want man's good in his stead, and man's freedom to err is accounted for as his opportunity to prove himself equal to a divine principle that shares this freedom with him (587). Hence also that the relationship between man and God can be called love: "I worship [*adore*] this supreme power and I am touched by his kindness. . . . It is not a natural consequence of our self-love to honor what protects us and to love what wants our good?" (583). Like the wild metaphor "giant" which, in the *Essay on the Origins of Language*, becomes "man," the spontaneous metaphor "God" can then be institutionalized and quantified into a contractual relationship in which God is said to *owe* something to man, and to pay him for the price of labors accomplished in his behalf. The pro- or regression from love to economic dependence is a constant characteristic of all moral or social systems based on the authority of noncontested metaphorical systems.

On the other hand, however, this God who is so much like us turns out to be as completely alien, unknowable, and "outside" as a pure sensation is before it has been organized by judgment: ". . . as soon as I try to contemplate [God] in himself, as soon as I try to discover where he is, what he is, what his substance is, he eludes me and my troubled mind no longer perceives anything" (581). When combined with all the previous passages on the indeterminacy of judgment and on its irresistible tendency to see seductive similarities where they do not exist, this passage is not at all similar to the kind of theological humility one would find, for example, in Malebranche. The manner in which God is said to be incomprehensible in his relation to his own being is precisely the same as that in which he is made all too comprehensible in his relation to man; the mystery of the parousia is not compatible with that of a divine presence showing itself providentially concerned as the voice of an individual moral conscience. One is reminded of Kant in the *Critique of Judgment:* "If one can call a mere representation a cognition, then all our knowledge of God is symbolical and whoever schematizes this knowledge by means of properties such as judgment, will, etc., which demonstrate only the objective reality of earthly creatures, lapses into anthropomorphism, just as he lapses into deism if he omits all elements of intuition."[20]

The logical pattern of these developments is always the same

20. Kant, *Kritik der Urteilskraft* (Stuttgart, 1924), § 59, p. 213.

and repeats the aporia of judgment. A concept such as judgment, will, or freedom operates deconstructively as a principle of differentiation but then, because of the referentiality inherent in the linguistic model, reintegrates by an act of the mind what it had taken apart on the level of intuition. The correlative of this second operation, regardless of whether it be called the *meaning* of a judgment, the *self* that wills, or the *God* that freely invents, recovers in its turn the attributes of (natural) existence, and can therefore again be deconstructed by the same system. The original metaphor is shown to be based on a misleading assumption of identity, but the utterance of this negative insight is itself a new metaphor that engenders its own semantic correlative, its own proper meaning: we move from sensation to judgment, for example, or from nature to God, but what appears to be a hypostasis is in fact even more vulnerable, logically speaking, than the entity it claims to supersede. A system of this type is bound to produce bewildering patterns of valorization.

The text of the *Profession de foi* becomes indeed increasingly saturated with value judgments. It starts out (570 ff.) in a relatively detached and analytical mode but, as the argument progresses, it modulates towards highly theatrical oratorical effects. There is a corresponding shift from the relatively "cold" values of truth and falsehood (which become values only because of the possibility of error) to the more turgid values of good and evil. The dynamic emphasis was present from the start, since judgment is consistently being described as an *act* and as a *power* [puissance]. From the moment, however, that one reaches such metaphors as the will that allow for the localization of the active principle within particular entities (such as the self), the tension is bound to increase: the incomprehensibility of the link between will and motion problematizes the relationship between the intent and the direction of the movement, and the solipsistic immanence of the will ("I know the will only through the feeling of my own will . . .") threatens the very possibility of motion with paralysis. The binary inside/outside pattern, which could be considered as a merely spatial organization without implying valorization, is now activated by a play of resistances and impulses; from being epistemological, the language of the *Profession de foi* becomes ethical. But since the "prime mover" of judgment is aberrant and represents as a deliberate movement what is, in fact, a suspended inability to know whether or where it should go (and is thus, in truth, neither "prime" nor "mover"), the system of valorization that links the modalities of judgment to the values of the will can never be consistent. Aberrations of moral judgment are a consequence of epistemological and rhetorical indeterminations.

The *Profession de foi* acts out this inconsistent transformation of structures into values. The referentiality inherent in judgment becomes more and more manifest and moves the text closer and closer to a world of practical reason which will finally end up in political realities. The theistic orthodoxy always associated the structures of inwardness and exteriority with the values of good and evil by linking inside with good and outside with evil. The positive valorization of inwardness is part of the historical tradition of pietism out of which Rousseau is writing. One remembers the vicar's exhortation: "Let us look into ourselves [*Rentrons en nous-mémes*], my young friend. . . ." Inwardness is the metaphor of virtue, and vice versa. But the text fails to respect the necessity of this linkage and it crosses and uncrosses the system established by the inside/outside and the good/evil polarities at will. We are told, for instance, that "As I meditated on the nature of man, I seemed to discover two distinct principles in him. The first elevated him to the study of eternal truths, to love of justice and moral beauty, to those realms of the intellectual world that the wise delight in contemplating. The second drew him downward *into himself*, subjected him to the power of his senses and the passions that are their ministers, and counteracted, through them, everything inspired in him by the first principle" (583, my italics). More explicitly still, a few pages later, evil is again directly associated with inwardness and, by implication, the love of beauty and of virtue directed towards the outside: "If you take away from our hearts that love of what is beautiful, you will take away all the charm of life. A man whose vile passions have stifled those exquisite feelings in his narrow soul, and who, by focussing all his attention *within himself* [au dedans de lui], has come to love no one but himself, is no longer enraptured by anything, . . . such a wretched man no longer feels or lives; he is already dead" (596, my italics). Yet, separated from this passage by only the one paragraph, the following statement again reverses the pattern: "The wicked man fears and avoids himself; he lifts his spirits by going *outside* himself; he looks around him with anxiety, seeking something that will divert him . . . derisive laughter is his only pleasure. The virtuous man, however, finds only joy, and the source of that joy is *in himself*; he is cheerful alone as in company; he does not draw his contentment from those around him: he communicates it to them" (597, my italics). One can argue, of course, that, psychologically speaking, there can just as well be a "bad" as a "good" inwardness. But this has little bearing upon a text that is not set up along psychological lines but structured by means of a differential inside/outside axis; in such a text, the values associated with these two dimensions will necessarily carry a decisive exegetic weight.

The occurrence of such systematic value-displacements thus acquires central importance in the reading of the *Profession de foi*. They are not simply chiasmic reversals allowing the (inside) good to be called "evil" and the (outside) evil to be called "good." The system is not symmetrical, since it postulated, from the start, the nonidentity of inside and outside, the "supplementarity" of the one with regard to the other. On the level of judgment, the asymmetry leads to the play of contradictions and paradoxes, the logical tensions that have earned Rousseau the frequent accusation of sophistry. Deconstructive readings can point out the unwarranted identifications achieved by substitution, but they are powerless to prevent their recurrence even in their own discourse, and to uncross, so to speak, the aberrant exchanges that have taken place. Their gesture merely reiterates the rhetorical defiguration that caused the error in the first place. They leave a margin of error, a residue of logical tension that prevents the closure of the deconstructive discourse and accounts for its narrative and allegorical mode. When this process is described in terms of will or freedom and thus transferred to the level of reference, the differential residue is bound to become manifest as an empirical awareness that *affects* and indeed constitutes a world in which it now appears to be "taking place"; a mind, a consciousness, a self. The abstract attributes of truth and falsehood grow more and more concrete and find themselves a place, a stage on which to act out the temporal sequence of their occurrence. Judgment becomes a "spectacle" (596), a pathetic action that affects us like a theatrical representation. Trying to persuade his interlocutor of the quality of virtue, the vicar resorts as by instinct to analogies from the theatre: "When you see a play, which characters win your sympathy?" (596), he asks. As the confusion between structure and value increases, the tone and the terminology of the text glide almost imperceptibly from the language of judgment to the language of the affections, and judgment finally openly declares itself to be another name for "sentiment" (still distinct, at this point, from "sensation," *against* which, it will be remembered, judgment was originally defined). The ambiguously valorized "inner" world of consciousness, of which it can no longer be said whether it is the seat of good or evil, becomes the affective space engendered by this ethical indecisiveness: "The acts of our conscience are not judgments, but feelings. Although all our ideas come from outside us, the feelings that evaluate them are inside ourselves, and it is solely by those feelings that we know the fitness or unfitness that exists between us and those things which we must respect or shun" (599).

The principle of valorization according to which this evaluation can be carried out has itself to become increasingly literal. The eudaemonic polarity of pleasure and pain replaces the moral polarity of good and evil. The text behaves as if, at this point (599), the question that had opened up its entire inquiry had been decisively answered. We are now supposed to know the answer to the critical "But who am I?" (570) that was to sanction the recourse to immanent evidence in the understanding of our being-in-the-world. What has in fact been established is the gradual loss of authority of any immanent judgment or any immanent value whatsoever. At the same time, and by means of the same argument, the alternative recourse to a transcendental source of authority, such as nature, or God, has also been definitively foreclosed. The aporia of truth and falsehood has turned into the confusion of good and evil and ended up in an entirely arbitrary valorization in terms of pain and pleasure. Virtue becomes finally justified in terms of an erotic pleasure principle, a moral libido that seems not easily compatible with the piety of the inner voice of conscience but that consistently acts out the rhetorical system of the text.

The turn towards eudaemonic valorization is more apparent, for obvious reasons, in the so called *Lettres morales* addressed by Rousseau to Sophie d'Houdetot, a text that is ancillary to the *Profession de foi* and that dates from 1757. In this text, virtue is spoken of in terms of a narcissistic economy of personal well-being, accessible only to those who can afford a great deal of leisure: "Every month, take a span of two or three days away from your pleasures and your business, and devote it to the most important task of all. . . . I don't expect you to concentrate from the start on profound meditations, I only insist that you keep your soul in a state of quiet languor that will allow it to turn inward upon itself and to exclude whatever is alien to its own being. In that state, you may ask, what will I do? Nothing at all. Just let natural unrest take over; in solitude, it will not take long to manifest itself, whether we want it or not. . . . Just as one rewarms a numbed part of the body by rubbing it delicately, so the soul, numbed by a long state of inaction, revives in the gentle warmth of a well-tempered motion. . . . One must remind it of the affections that have caused it pleasure, but not by ways of the senses; it must happen by the proper feelings and by intellectual pleasures. . . . Whatever state the soul may be in, a feeling of pleasure at doing the right thing remains and serves as a foothold for all other virtues. It is by cultivating this feeling that one comes to love and to find pleasure in one's own company" (1115–16). The language of self-seduction is less obvious in the mouth of the vicar, but he is saying nothing else when virtue is called "the charm of life" (596) or "the pure voluptuousness born from self-satisfaction" (591).

The point is not that the foundation of moral judgment in the pleasure principle is in any way ethically or psychologically wrong. Such returns to the physiological foundations of the notions of right and wrong are not at all surprising in the century of *morale sensitive,* nor for that matter in any other century; without even having recourse to Freud, we can refer, for instance, to the importance given by Nietzsche to the pleasure/pain polarity in his critique of metaphysical concepts.[21] What matters here is that the reintroduction of these notions, at this point in the *Profession de foi,* illustrates the viciously circular (in the Nietzschean sense) structure of Rousseau's theological discourse. For he has no illusions about the consistency of eudaemonic systems of valorization. The association of virtue with pleasure (as in the text from the *Lettres morales* that has just been quoted) can at once be reversed and the self-love turn into the *amour propre* which is at the base of bad faith and of bad judgment: "The practice of virtue naturally flatters our vanity [*amour propre*] by an idea of superiority. We remember good deeds as proof that we have the strength to satisfy even the needs of others after our own needs have been fulfilled. This feeling of *power* [puissance] makes life more pleasant and makes us cohabitate more easily with ourselves" (1116). But the ambivalence of this will-to-power morality is not the main complication of our text. The sliding pro- or regression from judgment to feeling, from epistemology to eudaemony, a motion which takes place entirely within the conceptual system that consti

21. For example in Friedrich Nietzsche, *The Will to Power,* translated by Walter Kaufmann and R. J. Hollingdale (New York, 1968), pp. 371–74, sections 699–703.

tutes the text of the *Profession de foi* and is therefore accounted for, at all times, by its logic, requires, as a thematic assertion, the necessary reintroduction of the rhetorical structure that was explicitly banned at the start. The serpent bites its own tail. The vicar has to reaffirm, at the end of his argument, the priority of the category against which his argument has been consistently directed. He has to restate his belief in the metaphorical analogy between mind and nature: ". . . we feel before we know, and just as we do not learn to will our own good and avoid what is harmful to us, but receive that will from nature, love of good and hatred of evil are as natural to us as self-love" (599). The equation of will with nature is precisely what the vicar's judgment persistently puts in question. Within the context of this deconstruction, the final part of this quotation can be read ironically, since nothing could be more problematic than the naturalness of self-love, a passion which, like all passions, merely repeats the aberrations of figural language. Nothing therefore prevents the deconstructive labor that has brought us to this point from starting all over again.

The naïve historical question from which we started out—should the *Profession de foi* be called a theistic text?—must remain unanswerable. The text both is and is not the theistic document it is assumed to be. It is not the simple negation of the faith it seems to proclaim, since it ends up by accounting in a manner that cannot be refuted for the necessary occurrence of this faith. But it also denounces it as aberrant. A text such as the *Profession de foi* can literally be called "unreadable" in that it leads to a set of assertions that radically exclude each other. Nor are these assertions mere neutral constations; they are exhortative performatives that require the passage from sheer enunciation to action. They compel us to choose while destroying the foundations of any choice. They tell the allegory of a judicial decision that can be neither judicious nor just. As in the plays of Kleist, the verdict repeats the crime it condemns. If, after reading the *Profession de foi,* we are tempted to convert ourselves to "theism," we stand convicted of foolishness in the court of the intellect. But if we decide that belief, in the most extensive use of the term (which must include all possible forms of idolatry and ideology) can once and forever be overcome by the enlightened mind, then this twilight of the idols will be all the more foolish in not recognizing itself as the first victim of its occurrence. One sees from this that the impossibility of reading should not be taken too lightly.

11   Promises

(Social Contract)

THE CONNECTION BETWEEN THE POLITICAL AND THE religious writings of Rousseau is enigmatic and, at first sight, entirely contradictory. Rousseau's theology and his political theory seem to lead in opposite directions. There have been excellent books written about Rousseau's political theory that don't even mention his religious concerns, and vice versa.[1] Yet the second part of the *Nouvelle Héloïse* combines the discussion of political institutions with theological considerations and at least suggests a close, albeit unformulated interrelationship between both. And the *Social Contract*, which obviously proposes a model for political institutions and reflects on the authority of legal language, has to reintroduce religious themes at at least one crucial point.[2] The difficulty may well stem from the use of such thematic terms as "political" or "religious," as if their referential status were clearly established and could be understood without regard for the rhetorical mode of their utilization.

1. E.g., Mario Einaudi, *The Early Rousseau* (Ithaca, N.Y., 1967) or, in the other direction, Louis Althusser, "Sur le *Contract Social* (Les Décalages)" in *L'impensé de J. J. Rousseau, Cahiers pour l'analyse*, vol. 8 (Paris, 1970). pp. 5–42. The problem of the relationship between Rousseau's theology and his political theories is, of course, of central importance in all historical and thematic studies of Rousseau's work as a whole, for example, in the books and articles of Robert Derathé, Pierre Burgelin, Henri Gouhier, Jean Starobinski, Roland Grimsley and others. The notes to the third volume of the Pléiade edition (*Ecrits politiques*) reflect the present state of the question in academic Rousseau interpretation. The polemical implications of the reading that is here being suggested have not been developed, since the emphasis falls on the theoretical status of misreading in general rather than on actual (mis)-readings of their history.

2. Particularly in the section on the lawgiver (*Social Contract*, book 2, chapter 7, pp. 381 ff.) and in the penultimate section of the text (*Social Contract*, book 4, chapter 8, pp. 460–69). All quotations are from J. J. Rousseau, *Oeuvres complètes*, ed. Bernard Gagnebin and Marcel Raymond (Paris: Gallimard [Bibliothèque de la Pléiade], 1964), vol. 3. Translations are my own or based on the version established by Lowell Bair in *The Essential Rousseau* (New York: Random House, 1974) with occasional modifications.

It may be just as difficult to decide upon the rhetorical status of theoretical texts such as the *Profession de foi* and the *Social Contract* as on a fiction such as the *Nouvelle Héloïse*. The difference between a fictional and a theoretical text carries very little weight in the case of Rousseau. By reading the unreadability of the *Profession de foi*, we found it to be structured exactly like the *Nouvelle Héloïse*: the deconstruction of a metaphorical model (called "love" in the *Nouvelle Héloïse*, "judgment" in the *Profession*) leads to its replacement by homological text systems whose referential authority is both asserted and undermined by their figural logic. The resulting "meanings" can be said to be ethical, religious, or eudaemonic, but each of these thematic categories is torn apart by the aporia that constitutes it, thus making the categories effective to the precise extent that they eliminate the value system in which their classification is grounded. If we choose to call this pattern an allegory of unreadability or simply an allegory, then it should be clear that the *Profession de foi*, like *Julie*, is an allegory and that no distinction can be made between both texts from the point of view of a genre theory based on rhetorical models. The fact that one narrates concepts whereas the other narrates something called characters is irrelevant from a rhetorical perspective.

But if the *Profession de foi* is an allegory of (non)signification, can the same still be said of the *Social Contract*? Again, no reliable answer can be given by merely quoting or paraphrasing the text without reading it. And to read the *Social Contract* is, for instance and among other things, to determine the relationship between general will and particular will, two notions that obviously play a predominant part in the organization of the text.

A first difficulty in the use of the polarity between the general and the particular will is lexicological and stems from the apparently interchangeable use of the terms "natural" (as in *religion naturelle*, *droit naturel*, etc.) and "particular" or "individual," both used in opposition to "civil" or "collective." Rousseau follows common usage in speaking of natural law, natural religion, or natural freedom (p. 293); he does not use "volonté naturelle" however, but would rather have chosen, in opposition to "volonté générale," the term "volonté particulière."[3] Yet, taken literally, "particular" is clearly not the same

3. The specific expression "volonté particulière" occurs rarely or not at all in this form, but Rousseau speaks frequently of "fait," "droit" (pp. 306, 307), "objet" (p. 378) or "acte" (p. 287) "particulier" in a way that leaves no doubt that what is in conflict when "man" is opposed to "citizen" are the categories of particularity and

as "natural"; if we say, for example, that the first part of the *Nouvelle Héloïse* deals with the particular, or individual, relationships between Julie and Saint-Preux in contrast to the second part which, at least at times, deals with public, collective relationships between the inhabitants of Clarens, it does not follow that, in the first three books, Julie and Saint-Preux are in the state of nature as the term is used in the *Second Discourse*. A certain amount of confusion results from Rousseau's interchangeable use of "natural" and "particular," especially since his sense of the complexities of selfhood puts the individuals he portrays far beyond the simplicity of the state of nature. This is true of fictional entities such as the "characters" of the *Nouvelle Héloïse* (if one wishes to consider them as such) as well as of actual human beings, including Rousseau himself, in the autobiographical writings. It would be absurd, for instance, to consider the *Confessions* as more "natural" than the *Social Contract* because it deals with individual experiences rather than with societies. The case of *Emile* is somewhat different, since the diegetic narrative is supposed to follow the history of an empirical human being from the start and along chronological lines.[4] This forces upon us the contrast between a "natural" child and a corrupted citizen, an antithetical pattern of innocence and experience. The rhetorical mode of *Emile* produces the opposition between nature and society as a textual necessity. No such polarity functions in the *Confessions*, since Rousseau never claims to narrate anything about the child Jean-Jacques that is not directly remembered by him. He is thus at least twice removed from the preconscious condition of nature: the experiences of a highly self-conscious and "dénaturé" child are told by the disfigured figure of a highly self-conscious narrator.

The lexicological confusion between "natural" and "particular" thus has only limited theoretical interest, although it certainly has been responsible for many aberrations in the interpretation of Rousseau. It nevertheless provides a point of entrance into the remarkably smooth and homogeneous textual surface of the *Social Contract*. For it again attracts attention to the danger of hypostatizing such concepts as "nature," "individual" or "society" as if they were the desig-

---

generality. The same polarity opposes private to public in such expressions as "personne publique" and "personne privée."

4. A problem that does not arise in the *Second Discourse* where the natural origin of mankind is a fiction and the diachrony of the narrative only exists on the level of the signifier.

nation of substantial entities. Rousseau can legitimately shift these terms around and confuse the names of two such divergent semantic fields as those covered by "nature" and "particularity" because they designate relational properties, patterns of relational integration or disintegration, and not units or modes of being. This may be easier to admit in the case of superstuctures such as civil society, or the arts, or technology, but it pertains to the term nature as well. Rousseau calls natural any stage of relational integration that precedes in degree the stage presently under examination. In the analysis of conceptualization, the "natural" stage that precedes the concept is denomination; in the analysis of metaphor, the natural figure would be metonymy; in the critique of judgment, it is sensation or perception; in the case of generality, any previous mode of particularity, etc. The deconstruction of a system of relationships always reveals a more fragmented stage that can be called natural with regard to the system that is being undone. Because it also functions as the negative truth of the deconstructive process, the "natural" pattern authoritatively substitutes its relational system for the one it helped to dissolve. In so doing, it conceals the fact that it is itself one system of relations among others, and it presents itself as the sole and true order of things, as nature and not as structure. But since a deconstruction always has for its target to reveal the existence of hidden articulations and fragmentations within assumedly monadic totalities, nature turns out to be a self-deconstructive term. It engenders endless other "natures" in an eternally repeated pattern of regression. Nature deconstructs nature, hence the ambiguous valorization of the term throughout Rousseau's works. Far from denoting a homogeneous mode of being, "nature" connotes a process of deconstruction redoubled by its own fallacious retotalization. In the opposition between private and public, or particular and general, the first term is the "natural" counterpart of the second, provided one reads "natural" as has just been suggested. We conclude that there is no structural difference between the couple linking "volonté particulière" to "volonté générale" and, on the other hand, such pairings as "droit" or "religion naturelle" "de l'homme" with "droit" or "religion civile" "du citoyen."

Any Rousseau text that puts such polarities into play will therefore have to set up the fiction of a natural process that functions both as a deconstructive instrument and as the outcome of the deconstruction. Frequently enough, the fiction is provided by a contemporary or traditional text written by someone else: in the *Profession de foi*, it was primarily Helvétius and Quesnay that were thus being used; in the first version of the *Social Contract*, Diderot's *Encyclopédie* entry on "Droit naturel" furnishes the appropriate target. Lacking a suitable formulation, Rousseau sets one up himself, thus conveying an impression of self-contradiction that has considerably enriched, if not clarified, the history of his interpretation. This is in part what happens in the *Second Discourse*, where neither Hobbes, nor Condillac, nor any of the other polemical opponents, provides an adequate natural model and where Rousseau therefore has to invent one himself. A similar, somewhat more complex instance of the same strategy occurs in a text that has close affinities with some aspects of the Social *Contract*, the fragment that the editors of the Pléiade edition have included under the title "Du bonheur public."

Although the fragmentary state of "Du bonheur public" (as well as the fact that it originated as an occasional improvisation in reply to a questionnaire sent out by the Société économique de Berne) makes a sustained reading difficult, the notes nevertheless illustrate the odd logical shape of Rousseau's political discourse. And because it deals with the opposition between private and public values as they relate to the political constitution of the State, the brief text is like a blueprint for the more elaborate structure that supports the *Social Contract*. In truth, "Du bonheur public" is not based on a dialectic of private as opposed to public or social identity; it considers the possibility of a readable semiology of private happiness that would be based on analogies between inside feelings and their outside manifestations only in order to reject it out of hand: "Happiness is not pleasure; it is not a fleeting stirring of the soul, but a permanent and entirely inward feeling, that can only be evaluated by the person who experiences it. No one can therefore decide with certainty if someone else is happy, nor can he, as a result of this, come to know with certainty the *signs* that bear witness to the happiness of individuals" (p. 510, my italics).[5] Consequently, there can be no easy metaphorical totalization from personal to social well-being, based on an analogical resemblance between both: "It is . . . not by the feeling that the citizens have of their happiness, not consequently by their happiness itself that one can judge the prosperity of the State" (p.

---

5. A little further in the text, Rousseau also speaks of ". . . the true *signs* that might characterize the well-being of a people" (p. 512, my italics).

513), or: "If I had deduced the idea of happiness collectively from the particular state of happiness of every citizen that makes up the State, I could have said something that would have been easier to grasp for many readers, but aside from the fact that no conclusions could ever have been drawn from these metaphysical notions that depend on the way of thinking, the mood and the disposition of each individual, I would have given a very inaccurate definition" (p. 512). The text takes the deconstruction of a private inwardness that could be equated with a natural inwardness for granted; the spontaneous manifestations of the happy consciousness are so unnatural as to be entirely unfathomable and beyond observation. The actual evocation of private happiness, so freely developed in many other Rousseau texts such as the *Confessions* or the *Rêveries,* does not even require formulation here. Yet it operates as a totalizing power based on natural properties, and it at once replaces the dismissed, natural affectivity of the individual subject by a natural affectivity of the group that can be interpreted precisely as the self has just been shown *not* to be. Natural societies in which "men [will be] social [*civils*] by nature . . ." (p. 510) are assumed to exist or (what amounts to the same thing) to have existed or to be conceivable in the future. In such societies, the semantics of affectivity, opaque in the case of individuals, are transparent and reliable: "[The] virtues [and the] vices [of political societies] are all apparent and visible, their inner feeling is a public one. . . . For any eye that can see, they are what they seem to be, and one can safely evaluate [*juger*] their moral being" (p. 510). This being granted, the totalization is bound to ensue without further delay: "[men] will be united, they will be virtuous, they will be happy, and their felicity will be the well-being of the Republic; for since they receive all their being from the State, they owe everything to the State. The Republic will own all they own and will be all they are" ("car n'étant rien que par la république ils ne seront rien que pour elle, elle aura tout ce qu'ils ont et sera tout ce qu'ils sont"). Such sentences automatically fall back into the familiar diction of "all" and "nothing," or "all" and "one," in the reconciliation "schon längst Eines und Alles genannt" (Hölderlin) of the pantheistic *hen kai pan.* The model for this utopia is the reconciliation of the most natural of groups, the family, with the State: "The family, pointing to its children, will say: it is in them that I flourish" (p. 511). It also reconciles moral virtue with economic wealth and makes property innocent by making it collective; the word "bien" can be used in its ethical register (as the opposite of "mal") as well as in the economic sense of "real" estate. That, in the sentence which speaks of "les biens, les maux . . ." of political societies (p. 510), "biens" also means wealth is clear from its use a few lines further on: "au trésor public, vous aurez joint les *biens* des particuliers" (p. 511, my italics).

As it denies the validity of the metaphor that unites the self with society, the text, by the same token, elaborates a new metaphor, the "natural" political society or family which, in its turn, fulfills the totalization that was denied to the first binary pair. But the logic of totalization works both ways, toward the *one* as well as toward the *all*, and the welfare of the natural society is bound to restore the well-being of the individual who relates to it as part relates to whole in an organic synecdoche, as the "member" relates to the "body" in the political unit. Therefore Rousseau has to state the very opposite of his initial assertion: ". . . do not imagine that the State could be happy when all its members are in distress. This ethical fiction that you call public happiness is, by itself, a chimera: if the feeling of well-being is not felt by anyone, it has no existence and no family can flourish if its children do not prosper" (p. 510). This is stated in the paragraph immediately following the one which denied the significance of any individual well-being for the society as a whole, and it will be followed, not much further, by the equally categorical assertion: ". . . [that it is] therefore not by [the] happiness [of the citizens] that one can measure the prosperity of the State."

The occurrence of such contradictions within the confines of a few lines obviously does not have the same effect in a tentative, unfinished and disjointed text as in a more continuous argument. On the other hand, one may well wonder, with equally good reason, whether the pattern of contradiction in this fragmented composition does not represent a more faithful outline of Rousseau's thought patterns, simply because the narrative developments and transitions that conceal incompatible affirmations merely by putting some space between them are lacking in this case. A text such as this one bears a close resemblance to what is generally referred to, rather inaccurately, as Nietzsche's aphoristic manner, as we know it from *Human all too human* on. This discontinuous format goes back, in Rousseau, at least as far as the notes to the *Second Discourse* and represents probably the most characteristic dimension of his style.

The reading of "Du bonheur public" is not completed when the figural pattern of contradiction has been pointed out. Short as it is, the text contains the elements necessary to the second deconstruction that can be grafted onto the first undoing of the "natural" metaphor, and that raises its figural status to the second power, making it into the figural deconstruction of the prior deconstruction of a figure. For the text also states, this time truly in the form of an aphorism, without further context: "The moral condition of a people is less the result of the absolute condition of its members than of the relationships among them" (p. 511). One is reminded of the structure of judgment as a posited relationship (in the *Profession de foi*) and also of the statement about love in the *Nouvelle Héloïse*: ". . . the source of happiness does not reside wholly in the desired object nor in the heart that possesses it, but in the relationship of the one to the other" (*Oeuvres complètes*, 2:225). An entirely different principle of organization is introduced by this description. If the principle of collectivization or generalization that constitutes what is here called a "people" does *not* operate between part and whole but is determined by the relationship that the different parts, as parts, establish between each other, then the rhetorical structure is no longer the same as in binary structures. The principle of differentiation no longer operates between two entities whose difference is both redundant (since it is posited from the start) and transcended (since it is suspended at the end); it now operates to reveal differences where a metaphorical totalization had created the illusion of an identity, a delusive generality in such words as "man," "self," "people," or "State," all of which suggest that, to the extent that they are men, or people, or States, all men, people, and States are essentially the same. Groups constituted on the basis of relationships which no longer claim to be natural engender different systems of interaction, in relation to themselves as well as to other groups or entities. Since the principle that establishes their *general* character as group is no longer a principle of necessity, but the result of an uncertain act of judgment ratified by convention, it follows that the principle of generalization that constituted it is by no means unique. The same entity can thus be inscribed within diverse systems that are not necessarily compatible. They can be considered from different points of view without necessarily allowing for a coordination of these various perspectives. Neither does their interference with other systems necessarily allow for specular exchanges or integrations.

The shift from a (deconstructed) binary model to this still un-

identified "other" model occurs in "Du bonheur public" when Rousseau abruptly changes ground, abandons the binary model that seeks
to derive political well-being from private happiness altogether, and
affirms, as a "very general idea . . . to which no reasonable man
could, I believe, refuse his assent" (p. 512) that ". . . the happiest
nation is the one that can most easily dispense with all others and the
most flourishing the one the others can least dispense with" ("la
nation la plus heureuse est celle qui peut le plus aisément se passer
de toutes les autres, et la plus florissante est celle dont les autres
peuvent le moins se passer" [p. 512]). The language shifts from the
qualitative and unfathomable "will to happiness" to an outspoken
will to power quantified in terms of economic and military interests.
The decisive relationship is no longer between constituting and constituted elements. Within a political entity, no necessary link connects individual to collective well-being; to pursue the problem of
this relationship (as "Du bonheur public" set out by doing) is to
pursue a false problem. It is not irrelevant to raise the question of the
"happiness" of a political entity such as a State, but it can only be
considered in terms of the relationship of one State to another. The
very concept of a political entity, be it a State, a class or a person, also
changes: an entity can be called political, not because it is collective
(constituted by a plurality of similar units), but precisely because it is
not, because it sets up relationships with other entities on a non-
constitutive basis. The encounter between one political unit and
another is not a generalization in which a structure is extended on
the basis of a principle of similarity (or of a proximity considered as
similarity) to include both under its common aegis. Just as the unit
itself is not the outcome of such a generalization, the relationships of
the units among each other are not stated in terms of affinities,
analogies, common properties or any other principle of metaphorical
exchange. They depend instead on the ability of one entity, regardless
of similarities, to keep the relationship to another contingent, "to be
able to dispense with all other [nations]." If this degree of autarchy is
achieved, relationships with other States are still possible, and
perhaps desirable, but they are no longer compulsory. To the extent
that a less fortunate State is unable to achieve this and remains
dependent for its existence on necessary links, it is not a truly political entity, not really a State at all. In other words, the structure
postulates the necessary existence of radical estrangement between
political entities. Autarchy, as it is here conceived, is not a principle
of autonomy, still less of totalization. The accent does not fall on

freedom as a positive force but on the ability to dispense with others; the worst that can happen politically is having to have recourse to "strangers." Such patterns of estrangement are an inevitable aspect of political structures; it is well known, for instance, that Rousseau refused to believe in perpetual peace and that, by consistently arguing against Hobbes that the state of war is not a natural state, he had to see war as a necessary moment in the political process: ". . . far from being natural to man, the state of war is born from peace, or at the least from the precautions men had to take in order to insure themselves of a durable peace."[6]

In its stress on separation and solitude, on the fragmented differentiation of entities rather than on their unity, the condition of political estrangement is reminiscent of the state of nature. This is not surprising, since the fiction of a natural "state" results from the deconstruction of metaphorical patterns based on binary models— which is exactly how Rousseau's definition of political happiness here comes into being, after the antithetical system that deduces public from private happiness has been allowed to destroy itself by running its course. For the same reason, the rediscovery of differential moments, such as those suggested by the term estrangement, also signals the inevitable relapse into patterns of totalization. The sentence that asserts the differentiation ("the happiest nation is the one that can most easily dispense with all others") also asserts the simultaneous reconstruction of an aberrant totality: "the most flourishing is the one the others can least dispense with." The shift from qualitative happiness [*nation heureuse*] to quantitative prosperity [*nation florissante*] is revealing. The synonymy of both terms is asserted as part of the system: ". . . if money makes the rich happy, it is less by its immediate possession than because it enables them, first to satisfy their needs and to carry out their will in all things, without having to depend on anyone, and second to exercise command over others and keep them in their dependence" (pp. 513–14).[7] Yet a shift is implied by the quantification, which is also a surreptitious reintroduction of

6. *Ecrits sur l'Abbé de Saint-Pierre*, 3:611. See also: "Hobbes' error is not to have established the presence of a state of war among independent men in a society, but to have assumed that this is the natural condition of the species, and to have made it the cause of the vices of which it is the effect" (*Social Contract*, first version, p. 288). Kant's famous text *On Perpetual Peace* (1795) is of course highly relevant here.

7. The point is further developed, in terms of a semiology of money, in the fragment "Le luxe, le commerce et les arts" (pp. 520 ff.). See also *Discours sur les richesses*, not included in the Pléiade edition, published by F. Bovet in 1853.

conceptual number metaphors into the deconstructed system. The
"happy" State is entirely self-sufficient and does not need to establish
relationships with any other nation, but the very strength resulting
from this independence allows it, almost in spite of itself, to assert its
power over others and make them in turn aware of their dependency: "The security, the conservation [of the State] require that it
become more powerful than all its neighbors. It can only augment,
nourish and exercise its power at their expense, and although it does
not have to look for subsistence beyond its boundaries, it nevertheless
always seeks for new members that reinforce its own strength [*qui
lui donnent une consistance plus inébranlable*]" (*Ecrits sur l'Abbé de
Saint-Pierre*, 3:605). The political power does not remain in its condition of fragmented isolation in which it is satisfied to consider the
other State as a pure stranger. Carried by the metaphorical structure
of the number system, it enters into relationships of comparison that
necessarily lead back to totalizations from part to whole: "Since the
size of the political body is entirely relative, it is forced to enter
steadily into comparison in order to know itself; it depends on everything that surrounds it, and must take an interest in everything that
happens outside, although it would want to remain self-confined,
without gains or losses. . . . Its very strength, making its relationships to others more constant, makes all its actions further-reaching
and all its quarrels more dangerous" (*Ecrits sur l'Abbé de Saint-
Pierre*, 3:605). Consciousness of selfhood [*se connaître*], whether
individual or political, is itself dependent on a relationship of power
and originates with this relationship. The danger of the situation is
not only the actual damage done to the others, but the reintroduction
of a master/slave relationship of mutual dependency within a system
that had come into being by overcoming the fallacies of this model.[8]
The fact that the strong and "happy" State comes to depend on the
dependency of the other as if it were a necessity dissolves the structure to which it owed its existence. For the master/slave relationship
is not the (non)relationship of pure estrangement that was posited as
the necessary condition for a political entity to come into being. It
clearly is a polarity susceptible of dialectical exchange: master and
slave are no strangers to each other, as little as the conquered State

---

8. ". . . the war (between two nations) can only cease when both of them
freely proclaim their renunciation of war. It follows that, as a consequence of the
relationship between master and slave, they continue even in spite of themselves, of
being in a state of war" (*Ecrits sur l'Abbé de Saint-Pierre*, 3:615).

remains a stranger to its conqueror. "Du bonheur public," like all the other allegorical Rousseau texts, reintroduces the metaphorical model whose deconstruction had been the reason for its own elaboration. It is therefore just as "unreadable" as the other allegories we have considered.

Does this mean that it can, without further qualification, be equated with such previously considered texts as *Julie* or the *Profession de foi*? It would then differ from them only thematically, by its political "content," but not rhetorically. If we are correct in assuming that the logical structure of "Du bonheur public" also operates as the organizing principle of the *Social Contract*—a point that remains to be shown—it would follow that the *Social Contract* could be called an allegory of the same type and for the same reason as the *Profession de foi*. This conclusion would, in a sense, make the consideration of the *Social Contract* and of Rousseau's political texts in general redundant for the rhetorical analysis of his work as a whole. It would merely confirm what we already know, that Rousseau's fictional as well as his discursive writings are allegories of (non)signification or of unreadability, allegories of the deconstruction and the reintroduction of metaphorical models. We would merely have gained yet another version of this same insight. This would not lead to a refinement of the question that remained precariously suspended at the end of the reading of the *Profession de foi*, when the referential power of the allegorical narrative seemed to be at its most effective when its epistemological authority was most throughly discredited. The political question would then only have a digressive importance in the reading of Rousseau; like the metaphor of selfhood, it would have no privileged interpretative function. Such a conclusion is not without consequence: for example, the naïve [*impensé*] distinction between a "literary" and a "political" Rousseau from which we started out as from the empirical *donnée* provided by the present state of Rousseau studies has, to a considerable extent, been overcome. It no longer makes sense to consider *Julie* as more or less "literary" than the *Social Contract*; neither can the assumed inconsistencies and contradictions of the political theorist be explained away by calling them "literary" and attributing them to the discrepancies between "l'analyse intellectuelle" and "l'élan du coeur."[9] One can no longer

9. The expression is by Pierre Burgelin in his introduction to the edition of the *Profession de foi du vicaire savoyard* (*Oeuvres complètes*, 4:cxliii).

call Rousseau an "admirable" writer and dismiss the political
theorist or, conversely, praise the rational rigor of the political
analyses while writing off the more disquieting aspects of the imagi-
native and autobiographical writings as more or less accidental
pathology. The rhetorical reading leaves these fallacies behind by
accounting, at least to some degree, for their predictable occurrence.
With the assistance of the political writings, it may however be
possible to take one further step.

"Du bonheur public" appears to be "privileged" in at least one
respect: it isolates a model for the elaboration and the comportment
of political entities that is more rigorous and systematic than the
models we have encountered up till now. It is true that this model
never asserts itself as an actual state of being (in all the meanings of
the term "state," be it as state of nature, state of war, the State, etc.).
It is at once overtaken by other rhetorical patterns, similar in structure to conceptual metaphors. But the question remains what is
being overtaken and how this "relapse" is to be understood. The
Social Contract, the most complete section of Rousseau's planned
treatise on political institutions, provides information on this point.
We are not here concerned with the technically political significance
of this text, still less with an evaluation of the political and ethical
praxis that can be derived from it. Our reading merely tries to define
the rhetorical patterns that organize the distribution and the movement of the key terms—while contending that questions of valorization can be relevantly considered only after the rhetorical status of
the text has been clarified.

That the *Social Contract* implies a deconstruction of a binary
metaphorical system similar to that operating between personal and
public happiness in "Du bonheur public" is hardly apparent in the
final text but becomes much more noticeable if one takes into account the earlier version known as the *manuscrit de Genéve*.[10] This
version begins with a genetic section that sets out to investigate "d'où
naît la nécessité des institutions politiques" (p. 281, my italics). The

___

10. In *Oeuvres complètes*, 3:279–346. This text has been known at least since
1882 and was published for the first time in 1887. It is part of C. E. Vaughan's still
authoritative edition of *The Political Writings of J. J. Rousseau* (Cambridge, England,
1915). The first section, entitled "Premières notions du corps social," is taken over in
the final version only from chapter 3 on (see p. 289). It deals with the development
leading up to the contract and thus establishes a transition between the *Second
Discourse* and the *Social Contract*.

section was subsequently omitted from the final version, and this omission has not made the interpretation of the *Social Contract* any easier. It has made it difficult, for example, to see in what way the structure of the political entity established on a contractual basis differs from that of an empirical or natural entity. The principle of totalization that organizes the first formal definition of the contract seems, in all respects, to be similar in kind to the organic link that binds part to whole in a metaphorical synecdoche. The social pact is determined as follows: "Everyone puts his will, his property, his strength, and his person in common, under the direction of the general will, and we receive as a body [*en corps*] each member as an inalienable part of the whole" (p. 290). The final version retains this definition, with some changes in wording that do not detract from its assumed holism. The metaphorical system that unites limb to body, one to all, individual to group, seems firmly established. A few paragraphs earlier in the same version, Rousseau has described a similar system: "There would exist a kind of common sensorium that would control the correspondence of all the parts; public good and evil would not only be the sum of particular virtues and vices as in a simple juxtaposition [*une simple aggrégation*], but it would reside in the link that unites them. It would therefore be larger than the sum, and far from having public well-being derive from the happiness of individuals, it would be its source" (p. 284).[11] The distinction between metonymic aggregates and metaphorical totalities, based on the presence, within the latter, of a "necessary link" that is lacking in the former, is characteristic of all metaphorical systems, as is the equation of this principle of totalization with *natural* process. After the deconstruction of the metaphorical model has taken place, the attribute of naturalness shifts from the metaphorical totality to the metonymic aggregate, as was the case for the "state of nature" in the *Second Discourse* or for "sensation" in the *Profession de foi*. However, at this point in the argument, the evocation of this natural synthesis—Rousseau makes the comparison with chemical compounds, whose properties are distinct from the properties of their components—is not held up as the desirable wholeness that political units must try to emulate, but as the very opposite: they are precisely

11. The passage is crossed out in the manuscript (see 3:1413 n. 4) for reasons on which one can speculate. Its suppression is certainly not caused by a divergence with the general thrust of the argument, within which it fits perfectly well.

the misleading model after which no sound political system should be patterned. The synesthetic illusion of the common sensorium, just as the concomitant illusions of a universal language and a golden age,[12] is a mythical aberration of judgment devoid of truth and of virtue. It becomes pernicious when it is used as the foundation of a political society: the entire polemic with Diderot, in the *manuscrit de Genève,* is directed toward the necessity of devising a model for a political order that is not natural, in this sense of the term. Hence the categorical rejection, more explicit in the early version than in the final text, of the family as a suitable political model, precisely because the family is based on natural ties.[13] In this respect, the family is no better model for legality than imperialistic conquest or the enslavement of prisoners in time of war, and it is discussed under the same rubric as these anarchic manifestations of power. The same is true of the god-centered systems that occupy such a prominent place in the *Profession de foi* and that, in this context, begin by being dismissed altogether (although they will reappear in a different form later on in the *Social Contract*): the idea of a natural religion is as absurd as the idea of a natural law, and the text seems to be an even sharper attack on the vicar of the *Profession de foi* than on Diderot: ". . . if the notions of a great Being and of natural law were *innate* in all hearts, it would be quite superfluous to instruct people in either of them. . . . Let us therefore discard the sacred precepts of the various religions. Their abuse has caused as many crimes as their use can prevent, and let us give back to the Philosopher a question that the Theologian has treated only at the expense of mankind" (p. 286). The deconstruction of metaphorical totalities which, in "Du bonheur public," starts out from the relationship between private and public well-being here has a wider scope that encompasses all organic and

12. ". . . the happy existence of a golden age was always alien to the race of man, either for not having known it when it was within reach or for having lost it when they were capable of knowledge" (p. 283).

13. *Social Contract,* first version, p. 297. The final version (chap. 2, "Des premières sociétés," p. 352) seems to reverse this when it states: "The family is, if one so wishes (*si l'on veut*), the first model of political societies." But the passage uses the same metaphor of the "link" negatively ("Still, the children remain linked [*liés*] to the father for only as long as they need him in order to survive. As soon as this need ceases, the natural link dissolves") and concludes that actual families are in fact not natural but political institutions: "If they remain together, it is no longer for natural reasons but by their own will, and the family itself remains in existence only by convention" (p. 352).

theotropic ideologies. It is not carried out in a detailed analysis, as was the case in some of the other texts, but asserted sweepingly, as if it could be taken for granted. If the formal definition of the contract then seems to relapse into the figure which has just been decisively condemned, then this can certainly not be true without further qualification. The definition is far from telling all there is to tell about the structure of the contract, perhaps because a degree of complexity has been reached that no longer allows for definitional language.

As the mechanics of the contractual convention are being elaborated in more detail, it becomes apparent that the constitutive power of the contract, the manner in which it engenders entities, is no dialectical synthesis or any other system of totalization. The general will is by no means a synthesis of particular volitions. Rousseau starts out instead from the opposite assertion and postulates the incompatibility between collective and individual needs and interests, the absence of any links between the two sets of forces: the general will is "a pure act of reason that operates without regard for the passions [*dans le silence des passions*] . . . ." (p. 286) but "where is the person who can thus sever himself from his own desires and . . . can he be forced to consider the species in general in order to impose upon himself duties of which he cannot perceive the link with his own, particular constitution?" (p. 286). It is clear that when Rousseau, in the next paragraph, speaks of "the art of generalizing ideas" in order to orient them toward the general will, the act of generalizing must then have a very different figural structure than such metaphorical processes as, for example, conceptualization, love, or even judgment.

The simplest way to gain insight into the process or function that is being described may be by way of its most naïve, spatial version, in the section of the *Social Contract* entitled, in the *manuscrit de Genève*, "Du domaine réel" (pp. 293—94). Considered from a geopolitical point of view, the State is not primarily a set of individuals, but a specific piece of land; Rousseau praises the wisdom implied in the modern custom of calling a monarch King *of France*, or *of England*, rather than, as was the case in Antiquity, King of the Persians or of the Macedonians. "By thus holding the land, [the kings] are certain to hold its inhabitants" (p. 293). This terminology is said to be more precise because the original possesion of the land is, in fact, arbitrary and "natural," in the anarchic sense of the term. One could call it metonymic, simply based on the fact that one happened to be in the proximity of this particular piece of terrain, and this "right of first occupancy" may be "less absurd, less repellent than the right of conquest" but nevertheless, "on close examination . . . it is not more legitimate" (p. 293).

A specific piece of landed property within the State is the result of a contractual convention that involves both the citizen and the State; it is only when the State is thus involved that one can speak of property rather than of mere possession. Although property, unlike possession, will exist and function within a legal context that is no longer based on mere physical inequality, it is not in itself more legitimate, if only because the State itself, on which it depends, is such an arbitrary entity: ". . . since the powers of the State are incomparably larger than those of each individual, public possession is, in practice, stronger and more irrevocable, without being more legitimate" (p. 293). The contractual instrument that is thus consti- tuted exists as a pradoxical juxtaposition or interference of relational networks. On the one hand, as private property, objects of possession used for the fulfillment of individual needs and desires [jouissance], the relationship between the owner and the land, or dwelling, is entirely literal. It is perfectly defined in its identity by its objective dimensions, and the inscribed signs by means of which these dimen- sions are designated (be it as a fence, or as a "nontrespassing" sign) is semantically unambiguous. A principle of functional identification between the owning subject and the owned object is implied. This identification, as we saw, is not natural and legitimate, but contrac- tual. There is nothing legitimate about property, but the rhetoric of property confers the illusion of legitimacy. The contract is self- reflective; it is an agreement *du même au même* in which the land defines the owner and the owner defines the land. One could say, with equal justice, that the private owner contracts with himself or that the private property contracts with itself; the identity of the owner is defined by the identity of the land. Thus it is that Marcel, in Proust's novel, understands the fascination of the *proper* names of the aristocracy because it is impossible to distinguish their names from the geographical names of their landed estate. There can be no more seductive form of onomastic identification. The fascination of the model is not so much that it feeds fantasies of material possession (though it does this too, of course) but that it satisfies semiological fantasies about the adequation of sign to meaning seductive enough to tolerate extreme forms of economic oppression.

On the other hand, Rousseau stresses that property can also be considered from a public point of view as part of the rights and duties of the State: "This is how the united and contiguous land of private owners becomes public territory, and how rights of sovereignty, extending from the subjects to the land they occupy, become both 'real' and personal . . ." (p. 293). But the relationship that governs the public aspect of the property is not the same as the one that determines its private identity. The difference becomes apparent in the way in which the property's "inside" relates to what lies beyond its boundaries. When considered from the private point of view, this relationship is still governed by patterns of genuine similarity. The relation of one private property to another is a relationship between two units that are similarly constituted, and it therefore suffices to respect the principle of this constitution in order to have a reliable system of arbitration available in the adjudication of any conflict that may arise between the two owners. Neighbors can have any number of conflicts with each other, but whether they want it or not, they remain neighbors and not strangers; as far as their mutual property rights are concerned, they can always be derived from the proprietary status they have in common, in the form of a deed or any other instrument of ownership. Local obscurities in the phrasing of the deed can be clarified and the deed is, in principle, a denominative text that is entirely readable to all parties. Therefore, though it is never g.uranteed, peace between neighbors is at least legally conceivable. But the same is not true when the property is considered within a context of public interests, especially when they involve the interests of the State with regard to other States. The contractual constitution of a State may or may not be similar to that of another, but this question is irrelevant with regard to territorial conflict and integrity. From that point of view, the other State is, per definition, a hostile stranger: ". . . the Greeks often called peace treaties the treaties established between two people who were not at war. The words for stranger and for enemy have long been synonyms for many ancient people, including the Romans" (p. 288). When considered privately, property is a structure based on similarity and on the integration of shared needs and desires; when considered publicly, the same property functions as a structure of necessary estrangement and conflict. This hostility is the foundation of the State's political integrity and can therefore be valorized positively: it protects property "with all its strength against the outsider [*contre l'Etranger*]" and it enables Rousseau to speak approvingly of "what is admirable in this alienation" (p. 294).

From a rhetorical perspective, the interest of the structure is that the same single entity (a specific piece of land) can be considered as the referent of two entirely divergent texts, the first based on the proper meaning engendered by a consistent conceptual system, the second on the radical discontinuity and estrangement of noncomparable systems of relationship that allow for no acts of judgment and, consequently, for no stable meaning or identity. The semiological systems at work within each of these systems are entirely different: the one is monological and controlled in all its articulations, the second at the mercy of contingencies more arbitrary even than the strength based on numerical power. Yet, in its absence, the first could never have come into being. The power of property is vested "in the distinction between the rights that the sovereign and the owner have over the same fund" (p. 294). Behind the stability and the decorum of private law lurk the "brigands" and the "pirates" (p. 288) whose acts shape the realities of politics between nations, the most difficult adjustment being the necessity of considering these mixed standards as entirely honorable (p. 288).

The pattern may seem crude and literal when it is applied to material property, but it pervades all aspects of the political society. The social contract is best characterized, not by the conceptual language of its formal definition, but by the *double rapport* that we found operative in the determination of property rights and that also characterizes the pact in its most fundamental form, of which property is only a derived, particular version. The expression *double rapport* is used in a difficult and controversial passage that formulates a distinction in the degree to which the contract is binding for the individual citizen as compared to the degree to which it is binding for the sovereign: ". . . the act of original confederation includes a reciprocal commitment between the public and the private sector. Each individual, contracting so to speak with himself, is committed in a double relationship, namely as member of the sovereign authority with regard to individuals and as member of the State with regard to the sovereign authority . . ." (p. 290). We know from empirical experience that the individual is subjected to a more stringent legal control than the executive power which has much more leeway in its actions and initiatives, in international politics, for example, where it is expected to resort to war and to violence in a manner that could not be tolerated in relationships between individuals. Rousseau accounts for this by stressing that the private interests of the individual (which can be called his commitments toward himself) have nothing in common with his political, public interests and obligations. The former do precisely *not* derive from the latter as part derives from whole; the sentence "there is considerable difference between a commitment toward oneself and a commitment toward a whole of which one is a part" (p. 290) is true because no metaphorical totalization is allowed to intervene. The double relationship of the individual toward the State is thus based on the coexistence of two distinct rhetorical models, the first self-reflective or specular, the other estranged. But what the individual is estranged from is precisely the executive activity of his own State as *souverain*. This power is unlike him and foreign to him because it does not have the same double and self-contradictory structure and therefore does not share in his problems and tensions. The *souverain* can consider himself "under one single and identical relationship" and, with regard to any outsider, including the individual citizen, it can become "a single Being or an individual" ("à l'égard de l'étranger, il devient un Etre simple ou un individu" [p. 291]). Unlike the "individual," who is always divided within himself, the executive is truly in-dividual, un-divided.

The passage becomes clearer in its implications if one takes into account the precise meaning of the terminology. What Rousseau calls the "souverain" (which can, with some historical hindsight, be translated as the executive power) is, of course, not a person but specifically the political body when it is active as distinct from this same body as a mere entity, the carrier, or ground, as it were, of the action that it makes possible by its existence: ". . . the sovereign authority, by its very nature, is only a moral person, whose existence can only be abstract and collective. The idea that is linked to this term cannot be equated with that of a single individual (pp. 294–95). "This public person thus constituted by the union of all the others . . . is called by its members the *State* [*Etat*] when it is passive, the *Sovereign* [*Souverain*] when it is active . . ." (p. 290). The individual's private will (like his private property) is clear and comprehensible in itself, but devoid of any general interest or signification beyond himself. The same is still true of the relationship between several private volitions. Only with the "double relationship" does the possibility of generalization come into being but, at the same moment, the continuity between purpose and action that remained preserved on the private level is disrupted. It follows that the divergence which prevails, within the State, in the relationship between the citizen and the executive is in fact an unavoidable estrangement between political rights and laws on the one hand, and political action and history on the other. The grounds for this alienation are best understood in terms of the rhetorical structure that separates the one domain from the other. The passage, as is well known, was to be one of the main considerations in condemning Rousseau as politically subversive.[14] It proves however that he had a much more developed sense of political praxis than the magistrates of the city of Geneva; he certainly never meant to imply that the executive has the right to change the constitution at its own will, but merely to caution against the fact that it would always be tempted and have the power to do just that, and that therefore the State needs legislation to protect it against the persistent threat of its own executive branch. And, as his admiration for Moses indicates, Rousseau is equally convinced of the need for durable institutions or States. But precisely because it is not rooted in the contract itself, durability has to be legislated. The *Social Contract* does not warrant belief in a suprahistorical political model that, in the words of the 1738 *Edit de Médiation* of the State of Geneva, would make the political State "perpetual."[15] For this would reduce the double structure of the constitutional text to a monological signification and cause the State to relapse into the kind of aberrant natural model of which the end of the *Second Discourse* gives a fictional description. The declaration of the "permanence" of the State would thus greatly hasten its dissolution. It follows however that the meaning of the contractual text has to remain suspended and undecidable: "there can be no fundamental Law that is binding for the entire body of the people" (p. 291) and ". . . since the decisions of the executive, as executive, concern only itself, it is always free to change them" (p. 316). Revolution and legality by no means cancel each other out, since the text of the law is, per definition, in a

14. See Derathé's note (3:1447) on the objections of Jean-Robert Tronchin, Chief Prosecutor for the Republic of Geneva and his complaint that, for Rousseau, "the constitutive laws of all governments were never to be considered as irrevocable." This led to the condemnation of the *Social Contract* as "destructive of all government."

15. See J. S. Spink, *Jean Jacques Rousseau et Genève* (Paris, 1934). p. 23.

condition of unpredictable change. Its mode of existence is necessarily temporal and historical, though in a strictly nonteleological sense.

The structure of the entity with which we are concerned (be it as property, as national State or any other political institution) is most clearly revealed when it is considered as the general form that subsumes all these particular versions, namely as legal *text*. The first characteristic of such a text is its generality: ". . . the object of the Law must be general, like the will that dictates it. It is this double universality that determines the legality of the Law." At first sight, it seems that this generality is rooted in the selective applicability of the law to the part that makes up the political whole, as the exclusion of the part that does not partake of this whole: "This is why the general will of an entire people is not general for a foreign individual [*un particulier étranger*], for this individual is not a member of this people" (p. 327). But it turns out that the estrangement is not (as it still misleadingly appeared to be in the case of territorial property models) the result of some spatial, temporal, or psychological nonpresence, but that it is implied by the very notion of particularity itself. To the extent that he is particular, *any* individual is, as individual, alienated from a law that, on the other hand, exists only in relation to his individual being. "For at the moment that a people consider a particular object, *even if it be one of its own members*, a relation is created between whole and part that makes them into two separate beings. The part is one of these beings, the whole minus this part the other. But the whole minus a part is not the whole and as long as the relationship persists, there is no whole, only two unequal parts" (p. 327, my italics). This statement is repeated whenever the mode of applicability of the law to particular citizens is under discussion. ". . . there is no general will acting upon a particular object" but the particularity of the legal subject, to which the law is made to apply, is independent of its being inside or outside the precinct of the State; the categories of inside and outside do not function as the determining principle of an unavoidable estrangement. That the *extra-muros* individual is estranged from the law is obvious: "If [the particular object] is outside the State, a will that is estranged from him is not general in relation to him . . ." (p. 378). But the same applies necessarily to the individual *intra-muros*, simply because he is individual or particular: "Indeed, this particular object is either within the State, or without it. . . . If the object is within the State, then it is a part of it. A relation is then created between the whole and the part that makes them into two separate beings. The part is one of them, the whole minus the part the other. But the whole minus a part is not the whole . . . etc." (pp. 378–79).

From the point of view of the legal text, it is this generality which ruthlessly rejects any particularization, which allows for the possibility of its coming into being. Within the textual model, particularization corresponds to reference, since reference is the application of an undetermined, general potential for meaning to a specific unit. The indifference of the text with regard to its referential meaning is what allows the legal text to proliferate, exactly as the preordained, coded repetition of a specific gesture or set of gestures allows Helen to weave the story of the war into the epic. As a text, the *Social Contract* is unusual among Rousseau's works because of its impersonal, machinelike systematicity: it takes a few key terms, programs a relationship between them, and lets mere syntax take its course. It is, for instance, the only Rousseau text to make explicit and repeated use of mathematical ratios. By suppressing the genealogy of the key terms from the final version, this quasi-mechanical pattern becomes even more evident. "I shall go directly to my subject without first demonstrating its importance" Rousseau announces at the start of the final text (p. 351), but the early version still felt the need to make explicit what is taken for granted later on: "I describe the mainsprings [of the social body] and its various parts, and I assemble them into place. I make the machine ready to go to work; others, wiser than I am, will regulate its movements" (p. 281).

We have moved closer and closer to the "definition" of *text*, the entity we are trying to circumscribe, a law being, in its facticity, more like an actual text than a piece of property or a State. The system of relationships that generates the text and that functions independently of its referential meaning is its grammar. To the extent that a text is grammatical, it is a logical code or a machine. And there can be no agrammatical texts, as the most grammatical of poets, Mallarmé, was the first to acknowledge.[16] Any nongrammatical text will always be read as a deviation from an assumed grammatical norm. But just as no text is conceivable without grammar, no grammar is conceivable without the suspension of referential

16. "Quel pivôt, j'entends, dans ces contrastes, à l'intelligibilité? il faut un garantie—La Syntaxe—" (*Le Mystère dans les lettres*, Pléiade edition [Paris, 1945], p. 385).

meaning. Just as no law can ever be written unless one suspends any consideration of applicability to a particular entity including, of course, oneself, grammatical logic can function only if its referential consequences are disregarded.

On the other hand, no law is a law unless it also applies to particular individuals. It cannot be left hanging in the air, in the abstraction of its generality. Only by thus referring it back to particular praxis can the *justice* of the law be tested, exactly as the *justesse* of any statement can only be tested by referential verifiability, or by deviation from this verification. For how is justice to be determined if not by particular reference? "Why is the general will always right, and why do all citizens constantly desire the well-being of each, if it were not for the fact that no one exists who does not secretly appropriate the term *each* and think of himself when he votes for all [*il n'y a personne qui ne s'approprie en secret ce mot* chacun *et qui ne songe à lui-même en votant pour tous*]? Which proves that the equality of right and the notion of justice that follows from it derive from the preference that each man gives to himself, and therefore from the nature of man" (p. 306).[17] There can be no text without grammar: the logic of grammar generates texts only in the absence of referential meaning, but every text generates a referent that subverts the grammatical principle to which it owed its constitution. What remains hidden in the everyday use of language, the fundamental incompatibility between grammar and meaning, becomes explicit when the linguistic structures are stated, as is the case here, in political terms. The preceding passage makes clear that the incompatibility between the elaboration of the law and its application (or justice) can only be bridged by an act of deceit. "S'approprier en secret ce mot *chacun*" is to steal from the text the very meaning to which, according to this text, we are not entitled, the particular *I* which destroys its generality; hence the deceitful, covert gesture "en secret," in the foolish hope that the theft will go unnoticed. Justice is unjust; no wonder that the language of justice is also the language of guilt and that, as we know from the *Confessions*, we never lie as much as when we want to do full justice to ourselves, especially in

17. Rousseau suppressed the all-important specification "en secret" in "s'approprier [en secret] ce mot *chacun* . . ." in the final version (p. 373). The self-censorship that operates between earlier and later versions of texts can, in cases such as this, reveal more than it conceals: how could one be more secretive than by trying to hide "the secret"?

self-accusation. The divergence between grammar and referential meaning is what we call the figural dimension of language. This dimension accounts for the fact that two enunciations that are lexicologically and grammatically identical (the one being, so to speak, the quotation of the other and vice versa) can, regardless of context, have two entirely divergent meanings. In exactly the same way Rousseau defines the State or the law as a "double relationship" that, at closer examination, turns out to be as self-destructive as it is unavoidable. In the description of the structure of political society, the "definition" of a text as the contradictory interference of the grammatical with the figural field emerges in its most systematic form. This is not unexpected, since the political model is necessarily diaphoric and cannot pretend to ignore the referential moment entirely. We call *text* any entity that can be considered from such a double perspective: as a generative, open-ended, non-referential grammatical system and as a figural system closed off by a transcendental signification that subverts the grammatical code to which the text owes its existence. The "definition" of the text also states the impossibility of its existence and prefigures the allegorical narratives of this impossibility.

In the *Social Contract*, the model for the structural description of textuality derives from the incompatibility between the formulation and the application of the law, reiterating the estrangement that exists between the sovereign as an active, and the State as a static, principle. The distinction, which is not a polarity, can therefore also be phrased in terms of the difference between political action and political prescription. The tension between figural and grammatical language is duplicated in the differentiation between the State as a defined entity (Etat) and the State as a principle of action (Souverain) or, in linguistic terms, between the constative and the performative function of language. A text is defined by the necessity of considering a statement, at the same time, as performative and constative, and the logical tension between figure and grammar is repeated in the impossibility of distinguishing between two linguistic functions which are not necessarily compatible. It seems that as soon as a text knows what it states, it can only act deceptively, like the thieving lawmaker in the *Social Contract*, and if a text does not act, it cannot state what it knows. The distinction between a text as narrative and a text as theory also belongs to this field of tension.

Especially in the final version, with the conceptual genealogy and the metaphorical deconstruction omitted, the *Social Contract* does not seem to be a narrative but a theory, a constitutional machine to which Rousseau was to resort for the elaboration of specific constitutions. If this were the case, then the text of the law and the law of the text would fully coincide and generate both the *Social Contract*, as a master text, and a set of contractual rules on which the constitution of any State could be founded, or from which the suitability of a given territory to be made into a State could be deduced. It turns out, however, that the "law of the text" is too devious to allow for such a simple relationship between model and example, and the theory of politics inevitably turns into the history, the allegory of its inability to achieve the status of a science. The passage from constative theory to performative history is very clearly in evidence in the *Social Contract*. The text can be considered as the theoretical description of the State, considered as a contractual and legal model, but also as the disintegration of this same model as soon as it is put in motion. And since the contract is both statutory and operative, it will have to be considered from this double perspective.

The legal machine, it turns out, never works exactly as it was programmed to do. It always produces a little more or a little less than the original, theoretical input. When it produces more, things go almost too well for the State: ". . . the more [the] natural forces [of man] are withered away and eliminated, and the more his ac- quired forces are stable and powerful, the more solid and perfect the institution will be. Legislation reaches the highest point it can reach when each citizen can act only through the others and when *the acquired power of the whole is equal or superior* to the sum of the natural forces of all individuals" (p. 313, my italics). The result of this supplementary efficiency of the political process is stated in (metaphorical) terms that are not entirely reassuring, neither physi- cally nor epistemologically, since they suggest a substitutive process that is far from harmless: to found a State is "to substitute a frag- mentary and moral existence for a physical and autonomous one," and this reductive substitution is called to kill, to annihilate, and "to mutilate, so to speak, the human constitution in order to strengthen it" ("mutiler en quelque sorte la constitution de l'homme pour la renforcer" [p. 313]).[18] A somewhat cryptic and isolated note by Rous- seau would seem to fit the situation: "I created a people, and I was

---

18. The final version deletes "mutiler" and replaces it by the innocuous "al- térer." The emendation is pointed out, without comment, by Derathé (p. 1462, n. 7).

unable to create men" ("J'ai fait un peuple et n'ai pu faire des hommes" [p. 500]). The thing to worry about is perhaps not so much the redoubtable power that the State can generate as the fact that this power is not necessarily equal to the power that went into its production. For at other moments, the supplementary or differential structure of the input/output relationship can take on a negative as well as a positive sign: "The general will is rarely that of all, and the public strength is always less than the sum of individual strengths. As a result, we find in the wheels of the State an equivalent of the principle of inertia in machines [*on trouve dans les ressorts de l'état un equivalent aux frottements des machines*]. This counterforce has to be kept to a minimum or, at the very least, it must be computed and deduced beforehand from the total power in order to set up a proper ratio between the means one uses and the effect one wishes to produce" (p. 287).[19] The transformation of the generative power of theory and of grammar into a quantitative economy of *loss*,[20] a kind of political thermodynamics governed by a debilitating entropy, illustrates the practical consequences of a linguistic structure in which grammar and figure, statement and speech act do not converge.

Regardless of whether the differentiation engenders excess or default, it always results in an increasing deviation of the law of the State from the state of the law, between constitutional prescription and political action. As in the *Profession de foi*, this differential structure engenders an affectivity and a valorization, but since the difference is one of epistemological divergence between a statement and its meaning, the affect can never be a reliable criterion of political value judgment. As we already know from "Du bonheur public," the eudaemony of politics is not an exact science: "In order for everyone to want to do what he has to do according to the commitment of the social contract, everyone has to know what he should want. What he should want is the common good; what he should avoid is public evil. But since the existence of the State is only ideal and conventional, its members possess no common and natural sensibility

19. "One cannot avoid, in politics as in mechanics, acting weakly or slowly, and losing strength or time" (*Social Contract*, first version, p. 296).

20. See also *Ecrits sur l'Abbé de Saint-Pierre*: "Consider to what extent, in the aggregate of the body politic, the public power is inferior to the sum of particular powers, how much inertia there is, so to speak, in the play of the entire machine, and one will have to conclude that the weakest man disposes proportionately of more strength for his survival than the strongest State for his" (3:606).

through which, without mediation, they are forewarned by a pleasurable impression of what is useful to the State and by a painful impression of what could harm it" ("ses membres n'ont aucune sensibilité naturelle et commune, par laquelle, immédiatement avertis, ils reçoivent une impression agréable de ce qui lui est utile, et une impression douloureuse sitôt qu'il est offensé" [p. 309]. The affective code is unreadable, which is equivalent to stating that it is not, or not merely, a code.

The discrepancy within the contractual model (here claimed to be the linguistic model in general) will necessarily manifest itself phenomenologically, since it is defined, in part, as the passage, however unreliable, from "pure" theory to an empirical phenomenon. The noncoincidence of the theoretical statement with its phenomenal manifestation implies that the mode of existence of the contract is temporal, or that time is the phenomenal category produced by the discrepancy. Considered performatively, the speech act of the contractual text never refers to a situation that exists in the present, but signals toward a hypothetical future: "Far from preventing the evils that attack the State, [the members of the State] are rarely on time to remedy them when they begin to perceive their effects. One has to foresee them well in advance in order to avoid or to cure them" (p. 309). All laws are future-oriented and prospective; their illocutionary mode is that of the *promise*.[21] On the other hand, every promise assumes a date at which the promise is made and without which it would have no validity; laws are promissory notes in which the present of the promise is always a past with regard to its realization: ". . . the law of today should not be an act of yesterday's general will but of today's; we have not committed ourselves to do what the people wanted but what they want. It follows that when the Law speaks in the name of the people, it is in the name of the people of today and not of the past" (p. 316). The definition of this "people of today" is impossible, however, for the eternal present of the contract can never apply as such to any particular present.

The situation is without solution. In the absence of an *état présent*, the general will is quite literally voiceless. The people are a

21. In *The Genealogy of Morals*, Nietzsche also derives the notion of a transcendental referent (and the specificity of "man") from the possibility of making promises. See, for example, Friedrich Nietzsche, *Werke*, edited by Karl Schechta (Munich, 1955), 2:805, 826.

helpless and "mutilated" giant, a distant and weakened echo of the Polyphemos we first encountered in the *Second Discourse*.[22] "Does the body political possess an organ with which it can state [*énoncer*] the will of the people? Who will give it the necessary foresight to shape the people's actions and to announce them in advance, and how will it pronounce them when the need arises? How could a blind mob, which often does not know what it wants because it rarely knows its own good, carry out by itself as huge and difficult an enterprise as the promulgation of a system of Law" (p. 380)? Yet it is this blind and mute monster which has to articulate the promise that will restore its voice and its sight: "The people subject to the Law must be the authors of the Law" (p. 390). Only a subterfuge can put this paralysis in motion. Since the system itself had to be based on deceit, the mainspring of its movement has to be deceitful as well.

The impostor is clearly enough identified: Rosseau calls him the "lawgiver." It has to be an individual, since only an individual can have the sight and the voice that the people lack. But this individual is also a rhetorical figure, for his ability to promise depends on the metaleptic reversal of cause and effect: "For a people to appreciate the sound maxims of politics and to follow the fundamental rules of political reason [*la raison d'Etat*], effect should become cause, and the social spirit that the institutions are to produce should preside over their elaboration. Men should be, prior to the laws, what they are to become through them" (p. 383). The metaphor engendered by this metalepsis is equally predictable. It can only be God, since the temporal and causal reversal that puts the realization of the promise before its utterance can only occur within a teleological system oriented toward the convergence of figure and meaning. Since the *Social Contract* is nothing of the sort, it is entirely consistent that it should introduce the notion of divine authority at this particular point and have to define it as a simulacrum: "If prideful philosophy and blind partisan spirit continue to regard [the lawgiver] as a fortunate impostor, true political minds admire in the institutions they created, the forceful genius that presides over enduring laws" (p. 384). When the truly political mind is also a philosopher, he will no longer be "prideful," but this lawgiver will be no less of an impostor, albeit no longer a fortunate one. The metaphorical substitution of one's own for the divine voice is blasphemous, although the necessity

22. See Chapter 7, p. 153, n. 29.

for this deceit is as implacable as its eventual denunciation, in the future undoing of any State or any political institution.

Is Rousseau himself the "lawgiver" of the *Social Contract* and his treatise the Deuteronomy of the modern State? If this were the case, then the *Social Contract* would become a monological referential statement. It could not be called an allegory, nor a text in our sense, since the exposure of the deceit would have to come from outside evidence not provided by the text itself. Since it implicitly and explicitly denies, in chapter 7 of book 2 ("Du législateur") and again in the related chapter 8 of book 4 ("De la religion civile"), any form of divine inspiration for itself, it is clear that Rousseau does not identify himself with any of the major legislators, be it Moses, Lycurgus, or Christ; instead, by raising the suspicion that the Sermon on the Mount may be the Machiavellian invention of a master politician, he clearly undermines the authority of his own legislative discourse. Would we then have to conclude that the *Social Contract* is a deconstructive narrative like the *Second Discourse*? But this is not the case either, because the *Social Contract* is clearly productive and generative as well as deconstructive in a manner that the *Second Discourse* is not. To the extent that it never ceases to advocate the necessity for political legislation and to elaborate the principles on which such a legislation could be based, it resorts to the principles of authority that it undermines. We know this structure to be characteristic of what we have called allegories of unreadability. Such an allegory is metafigural: it is an allegory of a figure (for example, metaphor) which relapses into the figure it deconstructs. The *Social Contract* falls under this heading to the extent that it is indeed structured like an aporia: it persists in performing what it has shown to be impossible to do. As such, we can call it an allegory. But is it the allegory of a figure? The question can be answered by asking what it is the *Social Contract* performs, what it keeps doing despite the fact that it has established that it could not be done. What the *Profession de foi* keeps doing is to assert the metaphorical analogy between mind and nature against which the text has generated its own argument; it keeps listening, in other words, to the voice of conscience (or of God) affectively, although it no longer can believe it. What Julie keeps doing, at the end of part 3 of the novel, is to "love" Saint-Preux and God as if they were interchangeable. To listen and to love are referential transitive acts that are not self-positing. What the *Social Contract* keeps doing however is to promise, that is, to perform the very

illocutionary speech act which it has discredited and to perform it in
all its textual ambiguity, as a statement of which the constative and
the performative functions cannot be distinguished or reconciled.

That the *Social Contract* denies the right to promise is clear
from the fact that the legislator has to invent a transcendental principle of signification called God in order to perform the metalepsis
that reverses the temporal pattern of all promissory and legal statements. Since God is said to be, within this perspective, a subterfuge,
it follows that the *Social Contract* has lost the right to promise anything. Yet it promises a great deal. For example: ". . . far from
thinking that we can have neither virtue nor happiness and that
providence [*le ciel*] has abandoned us without shelter to the degradation of the species, let us extract from evil itself the remedy that must
cure it. Let us if possible improve by new institutions [*de nouvelles
associations*] the shortcomings of society in general. . . . Let our
interlocutor see in a better constitution of things the reward for
virtuous deeds, the punishment of evil and the harmonious accord of
justice and well-being" (p. 288). Or: ". . . it becomes obvious that
individuals do not really give up anything when they enter into the
social contract. Their new situation is genuinely preferable to the old
one, before the contract. Instead of an alienation, they have exchanged an uncertain and precarious way of life against a better and
more secure one; instead of natural independence, they now have
freedom; instead of the power to harm others, they now have their
own security; and instead of their individual strength, which others
might overcome, they now have rights which the social union makes
invincible" (p. 375). Several other instances could be quoted, some
explicit, some all the more suggestive because they are all-pervasive
in their connotations; it is impossible to read the *Social Contract*
without experiencing the exhilarating feeling inspired by a firm
promise.

The reintroduction of the promise, despite the fact that its impossibility has been established (the pattern that identifies the *Social
Contract* as a *textual* allegory), does not occur at the discretion of the
writer. We are not merely pointing out an inconsistency, a weakness
in the text of the *Social Contract* that could have been avoided by
simply omitting sentimental or demagogical passages. The point is
not that the *Social Contract* relapses into textual activism because it
does so explicitly, in sections and passages that can be isolated and

quoted by themselves. Even without these passages, the *Social Contract* would still promise by inference, perhaps more effectively than if Rousseau had not had the naïveté, or the good faith, to promise openly. The redoubtable efficacy of the text is due to the rhetorical model of which it is a version. This model is a fact of language over which Rousseau himself has no control. Just as any other reader, he is bound to misread his text as a promise of political change. The error is not within the reader; language itself dissociates the cognition from the act. *Die Sprache verspricht (sich);* to the extent that is necessarily misleading, language just as necessarily conveys the promise of its own truth. This is also why textual allegories on this level of rhetorical complexity generate history.

12   Excuses

(Confessions)

POLITICAL AND AUTOBIOGRAPHICAL TEXTS HAVE IN COM-
mon that they share a referential reading-moment explicitly built in
within the spectrum of their significations, no matter how deluded
this moment may be in its mode as well as in its thematic content:
the deadly "horn of the bull" referred to by Michel Leiris in a text that
is indeed as political as it is autobiographical.[1] But whereas the
relationship between cognition and performance is relatively easy to
grasp in the case of a temporal speech act such as *promise*—which,
in Rousseau's work, is the model for the *Social Contract*—it is more
complex in the confessional mode of his autobiographies. By reading
a central passage from the *Confessions*, I attempt to clarify the relationship between critical procedures that start out from the discourse of the subject and procedures that start out from political
statements.

Among the various more or less shameful and embarassing
scenes from childhood and adolescence related in the first three
books of the *Confessions*, Rousseau singled out the episode of Marion
and the ribbon as of particular affective significance, a truly primal
scene of lie and deception strategically placed in the narrative and
told with special *panache*. We are invited to believe that the episode
was never revealed to anyone prior to the privileged reader of the
Confessions "and . . . that the desire to free myself, so to speak, from
this weight has greatly contributed to my resolve to write my confessions" (86).[2] When Rousseau returns to the *Confessions* in the later
Fourth Rêverie, he again singles out this same episode as a paradig-

1. "De la littérature considérée comme une tauromachie," in Michel Leiris,
L'âge d'homme (Paris: Gallimard, 1946). The essay dates from 1945, immediately
after the war.
2. Page numbers are from J. J. Rousseau, *Oeuvres complètes, Les confessions,
autres textes autobiographiques*, ed. Bernard Gagnebin and Marcel Raymond (Paris:
Gallimard [Bibliothèque de la Pléiade], 1959), vol. 1. The passage concludes Book II
of the *Confessions* and appears on pp. 85–87.

matic event, the core of his autobiographical narrative. The selection is, in itself, as arbitrary as it is suspicious, but it provides us with a textual event of undeniable exegetic interest: the juxtaposition of two confessional texts linked together by an explicit repetition, the confession, as it were, of a confession.

The episode itself is one in a series of stories of petty larceny, but with an added twist. While employed as a servant in an aristocratic Turin household, Rousseau has stolen a "pink and silver colored ribbon." When the theft is discovered, he accuses a young maidservant of having given him the ribbon, the implication being that she was trying to seduce him. In public confrontation, he obstinately clings to his story, thus casting irreparable doubt on the honesty and the morality of an innocent girl who has never done him the slightest bit of harm and whose sublime good nature does not even flinch in the face of dastardly accusation: "Ah Rousseau! I took you to be a man of good character. You are making me very unhappy but I would hate to change places with you" (85). The story ends badly, with both characters being dismissed, thus allowing Rousseau to speculate at length, and with some relish, on the dreadful things that are bound to have happened in the subsequent career of the hapless girl.

The first thing established by this edifying narrative is that the *Confessions* are not primarily a confessional text. To confess is to overcome guilt and shame in the name of truth: it is an epistemological use of language in which ethical values of good and evil are superseded by values of truth and falsehood, one of the implications being that vices such as concupiscence, envy, greed, and the like are vices primarily because they compel one to lie. By stating things as they are, the economy of ethical balance is restored and redemption can start in the clarified atmosphere of a truth that does not hesitate to reveal the crime in all its horror. In this case, Rousseau even adds to the horror by conjuring up, in the narrative of the *Confessions* as well as that of the *Promenade*, the dire consequences that his action may have had for the victim. Confessions occur in the name of an absolute truth which is said to exist "for itself" ("pour elle seule," [1028]) and of which particular truths are only derivative and secondary aspects.

But even within the first narrative, in Book II of the *Confessions*, Rousseau cannot limit himself to the mere statement of what "really" happened, although he is proud to draw attention to the fullness of a self-accusation whose candor we are never supposed to suspect: "I have been very thorough in the confession I have made, and it could certainly never be said that I tried to conceal the blackness of my crime" (86). But it does not suffice to tell all. It is not enough to *confess*, one also has to *excuse*: "But I would not fulfill the purpose of this book if I did not reveal my inner sentiments as well, and if I did not fear to *excuse* myself by means of what conforms to the truth" ("que je [ne] craignisse de m'*excuser* en ce qui est conforme à la vérité" [86, my italics]). This also happens, it should be noted, in the name of truth and, at first sight, there should be no conflict between confession and excuse. Yet the language reveals the tension in the expression: *craindre* de m'excuser. The only thing one has to fear from the excuse is that it will indeed exculpate the confessor, thus making the confession (and the confessional text) redundant as it originates. *Qui s'accuse s'excuse;* this sounds convincing and convenient enough, but, in terms of absolute truth, it ruins the seriousness of any confessional discourse by making it self-destructive. Since confession is not a reparation in the realm of practical justice but exists only as a verbal utterance, how then are we to know that we are indeed dealing with a *true* confession, since the recognition of guilt implies its exoneration in the name of the same transcendental principle of truth that allowed for the certitude of guilt in the first place?

In fact, a far-reaching modification of the organizing principle of truth occurs between the two sections of the narrative. The truth in whose name the excuse *has to be* stated, even at Rousseau's assumed "corps défendant," is not structured like the truth principle that governs the confession. It does not unveil a state of being but states a suspicion, a possible discrepancy that might lead to an impossibility to know. The discrepancy, of course, is between the "séntiment intérieur" that accompanied (or prompted?) the act and the act itself. But the spatial inside/outside metaphor is misleading, for it articulates a differentiation that is not spatial at all. The distinction between the confession stated in the mode of revealed truth and the confession stated in the mode of excuse is that the evidence for the former is referential (the ribbon), whereas the evidence for the latter can only be verbal. Rousseau can convey his "inner feeling" to us only if we take, as we say, his *word* for it, whereas the evidence for his theft is, at least in theory, literally available.[3] Whether we believe him

3. This is so even within the immediate situation, when no actual text is

or not is not the point; it is the verbal or nonverbal nature of the evidence that makes the difference, not the sincerity of the speaker or the gullibility of the listener. The distinction is that the latter process necessarily includes a moment of understanding that cannot be equated with a perception, and that the logic that governs this moment is not the same as that which governs a referential verification. What Rousseau is saying then, when he insists on "sentiment intérieur," is that confessional language can be considered under a double epistemological perspective: it functions as a verifiable referential cognition, but it also functions as a statement whose reliability cannot be verified by empirical means. The convergence of the two modes is not a priori given, and it is because of the possibility of a discrepancy between them that the possibility of excuse arises. The excuse articulates the discrepancy and, in so doing, it actually asserts it as fact (whereas it is only a suspicion). It believes, or pretends to believe, that the act of stealing the ribbon is both this act as a physical fact (he removed it from the place where it was and put it in his pocket, or wherever he kept it), as well as a certain "inner feeling" that was somehow (and this "how" remains open) connected with it. Moreover, it believes that the fact and the feeling are not the same. Thus to complicate a fact certainly is: to act. The difference between the verbal excuse and the referential crime is not a simple opposition between an action and a mere utterance about an action. To steal is to act and includes no necessary verbal elements. To confess is discursive, but the discourse is governed by a principle of referential verification that includes an extraverbal moment: even if we confess that we *said* something (as opposed to *did*), the verification of this verbal event, the decision about the truth or falsehood of its occurrence, is not verbal but factual, the knowledge that the utterance actually took place. No such possibility of verification exists for the excuse, which is verbal in its utterance, in its effect and in its authority: its purpose is not to state but to convince, itself an "inner" process to which only words can bear witness. As is well known at least since Austin,[4] excuses are a complex instance of what he termed perform-

---

present. Someone's sentiments are accesible only through the medium of mimicry, of gestures that require deciphering and function as a language. That this deciphering is not necessarily reliable is clear from the fact that the facial expression of, say, a thief at the moment he is caught red-handed is not likely to weigh heavily as evidence in a court of law. Our own sentiments are available to us only in the same manner.

4. See, for example, J. L. Austin, "Performative Utterances" and "A Plea for

ative utterances, a variety of speech act. The interest of Rousseau's text is that it explicitly functions performatively as well as cognitively, and thus gives indications about the structure of performative rhetoric; this is already established in this text when the confession fails to close off a discourse which feels compelled to modulate from the confessional into the apologetic mode.[5]

Neither does the performance of the excuse allow for a closing off of the apologetic text, despite Rousseau's plea at the end of Book II: "This is what I had to say on this matter. May I be allowed never to mention it again" (87). Yet, some ten years later, in the *Fourth Rêverie*, he tells the entire story all over again, in the context of a meditation that has to do with the possible "excusability" of lies. Clearly, the apology has not succeeded in becalming his own guilt to the point where he would be allowed to forget it. It doesn't matter much, for our purpose, whether the guilt truly relates to this particular act or if the act is merely made to substitute for another, worse crime or humiliation. It may stand for a whole series of crimes, a general mood of guilt, yet the repetition is significant by itself: what-

Excuses," in *Philosophical Papers*, ed. J. O. Urmson and G. J. Warnock (Oxford, 1961).

5. The usual way of dealing with this recurrent pattern in Rousseau's writings is by stressing the bad faith of his commitment to a *morale de l'intention*, the ethical stance for which he was taken severely to task by Sartre. In his commentary on the passage, Marcel Raymond, though less severe, takes the same approach: "By revealing his 'inner feelings' [*dispositions intérieures*'] which were good . . . it appears that after having stigmatized his misdeed he gradually begins to justify it. The same gliding and swerving motion can be observed more than once in the *Confessions*, especially when Rousseau accounts for the abandonment of his children. He is always led to distinguish the intent from the act" (1273–74). It can, however, be shown that Rousseau's ethics is much rather a *morale de pratique* than a *morale de l'intention*, and that this analysis therefore does not account for the genuinely pre-Kantian interest of his ethical language and theory. The extensive possibilities of bad faith engendered by the distinction between the actual event and the inner feeling are abundanelty present throughout Rousseau, but they don't govern the more puzzling and interesting movements and coinages of the text. Whether the link between "inner" feeling and "outer" action can be called intentional is precisely the burden of the interpretation and cannot be asserted without further evidence. If we are right in saying that "*qui s'accuse s'excuse*," then the relationship between confession and excuse is rhetorical prior to being intentional. The same assumption of intentional apologetics, controlled by the narrative voice, underlies the recent readings of the *Confessions* by Phillippe Lejeune in *Le pacte autobiographique* (Paris, 1976) and "Le peigne cassé," *Poétique* 25 (1976): 1–30.

ever the content of the criminal act may have been, the excuse presented in the *Confessions* was unable to satisfy Rousseau as a judge of
Jean-Jacques. This failure was already partly inscribed within the
excuse itself and it governs its further expansion and repetition.

Rousseau excuses himself from his gratuitous viciousness by
identifying his inner feeling as *shame* about himself rather than any
hostility towards his victim: ". . . the presence of so many people
was stronger than my repentance. I hardly feared punishment, my
only fear was shame; but I feared shame more than death, more
than the crime, more than anything in the world. I wished I could
have sunk and stifled myself in the center of the earth: unconquera-
ble shame was stronger than anything else, shame alone caused my
impudence and the more guilty I became, the more the terror of
admitting my guilt made me fearless" (86).

It is easy enough to describe how "shame" functions in a context
that seems to offer a convincing answer to the question: what is
shame or, rather, what is one ashamed of? Since the entire scene
stands under the aegis of theft, it has to do with possession, and
desire must therefore be understood as functioning, at least at times,
as a desire to possess, in all the connotations of the term. Once it is
removed from its legitimate owner, the ribbon, being in itself devoid
of meaning and function, can circulate symbolically as a pure signifier and become the articulating hinge in a chain of exchanges and
possessions. As the ribbon changes hands it traces a circuit leading to
the exposure of a hidden, censored desire. Rousseau identifies the
desire as his desire for Marion: "it was my intention to give her the
ribbon" (86), i.e., to "possess" her. At this point in the reading
suggested by Rousseau, the proper meaning of the trope is clear
enough: the ribbon "stands for" Rousseau's desire for Marion or,
what amounts to the same thing, for Marion herself.

Or, rather, it stands for the free circulation of the desire between Rousseau and Marion, for the reciprocity which, as we know
from *Julie*, is for Rousseau the very condition of love; it stands for the
substitutability of Rousseau for Marion and vice versa. Rousseau desires Marion as Marion desires Rousseau. But since, within the atmosphere of intrigue and suspicion that prevails in the household of
the Comtesse de Vercellis, the phantasy of this symmetrical reciprocity is experienced as an interdict, its figure, the ribbon, has to be
stolen, and the agent of this transgression has to be susceptible of
being substituted: if Rousseau has to be willing to steal the ribbon,

then Marion has to be willing to substitute for Rousseau in performing this act.[6] We have at least two levels of substitution (or displacement) taking place: the ribbon substituting for a desire which is itself
a desire for substitution. Both are governed by the same desire for
specular symmetry which gives to the symbolic object a detectable,
univocal proper meaning. The system works: "I accused Marion of
having done what I wanted to do and of having given me the ribbon
because it was my intention to give it to her" (86). The substitutions
have taken place without destroying the cohesion of the system,
reflected in the balanced syntax of the sentence and now understandable exactly as we comprehend the ribbon to signify desire.
Specular figures of this kind are metaphors and it should be noted
that on this still elementary level of understanding, the introduction
of the figural dimension in the text occurs first by ways of metaphor.

The allegory of this metaphor, revealed in the "confession" of
Rousseau's desire for Marion, functions as an excuse if we are willing
to take the desire at face value. If it is granted that Marion is desirable, or Rousseau ardent to such an extent, then the motivation for
the theft becomes understandable and easy to forgive. He did it all
out of love for her, and who would be a dour enough literalist to let a
little property stand in the way of young love? We would then be
willing to grant Rousseau that "viciousness was never further from
me than at this cruel moment, and when I accused the hapless girl, it
is bizarre but it is true that my friendship for her was the cause of
my accusation" (86). Substitution is indeed bizarre (it is odd to take
a ribbon for a person) but since it reveals motives, causes, and
desires, the oddity is quickly reduced back to sense. The story may be
a rebus or a riddle in which a ribbon is made to signify a desire, but
the riddle can be solved. The delivery of meaning is delayed but by no
means impossible.

This is not the only way, however, in which the text functions.
Desire conceived as possession allows for the all-important introduction of figural displacement: things are not merely what they seem to
be, a ribbon is not just a ribbon, to steal can be an act of love, an act
performed by Rousseau can be said to be performed by Marion and,
in the process, it becomes more rather than less comprehensible, etc.
Yet the text does not stay confined within this pattern of desire. For

6. It is therefore consistent that, when the scheme ends in disaster, Marion
would say: "Je ne voudrois pas être à votre place" (85).

one thing, to excuse the crime of theft does not suffice to excuse the
worse crime of slander which, as both common sense and Rousseau
tell us, is much harder to accept.[7] Neither can the shame be accounted for by the hidden nature of the desire, as would be the case
in an oedipal situation.[8] The interdict does not weigh very heavily
and the revelation of Rousseau's desire, in a public situation that does
not allow for more intimate self-examination, hardly warrants such
an outburst of shame. More important than any of these referential
considerations, the text is not set up in such a way as to court
sympathy in the name of Marion's erotic charm, a strategy which
Rousseau uses with some skill in many other instances including the
first part of *Julie.* Another form of desire than the desire of possession
is operative in the latter part of the story, which also bears the main
performative burden of the excuse and in which the crime is no
longer that of theft.

The obvious satisfaction in the tone and the eloquence of the
passage quoted above, the easy flow of hyperboles (". . . je la crai-
gnois [la honte] plus que la mort, plus que le crime, plus que tout au
monde. J'aurois voulu m'enforcer, m'étouffer dans le centre
de la terre . . ." [86]), the obvious delight with which the desire
to hide is being revealed, all point to another structure of desire
than mere possession and independent of the particular target of
the desire. One is more ashamed of the exposure of the desire to
expose oneself than of the desire to possess; like Freud's dreams of
nakedness, shame is primarily exhibitionistic. What Rousseau *really*
wanted is neither the ribbon nor Marion, but the public scene of
exposure which he actually gets. The fact that he made no attempt to
conceal the evidence confirms this. The more crime there is, the
more theft, lie, slander, and stubborn persistence in each of them,
the better. The more there is to expose, the more there is to be
ashamed of; the more resistance to exposure, the more satisfying the
scene, and, especially, the more satisfying and eloquent the belated
revelation, in the later narrative, of the inability to reveal. This desire

7. "To lie for one's own advantage is deceit, to lie for the benefit of another is
fraudulent, to lie in order to harm is slander; it is the worst kind of lie" (*Fourth
Rêverie*, 1029).

8. The embarrassing story of Rousseau's rejection by Mme. de Vercellis, who is
dying of a cancer of the breast, immediately precedes the story of Marion, but
nothing in the text suggests a concatenation that would allow one to substitute
Marion for Mme. de Vercellis in a scene of rejection.

is truly shameful, for it suggests that Marion was destroyed, not for
the sake of Rousseau's saving face, nor for the sake of his desire for
her, but merely in order to provide him with a stage on which to
parade his disgrace or, what amounts to the same thing, to furnish
him with a good ending for Book II of his *Confessions*. The structure
is self-perpetuating, *en abîme*, as is implied in its description as
exposure of the desire to expose, for each new stage in the unveiling
suggests a deeper shame, a greater impossibility to reveal, and a
greater satisfaction in outwitting this impossibility.

The structure of desire as exposure rather than as possession
explains why shame functions indeed, as it does in this text, as the
most effective excuse, much more effectively than greed, or lust, or
love. Promise is proleptic, but excuse is belated and always occurs
after the crime; since the crime is exposure, the excuse consists in
recapitulating the exposure in the guise of concealment. The excuse
is a ruse which permits exposure in the name of hiding, not unlike
Being, in the later Heidegger, reveals itself by hiding. Or, put differently, shame used as excuse permits repression to function as revelation and thus to make pleasure and guilt interchangeable. Guilt is
forgiven because it allows for the pleasure of revealing its repression.
It follows that repression is in fact an excuse, one speech act among
others.

But the text offers further possibilities. The analysis of shame as
excuse makes evident the strong link between the performance of
excuses and the act of understanding. It has led to the problematics
of hiding and revealing, which are clearly problematics of cognition.
Excuse occurs within an epistemological twilight zone between
knowing and not-knowing; this is also why it has to be centered on
the crime of lying and why Rousseau can excuse himself for everything provided he can be excused for lying. When this turns out not
to have been the case, when his claim to have lived for the sake of
truth (*vitam impendere vero*) is being contested from the outside, the
closure of excuse ("qu'il me soit permis de n'en reparler jamais")
becomes a delusion and the *Fourth Rêverie* has to be written.

The passage also stakes out the limits of how this understanding
of understanding then is to be understood. For the distinction between desire as possession and desire as exposure, although it unde-
niably is at work within the text, does not structure its main movement. It could not be said, for instance, that the latter deconstructs
the former. Both converge towards a unified signification, and the
shame experienced at the desire to possess dovetails with the deeper

shame felt at self-exposure, just as the excuse for the one conspired with the excuse for the other in mutual reinforcement. This implies that the mode of cognition as hiding/revealing is fundamentally akin to the mode of cognition as possession and that, at least up till this point, to know and to own are structured in the same way. Truth is a *property* of entities, and to lie is to steal, like Prometheus, this truth away from its owner. In the deviousness of the excuse pattern, the lie is made legitimate, but this occurs within a system of truth and falsehood that may be ambiguous in its valorization but not in its structure. It also implies that the terminology of repression and exposure encountered in the passage on shame is entirely compatible with the system of symbolic substitutions (based on encoded significations arbitrarily attributed to a free signifier, the ribbon) that govern the passage on possessive desire ("Je l'accusai d'avoir fait ce que je voulois faire . . ." [86]). The figural rhetoric of the passage, whose underlying metaphor, encompassing both possession and exposure, is that of unveiling, combines with a generalized pattern of tropological substitution to reach a convincing meaning. What seemed at first like irrational behavior bordering on insanity has, by the end of the passage, become comprehensible enough to be incorporated within a general economy of human affectivity, in a theory of desire, repression, and self-analyzing discourse in which excuse and knowledge converge. Desire, now expanded far enough to include the hiding/revealing movement of the unconscious as well as possession, functions as the *cause* of the entire scene (". . . it is bizarre but true that my friendship for her was the *cause* of my accusations" [86]), and once this desire has been made to appear in all its complexity, the action is understood and, consequently, excused—for it was primarily its incongruity that was unforgivable. Knowledge, morality, possession, exposure, affectivity (shame as the synthesis of pleasure and pain), and the performative excuse are all ultimately part of one system that is epistemologically as well as ethically grounded and therefore available as meaning, in the mode of understanding. Just as in a somewhat earlier passage of the *Confessions* the particular injustice of which Rousseau had been a victim becomes, by metaphorical synecdoche, the paradigm for the universal experience of injustice,[9] the episode ends up in a generalized economy of rewards and punishments. The injury done to Marion is

9. See the episode of Mlle Lambercier's broken comb in Book I of the *Confessions*, especially p. 20.

compensated for by the subsequent suffering inflicted on Rousseau by nameless avengers acting in her stead.[10] The restoration of justice naturally follows the disclosure of meaning. Why then does the excuse fail and why does Rousseau have to return to an enigma that has been so well resolved?

We have, of course, omitted from the reading the other sentence in which the verb "excuser" is explicitly being used, again in a somewhat unusual construction; the oddity of "que je craignisse de m'excuser" is repeated in the even more unusual locution: "Je m'excusai sur le premier objet qui s'offrit" ("I excused myself upon the first thing that offered itself" [86]), as one would say "je me vengeai" or "je m'acharnai sur le premier objet qui s'offrit."[11] The sentence is inserted, it is true, within a context that may seem to confirm the coherence of the causal chain: ". . . it is bizarre but it is true that my friendship for her was the cause of my accusation. She was present to my mind, I excused myself on the first thing that offered itself. I accused her of having done what I wanted to do and of having given me the ribbon because it was my intention to give it to her . . ." (86). Because Rousseau desires Marion, she haunts his mind and her name is pronounced almost unconsciously, as if it were a slip, a segment of the discourse of the other. But the use of a vocabulary of contingency ("le premier objet qui s'offrit") within an argument of causality is arresting and disruptive, for the sentence is phrased in such a way as to allow for a complete disjunction between Rousseau's desires and interests and the selection of this particular name. Marion just happened to be the first thing that came to mind; any other name, any other word, any other sound or noise could have done just as well and Marion's entry into the discourse is a mere effect of chance. She is a free signifier, metonymically related to the

10. "If this crime can be redeemed, as I hope it may, it must be by the many misfortunes that have darkened the later part of my life, by forty years of upright and honorable behavior under difficult circumstances. Poor Marion finds so many avengers in this world that, no matter how considerably I have offended her, I have little fear that I will carry this guilt with me. This is all I had to say on this matter. May I be allowed never to mention it again" (87).

11. The editor of the Pléiade Rousseau, Marcel Raymond, comments on the passage and quotes Ramon Fernandez (De la personnalité, p. 77): "He accuses her as if he leaned on a piece of furntiture to avoid falling." Raymond speaks of "an almost dreamlike movement dictated by an unconscious which suddenly feels itself accused and by which he transfers the 'misdeed' upon the other, on his nearby partner" (1273).

part she is made to play in the subsequent system of exchanges and substitutions. She is, however, in an entirely different situation than the other free signifier, the ribbon, which also just happened to be ready-to-hand, but which is not in any way itself the object of a desire. Whereas, in the development that follows and that introduces the entire chain leading from desire to shame to (dis)possession to concealment to revelation to excuse and to distributive justice, Marion can be the organizing principle because she is considered to be the hidden center of an urge to reveal. Her bondage as target liberates in turn the free play of her symbolical substitutes. Unlike the ribbon, Marion is not herself divested of positive signification, since no revelation or no excuse would be possible if her presence within the chain were not motivated as the target of the entire action. But if her nominal presence is a mere coincidence, then we are entering an entirely different system in which such terms as desire, shame, guilt, exposure, and repression no longer have any place.

In the spirit of the text, one should resist all temptation to give any significance whatever to the sound "Marion." For it is only if the act that initiated the entire chain, the utterance of the sound "Marion," is truly without any conceivable motive that the total arbitrariness of the action becomes the most effective, the most efficaciously performative excuse of all. The estrangement between subject and utterance is then so radical that it escapes any mode of comprehension. When everything else fails, one can always plead insanity. "Marion" is meaningless and powerless to generate by itself the chain of causal substitutions and figures that structures the surrounding text, which is a text of desire as well as a desire for text. It stands entirely out of the system of truth, virtue, and understanding (or of deceit, evil, and error) that gives meaning to the passage, and to the *Confessions* as a whole. The sentence: "je m'excusai sur le premier objet qui s'offrit" is therefore an anacoluthon,[12] a foreign element that disrupts

12. Classical rhetoric mentions anacoluthon especially with regard to the structure of periodical sentences, when a shift, syntactical or other, occurs between the first part of the period (protasis) and the second part (apodosis). Heinrich Lausberg in *Handbuch der Literarischen Rhetorik* (Munich, 1960), 1:459, § 924, gives an example from Vergil: "quamquam anima meminisse horret luctuque refugit, incipiam" (*Aeneid* 2, 12). The following example from Racine is frequently quoted: "Vous voulez que ce Dieu vous comble de bienfaits / Et ne l'aimer jamais." Anacoluthon is not restricted to uninflected parts of speech but can involve nouns or inflected shifters such as pronouns. It designates any grammatical or syntactical discontinuity in which a construction interrupts another before it is completed. A

the meaning, the readability of the apologetic discourse, and reopens what the excuse seemed to have closed off. How are we to understand the implications of this sentence and what does it do to the very idea of understanding which we found to be so intimately bound up with and dependent upon the performative function itself?

The question takes us to the *Fourth Rêverie* and its implicit shift from reported guilt to the guilt of reporting, since here the lie is no longer connected with some former misdeed but specifically with the act of writing the *Confessions* and, by extension, with all writing. Of course, we always were in the realm of writing, in the narrative of the *Confessions* as well as in the *Rêverie*, but the thematization of this fact is now explicit: what can be said about the interference of the cognitive with the performative function of excuses in the *Fourth Rêverie* will disseminate what existed as a localized disruption in the *Confessions*.

With the complicity of the casual, ambling, and free-associating mode of the *Rêverie*, the text allows itself a puzzling lack of conclusiveness. Cast in the tone of a pietistic self-examination, it sounds severe and rigorous enough in its self-accusation to give weight to the exoneration it pronounces upon its author—until Rousseau takes it all back in the penultimate paragraph which decrees him to be "inexcusable" (1038). There is also a strange unbalance between the drift of the argument, which proceeds by fine distinctions and ratiocinations, and the drift of the examples, which do not quite fit their declared intent. The claim is made, for example, that, in the *Confessions*, Rousseau left out several episodes because they showed him in too favorable a light; when some of these incidents are then being told in order to make the disfigured portrait more accurate, they turn out to be curiously irrelevant. They do not show Rousseau in all that favorable a light (since all he does is *not* to denounce playing companions who harmed him by accident and from whose denunciation he would, at the time, have stood to gain very little) and they are, moreover, most unpleasant stories of physical assault, bloody mutilation, and crushed fingers, told in such a way that one remembers the pain and the cruelty much better than the virtue they are supposed to illustrate. All this adds to the somewhat uncanny

---

striking instance of the structural and epistemological implications of anacoluthon occurs in Proust in the description of the lies used by Albertine ("La prisonniere," *A la recherche du temps perdu* [Paris: Pléiade, 1954], 3:153). For Rousseau's own description of an anacoluthon-like situation, see note 16.

obliqueness of a slightly delirious text which is far from mastering the effects it pretends to produce.

The implications of the random lie in the Marion episode ("je m'excusai sur le premier objet qui s'offrit") are distributed, in the *Fourth Rêverie*, over the entire text. The performative power of the lie as excuse is more strongly marked here, and tied specifically to the absence of referential signification; it also carries, in this literary context, a more familiar and reputable name since it is now called *fiction*: "To lie without intent and without harm to oneself or to others is not to lie: it is not a lie but a fiction" (1029). The notion of fiction is introduced in the same way that the excuse of randomness functions in the *Confessions*. Within the airtight system of absolute truth it produces the almost imperceptible crack of the purely gratuitous, what Rousseau calls "un fait oiseux, indifférent à tous égards et sans conséquence pour personne . . ." ("a fact that is totally useless, indifferent in all respects and inconsequential for anyone" [1027]). There is some hesitation as to whether such "perfectly sterile truths" are at all conceivable, or if we possess the necessary judgment to decide authoritatively whether certain statements can be to that extent devoid of any significance. But although the text vacillates on this point, it nevertheless functions predominantly as if the matter had been settled positively: even if such truths are said to be "rares et difficiles," it is asserted that the "truth" of such "useless facts" can be withheld without lying: "Truth deprived of any conceivable kind of usefulness can therefore not be something due [*une chose due*], and consequently the one who keeps it silent or disguises it does not lie" (1027). Moreover, "I have found there to be actual instances in which truth can be withheld without injustice and disguised without lying" (1028). Some speech acts (although they might better be called silence acts) therefore escape from the closed system in which truth is property and lie theft: ". . . how could truths entirely devoid of use, didactic or practical, be a commodity that is due [*un bien dû*], since they are not even a commodity? And since ownership is only based on use, there can be no property where there can be no use" ("où il n'y a point d'utilité possible il ne peut y avoir de propriété" [1026]. Once this possibility is granted, these free-floating "truths" or "facts," utterly devoid of value ("*Rien* ne peut être dû de ce qui n'est bon à *rien*" [1027]) are then susceptible of being "used" as an excuse for the embellishments and exaggerations that were innocently added to the *Confessions*. They are mere "détails oiseux" and to call them lies would be, in Rousseau's words, "to have a conscience that is more delicate than mine" (1030). The same paragraph calls these weightless, airy non-substances fictions: "whatever, albeit contrary to truth, fails to concern justice in any way, is mere fiction, and I confess that someone who reproaches himself for a pure fiction as if it were a lie has a conscience that is more delicate than mine" (1030). What makes a fiction a fiction is not some polarity of fact and representation. Fiction has nothing to do with representation but is the absence of any link between utterance and a referent, regardless of whether this link be causal, encoded, or governed by any other conceivable relationship that could lend itself to systematization. In fiction thus conceived the "necessary link" of the metaphor has been metonymized beyond the point of catachresis, and the fiction becomes the disruption of the narrative's referential illusion. This is precisely how the name of Marion came to be uttered in the key sentence in the *Confessions*: "je m'excusai sur le premier objet qui s'offrit," a sentence in which any anthropomorphic connotation of seduction implied by the verb "s'offrir" has to be resisted if the effectiveness of the excuse is not to be undone and replaced by the banality of mere bad faith and suspicion. Rousseau was making whatever noise happened to come into his head; he was saying nothing at all, least of all someone's name. Because this is the case the statement can function as excuse, just as fiction functions as an excuse for the disfigurations of the *Confessions*.

It will be objected that fiction in the *Rêverie* and the denunciation of Marion are miles apart in that the former is without consequence whereas the latter results in considerable damage to others. Rousseau himself stresses this: "whatever is contrary to truth and hurts justice in any conceivable way is a lie" (1030), and also "the absence of a purposefully harmful intent does not suffice to make a lie innocent; one must also be assured that the error one inflicts upon one's interlocutor can in no conceivable way harm him or anyone else" (1029). But the fiction, in the *Confessions*, becomes harmful only because it is not understood for what it is, because the fictional statement, as it generates the system of shame, desire, and repression we described earlier, is at once caught and enmeshed in a web of causes, significations, and substitutions. If the essential non-signification of the statement had been properly interpreted, if Rousseau's accusers had realized that Marion's name was "le premier objet qui s'offrit," they would have understood his lack of guilt as well as Marion's innocence. And the excuse would have extended

from the slander back to the theft itself, which was equally unmotivated: he took the ribbon out of an unstated and anarchic fact of
proximity, without awareness of any law of ownership. Not the
fiction itself is to blame for the consequences but its falsely referential reading. As a fiction, the statement is innocuous and the error
harmless; it is the misguided reading of the error as theft or slander,
the refusal to admit that fiction is fiction, the stubborn resistance to
the "fact," obvious by itself, that language is entirely free with regard
to referential meaning and can posit whatever its grammar allows it to
say, which leads to the transformation of random error into injustice.
The radical irresponsibility of fiction is, in a way, so obvious, that it
seems hardly necessary to caution against its misreading. Yet its
assertion, within the story of the *Confessions*, appears paradoxical
and far-fetched to the point of absurdity, so much so that Rousseau's
own text, against its author's interests, prefers being suspected of lie
and slander rather than of innocently lacking sense. It seems to be
impossible to isolate the moment in which the fiction stands free of
any signification; in the very moment at which it is posited, as well as
in the context that it generates, it gets at once misinterpreted into a
determination which is, *ipso facto*, overdetermined. Yet without this
moment, never allowed to exist as such, no such thing as a text is
conceivable. We know this to be the case from empirical experience
as well: it is always possible to face up to any experience (to excuse
any guilt), because the experience always exists simultaneously as
fictional discourse and as empirical event and it is never possible to
decide which one of the two possibilities is the right one. The indecision makes it possible to excuse the bleakest of crimes because, as a
fiction, it escapes from the constraints of guilt and innocence. On the
other hand, it makes it equally possible to accuse fiction-making
which, in Hölderlin's words, is "the most innocent of all activities," of
being the most cruel. The knowledge of radical innocence also performs the harshest mutilations. Excuses not only accuse but they
carry out the verdict implicit in their accusation.

This other aspect of radical excuse is also conveyed by the text of
the *Rêverie*, though necessarily in a more oblique manner. In telling
another instance of a situation in which he lied out of shame—a less
interesting example than the ribbon, because there is nothing enigmatic about a lie which, in this case, is *only* a defense[13]—Rousseau

13. In this case he is being provoked into lying by the half-teasing, half-
malicious questions of a woman inquiring whether he ever had children.

writes: "It is certain that neither my judgment, nor my will dictated my reply, but that it was the automatic result [*l'effet machinal*] of my embarrassment" (1034). The machinelike quality of the text of the lie is more remarkable still when, as in the Marion episode, the disproportion between the crime that is to be confessed and the crime performed by the lie adds a delirious element to the situation. By saying that the excuse is not only a fiction but also a machine one adds to the connotation of referential detachment, of gratuitous improvisation, that of the implacable repetition of a preordained pattern. Like Kleist's marionettes, the machine is both "anti-grav," the anamorphosis of a form detached from meaning and capable of taking on any structure whatever, yet entirely ruthless in its inability to modify its own structural design for nonstructural reasons. The machine is like the grammar of the text when it is isolated from its rhetoric, the merely formal element without which no text can be generated. There can be no use of language which is not, within a certain perspective thus radically formal, i.e. mechanical, no matter how deeply this aspect may be concealed by aesthetic, formalistic delusions.

The machine not only generates, but also suppresses, and not always in an innocent or balanced way. The economy of the *Fourth Rêverie* is curiously inconsistent, although it is strongly thematized in a text that has much to do with additions and curtailments, with "filling holes" ("remplir les lacunes" [1035]) and creating them. The parts of the text which are destined to be mere additions and exemplifications acquire autonomous power of signification to the point where they can be said to reduce the main argument to impotence. The addition of examples leads to the subversion of the cognitive affirmation of innocence which the examples were supposed to illustrate. At the end of the text, Rousseau knows that he cannot be excused, yet the text shelters itself from accusation by the performance of its radical fictionality.

The literal censorship and curtailment of texts appears prominently in several places. A quotation from Tasso provides a first example: Rousseau compares his own resolve not to denounce his playing companion to Sophronie's sacrificial lie when, in order to save the life of the Christians, she confessed to a crime (the theft of a religious icon) that did not take place. The comparison borders on the ludicrous, since Rousseau's discretion is in no way equivalent to a sacrifice. But the quotation which Rousseau now inserts into the text serves a different function. It is a passage which he had omitted, without apparent reason, from the translation he made of the Second Canto of Tasso's epic[14] at an earlier date. Any mention of Tasso, in Rousseau, always carries a high affective charge and generates stories clustering around dubious translations, literary falsifications, textual distortions, fallacious prefaces as well as obsessions of identification involving erotic fantasies and anxieties of insanity.[15] Limiting oneself, in this context, to the obvious, the insertion of the quotation must be an attempt to restore the integrity of a text written by someone of whom Rousseau himself had said "that one could not suppress from his work a single stanza, from a stanza a single line, and from a line a single word, without the entire poem collapsing. . . ."[16] But the restoration occurs as an entirely private and secretive gesture, not unlike the citizen stealing "en secret" the word "chacun" and thinking of himself when he votes for all.[17] Such a secretive reparation enforces the shamefulness of the crime as well as destroying any hope that it could be repaired. The mutilation seems

14. The translation is available in several of the early Rousseau editions, for example in *Oeuvres complètes de J. J. Rousseau* (Aux deux ponts: chez Sanson et Compagnie, 1792), 4:215–47. It is printed in bilingual version and even the early editors had observed and indicated the absence of the passage which was later to be quoted in the *Fourth Rêverie* (ibid., 229).

15. On Rousseau and Tasso, one finds general observations, not very informative in this context, in several articles, mostly by Italian authors, mentioned by Bernard Guyon in his notes to the Pléiade edition of the *Nouvelle Héloïse* (2:1339).

16. The statement is not a quotation from Rousseau but is reported by Corancez in *De J. J. Rousseau* (Extrait du Journal de Paris, # 251, 256, 259, 260, 261, An 6, 42–43). The sequel of the statement, in which Rousseau describes the one exception to the organic integrity of Tasso's work, is equally interesting for our purposes and could be read as Rousseau's description of an anacoluthon: ". . . sans que le poème entier ne s'écroule, tant (le Tasse) était précis et ne mettait rien que de nécessaire. Eh bien, ôtez la strophe entiére dont je vous parle; rien n'en souffre, l'ouvrage reste parfait. Elle n'a rapport ni à ce qui précède, ni à ce qui suit; c'est une pièce absolument inutile. Il est à présumer que le Tasse l'a faite involontairement et sans la comprendre lui-même; mais elle est claire." Corancez could not remember the stanza Rousseau quoted, but it has been tentatively identified as stanza 77 of Canto XII of *Jerusalem Delivered*. See L. Proal. *La psychologie de J. J. Rousseau* (Paris: F. Alcan, 1923), p. 327 and *Oeuvres complètes*, 1:1386–87, which Rousseau chose to read as the prefiguration of his own persecutions. Corancez tells the story as an instance of Rousseau's growing paranoia and, in the same article, he reports Rousseau's death as suicide. His article is written in defense, however, of Rousseau's memory.

17. *Social Contract* (3:306).

to be incurable and the prothesis only serves to mark this fact more strongly. The accusation that hangs over the entire *Fourth Rêverie* and against which the excuse tries to defend itself seems to have to do with a threat of textual mutilation, itself linked to the organic and totalizing synechdocal language by means of which Rousseau refers to the unity of Tasso's work.

The omission and surreptitious replacement of the Sophronie passage is at most a symptom, all the more so since "Tasso," in Rousseau, implies a threat as well as a victim, a weapon as well as a wound. The mutilation is not just the excision of one specific piece of text. Its wider significance becomes more evident in another literary allusion in the *Fourth Promenade*, the reference to Montesquieu's conventionally deceptive preface to *Le Temple de Gnide*. By pretending that his work is the translation of a Greek manuscript, the author shelters himself from the possible accusation of frivolity or licentiousness, knowing that the reader who is enlightened enough not to hold his levity against him will also be sufficiently informed about literary convention not to be taken in by the phony preface. Rousseau treats Montesquieu's hoax without undue severity ("Could it have occurred to anyone to incriminate the author for this lie and to call him an impostor?" [1030]), yet behind this apparent tolerance stands a much less reassuring question. As we know from the "Préface dialoguée" to the *Nouvelle Héloïse*, the preface is the place in the text where the question of textual mastery and authority is being decided and where, in the instance of *Julie*, it is also found to be undecidable. With this threatening loss of control the possibility arises of the entirely gratuitous and irresponsible text, not just (as was apparently the case for Montesquieu or for naïve readers of *Julie*) as an intentional denial of paternity for the sake of self-protection, but as the radical annihilation of the metaphor of selfhood and of the will. This more than warrants the anxiety with which Rousseau acknowledges the lethal quality of all writing. Writing always includes the moment of dispossession in favor of the arbitrary power play of the signifier and from the point of view of the subject, this can only be experienced as a dismemberment, a beheading or a castration. Behind Montesquieu's harmless lie, denying authorship of *Le Temple de Gnide* by the manipulation of the preface that "heads" the text, stands the much more dangerous ambivalence of the "beheaded" author.[18]

18. The same anxiety is apparent in another reference to prefaces in Rousseau,

But precisely because, in all these instances, the metaphor for the text is still the metaphor of text as body (from which a more or less vital part, including the head, is being severed), the threat remains sheltered behind its metaphoricity. The possible loss of authorship is not without consequences, liberating as well as threatening, for the empirical author, yet the mutilation of the text cannot be taken seriously: the clear meaning of the figure also prevents it from carrying out what this meaning implies. The undecidability of authorship is a cognition of considerable epistemological importance but, as a cognition, it remains ensconced within the figural delusion that separates knowing from doing. Only when Rousseau no longer confronts Tasso's or Montesquieu's but his own text, the *Confessions*, does the metaphor of text as body make way for the more directly threatening alternative of the text as machine.

Unlike the other two texts, where the distortion had been a suppression, the *Confessions* is at first guilty of disfiguring by excess, by the addition of superfluous, fictional embellishments, "I have never said less, but I have sometimes said more . . ." (1035), but a few lines later it turns out that this was not the case either, since Rousseau admits having omitted some of his recollections from the narrative merely because they showed him in too favorable a light. There is less contradiction between the two statements when it turns out that what he omitted are precisely stories that narrate mutilations or, in the metaphor of the text as body, suppressions. Both stories have to do with mutilation and beheading: he nearly loses a hand in the first and comes close to having his brains knocked out in the other. Thus to omit suppressions is, in a sense (albeit by syllepsis), to preserve an integrity, "ne jamais dire moins." If the stories that have been omitted threaten the integrity of the text, then it

---

interestingly enough also in connection with Tasso. To deny authorship in a preface in the name of truth (as Rousseau did in the case of *Julie*) does not only mean that one's authorship of all texts can be put in question but also that all texts can be attributed to one. This is precisely what happens to Rousseau when a malevolent (or commercially enterprising) editor, in what reads like a transparent parody of the "*Préface dialoguée*," attributes to him a poor translation of Tasso's *Jerusalem Delivered*, (see *Oeuvres complètes*, 1:1740 for the text of the editor's *préface*, and also *Oeuvres complètes*, 1:1386). Rousseau mentions the incident with some degree of paranoid anxiety in a letter to Mme. de Lessert of August 23, 1774, and among many other instances of false textual attribution, in the *Dialogues* (960). The chain that leads from Tasso to translation, to prefaces, to authorship, to beheading, and to insanity is ready to surface in any context of anxiety about truth and falsehood.

would be even easier to excuse him for not having included them than to excuse him for the superfluous ornaments he added to the recollection of his happier memories.

But in what way are these narratives threatening? As instances of Rousseau's generosity they are, as we already pointed out, more inept than convincing. They seem to exist primarily for the sake of the mutilations they describe. But these actual, bodily mutilations seem, in their turn, to be there more for the sake of allowing the evocation of the machine that causes them than for their own shock value; Rousseau lingers complacently over the description of the machine that seduces him into dangerously close contact: "I looked at the metal rolls, my eyes were attracted by their polish. I was tempted to touch them with my fingers and I moved them with pleasure over the polished surface of the cylinder . . ." (1036). In the general economy of the *Rêverie*, the machine displaces all other significations and becomes the raison d'être of the text. Its power of suggestion reaches far beyond its illustrative puspose, especially if one bears in mind the previous characterization of unmotivated, fictional language as "machinal." The underlying structural patterns of addition and suppression as well as the figural system of the text all converge towards it. Barely concealed by its peripheral function, the text here stages the textual machine of its own constitution *and* performance, its own textual allegory. The threatening element in these incidents then becomes more apparent. The text as body, with all its implications of substitutive tropes ultimately always retraceable to metaphor, is displaced by the text as machine and, in the process, it suffers the loss of the illusion of meaning. The deconstruction of the figural dimension is a process that takes place independently of any desire; as such it is not unconscious but mechanical, systematic in its performance but arbitrary in its principle, like a grammar. This threatens the autobiographical subject not as the loss of something that once was present and that it once possessed, but as a radical estrangement between the meaning and the performance of any text.

In order to come into being as text, the referential function had to be radically suspended. Without the scandal of random denunciation of Marion, without the "faits oiseux" of the *Confessions*, there could not have been a text; there would have been nothing to excuse since everything could have been explained away by the cognitive logic of understanding. The cognition would have been the excuse, and this convergence is precisely what is no longer conceivable as soon as the metaphorical integrity of the text is put in question, as soon as the text is said not to be a figural body but a machine. Far from seeing language as an instrument in the service of a psychic energy, the possibility now arises that the entire construction of drives, substitutions, repressions, and representations is the aberrant, metaphorical correlative of the absolute randomness of language, prior to any figuration or meaning. It is no longer certain that language, as excuse, exists because of a prior guilt but just as possible that since language, as a machine, performs anyway, we have to produce guilt (and all its train of psychic consequences) in order to make the excuse meaningful. Excuses generate the very guilt they exonerate, though always in excess or by default. At the end of the *Rêverie* there is a lot more guilt around than we had at the start: Rousseau's indulgence in what he calls, in another bodily metaphor, "*le plaisir d'*écrire" (1038), leaves him guiltier than ever, but we now have also the two companions of his youth, Pleince and Fazy, guilty of assault, brutality or, at the very best, of carelessness.[19] Additional guilt means additional excuse: Fazy and Pleince now both have to apologize and may, for all we know, have written moving texts about the dreadful things they did to Jean-Jacques who, in his turn, now has to apologize for having possibly accused them arbitrarily, as he accused Marion, simply because their names may have happened to occur to him for the least compelling of reasons.[20] No excuse can ever hope to catch up with such a proliferation of guilt. On the other hand, any guilt, including the guilty pleasure of writing the *Fourth Rêverie*, can always be dismissed as the gratuitous product of a textual grammar or a radical fiction: there can never be enough guilt around to match the text-machine's infinite power to excuse. Since guilt, in this description, is a cognitive and excuse a performative function of language, we are restating the disjunction of the perfor-

19. The description of the way in which Fazy injured Rousseau is ambiguous, since the narrative is phrased in such a way that he can be suspected of having done it with deliberation: ". . . le jeune Fazy s'étant mis dans la roue lui donna un demiquart de tour si adroitement qu'il n'y prit que le bout de mes deux plus longs doigts; mais c'en fut assez pour qu'ils fussent écrasés . . ." (1036).

20. For example, the fact that their names may have come to mind because of their phonic resemblance to the place names where the incidents are said to have taken place: the one involving Fazy occurs at Pâquis, the one involving Pleince at Plain-Palais.

mative from the cognitive: any speech act produces an excess of cognition, but it can never hope to know the process of its own production (the only thing worth knowing). Just as the text can never stop apologizing for the suppression of guilt that it performs, there is never enough knowledge available to account for the delusion of knowing.

The main point of the reading has been to show that the resulting predicament is linguistic rather than ontological or hermeneutic. As was clear from the Marion episode in the *Confessions*, the deconstruction of tropological patterns of substitution (binary or ternary) can be included within discourses that leave the assumption of intelligibility not only unquestioned but that reinforce this assumption by making the mastering of the tropological displacement the very burden of understanding. This project engenders its own narrative which can be called an allegory of figure. This narrative begins to vacillate only when it appears that these (negative) cognitions fail to make the performative function of the discourse predictable and that, consequently, the linguistic model cannot be reduced to a mere system of tropes. Performative rhetoric and cognitive rhetoric, the rhetoric of tropes, fail to converge. The chain of substitutions functions next to another, differently structure system that exists independently of referential determination, in a system that is both entirely arbitrary and entirely repeatable, like a grammar. The intersection of the two systems can be located in a text as the disruption of the figural chain which we identified, in the passage from the *Confessions*, as anacoluthon; in the language of representational rhetoric, one could also call it parabasis,[21] a sudden revelation of the discontinuity between two rhetorical codes. This isolated textual event, as the reading of the *Fourth Rêverie* shows, is disseminated throughout the entire text and the anacoluthon is extended over all the points of the figural line or allegory; in a slight extension of

---

21. The similarity between anacoluthon and parabasis stems from the fact that both figures interrupt the expectations of a given grammatical or rhetorical movement. As digression, aside, *"intervention d'auteur,"* or *"aus der Rolle fallen,"* parabasis clearly involves the interruption of a discourse. The quotation from Friedrich Schlegel appears among the formerly unavailable notes contemporary with the Lyceum and Atheneum Fragmenten. Friedrich Schlegel, *Kritische Friedrich-Schlegel-Ausgabe*, ed. Ernst Behler (Munich, 1963), 18:85, §668. The use of the term parabasis (or parekbasis) by Schlegel echoes the use of the device especially in the plays of Tieck.

Friedrich Schlegel's formulation, it becomes the permanent parabasis of an allegory (of figure), that is to say, irony. Irony is no longer a trope but the undoing of the deconstructive allegory of all tropological cognitions, the systematic undoing, in other words, of understanding. As such, far from closing off the tropological system, irony enforces the repetition of its aberration.

Index